D1562737

Mathematical Modelling

Mathematical Modelling

A Source Book of Case Studies

Edited by

I.D. Huntley
Sheffield City Polytechnic

and

D.J.G. James
Coventry Polytechnic

OXFORD NEW YORK TOKYO
OXFORD UNIVERSITY PRESS
1990

Oxford University Press, Walton Street, Oxford OX2 6DP
Oxford New York Toronto
Delhi Bombay Calcutta Madras Karachi
Petaling Jaya Singapore Hong Kong Tokyo
Nairobi Dar es Salaam Cape Town
Melbourne Auckland
and associated companies in
Berlin Ibadan

Oxford is a trade mark of Oxford University Press

Published in the United States
by Oxford University Press, New York

© Institute of Mathematics and its Applications, 1990

British Library Cataloguing in Publication Data
Mathematical modelling: a source book of case studies
1. Mathematical models, Applications
I. Huntley, Ian 1918– II. James, G.
611.8
ISBN 0–19–853657–7

Library of Congress Cataloging in Publication Data
Data available

Printed and bound in Great Britain by
Biddles Ltd, Guildford and King's Lynn

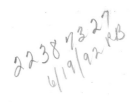

Preface

Mathematical modelling is not a new discovery, nor even a new activity. It has been with us throughout the ages and mathematicians such as Isaac Newton must be regarded as being outstanding mathematical modellers. It is, however, an area of mathematical education that has been much neglected, and the last few years have seen a move towards remedying the situation within undergraduate courses. This is seen as an attempt to remedy identified deficiencies relating to the ability of mathematics graduates to formulate problems and communicate results to the non-specialist.

It is important to distinguish between mathematical modelling and mathematical models. Both of these have a distinctive role to play in the teaching of mathematics but there is a great difference between the passive experience of seeing someone else's model and the active experience of formulating the model for oneself. In the passive mode, the student is concerned with applying a mathematical technique to a set-piece model with emphasis on obtaining a solution to the model. Such exercises have an important role to play in the teaching of mathematics, as they help to illustrate the usefulness of, and increase student motivation towards, the technique being taught. However, they do not, on their own, provide insight into the process of model formulation and, therefore, should not be regarded as mathematical modelling.

In practice, the situation of being faced with a model to which mathematical techniques can be applied directly is rarely met. Instead, an individual is likely to be confronted with a problem for which a solution is required; rarely will the problem be expressed in a mathematical form, and sometimes those posing it will not even be aware that mathematics can be of any assistance. The real challenge is to find relevant questions and answers from a situation that may initially look chaotic. This is a skill that to some extent can be nurtured and, therefore, should be the concern of mathematics educators. It is the development of such skills that is one of the main objectives of a course in mathematical modelling. Students should no longer take a passive role, but should be fully involved with the more active and demanding role of designing and developing the models for themselves.

The development of a course in mathematical modelling is not without its difficulties. For the students, the realisation that modelling does not comprise finding a unique answer to a well-defined mathematical problem, as previously encountered, takes a long time to dawn and requires a change of mental attitude towards problem solving. They generally lack confidence and feel insecure when faced with an imprecise problem which does not have a unique mathematical formulation or solution. A teacher new to modelling also faces problems, not least because it is a difficult subject to teach. In addition to developing, in the student, skills in the understanding of concepts and techniques, the teacher needs to be concerned with developing innovative skills and an ability to interact between the abstract world of mathematics and the real world of the situation being modelled. There are two specific issues that have been highlighted by experienced teachers, which are worth bearing in mind when designing a modelling course. The first concerns the level of mathematics required of the student. Clearly, in order to formulate effectively a mathematical model, a student needs to have a good understanding of the mathematics being used. It is unrealistic to expect a student to be capable of using newly assimilated mathematics, say in a parallel course of lectures, in a modelling context. It is important that the time lag between learning and vocational application is not overlooked and, consequently, when introducing case studies in a modelling course it is important that a suitable model, requiring only the mathematical knowledge of the student for its appraisal, be developed. There is general agreement, evident in the literature, amongst those that have been involved with its teaching, that mathematical modelling is not an appropriate vehicle for introducing new mathematical ideas and techniques. The second issue is concerned with a need to include, within the teaching programme, opportunities for a group activity. In particular, when faced with a new problem situation the importance of an initial brain-storming session cannot be overstressed, as even the most experienced modellers have acquired great satisfaction from participating in such sessions.

Much has been written on modelling methodology but, to date, there is no general consensus as to what constitutes such a methodology. Different people use different approaches to modelling, and the approach sometimes depends on the context. Without doubt, general experience as a mathematician and experience in a particular application area play a great part. It is fairly widely recognised, however, that there are a number of major steps in the modelling process; briefly these may be summarised as follows.

      i) Identify the problem
     ii) Formulate the model
   iii) Investigate the model
   iv) Validate the outcome
    v) Update if necessary

This is not to imply that the modelling process is always a linear, or linear with looping, sequencing of these stages. In some cases the modelling process may be even more complex, with the various stages intimately interwoven.

It is, therefore, clear that a course in mathematical modelling needs to be carefully structured, if it is to be successful and develop in the students the skills essential for good modelling. There is much to be said in favour of a workshop/studio approach to the teaching, where illustrative case studies can be developed interactively between the teacher and the class and students' assignments can be conducted in groups with, where appropriate, specific tasks allocated to individual members at various stages in the development of the model. The advantage of such an approach is also highlighted by Murphy and Page (1981, Int. J. Math. Educ. Sci. Technol., 12, p235), who draw a parallel with the teaching of design to engineering students.

A course format that has proven to be fairly successful is one having a three component pattern. During the first part, a series of short case studies is developed interactively between the teacher and the class in order to illustrate the modelling process. Ideally the studies chosen at this stage should be such that reasonable solutions may be obtained using only elementary mathematical techniques, thus allowing emphasis to be placed on model formulation whilst still dealing with the entire model building process. It is important, even at this stage, to give the students ample opportunity to participate and not allow a passive learning situation to develop. During the second part of the course a problem situation is presented and, after allowing a short period for discussion amongst the students, a possible model is developed interactively between the teacher and the class. The class is then divided into groups of three or four students, and each group asked to enhance the interactively-developed model or to consider a variation of the problem posed. Emphasis is not on the application of particular mathematical techniques but rather on seeking a reasonable solution to an open-ended problem using the most elementary mathematics possible. A range of case studies should be studied in order to illustrate the various aspects of, and approaches to, the modelling process. This part of the course serves very much as a confidence building stage in the students' development.

Each group is required to write a report and to report back orally to the class. Initially the standard of the report writing, and the presentation of results generally, is not of a particularly high standard, and a great deal of guidance is required. It is important that this important area is strongly stressed during the first two parts of the course.

During the final stage of the course students are involved with group project activity. Here each group, of three or four students, is presented with a problem statement and asked to investigate it fully. Ideally, case studies used should be of an extendable nature, allowing the possibility for each group member to undertake a specific task. During this stage of the course teachers should interfere as little as possible; rather, they should act simply as consultants giving advice as and when requested. There is merit in students being asked to submit individual reports, and ideally groups should also be required to report back orally to the class.

It is believed that this course structure will facilitate the students' progressive development and confidence in the modelling process and allow them to learn and develop the skills, particularly those of innovation and self-discovery, which are essential qualities in becoming a good model builder. As well as developing the students' modelling skills this approach will also improve their communication skills and their ability to participate in team work, both of which are highly valued attributes to any employer.

The collection of case studies included in this text are the result of a series of national workshops on the Teaching of Mathematical Modelling organised by the editors over a period of years. All the authors have, in their individual ways, been involved in teaching mathematical modelling. Each case study has a self-contained statement of the problem to be considered and this, in many cases, is accompanied by other material providing background and motivation. In developing an appropriate model the author(s) of each case study will have adopted a particular stance. The approach chosen will be based on the author's use of the study with a group of students and, for this reason, authors have provided comments and hints on handling the study in the teaching environment. In doing so, the intention is not to appear to be dogmatic; rather, it is felt that there are instances where the author's advice, based on experience, could be valuable to a teacher or student. However, it cannot be emphasised enough that there is no correct answer to any of the problems contained in this collection; others may take quite different approaches from those of the authors.

Although progress can be made with most of the case studies without the use of computers, readily available access to a microcomputer laboratory having suitable supporting software would be an advantage. The availability of such a facility can certainly enrich the teaching of a modelling course, particularly in the areas of demonstration, realisation and investigation of performance. There are also distinct advantages in using interactive simulation packages, in that they enable students to investigate readily more complicated models without recourse to programming, which can be time consuming and frequently distract from motivating the modelling aspects being pursued. However, there are dangers in over reliance on the use of computers and simulation packages, and one cannot stress too strongly the need for constructive use. They should play very much a supportive role, taking the drudgery out of the modelling exercise and enabling the student to devote more attention to the thought and understanding processes so essential in model building.

Whilst the text may be used in a variety of ways, its main purpose is to provide support material for an introductory undergraduate course in mathematical modelling. The case studies presented are categorised into four sections. Section 1 constitutes studies 1 to 5, which are suitable for use at the first stage of the course structure outlined earlier. Section 2 constitutes studies 6 to 17, which are suitable for use in the second stage of the course, whilst section 3 constitutes studies 18 to 24 which are suitable for use in the final stage. Section 4 constitutes the remaining case studies, which are suitable for use at various stages at the discretion of the teacher.

1990   Professor D.J.G. James
                                                 Coventry Polytechnic

                                                     Dr. I.D. Huntley
                                              Sheffield City Polytechnic

Acknowledgements

The Institute thanks the authors of the papers, the editors, Dr. I.D. Huntley (Sheffield City Polytechnic) and Professor D.J.G. James (Coventry Polytechnic) and also Miss D. Brown, Miss P. Irving and Miss K. Jenkins for typing the papers.

Contents

Some aspects of the process of formulation of mathematical models

1. INTRODUCTION

The increasing realisation of the importance of mathematical
modelling as a distinct part of the mathematics curriculum at
all levels of the educational system has engendered considerable work on the methodology of mathematical modelling.
Clements (1982) reviews the history and development of such
models and the interested reader will find further references
therein. What is methodology? A formal definition may perhaps
be that a methodology is an ideal type (in the social scien-
tific sense of a normative pattern) for a class of intellectual
activity. Such a definition sounds very abstruse and perhaps
not a little daunting but if it is examined in a little more
depth it is not so daunting as may, at first sight, seem. An
ideal type attempts to distill the essence of a system or
object so that the student of such objects may more readily
recognize the essential features of the objects and be better
fitted to deal with new examples of the object. Such types
also help in the classification, recognition and comparison of
unfamiliar objects. Mathematical modelling is indeed an
intellectual activity. A methodology of modelling (and it must
be recognized that there are different, complementary and
competing methodologies) is an attempt to describe the common
strands of that intellectual activity when applied to the
solution of a wide range of problems.

Of what use, therefore, is a methodology? What problems do we
incur if we lack one? We must certainly be sure that a
methodology does not become a strait jacket, stifling the
intellectual activity that it is intended to order and
facilitate. It is our contention that a methodology assists
both teacher and taught. The externalisation of the pattern
of intellectual activities (that is the recognition that a

pattern exists and the attempt to describe it in terms that
help others to understand and apply it) which lead to the
creation of a mathematical model or solution of a real world
problem helps to prevent the process from losing direction.

The creation and validation of a methodology, relies upon
observation of the common strands in the intellectual activity
of experienced and effective modellers and codification of that
observation in a way that can be effectively communicated to
others. The use of analogy and cross-disciplinary reference
are effective tools in describing methodologies.

In the spirit of enquiry into methodology several groups of
experienced teachers of mathematics and mathematical modelling
were brought together to work on some mathematical modelling
problems over a two day period. Each group consisted of four
members and the groups were each presented with a number of
problem statements, such as might be given to students (though
some members had reservations about the suitability of some of
the problems, at least in the form presented).

Owing to the limited time scale it was not practicable to
expect the groups to complete a modelling exercise and the
object of the study was confined to observing the way in which
the groups approached the initial stages of the modelling
problem, those which may be characterised as the formulation
of a model of a real world problem and the initial mathematical
solution of that model, at least as far as an assessment of its
feasibility. It is important to realise that our objective is
primarily to study the process not the product of the exercise.
We are concerned to discover how the participants went about
creating models, not to assess or criticise the models produced
(though these may well also be of interest to the reader).

What we hope to provide here is some quasi-experimental
evidence which may be used either for the validation of
previously proposed methodologies of modelling or for the
foundation of new advances in such methodologies. At the same
time, though, we anticipate that those relatively new to the
discipline will find some encouragement and enlightenment in
the description of the struggles and variety of approaches
adopted by different groups in response to identical problem
statements. Modelling is never a dull activity and never one
in which one finds right or wrong answers - merely greater or
lesser degrees of appropriateness of response.

2.   THE PROBLEM

The first problem statement that each group considered was
this:

"A common way of discouraging speeding on housing estates,
campuses and other restricted road systems is the construction
of 'sleeping policemen' or speed bumps. How does the highway
engineer decide on the precise design of a speed bump? What is
he trying to achieve? What is he trying to avoid? Give
advice."

3.   THE FIRST STAGE OF MODELLING

Observations of all the groups suggested that there was a
common pattern in their initial approaches to this problem.
Firstly a stage that could be characterised as perception of
the problem. In this stage the participants engaged in a free
ranging discussion of the problem, sharing their own experiences that related to the problem (for instance how their
driving is affected by bumps, how bumps are set out on their
home campuses or housing suburbs) and discussing the form the
answer might take. The important common quality of this
discussion was a relative lack of closely defined aim or goal.

It was apparent, from observation of the groups and records of
their deliberations at this stage, that all the groups found
this problem appealing and were well motivated to further and
deepening investigation. This is important in this context
when compared with one of the other mutual problems which,
almost without exception, failed to engage the attention of the
participants. One of the participants later commented that the
only way he could have got interested in this latter problem
was if someone paid him enough to solve it! This illustrates
one quality that problems need if they are to inspire students
or anyone else to make an effort to solve them - sufficient
interest for that group. The interest could be intrinsic to
the problem (which seemed to be the case for our groups with
the speed bump problem) or externally generated or imposed (as
in the case of the sufficient financial or academic reward for
solving a problem). In retrospect we were unclear to what
extent the actual wording or whole presentational mode of the
problem affected its intrinsic appeal. This would be an
interesting issue to investigate further.

During the perception stage the range of issues discussed by
the groups showed considerable overlap. The whole range of
topics discussed was roughly as follows:

(1)   Is this really a mathematical problem at all? Could the
      problem better be solved by experimentation? Has anyone
      ever actually designed an optimal speed bump?

(2)   What is the purpose of a speed bump? How does it work?
      Is it intended to cause direct discomfort to the driver
      or is it meant to slow him down because of his perception
      of the mechanical distress being caused to his vehicle?
      Is it intended to reduce maximum speed or average speed?
      How do safety considerations affect the design (e.g. could
      icing on speed bumps promote loss of control of vehicles
      and cause accidents)?

(3)   Is it the size and shape of an individual bump which is
      of interest or is it the spacing between bumps?

(4)   What type of vehicle is the bump expected to be effective
      against? How does a vehicle suspension unit work and how
      would it react to a speed bump? How do the suspension
      characteristics of buses, lorries, cars, milk floats,
      motor cycles etcetera differ?

(5)   What novel designs of bump might exist? Could troughs
      be used instead of bumps? Would diagonal bumps be more
      effective than ones at right angles to the kerbs?

(6)   What is the driver psychology of speed bumps? Would false
      speed bumps painted on the road be effective? How does
      the behaviour of company vehicle drivers differ from that
      of owner drivers?

It is particularly interesting to note that, at this stage when
the groups were being most creative and divergent in their
work, several of the main areas of discussion seemd to go
outside the areas defined by the problem statement. We feel
that this freedom is important and should be encouraged. It
is usually necessary to explore some areas peripheral to the
main problem before homing in on the problem to be solved.
Such exploration will both illuminate the main problem and
identify possible cross links with other problems or considerations. Some participants in one group, with particular
interests and expertise in applied mechanics, tended to become
over concerned with the vehicle suspension aspects of the
problem to the exclusion of other areas which other members of
their group wanted to explore. Another group agreed to begin
by each individually reporting his own initial ideas to the
whole group without interruption of discussion until all had
done this. This procedure had the effect of ensuring that the
ideas, queries and misgivings of all members were taken into

account in the ensuing general discussion and acted as an effective safeguard against the possibility of the group rushing off down the first potentially profitable avenue before considering all others. Such a procedure though might have drawbacks for student use, where it might be discouraging and emotivating for weaker or more introverted students.

The second generally identifiable stage was one that could be characterised as the choice and further elaboration of one aspect of the problem. Here the groups exhibited more convergent behaviour, reducing the range of options and homing in on one or maybe two promising avenues to explore in more depth. The mechanism of this homing in process was not entirely explicit but, in at least two cases, appeared to relate partly to the groups anticipation of being able to actually solve the model equations chosen. Thus the choice of model for the problem was not solely determined by the appropriateness of the model as an abstract representation of the problem but considerations of its properties as a whole problem solving aid (i.e. would this model be likely to yield usable conclusions?) were also taken into account.

To illustrate these points we will quote examples from the progress of two groups. One group, which we shall call the 'bump group', contained the predominance of applied mechanicians who quickly homed in on the bump profile/vehicle suspension interaction aspect of the problem. They took it that the function of the bump was to prevent speeding by imparting a suitable shock to the vehicle suspension which would deter the driver but not damage the vehicle. This led to an investigation of the magnitude of acceptable forces and caused this group to concentrate on the effects of a single bump. Another group, the 'spacing group', decided that the profile of bumps, as built on the highway, was liable to exhibit considerable variations and that detailed models of individual bumps would not yield the most useful information. Their reaction was to concentrate on the interaction between bump spacing and maximum achieved vehicle speed.

A comment we would make here is that each group's final choice of model seemed to be, at least in part, conditioned by their anticipation of success in drawing useful or interesting conclusions. This reinforces the comment above about 'whole problem solving' methods but also suggests that prior expertise in a group has considerable influence on the problem solving methods chosen.

4.   THE MODELS

Having commented on the process whereby the groups formulated
their models it will be of interest to outline here the models
formulated.   Sections 4(i) and 4(ii) are contributed by the
two groups referred to above and outline their models.   It is
appropriate to repeat here that these models were really only
preliminary attempts at solving the problem achieved in a
relatively restricted time span and should be viewed in that
light.

(i)   The 'bump' group's model

The group aimed to estimate the shock on the body of the car
transmitted by the suspension system when the car was driven
over a curved bump.   No distinction was to be made between the
wheels so the effect of the bump on an isolated single wheel
was studied.

Assumptions

(a)   speed of car, v, is constant

(b)   shape of the curve could be described by the cosine curve

$$z = a(1 - \cos \frac{\pi x}{L})$$

(c)   the suspension of a vehicle can be modelled by a spring
with constant k, natural length ℓ

(d)   motion over bump is governed by Newton's Laws

(e)   no damping involved.

Suggested model

The general layout is given in Figure 1.

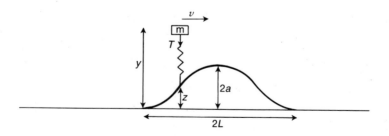

Figure 1   General arrangement of car passing over bump

Equations of motion are

$$m\ddot{y} = - mg - T$$

$$T = k(y - z - \ell)$$

thus

$$m\ddot{y} + ky = - mg + kz + k\ell.$$

In equilibrium position

$$kY = - mg + k\ell.$$

Choose new variable u such that $u = y - Y$ and substitute

$$m\ddot{u} + ku = kz$$

i.e.

$$m\ddot{u} + ku = ka(1 - \cos \frac{\pi x}{L}) = ka(1 - \cos \frac{\pi vt}{L}).$$

Solution gives

$$\dot{u} = A \cos\alpha t + B \sin\alpha t + a - ka(\cos \frac{\pi v}{L}t)/(k - \frac{m\pi^2 v^2}{L^2})$$

where $\alpha = (k/m)^{\frac{1}{2}}$.

Given initial conditions

$$\dot{u} = 0 \Rightarrow B = 0$$

$$u = 0 \Rightarrow A + a - ka/(k - \frac{m\pi^2 v^2}{L^2}) = 0$$

i.e.

$$A = a\left(k/(k - \frac{m\pi^2 v^2}{L^2}) - 1\right)$$

we have

$$u = a(1 - \cos\alpha t) + ka(\cos\alpha t - \cos \frac{\pi v}{L}t)/(k - \frac{m\pi^2 v^2}{L^2}).$$

From previous equation

$$m\ddot{u} = ka(1 - \cos\frac{\pi v}{L}t) - ka(1 - \cos\alpha t)$$

$$- k^2 a(\cos\alpha t - \cos\frac{\pi v}{L}t)/(k - \frac{m\pi^2 v^2}{L^2}) \ .$$

$$m\ddot{u} = ka\left\{1 - k/(k - \frac{m\pi^2 v^2}{L^2})\right\}(\cos\alpha t - \cos\frac{\pi v}{L}t) \ .$$

We may establish a non-dimensional variable

$$V^2 = \frac{kL^2}{m\pi^2}$$

(V can be thought of as some typical velocity and $\tau = \frac{L}{\pi V}$ as a representative time).

Substituting we obtain

$$m\ddot{u} = ka(\frac{v^2}{V^2})(\cos\frac{v}{V}\frac{t}{\tau} - \cos\frac{t}{\tau})/(1 - \frac{v^2}{V^2})$$

this being the force experienced by the wheel over the bump.

Estimation of Parameters

Typical mass of a car is 1000 Kg so that m = 250 Kg

Typical speed is v = 10 ms^{-1}

2a = .2 m   2L = .4m

k was estimated by one member (90 Kg) sitting on another's car and measuring its movement (10 cm) thus giving k ≑ 900

then V ≑ .1m/sec, τ ≑ 0.4 s

as v >> V then using these parameters

force ≑ 90(cos 200t - cos 2t)   where $0 < t < \frac{1}{20}$.

Model Evaluation

A graph of this expression does give a positive quantity for the interval $0 < t < 0.25$, giving a force of about 200 Kg in a very small interval of time.

The denominator gives a singularity when $v = V$. This is at extremely small velocities. It was thought that at these speeds, the damping assumption would be invalid and by adding damping due to a shock absorber this would be avoided. The equation plus a damping term was too difficult to solve during the time period but a numerical solution could easily be attained and it would be hoped that this would model lower speeds. It was also felt that it would be useful to calculate the jerk associated with the force. This was approximately equal to the derivative of the force but it was not clear how or which units this would be measured in.

(ii) The 'spacing' group's model

A model of the relation of vehicle velocity and bump spacing

The group eventually, after much discussion, decided to concentrate attention on minimising accidents on a housing estate by using appropriately spaced speed bumps to restrict all vehicles to some maximum speed, v_1.

Assume a single bump can reduce a vehicle's speed to v_0. The situation is as in Figure 2. The vehicle goes over a speed bump at v_0, accelerates up to velocity v_1 and slows to v_0 for the next bump (at separation D).

Our aim is now to choose v_0 and D in order to prescribe v_1, with constraints on cost (i.e. very frequent bumps will be expensive to build) and on acceptability (i.e. very frequent bumps will annoy the residents).

The combination v_0, D will clearly vary from vehicle to vehicle from given v_1, so the sensible course is to design for the 'worst case'. In practical terms, this might be a sports car or an unladen lorry - able to accelerate fast and decelerate fast. If we can restrict this 'worst case' vehicle to a maximum speed of v_1 throughout the estate (and v_1 is chosen so that a vehicle with poor brakes can still stop in a reasonable distance) then accidents should be minimised.

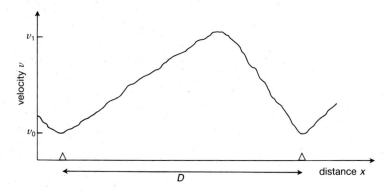

Figure 2 Form of velocity position graph for vehicle between
bumps

In order to proceed without an extensive literature search,
we now make the assumption that both acceleration and deceleration are constant. This assumption can always be improved
later but, given the rough and ready nature of our model, may
well be sufficient.

Letting acceleration = a
        deceleration = -b

and using formulae for constant acceleration gives

$$D = \frac{v_1^2 - v_0^2}{2} \left(\frac{1}{a} + \frac{1}{b}\right).$$

In order to get a feel for the meaning of this equation we now
want order of magnitude estimates for a and b.

Taking a 0-60 mph time of 10s and assuming constant acceleration throughout will give an estimate for a of 8.8 ft/s^2.
Similarly, the Highway Code estimates a constant deceleration
of 2g/3 when evaluating its braking distance, leading to
b = 21.5 ft/s^2. Thus our formula now becomes

$$D = 0.08 \ (v_1^2 - v_0^2) \ \text{ft}.$$

A figure near v_1 = 20 mph = 29 ft/s would seem reasonable on
a housing estate and corresponds to a Highway Code total

stopping distance of about 40 ft, (i.e. $2\frac{1}{2}$ Ford Cortina lengths), so we now have

$$D = 0.08 \ (860 - v_O^2) \ \text{ft}$$

as sketched in Figure 3.

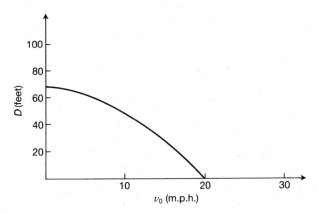

Figure 3   D as a function of v_O for v_1 = 20 mph

Thus, even if the bumps slow vehicles down to 5 mph they must still be positioned every 65 ft - a combination almost sure to displease the residents.

In fact, we might conclude that:

"Reasonable bumps can't slow a maniac down and any system that slows a maniac down isn't reasonable."

To be more realistic we might turn the problem round, letting D be given and using the formula to find v_O. A reasonable value might be D = 150 ft (i.e. 10 Cortinas), so we now have

$$v_1^2 = v_O^2 + 1875$$

for velocities in ft/s or

$$v_1^2 = v_O^2 + 872$$

for velocities in mph. For the minimal value v_0 = 5 mph this gives v_1 = 30 mph, an answer not very sensitive to v_0.

Conclusions

Although based entirely on constant acceleration and deceleration (and hence capable of improvement) our model shows clearly that the maximum speed attained on the housing estate is fairly insensitive to the speed over the bump v_0 ft/s.

Attention should be focussed on finding out what the residents regard as an acceptable bump separation D ft, and the formula

$$D = 0.08 \ (v_1^2 - v_0^2)$$

used to predict the maximum speed v_1 ft/s.

5.   GENERAL COMMENTS

A question was raised concerning the value of using groups to work on these problems. It is interesting to ask when group working has significant advantages and when disadvantages. It was observed in each group that different members contributed to the progress of particular lines of investigation sequentially. An initial idea could come from one member which then engendered further ideas to expand the approach from others. In this way the group appears to exhibit synergistic properties, the product of several modellers is more than the sum of their original individual ideas. This seemed to hold good during the problem perception and choice and formulation phases but, once the groups were well advanced in the choice of a model, the detailed formation of the equations and their manipulation and solution was seen to be much more suitable for individual working.

It is apparent that group problem solving has its strong points, but it must not be ignored that certain phases of the modelling cycle are not necessarily best or even ever appropriately tackled by groups. The teacher of modelling must make sure that students become aware of the distinction between activities that are enhanced by a group approach and those that are hindered. The use of a methodology can perhaps be helpful in ensuring that such points do become apparent.

Another interesting observation was that no group actually claimed to be following a particular methodology, yet no serious disagreements appeared about how to proceed at any

stage of the problem. It was apparent that the internal
models of the modelling process that each participant worked
with were in sufficient agreement that no conflict arose. We
feel that this indicates an important aspect in the use of
methodologies. Methodologies are useful frameworks for the
organisation of intellectual activity. For the teacher they
help to clarify his other ideas about what exactly he or she
is trying to teach. For the student they provide a logical
framework through which to order the detailed or specific
lessons about modelling which he or she is learning. Methodologies, followed too slavishly, however, become stultifying.
The methodology must provide a background pattern to the
intellectual processes not a close strait jacket. Too often
students let methodologies that they have learnt restrict too
closely the scope of their investigations. Intellectual rules
are made to be broken!

All the groups were seen to use diagrams extensively. Our
observation is that students new to modelling are often
reluctant to be sufficiently pictorial in their thinking and
exploratory work on a problem. The copious use of pictures by
our experienced modellers suggest that they have learnt by
experience that this is a profitable tactic. On the other
hand, certain forms of conventional diagram (conventional in
the sense of containing the symbolism of a particular method
of solution) can restrict the wide ranging and peripheral
thinking which we feel is important in the early stage of the
problem. Diagrams can therefore be seen as a double edged
sword.

6. CONCLUSION

The experiences of the several groups of teachers of mathematical modelling undertaking some modelling problems have
been used here in an attempt to elucidate and demonstrate
some important practical points about the initial stages of
the mathematical modelling process. The results certainly
illustrate the important point that modelling is an open ended
activity and that the result of asking a particular question
to different modellers can be a range of different models with
various emphases. Of the other points that have emerged
perhaps the most important is the contrast between the
initially divergent, wide/ranging, idea generating discussion
and the subsequent convergent, concentrated development of the
more detailed model that ensued once the groups had identified
the problem aspect or model that seemed to them to offer the
most insight into the problem.

7.   FURTHER COMMENTS ON SPEED BUMPS

The design of speed bumps has subsequently been undertaken as a project by a group of undergraduate students. During this work more information was gathered on the current state of the art in the design of speed bumps. Legislation for the use of speed bumps on public roads was introduced in 1983 (Ministry of Transport, 1983). Prior to this the Transport and Road Research Laboratory had undertaken some work concerning the operation and design of speed bumps which is described in Watts (1973), Sumner and Baguley (1979) and Baguley (1981). Most of this work was heuristic, experimental and subjective in nature though some work was also pursued using dynamic models of vehicle suspensions.

REFERENCES

Baguley, C., 1981, Speed control humps - further public road trials. TRRL report 1017.

Clements, R.R., 1982, The development of methodologies of mathematical modelling. *Teaching Mathematics Applics.*, **1**, 125.

Department of Transport, 1983, The Highways (Road Humps) Regulations 1983. Statutory Instrument 1983 No. 1087.

Sumner, R. and Baguley, C., 1979, Speed control humps on residential roads. TRRL report 878.

Watts, G.R., 1973, Road humps for the control of vehicle speeds. TRRL report 597.

Part I: Simple illustrative examples

1

Estimating route lengths

RAY ABRINES *Kingston Polytechnic* and
PETER HUDSON *Teesside Polytechnic*

1.1   PROBLEM STATEMENT

When planning a journey in advance, one of the factors that
might be considered important is the length of the route to
be taken. To obtain a rough estimate, the following rule of
thumb, for use in conjunction with Ordnance Survey maps, is
proposed:

> "Count the number of grid squares which the route
> enters, and then multiply this number by an appro-
> priate factor to give the length of the route."

In what way could this be regarded as a reasonable rule?

Investigate the possible values of the factor and its
dependence on different types of routes.

1.2   INTRODUCTION

The above problem should be within the capabilities of sixth
formers studying A-level mathematics, and students following
degree or diploma courses which incorporate an introductory
modelling unit. It is recommended as an initial modelling
exercise immediately after two or three lectures on the
principles and methodology of modelling and their illustration
with one or two simple examples. Weaker students will
possibly need some assistance with the integration involved in
the model analysis. Also with the increasing use of micro-
computers in schools, some students will no doubt find the
prospect of a computer simulation model appealing.

Such a model can give rise to some interesting statistical data
and their interpretation. Students are likely to want to refer
to Ordnance Survey maps and it is recommended that they are
made readily available when the problem statement is issued.
Ordnance Survey maps are currently based on a 2x2 cm grid with
a scale of 2 cm to 1 km so that any prediction is likely to
relate the route length in km to the number of grid squares.
However, because the layman still tends to work in miles, it
may be more convenient to suggest a relation for distances
measured in miles. The scale factor for conversion of km to
miles is 0.6124.

Initially students are likely to embark upon a data collecting
exercise involving the actual measurement of route lengths
and the counting of the number of grid squares which the route
enters. They may also wish to get a feel for the problem by
drawing their own routes and, for this purpose, graph paper is
ideal and should be issued with the problem statement.

As an alternative approach a data collection sheet similar to
that illustrated in Figure 1.1 is issued to the whole class
before the problem is set. This requires each student to
provide some five lines of data. All the data collected in
this way can then be entered onto a summary sheet and issued
to the groups attempting the problem. This provides valuable
practice in real data collection and interpretation and
experience in checking and questioning data. It is important
not to ask for too much detail, such as variables which only
come to light in the refinement of the model, nor to insist
that the data is in some precise form. Variations are useful
to suggest ideas or problems which may not have occurred to
the modeller and to allow him to experience some of the difficulties inherent in real life data. Note also that scale,
grid square size and units are all requested to provide a
possible check on the data submitted.

It is recommended that the class is split into small groups to
work on the problem with each student making his own notes of
the group discussions in order to write his own personal report
to be submitted for assessment purposes. It is helpful to
begin each practical session with a brief summary of useful
guidelines to modelling with the final session including
advice on writing reports. Without a computer simulation
three one-hour sessions should suffice.

1.3 MODEL FORMULATION

The essential variables in the statement of the problem are
the length L of the route and the number N of grid squares into

Take an Ordnance Survey map from either the One-inch Series or from the 1:50000 Series or any other similar map broken up into regular grid squares and complete the table below . This requires you to measure the distance between any two places on your map using a map measurer or a piece of string and also to count the number of grid squares through which the route you choose passes . In some cases you may judge that the route intersects the grid square at a corner . The number of these should be entered in the corner column.

Indicate whether your route is relatively straight (S) or highly curved (C) . Leave blank if you feel it could not be described as either.

No.	Place A	Place B	Distance between A and B in km/ miles	No. of grid squares	No. of corners	Type of route
1						
2						
3						
4						
5						

Map used :
Scale   :
Size of grid square in cm/in :

Name : ....

Figure 1.1 Data Calculation Sheet

which the route enters. It is required to investigate the existence of a relationship of the form

$$L = \text{constant} \times N \qquad (1)$$

The experience of collecting the data makes it seem unlikely that the constant would be the same for any type of route which may vary from almost a straight line to a possible combination of wave-like or spiral or circular type routes. It thus appears to be more reasonable to reformulate (1) into

$$L = k(R) \times N \qquad (2)$$

where k is a factor depending upon the route type R. Nevertheless for simplicity we initially consider only relatively
straight routes. Assume that the route can be approximated by
a series of straight lines in each of the grid squares. Then,
if L_{AV} is the average length of all straight line routes
through a grid square the average value of the factor k is L_{AV}.

(It is assumed that the contribution from the first and last
grid squares is equivalent to one grid square. This is consistent with what happens with the particular case of a
circular route.) Owing to the possible variations of routes
between any two points, even relatively straight ones, it is
clear that no exact deterministic model can be formulated in
the general case. I will therefore represent only the average
value of k for a large number of routes.

Consider then an arbitrary straight line AB making an angle θ
with the horizontal grid line of the grid square CDEF (Figure
1.2). Let BD = x. By symmetry about PQ, we need only consider
straight lines parallel to AB from D to the midpoint of EH and then
allow θ to vary from O to $\pi/2$. Figure 1.2 indicates the two
possibilities for $\theta < 45°$. Similar diagrams may be drawn for
$\theta > 45°$.

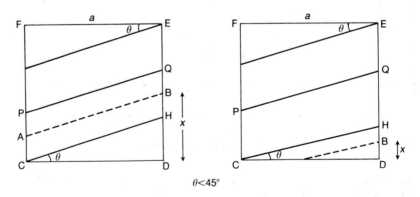

$\theta < 45°$

Figure 1.2 A grid square

Let a be the length of a side of the grid square. Then the
average length of all straight line paths making an angle θ
with CD is

$$\frac{2}{a(1+\tan\theta)} \left[\int_0^{a\,\tan\theta} x\,\mathrm{cosec}\theta\;dx + \int_{a\,\tan\theta}^{\frac{a}{2}(1+\tan\theta)} a\,\sec\theta dx \right]$$

$$= \frac{a}{(\sin\theta+\cos\theta)}$$

Thus the average length of all straight line paths for all directions is

$$L_{AV} = \frac{2}{\pi} \int_0^{\frac{\pi}{2}} \frac{a}{(\sin\theta+\cos\theta)}\;d\theta = \frac{2\sqrt{2}a}{\pi} \int_0^{\frac{\pi}{4}} \sec\theta d\theta$$

$$= \frac{2\sqrt{2}a}{\pi} \left[\ln|\sec\theta+\tan\theta| \right]_0^{\frac{\pi}{4}}$$

$$= \frac{2\sqrt{2}a}{\pi} \ln\,(1+\sqrt{2}) \doteq 0.79a$$

This stochastic model thus predicts that if L is measured in km, L = 0.79N and if L is measured in miles, L = 0.49N.

1.4 MODEL VALIDATION

Before examining the data obtained it is necessary to consider any possible ambiguities in counting the number N of grid squares, whether to include the squares containing the start and finish of a route is not clear but can be resolved satisfactorily by considering circular routes for which the start and the finish are coincident and thus lie in the same square. It is therefore reasonable and consistent to count the number of times the route passes from one grid square to a neighbouring one with the implication that the square containing the finish is counted but that containing the start is not. Whether a route is counted as having entered a particular grid square when it is close to a corner may also be doubtful but can be resolved satisfactorily by imagining the position to be magnified. This indicates that a corner intersection should be counted into the total for N. In this way a difference of opinion as to whether the route intersects a square at a corner leads to the same count. However provided that there is a consistent approach to the definition of a

corner intersection (even if it is subjective) it must be more
accurate to exclude it from the count.

An alternative method for calculating N is provided by considering the intersections of the route with the horizontal and
vertical grid lines. Each time a route enters a new square it
must cross either a vertical grid line or a horizontal grid
line. Thus if the number of times the route crosses a vertical
grid line, N_V, is added to the number of times it crosses a

horizontal grid line, N_H, the sum is equal to the number of

times the route enters a new square. The only possible
exception is when the route is allowed to pass through a
corner of a square. To be consistent with the counting of
corners in the previous paragraph, a corner intersection must
be counted as both a horizontal and a vertical crossing. But
the number of corners must be subtracted from the total N count
if the corner intersections were excluded as suggested in the
previous paragraph.

A considerable amount of data has been obtained for validation
purposes consisting of both "real-life" and simulated data.
They consist of:

> 25 routes including motorways, A roads, B roads and
> unclassified roads taken from Ordnance Survey Sheet
> 93 (Cleveland and Darlington) for which the ratio
> L/N varied between 0.74 and 1.00 with a mean of 0.83,
> when L is measured in km. (The corresponding ratios
> for measurements in miles are 0.46, 0.62 and 0.51
> respectively.)

> 28 relatively straight routes and 7 highly curved
> routes taken from miscellaneous Ordnance Survey maps
> for the South-East of England for which the ratio
> L/N varied between 0.63 and 1.27 with a mean of 0.89
> when L is measured in km. (The corresponding ratios
> for measurements in miles are 0.39, 0.79 and 0.55
> respectively.)

> 5000 simulated routes described in detail in the next
> section for which the ratio L/N varied between 0.42
> and 2.15 with a mean of 0.79 when L is measured in km.
> (The corresponding ratios for measurements in miles
> are 0.26, 1.33 and 0.49 respectively.)

1.5 MODEL SIMULATION

In order to obtain a large amount of data, 'real-life' calculations are not practical. (Note, however, that much work can

be avoided if use is made of published distances between
specified towns, when it is only necessary to count the number
of grid squares.) It is clearly an advantage to use the
computer to simulate a large number of different types of
routes and to perform the necessary statistical calculations.
To this end Raggett (1982) has written a program for the BBC
microcomputer which graphically represents the route and
calculates the average value, least value and greatest value
of the ratio L/N for 100 runs and for one of five possible
types of routes. The possible types of routes are determined
by the value of the maximum angle A for the random deviations
from the straight line path in either direction, at each step
length. They are

(a) Roman roads . . . straight line routes (A = 0);
(b) Motorways . . . . almost straight line routes (A = $\pi/9$);
(c) A roads . . . . . relatively direct routes (A = $\pi/6$);
(d) S roads . . . . . circuitous routes (A = $\pi/4$);
(e) Local walks . . . circular circuitous routes (A = $\pi/4$)
     (with deviations only allowed in one direction to ensure
     that the route describes approximate anticlockwise
     circles).

This program has been modified to run on a mainframe computer
without graphical output but to include a histogram of the
ratio values for each 100 runs and for each value between 0.2
and 1.2 at step lengths of 0.05. A listing of either program
is available on request.

The mainframe program was run ten times for each type of
route. The results are summarised in Table 1.1 and typical
histograms for each route type illustrated in Figure 1.3. For
the last two runs for each type of route the statistics were
also calculated for those simulations which included at least
nine grid squares and these results are given in Table 1.2.

1.6 CONCLUSIONS

Because of the stochastic nature of the problem it is clear
that no factor exists which would provide a reasonably good
approximation to the length of a route for any type of route
and for any starting and finishing points and this is confirmed
in the simulated data. Although the average agrees with the
prediction of the theoretical model there is a very large
variation in k values from 0.42 to 2.15. The proposed rule of
thumb would therefore be completely unsatisfactory as a general
rule to apply to the length of any route. However the
variation in k values for routes which enter at least nine grid
squares is considerably reduced ranging from 0.45 to 1.15.

TABLE 1.1

Results for 1000 simulations of each route type

Route Type	Distance measured in miles Values of ratio L/N			Distance measured in km Values of ratio L/N		
	Least	Greatest	Average	Least	Greatest	Average
(a)	0.27	0.99	0.51	0.44	1.60	0.82
(b)	0.27	1.33	0.50	0.44	2.15	0.81
(c)	0.29	1.17	0.49	0.47	1.89	0.79
(d)	0.26	1.05	0.48	0.42	1.69	0.77
(e)	0.29	1.22	0.43	0.47	1.97	0.77
all	0.26	1.33	0.49	0.42	2.15	0.79

TABLE 1.2

Results for simulations which gave at least nine grid squares

Route Type	Distance measured in miles Values of ratio L/N			Distance measured in km Values of ratio L/N			Number of Simulations
	Least	Greatest	Average	Least	Greatest	Average	
(a)	0.28	0.71	0.47	0.45	1.15	0.76	146
(b)	0.30	0.64	0.45	0.48	1.03	0.74	162
(c)	0.30	0.69	0.45	0.48	1.11	0.74	142
(d)	0.31	0.65	0.45	0.50	1.05	0.73	154
(e)	0.29	0.62	0.44	0.47	1.00	0.71	141
all	0.28	0.71	0.46	0.45	1.15	0.74	750

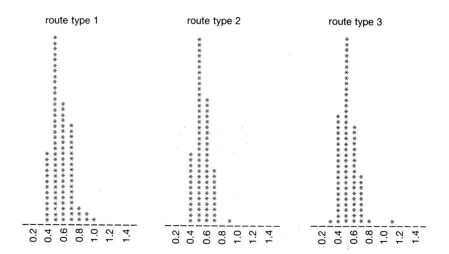

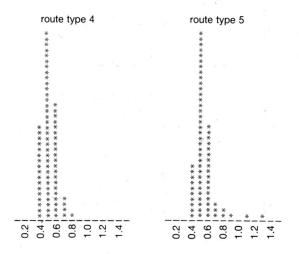

Figure 1.3   Histograms for the route L/N in a simulation of 100 routes for each of the five types of routes (L measured in miles)

The majority of the rogue high values occur for the shorter routes. The histograms indicate that the distribution skews slightly to the right with about three-quarters of the values lying between 0.55 and 0.95.

Contrary to the original intuitive idea that the factor may be dependent on the type of route, Tables 1.1 and 1.2 and the histograms seem to indicate that there is very little to choose between the average values of the ratio for the different types of routes although the ratio does appear to decrease slightly consistently as the type of route varies from type (a) to type (e).

We conclude that the average value of the ratio L/N is about 0.75 for a large number of routes with an error of about $\pm$ 0.2 for sufficiently long routes (N > 9). However we must also conclude that this rule is not useful for obtaining a rough estimate. In any case it is debatable whether it is easier to calculate N rather than L, particularly when L is not required too accurately. It must also be realised that these map measurements would not take the height of the road into account, however accurately they are made, and in mountainous districts this would be significant.

Despite the fact that the model is not useful for estimating route lengths it is an interesting example simple enough to serve as an introductory exercise in mathematical modelling and close enough to the student's own experience to give him confidence in discussing the problem adequately. It is also sufficiently profound to yield other interesting problems such as:

What is the relationship between L or N and the distance between starting and finishing points as the crow flies?

Is it possible to approximate the route by nonlinear curves in each grid square without too much mathematical complexity?

Is there a lower limit to the ratio L/N for all but certain pathological routes (note that the 5000 simulated routes gave L/N > 0.45)?

Would larger scale or smaller scale maps give different average values?

Finally it is interesting to note the relationship between
this problem and the problem

> "What is the average value of the rectilinear distance
> between the ends of a string thrown down at random
> on a horizontal table?"

which was set by Professor Synge in 1968 and on which several
substantial papers have been written [Synge (1970), Clarke
(1971), Kingman (1982)].

1.7 REFERENCES

Clarke, L.E., 1971, *Math. Gaz.*, 55, 404-407.

Kingman, J.F.C., 1982, *J.R. Statist. Soc. B*, 44, 109-138.

Raggett, G., 1982, Private communications

Synge, J.L., 1968, *Math. Gaz.*, 52, 165.

Synge, J.L., 1970, *Math. Gaz.*, 54, 250-260.

2

Forest management

IAN HUNTLEY *Sheffield City Polytechnic*

2.1 INTRODUCTION

The forest manager faces many interesting biological and
economic problems, among them the following:

> how many trees to plant per acre,
> how often and how much to thin,
> when to harvest the forest,
> what the yield will be.

To help him make the correct decisions the Forestry Commission
produces management tables (see Bradley, Christie and Johnson,
1966), which set out what is expected of the various species of
trees. Simplified examples of two of these, for the particular
case of Douglas Fir, are shown in Figures 2.1 and 2.2.

The commercial value of a stand of trees is determined by the
volume and the quality of the timber the trees can produce, and
clearly depends on the age of the trees. Although the management tables give excellent guidelines on what yield to expect
in any given year, they contain no economic considerations.
Thus it is difficult for the forest manager to know exactly
when to harvest: should he harvest early and have the profit
available to reinvest, or should he wait until later and get a
greater volume of timber and hence a greater return.

It is recognisable that a young tree has no commercial value,
and that the value increases with age as the volume of usable
timber increases. Eventually the tree approaches maturity,
its growth ceases and its value reaches a plateau. Ultimately
decay sets in and the value declines to zero.

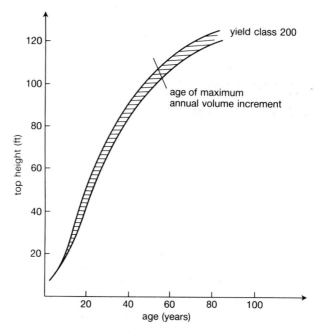

Figure 2.1   Yield class curve for Douglas Fir

(A yield class of 200 is average for this species and indicates
a potential annual volume increment of 200 hoppus ft/acre;
1 hoppus ft is 1.273 cu ft.)

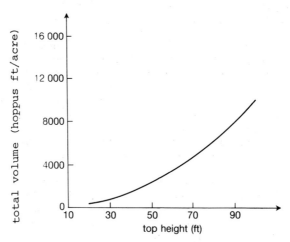

Figure 2.2   Production class curve for Douglas Fir

(1 hoppus ft/acre is 0.089 m^3/ha.)

Although the details of this process depend on the species of
tree and the use to which the timber is to be put, the general
pattern is common to all commercial trees. The problem for the
forestry manager, then, is to use the management curves to
produce a profit versus age graph and then to try to decide when
to fell a given stand of trees.

The first part of this is relatively straightforward: current
timber and felling costs are known, and graphs such as Figures
2.1 and 2.2 give the expected yields. Figure 2.3 gives an
example of a typical graph of commercial value (known as net
stumpage value) against age for the case of Douglas Fir, and
includes the returns from thinning at each stage. We take this
graph as our starting point, and now want to use it to advise
the forest manager on the policy needed to produce a maximum
profit.

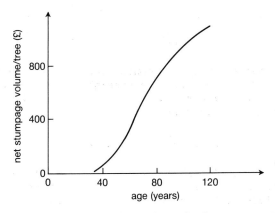

Figure 2.3 Commercial value of a single tree - Douglas Fir

2.2 FIRST THOUGHTS

Assuming that the commercial value V(t) is known as in Figure
2.3, it would seem obvious that we merely choose the value of
t which makes V(t) maximum, so that for Douglas Fir we harvest
when the trees are about 120 years old.

This, however, ignores the fact that a given amount of cash we
have on hand now is more valuable to us than the same amount
received at some later date. [This is true even without
inflation, since money on hand may be invested to produce more
money.] The standard method to account for this is to discount
all monies back to present day values, and obtain what is known
as the Net Present Value. This may be done in two ways:

discretely (for example annually) using a factor $(1+i)^{-n}$, where i is the discrete interest rate and n denotes the time;

continuously, using factor e^{-rt}, where r is the continuous interest rate and t the time.

The approaches are very similar, and for convenience we here discount the stumpage value by the factor e^{-rt}, where r is the continuous interest rate, and obtain the present value of the future earnings as

$$PV = e^{-rt}.V(t).$$

To obtain the year t=T at which the present value will be maximum we differentiate this expression and set the answer to zero, to obtain

$$\frac{V'(T)}{V(T)} = r.$$

The appendix contains the data concerning V(t) from which Figure 2.3 was drawn, and it is a straightforward matter to fit this data set with a least squares line. A good fit is obtained with the straight line

$$V(t) = 13.26\ t - 451.8$$

and we may now plot $V'(T)/V(T)$, known as the relative growth rate. This is shown in Figure 2.4, where the portion of the graph to the left of the asymptote is not meaningful in reality.

Knowing the prevailing interest rate r, we may now read off the age T at which the tree should be felled. For instance, if r = 10% = 0.1 (corresponding to an annually compounded interest rate of 10.5%), we would choose to harvest Douglas Fir at an age of about 50 years.

2.3 FURTHER THOUGHTS

The solution above ignores an important aspect of the forest rotation problem: once the trees are removed from a given area, the land is available for new forest growth. Clearly, the longer the felling of the existing forest is delayed, the longer it takes to acquire revenue from future harvests.

We also notice that after each successive harvest we are faced with a problem identical to the original one: when should the

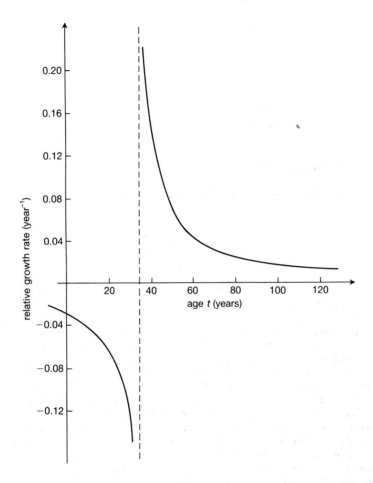

Figure 2.4   Relative growth rate against age - Douglas Fir

next crop of timber be cut? Thus, assuming a fairly stable
economic climate, it follows that each crop should be allowed
to grow for the same time T.

Letting V now include the sum of felling and replanting, we
can generalise our original solution to obtain the total
present value of all future harvests as

$$PV = e^{-rt}.V(T) + e^{-2rT}.V(2T-T) + \ldots$$

$$= \sum_{n=1}^{\infty} e^{-nrT}.V(T)$$

$$= \frac{V(T)}{e^{rT} - 1}$$

where we assume an infinite time horizon.

Maximising this expression with respect to T then requires that

$$\frac{V'(T)}{V(T)} = \frac{r}{1 - e^{-rT}}$$

which is known as the Faustmann formula after a 19th century German forester.

To obtain the optimal rotation period T, we must solve the above equation. The left-hand side we have seen before: it is the relative biological growth rate sketched in Figure 2.4. Thus if we graph the right-hand side (known as the relative economic growth rate) also, and superimpose the two, we may read off the value of T for any interest rate r. This is shown in Figure 2.5. It is clear that, since Douglas Fir takes a considerable time to mature, the effect of crop rotation is very small. The Appendix also contains figures for European Larch, however, a tree which matures much earlier; a similar analysis then shows a much more marked effect. Graphs such as these are of great value to forestry management.

2.4 PARTING COMMENTS

1. It could well be claimed that the manager ought to be maximising the average annual yield $V(T)/T$. Confirm that this corresponds to zero discounting $(r=0)$.

2. The Faustmann model can be used to predict the response of the forestry industry to a change in the demand for forest products or in the relative cost of logging. For further details see Clark (1976).

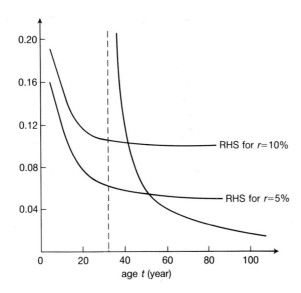

Figure 2.5 Graphical determination of the optimal rotation
period T

REFERENCES

Bradley, R.T., Christie, J.M. and Johnson, D.R., 1966, Forest
    Management Tables.   HMSO.

Clark, C.W., 1976, Mathematical Bioeconomics. Wiley
    Interscience.

Pearse, P., 1967, The Optimal Forest Rotation. *Forestry
    Chronical,* 43, 178-195.

APPENDIX

Typical net stumpage values, V(t), for Douglas Fir and
European Larch (from Pearse, 1967).

Age (years)	Fir value ($)	Larch value ($)
20	0	0
30	0	60
40	43	132
50	143	198
60	303	258
70	497	319
80	650	368
90	805	405
100	913	429
110	1000	
120	1075	

3

Apportionment

DAVID BURGHES *Exeter University*

3.1 BACKGROUND INFORMATION

The apportionment of the members of the House of Representatives in the U.S.A. is referred to in the Constitution, Article 1, Section 3.2:

"Representatives and direct taxes shall be apportioned among the several states ... according to their respective numbers ... The number of Representatives shall not exceed one for every thirty thousand, but each state shall have at least one representative".

Originally the number of representatives was set at 65 but Congress does have the power to vary the size of the House. This has steadily increased until, in 1910, it was set at 435, which is the present size of the House.

The constitution does not though expressly state what system of apportionment should be used, and in 1881, while considering reapportionment of the members, Congress discovered the following startling fact. Using their current method of appointment, the state of Alabama would be entitled to 8 representatives in a House having 299 members, but in a House having 300 members it would only receive 7 representatives! This strange occurrence, known as the "Alabama Paradox", was in fact no isolated incident.

The method of apportionment being used at this time was called the Vinton method, and we will illustrate its use with the following example:

In a college, there are

    (i)   103 staff members in the Science Faculty
   (ii)   63 staff members in the Arts Faculty
  (iii)   34 staff members in the Education Faculty

and the college has 20 members elected to its governing body,
Senate, from the three faculties, the number from each faculty
in proportion to the staff size of that faculty.

Faculty	Staff Nos.	% of Staff	Exact No. of Senate Representatives
SCIENCE	103	51.5	10.3
ARTS	63	31.5	6.3
EDUCATION	34	17.0	3.4
TOTALS	200	100	20.0

But clearly representatives of each faculty must be whole
numbers. In this way we obtain the following whole
representatives:

Science	10
Arts	6
Education	3

giving 19 members. The Vinton method allocates the final seat
to the faculty with the highest fractional part, which in this
example is the Education Faculty, with 0.4. So we obtain the
table:

Faculty	% Staff	Exact No. in 20 seat Senate	No. of seats
SCIENCE	51.5	10.3	10
ARTS	31.5	6.3	6
EDUCATION	17.0	3.4	4
TOTALS	100	20.0	20

For a 21 seat allocation we have the following table:

Faculty	% Staff	Exact No. in 21 seat Senate	No. of seats
SCIENCE	51.5	10.815	11
ARTS	31.5	6.615	7
EDUCATION	17.0	3.570	3
TOTALS	100	21.0	21

The whole number allocation gives 10 to Science, 6 to Arts and 3 to Education, giving a total of 19 seats. The remaining two seats are allocated to the two higher fractional parts, which gives one more to each of Science and Arts.

The final result now gives only 3 seats to Education - a decrease of 1 despite an increase in the total number of seats! At first this does indeed seem a paradox. We will give you another set of figures to try out, by which time you should be starting to think about how best to get out of this paradox.

3.2   PROBLEM STATEMENT

The populations of the five states that comprise the Kingdom of Jedesland are given in the table below:

State	Population
Floodland	9061
Galeland	7179
Hailland	5259
Snowland	3319
Rainland	1182

At present the ruling Council for the Kingdom of Jedesland has 26 members, the number of members being decided according to the respective populations of the states and using the Vinton method of apportionment (see Section 3.1). The ruling Council has decided to increase its size to 28, but the state of Snowland has threatened to declare itself independent and leave the Kingdom.

Can you explain why the state of Snowland is contemplating such serious action, and can you provide a suitable solution to the crisis?

3.3   THE CRISIS

The impending U.D.I. by the state of Snowland is due to the
effect of the 2-seat increase in the ruling Council of the
Kingdom of Jedesland.   The figures for the allocation of the
seats to the five member states, according to the Vinton
method are given below.

(i)   26-seat Council

State	Population	% Population	Exact Quota	Allocation
Floodland	9061	34.850	9.061	9
Galeland	7179	27.612	7.179	7
Hailland	5259	20.227	5.259	5
Snowland	3319	12.765	3.319	4
Rainland	1182	4.546	1.182	1
Totals	26000		26.0	26

(ii)   28-seat Council

State	Exact Quota	Allocation	Change from above
Floodland	9.758	10	+1
Galeland	7.731	8	+1
Hailland	5.664	6	+1
Snowland	3.574	3	-1
Rainland	1.273	1	0
Totals	28.0	28	

The 2-seat increase in the ruling Council leads to an extra
seat for the states of

Floodland, Galeland, Hailland

but for Snowland, a seat is lost!   So it is clear now why a
crisis has occurred - the state government of Snowland will
certainly not tolerate such a result.

3.4 MATHEMATICAL REPRESENTATION OF APPORTIONMENT

Let $\underset{\sim}{p} = (p_1, p_2, \ldots, p_s)$ be the populations of s states where each $p_i > 0$, and denote the size of the Council by h. In general, we want to find for each h > 0, an apportionment i.e. an s-tuple $(a_1, \ldots, a_s)$ such that $\sum_i a_i = h$.

The "ideal" or strictly proportional number of representatives for state j is given by

$$q_j(\underset{\sim}{p}, h) = p_j h / \sum_i p_i$$

We call this the exact quota. If q_j is integer for all j then $a_j = q_j$ is the perfect solution. This is of course unlikely to occur. Otherwise each state should receive at least its lowest quota, $\lfloor q_j \rfloor$, the largest integer less than or equal to j; but no more than its upper quota $\lceil q_j \rceil$, the smallest integer greater than or equal to q_j.

So any method of apportionment should "satisfy quota", that is the apportionment for each j satisfies

$$\lfloor q_j \rfloor \leq a_j \leq \lceil q_j \rceil$$

Further if we denote a method of apportionment by

$$\underset{\sim}{f} = (a_1, a_2, \ldots, a_s)$$

then $\underset{\sim}{f} = \underset{\sim}{f}(\underset{\sim}{p}, h)$ and in order to avoid the "Alabama paradox" we require

$$\underset{\sim}{f}(\underset{\sim}{p}, h + 1) \geq \underset{\sim}{f}(\underset{\sim}{p}, h)$$

for all h and each component of $\underset{\sim}{f}$. We call such apportionment "house monotone".

In mathematical terms, we are looking for a function $\underset{\sim}{f}(p, h)$ so that the apportionment

$$\underset{\sim}{f} = (a_1, a_2, \ldots, a_s)$$

satisfies

(i) $\lfloor q_j \rfloor < a_j < \lceil q_j \rceil$

(ii) $a_j(\underset{\sim}{p}, h + 1) \geq a_j(\underset{\sim}{p}, h)$ for all h and j

The Vinton method used in the earlier sections clearly satisfies condition (i), but not (ii).

3.5   SOME POSSIBLE SOLUTIONS

(i)   Modified Vinton Method

There have been many attempts to alter the Vinton method in order to produce a "house monotone" method. One such example is the so-called "Modified Vinton" method in which each state is given its lower quota $\lfloor q_j \rfloor$. The states are then ordered by $e_j = (q_j - \lfloor q_j \rfloor)/p_j$ into a priority list where

$$e_{j_1} \geq e_{j_2} \geq \dots\dots\dots$$

The additional seats, in number $h - \sum_i \lfloor q_j \rfloor$, are given according to the priority in the list. Note that this method is identical to the Vinton method, except the measure e_j is used instead of

$$q_j - \lfloor q_j \rfloor.$$

The following tables show its use for a 26, 27, 28 and 29 seat Council.

This method certainly gives a different apportionment, and the "Alabama paradox" is not exhibited in the 26-, 27- and 28- seat Council. Unfortunately (as the governor of Hailland will be quick to point out) for a 29-seat Council Hailland has lost one of its seats! So this method does not give a "house monotone" apportionment.

(i) 26-seat Council

State	Population p_j	Exact Quota q_j	Lower Quota $\lfloor q_j \rfloor$	$q_j - \lfloor q_j \rfloor$	$(q_j - \lfloor q_j \rfloor)/p_j$	Allocation
Floodland	9061	9.061	9	0.061	0.0000067	9
Galeland	7179	7.179	7	0.179	0.0000249	7
Hailland	5259	5.259	5	0.259	0.0000492	5
Snowland	3319	3.319	3	0.319	0.0000961	3
Rainland	1182	1.182	1	0.182	0.0001539*	2

(ii) 27-seat Council

State	Population p_j	Exact Quota q_j	Lower Quota $\lfloor q_j \rfloor$	$q_j - \lfloor q_j \rfloor$	$(q_j - \lfloor q_j \rfloor)/p_j$	Allocation
Floodland	9061	9.410	9	0.410	0.0000452	9
Galeland	7179	7.455	7	0.455	0.0000633	7
Hailland	5259	5.461	5	0.461	0.0000876	5
Snowland	3319	3.447	3	0.447	0.0001346*	4
Rainland	1182	1.227	1	0.227	0.0001920*	2

(iii) 28-seat Council

State	Population p_j	Exact Quota q_j	Lower Quota $\lfloor q_j \rfloor$	$q_j - \lfloor q_j \rfloor$	$(q_j - \lfloor q_j \rfloor)/p_j$	Allocation
Floodland	9061	9.758	9	0.758	0.0000836	9
Galeland	7179	7.731	7	0.731	0.0001018	7
Hailland	5259	5.663	5	0.663	0.0001260*	6
Snowland	3319	3.574	3	0.574	0.0001729*	4
Rainland	1182	1.273	1	0.273	0.0002309*	2

(iv) 29-seat Council

State	Population p_j	Exact Quota q_j	Lower Quota $\lfloor q_j \rfloor$	$q_j - \lfloor q_j \rfloor$	$(q_j - \lfloor q_j \rfloor)/p_j$	Allocation
Floodland	9061	10.106	10	0.106	0.0000117	10
Galeland	7179	8.007	8	0.007	0.0000009	8
Hailland	5259	5.866	5	0.866	0.0001646	5
Snowland	3319	3.702	3	0.702	0.0002115*	4
Rainland	1182	1.318	1	0.318	0.0002690*	2

(ii) Huntington Method

In 1921, E.V. Huntington, Professor of Mathematics at Harvard, investigated "house monotone" methods of apportionment. He realised that the key quantity in any method is that of "amount of inequality" between the representation of two states, and that an appropriate measure for this inequality is needed.

For a population $\underset{\sim}{p} = (p_1, p_2, \ldots, p_s)$, and an apportionment $\underset{\sim}{a} = (a_1, a_2, \ldots, a_s)$ for h, consider the quantity

$$p_i/a_i$$

which represents the average number of constituents per member for state i.   If

$$p_i/a_i > p_j/a_j$$

then state j is "better off" than state i.   In this case, the state j has fewer constituents per member of the Council than state i; we can rewrite the inequality as

$$\frac{p_i a_j}{a_i p_j} > 1$$

or

$$T = \frac{p_i a_j}{a_i p_j} - 1 > 0$$

This measure T represents the relative difference between the apportionments for states i and j where state j is better off than i; for we can write

$$T = \frac{(p_i/a_i) - (p_j/a_j)}{(p_j/a_j)}$$

We clearly want T to be as small as possible - in fact, in the ideal situation T = 0 for all i,j. Huntington used the principle that if a transfer of one representative from state

j to state i lessens the value of T, then it should be made.
He defined the apportionment as STABLE when no such transfer
is justified. Suppose we have such a stable system of
apportionment, but that we have now to allocate one extra seat.

If the seat is given to state i, then it will have a_i + 1 seats
and now be "better off" than state j, with measure

$$T = \frac{p_j(a_i + 1)}{a_j\, p_i} - 1$$

whereas if state j gains the extra seat, it will certainly be
better off than i and the measure is

$$T_2 = \frac{p_i(a_j + 1)}{a_i\, p_j} - 1$$

The extra seat will go to state i if $T_1 < T_2$, and state j if
$T_2 < T_1$. Thus if

$$\frac{p_j(a_i + 1)}{a_j\, p_i} - 1 < \frac{p_i(a_j + 1)}{a_i\, p_j} - 1$$

then state i gets the extra seat. The inequality leads to

$$\frac{p_j(a_i + 1)}{a_j\, p_i} < \frac{p_i(a_j + 1)}{a_i\, p_j}$$

or

$$\frac{p_j^2}{a_j(a_j + 1)} < \frac{p_i^2}{a_i(a_i + 1)}$$

So we conclude that the seat goes to the state which has the
largest value of $Q = p^2/a\,(a + 1)$ or $p/\sqrt{a(a + 1)}$.

In the usual application of Huntington's method (or "equal
proportion" - E.P. for short), we start by allocating one seat
to each state, and then evaluate the number Q for each state.

The state with the largest value of Q is allocated the seat, and the process continues. A quick way to see how 26 or 28 seats would be allocated is to form the table below.

Floodland	Galeland	Hailland	Snowland	Rainland
$\dfrac{9061}{\sqrt{1.2}}$	$\dfrac{7179}{\sqrt{1.2}}$	$\dfrac{5259}{\sqrt{1.2}}$	$\dfrac{3319}{\sqrt{1.2}}$	$\dfrac{1182}{\sqrt{1.2}}$
$\dfrac{9061}{\sqrt{2.3}}$	$\dfrac{7179}{\sqrt{2.3}}$	$\dfrac{5259}{\sqrt{2.3}}$	$\dfrac{3319}{\sqrt{2.3}}$	$\dfrac{1182}{\sqrt{2.3}}$
$\dfrac{9061}{\sqrt{3.4}}$	$\dfrac{7179}{\sqrt{3.4}}$	...	...	...
...	...	...	...	...

This leads to the following table:

Floodland		Galeland		Hailland		Snowland		Rainland
6407	- 6	5076	- 7	3719	- 8	2347	- 12	836
3699	- 9	2931	- 10	2147	- 13	1355	- 20	483
2616	- 11	2072	- 14	1518	- 18	958	- 27	...
2026	- 15	1605	- 17	1176	- 23	742		...
1658	- 16	1311	- 21	960		...		...
1401	- 19	1108	- 24	811		...		...
1211	- 22	959		...		...		...
1070	- 25	846		...		...		...
957	- 26	...		...		...		...
866	- 28	...		...		...		...

Five seats have already been allocated (one to each state), and the following seats are allocated according to the numerical ordering in the table. The seat allocation is numbered on the table above. So we obtain the following allocations.

	Council Size		
	26	27	28
Floodland	10	10	11
Galeland	7	7	7
Hailland	5	5	5
Snowland	3	4	4
Rainland	1	1	1

Although the Huntingdon method replaced the Vinton method for the allocation of extra seats to the House of Representatives in the U.S.A. it does have one serious drawback. Although by its construction it is house monotone, it unfortunately does not always satisfy "quota". For example, consider the allocation of 100 seats in the following table:

State	Population	Exact Quota	Allocation
A	9215	92.15	90
B	159	1.59	2
C	158	1.58	2
D	157	1.57	2
E	156	1.56	2
F	155	1.55	2
Totals	10,000	100	100

So although states B, C, D, E and F are within quota, the same is not true for state A - to satisfy quota, it should have either 92 or 93 seats - not 90! For further details see Huntingdon (1928).

(iii) Other Methods

There are many other methods that have been proposed for apportionment. Many of these are house monotone, but do not necessarily satisfy quota. For example, instead of using the formula

$$Q = p^2/a \, (a + 1) \quad \text{or} \quad Q^{\frac{1}{2}} = p/[a \, (a + 1)]^{\frac{1}{2}}$$

as in the Huntington method, we can replace $Q^{\frac{1}{2}}$ by

(a) $p/(a + \frac{1}{2})$ - Webster's method (or Major Fractions)

(b) $p/(a + 1)$ - Jefferson's method (or D'Hondt Rule)

(c) $p/\{2a(a + 1)/(2a + 1)\}$ - harmonic mean

In each case, though, we will find that these methods do not in general "satisfy quota". We will leave it to the reader to show this.

So we are still left with the problem of finding a method of apportionment which both "satisfies quota" and is "house monotone". Such methods do exist and the interested reader can find more details in Balinski and Young (1975).

3.6   A RESOLUTION OF THE CRISIS

In section 3.5 we have outlined some methods for apportionment, and, for example, the Huntington method does not give rise to the "Alabama paradox" type of situation. On the other hand these methods that are "house monotone" require allocating each seat on an individual basis, building up from a, say, 5-seat council, to a 26-seat council or 28-seat council in single steps. But, as we have seen, a 26-seat council apportioned according to the Huntington method does not give to the presently constituted council - so it will be difficult to convince all states of the worth of a 28 seat council, apportioned according to the Huntington method.

Luckily, wiser councils prevailed, and the Kingdom dropped its plan for a 28 seat council, returning to its original 26 seat council!

3.7   RELATED PROBLEMS

(i)   Ten seats on the halls of residence committee are to be apportioned to three halls A, B and C. There are 235 students in A, 333 in B and 432 in C. Use an apportionment method to allocate the seats.

(ii)   If the representation on the committee is increased to 15, how should the 5 new seats be distributed?

(iii)   Does the apportionment principle described above give an ideal method for apportioning members in the House of Representatives in accordance with the constitution?

REFERENCES

Balinski, M.L. and Young, H.P., 1975,　The Quota Method of
　Apportionment.　*Amer. Math. Mon.*, 701-730.

Huntington, E.V., 1928,　The Apportionment of Representatives
　in Congress.　*Trans. Amer. Math. Soc.*, 85-110.

4

The length of a roll of toilet paper

DON THATCHER *Leicester Polytechnic*

4.1 STATEMENT OF THE PROBLEM

Given a roll of paper find without unwrapping it the total
length of paper on the roll. A single sheet of paper is also
provided which may be used for measuring.

The problem is posed to a class in the above manner and has
been successfully undertaken by several classes where the
students have either worked individually or in groups of up to
10. Each group is given a toilet roll which is sealed
together with a single sheet of paper from which measurements
may be taken as required. No equipment is offered but, when
requested by the students, micrometers should be available (it
is quite common that students will have to be taught how to
use a micrometer - a useful exercise in itself). One of the
problems of having several groups in a class is that as soon
as one person or group has thought of an idea it tends to
spread rapidly to everyone else, despite this it is always
surprising how many different methods of solution are offered
by one class.

Working on their own students usually begin, quite correctly,
by drawing suitable sketches and introducing any necessary
variables. The three main sketches produced are as shown in
Figure 4.1.

Figure 4.1(a) is quickly discarded. In many cases not
because the students feel that the diagram is wrong, nor that
they feel the contribution due to the bump is negligible, but
because they do not know what to do next.

The important points to be brought out here are that the bump
is quite likely negligible and, in any case, when producing a

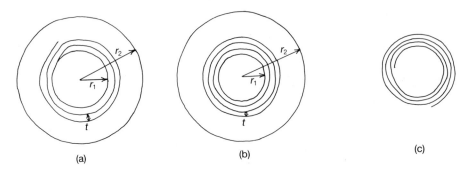

Figure 4.1 Sketches of paper roll
(a) 'reality'   (b) 'concentric circles'   (c) 'a spiral'

first model to keep it simple while making a note of the
factors that have not been taken into account - for possible
inclusion later.

The majority of students will eventually choose to use the
diagram shown in Figure 4.1(b)(or a derivative of it) and
probably choose it for the right reasons; that is, it gives a
reasonable representation of the problem and the mathematical
model should not be too difficult.

Having ignored the fact that the central core is circular the
diagram shown in Figure 4.1(c) is occasionally followed by a
few students either because the resultant mathematics is more
interesting (results given below) or in a genuine belief that
this is 'correct'.

4.2   VARIOUS MATHEMATICAL MODELS

4.2.1 *Direct Length Models*

The Concentric Circles of Figure 4.1(b)

$$\text{Thickness of paper} = t \quad \text{(as above)}$$
$$\text{Inner radius} = r_1$$
$$\text{Outer radius} = r_2$$

It is merely a case of writing down the length of paper in each
turn and summing over all such turns.

Suggestions for the length of the first turn are:-

$$2\pi r_1, \ 2\pi(r_1 + t), \ 2\pi(r + t/2)$$

and corresponding second turns of

$$2\pi(r_1 + t),\ 2\pi(r_1 + 2t),\ 2\pi(r_1 + 3t/2) \text{ etc.}$$

If there are n turns, the last length will be

$$2\pi(r_1 + (n-1)t),\ 2\pi(r_1 + nt),\ 2\pi(r_1 + (2n-1)t/2)$$

There is often much debate amongst students as to which is 'correct'. Eventually they make their own choice and proceed, resigned to the fact that they will produce different answers. Rarely does any one suggest that the difference between any two should be evaluated - it may well turn out to be negligible! Each forms an arithmetic progression with corresponding sum (total length).

$$2\pi n(r_1 + (n-1)t/2),\ 2\pi n(r_1 + (n+1)t/2),\ 2\pi n(r_1 + nt/2)$$

the difference between the first two being nt where nt is the total thickness of paper on the roll. For practical purposes this amount could be ignored, as it would be small compared with the overall length and small compared to the errors introduced through inaccurate measurement.

The number of turns n can then be calculated from

$$n = (r_2 - r_1)/t$$

which in the third case leads to

$$\text{total length} = \pi(r_2^2 - r_1^2)/t$$

The spiral of Figure 4.1(c)

Due to the relative complexity of the problem this is rarely undertaken.

All students who decide to tackle the problem this way choose the Archimedean spiral

$$r = t\theta \qquad \text{where r is the radius and } \theta \text{ is the angle.}$$

4.2.2 *The cross-sectional area methods*

Several groups base their model on

$$\text{Length of toilet roll} = \frac{\text{cross-sectional area of toilet papers}}{\text{thickness of a single sheet}}$$

The most natural technique to use here is to find the difference in areas between the circles formed using the inner and outer radii; that is,

$$\pi r_2^2 - \pi r_1^2$$

thus leading to

$$\text{length of the paper} = \pi (r_2^2 - r_1^2)/t$$

which we note is the same result as obtained previously!

This method, while offering an easier approach mathematically was no more accurate than methods above as it relies upon measurements and calculation of t, r_1, and r_2.

An alternative area method is to imagine that the toilet roll is cut, as shown in Figure 4.2, and opened out to form a trapezium.

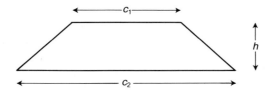

Figure 4.2   Trapezium cut

$$\text{Length of toilet roll} = \frac{\text{Area of trapezium}}{\text{Thickness of a single sheet}}$$

$$= \frac{(c_1 + c_2)h/2}{t}$$

$$= \frac{\pi (r_1 + r_2)(r_2 - r_1)}{t}$$

$$= \frac{\pi (r_2^2 - r_1^2)}{t}$$

4.2.3 Weighing methods

Many groups will consider weighing the given toilet roll and the single sheet of paper and then use the formula

Length of toilet roll =

$$\frac{\text{Weight of toilet roll}}{\text{Weight of single sheet}} \times \text{length of 1 sheet}$$

but will dismiss the method, regarding the actual weighing as impractical.

The few that do decide to pursue this model will have realised that very accurate weighings of a single sheet may be obtained using a chemical balance. A welcome trip to the Chemical Engineering Department is then undertaken. A single sheet may be easily weighed to an accuracy of 0.01g and by finding a similar inner core and weighing that, it is thus possible to find the weight of the toilet paper and hence the total number of sheets of paper, which in turn gives the total length.

2.4 MEASURING THE THICKNESS OF THE PAPER

There are several techniques used for measuring the thickness of the paper, examples being:

(a) Take the single sheet as it is and attempt to measure it. The relative error in this method is very high; many of the students using this method will suggest that the task is impossible rather than suspecting that they have a poor technique.

(b) Take the single sheet and fold it several times and then measure the thickness - a much improved result is obtained.

(c) It has been known for some students to show initiative(?) and collect all the single sheets in the class at that time, fold them a few times and then measure the total thickness - this tends to give the most accurate result.

(d) All members of a group individually measure the thickness and the group takes the average.

Great care has to be taken not to squash the paper too much when using the micrometer with similar care being taken when obtaining the radii. The radii will often be measured with a ruler. A useful point to bring out here is that of accuracy of data. The general belief amongst students (and staff) is

that published data is good while one's own data is poor. It
is worth pointing out that if the students' data were to be
published that would not change the quality of that data.

One other measurement has to be taken at the end of the
exercise, that being the length of the roll. The most
successful technique is to lay it, a length at a time, on the
floor of the classroom (it is at this point that colleagues
always look in and express their doubts about the topic of
Mathematical Modelling!)

4.3   RESULTS FROM A GROUP OF 11 STUDENTS

Data applies to a standard "Izal Medicated Toilet Roll"

The following methods were adopted:

4.3.1 Weighing Method

All weighings were carried out on a chemical balance accurate
to 0.01g.

All lengths were measured using a ruler accurate to 1mm.

        Total weight of toilet roll as provided = 157.22 g
        Weight of SIMILAR inner core   =   6.12 g
        Weight of SIMILAR paper wrapper   =   1.81 g

        Weight of toilet paper = 149.79 g

Each of the 11 students was given a single sheet of toilet
paper. The group weighed batches of 10 sheets, found the mean
weight and divided by 10 to give the weight of one sheet.

        Weight of single sheet = 0.4355 g

To measure the length of one sheet the mean of the lengths of
the 11 sheets was taken.

        Length of one sheet = 16.56 cm

    No. of sheets = Weight of roll/Weight of 1 sheet

                   = 149.29/0.4355

                   = 342.8 sheets

and length of roll = No. of sheets × length of 1 sheet

                   = 342.8 × 16.56

                   = 56.77 m

Comments:

(a)   The students observed that most toilet rolls have a
      fraction of a sheet at the end where it is attached to
      the cardboard core, and were therefore happy to accept
      0.8 of a sheet in 342.8 sheets.

(b)   The students experimented with the numbers to get a feel
      for errors - they concluded that the most significant
      error would be due to the weight of the core and wrapper,
      as they are obtained from SIMILAR toilet rolls.

4.3.2 Cross Sectional Area/Thickness Method

(a)

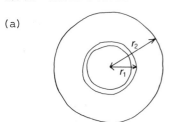

Measure r_1 and r_2 with a
ruler, and the thickness of
one sheet using a micrometer.
Taking the mean values for
the group
r_2 = 36.92mm, r_1 = 19.3mm,
t = 0.03735mm, giving

$$\text{Length} = \pi(r_2^2 - r_1^2)/t = \pi(36.92^2 - 19.3^2)/0.03735$$

$$= \underline{83.32m}$$

(b)

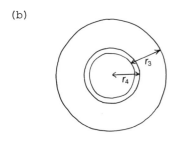

Measure r_3 and the thickness
of the core using a micrometer, and r_4 using a ruler

giving group mean values.
r_3 = 14.55mm, r_4 = 18mm

thickness of core = 0.78mm
Using the notation as in (a),
r_2 = 32.55mm, r_1 = 18.78mm,
t = 0.03735mm, giving

$$\text{Length} = \pi(32.55^2 - 18.78^2)/0.03735$$

$$= \underline{59.45m}$$

Comments:

Method (b) should be more accurate as it takes into account
the "natural compression" of the paper i.e. the sample sheets
and the actual roll both suffer similar compressions when
using the micrometer.

The actual length of paper was found by counting the total
number of sheets on the roll - giving

Length = No. of sheets × length of 1 sheet

= 336 × 16.56

= 55.64m

4.4 CONCLUSIONS

This problem is seen as a useful first modelling problem as it
incorporates many important features

- It is simple, the students understand the problem and do not
  have to be given large quantities of background information.

- There are several models that may be adopted, highlighting
  the point that most problems do not have just one answer.
  The mathematics required is in general very easy.

- The problem can be performed within the classroom within a
  small amount of time and the actual answer is known or can
  be found.

- Some data collection is required.

One disadvantage is that it is a contrived example, but some
of the techniques used here can be adopted when solving real
problems; for example "Air Gap Coiling of a Steel Strip"
(Huntley 1981).

REFERENCES

Huntley, I.D., 1981, Air Gap Coiling of Steel Strip. In:
    Case Studies in Mathematical Modelling (Eds., James, D.J.G.
    and McDonald, J.J.), Stanley Thornes (Pub) Ltd., Cheltenham,
    England.

5

Can water in a boat ever make it more stable?

GEORGE HALL   *Nottingham University*

5.1   STATEMENT OF PROBLEM

One day last summer, when I had some water in the bottom of
my dinghy, somebody said 'Does the water act like ballast to
make it more stable or like shifting cargo to increase the
risk of overturning?'

Stated in this way the problem is a general one and a satisfactory answer will have to be equally general. It is very
difficult, however, to find such an answer by a direct attack
on the problem. The alternative is to consider models of
boats with various shapes and investigate their stability both
with and without water. From these it may be possible to
generalize the results to apply to the complicated shapes of
real boats. The shapes of the models should be chosen in part
to approximate to real hulls and in part to display the
different factors that determine the result.

5.2   BACKGROUND - BUOYANCY

The weight of a boat (Mg) is a force acting downwards through
the centre of mass. When the boat floats in equilibrium this
force is exactly balanced by the upward thrust of the water on
the hull. Were the boat to be removed this upwater thrust
would exactly balance the downward force of the water that
would take its place (the displaced water). In other words,
as every schoolchild since the time of Archimedes knows, a
floating body displaces its own weight of water.

In equilibrium the upward and downward forces act in the same
line. When the boat heels in the wind, i.e. rotates sidewards
through a fore and aft axis, the forces remain parallel and
equal in magnitude but, in general, act in different lines so

that a couple is produced. In a stable design of boat this
will be a righting couple acting against the couple produced
by the wind and restoring its equilibrium when the wind drops.
The downward force always acts through the boat's centre of
mass (G) while the upward force acts through the centre of mass
of the 'displaced water', usually called the centre of buoyancy
(B). On heeling, one side of the hull emerges from the water
and the other is wetted so the displaced water is changed and
its centre of mass altered. Clearly, the geometry of the hull
has an important influence in determining stability.

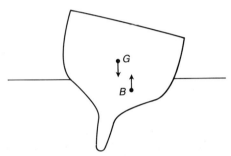

Figure 5.1   Centre of mass and centre of buoyancy

In principle, the stability of the boat under other distur-
bances should also be considered. Most boats are so much
longer than they are wide that a pitching displacement, i.e.
bows moving up and down, does not produce instability except
to the stomach. A yawing motion, i.e. a rotation about a
vertical axis, is also possible but, since this leaves the
centres of gravity and buoyancy unchanged, the equilibrium is
unaffected. Dynamical effects due to motion of the water
inside the boat can also be ignored since they constitute
another problem.

5.3   TEACHING NOTES

This problem involves modelling in an unusual sense. Model
shapes are required instead of model equations. Various shapes
of hull should be considered and, if necessary, a hint given
that multihulls occur as well as monohulls. It may be useful
to point out that the centre of mass of a triangular lamina is
at its centroid and to refer to other shapes.

Even when successful models have been found it is non-trivial
to formulate valid generalizations and conclusions.

The metacentre and centres of pressure are best avoided.

5.4   THE CYLINDRICAL BOAT OR CANOE

The simplest model of the underwater portion of a hull is a
hollow semi-circular cylinder. This is, perhaps, a reasonable
approximation to the shape of the canoe. When the cylinder
rotates the displaced water is unchanged so the centre of
buoyancy is fixed vertically below the axis of the cylinder.
For stability, the centre of gravity must lie below the
axis of the cylinder since this ensures a righting couple.

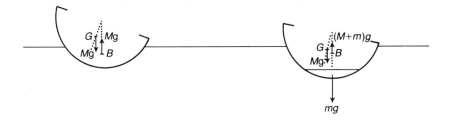

Figure 5.2   Righting Couple on Canoe with and without water

When water is added inside such a boat its weight (mg) will
add to the downward forces. It will also lower the boat in
the water and so increase the mass of displaced water to M + m.
If the inside of the hull is a coaxial cylinder then the water
maintains its position relative to the outside water when the
hull rotates. By taking moments about the axis it is clear
that, since the buoyancy and the weight of the internal water
always act through the axis, the righting couple is entirely
due to the weight of the boat and is unchanged by the water.
Thus the presence of water does not alter the stability of
this model boat.

5.5   THE TWO-CYLINDER BOAT OR CATAMARAN

The next simplest model of a boat consists of two circular
cylinders rigidly connected together. Although this most
closely copies a catamaran it also mimics certain features of
a broad beamed hull. When the boat heels, one cylinder rises
in the water and the other is depressed. The upward thrust
on the lower cylinder is then increased at the expense of that
on the higher one. It is this that produces the righting
couple. As the angle of heel increases one cylinder leaves the
water entirely and the other displaces twice its original
volume of water. The centre of buoyancy has then moved to the
vertical plane through the lower cylinder.

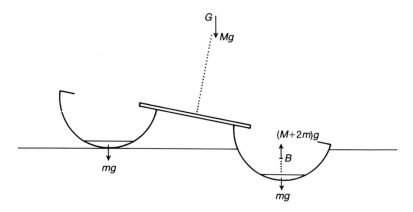

Figure 5.3 Righting Couple on Catamaran

If water enters both cylinders then, as with the single cylinder, the centres of gravity and of buoyancy and the cylinder axes all drop. Since the weight of the extra water in the lower cylinder always acts in the same line as the buoyancy when the upper cylinder is out of the water it contributes nothing to the righting couple. The weight of water in the upper cylinder, on the other hand, does give an additional couple in the correct sense so that the stability is slightly improved. Geometry shows that the angle of heel required to raise one cylinder out of the water is increased. The righting couple up to that angle is then greater than in the absence of water.

The model proves that there do exist boats whose stability is improved by water.

5.6 THE SQUARE-WALLED BOAT OR TANKER

Another simple model of boat has rectangular shape, c.f. a match box. This is a good approximation to an oil tanker and to certain dinghies. When such a boat heels, the edge on one side digs further into the water and the opposite side lifts up. This implies an appreciable sidewards movement of the centre of buoyancy and a large righting couple. It is this movement of B which makes the tanker so much more stable than the canoe.

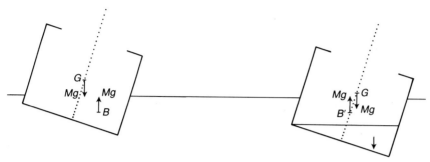

Figure 5.4 Righting Couple on Tanker

This water adds a downward force to the boat but because the
boat is lower in the water its weight is exactly cancelled by
the extra buoyancy. It is convenient to define a modified
buoyancy in which the cancellation is effected. This buoyancy
is then due to that part of the boat below water level which
is filled with air. In effect the surface of the water inside
can be treated as the bottom of the boat. The modified
buoyancy B' in Figure 5.4 is at the centre of the parallelogram
on the dotted medial line. For small angles of heel its
position is fixed in this line. If it lies below G, as shown,
the couple is in the wrong direction and the boat is unstable.
If B' is above G there will be a righting couple.

5.7 THE INTERNALLY PARTITIONED TANKER

A practical solution, often suggested, to this problem of
water flowing to the lowest point is to partition the boat
internally. This leads to the same model as connecting rigidly
together two tanker models. The medial partition prevents
water moving freely inside the boat and ensures that the major
part of the righting couple remains. The argument is similar
to that of the catamaran though any calculation of the effect
is much more complicated. Figure 5.5 shows that, because of
the partition, more air remains on the lower side and this
produces the couple required for stability.

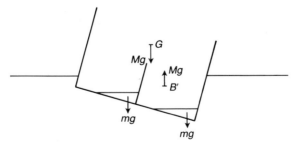

Figure 5.5 Effect of partition

5.8   A GENERAL ARGUMENT

The stability of most boats is due to the righting couple
produced by the greater volume of water displaced on the lower
side when the boat heels. If there is water inside and it is
free to move it will move on heeling to preserve a level
surface and hence to the lower side. The water displaced to
balance the boat's own weight will be the water that occupied
the volume of air above this internal water. In the end
internal water will eliminate that part of the righting couple
due to the wetted part of the bottom surface. Thus the general
consequence of water is reduced stability.

When the water inside the boat is constrained other effects
can be obtained. The traditional purpose of ballast is to
lower the boat in the water so that the broader parts of the
hull can be more fully submerged and so contribute more to the
righting couple. Such an effect can be obtained with water
ballast provided the water is sufficiently constrained to
prevent much movement and preferably towards the sides of the
boat.

REFERENCES

A more sophisticated approach to this problem is given in

Lamb, H., 1944 Statics Third Edition. CUP.

Muckle, W., 1975 Naval Architecture. for Marine Engineers.
   Newns-Butterworths.

Part II: Models for class development

6

Accident investigations

ROY SMITH *Leicester Polytechnic* and
JOHN HURST *Coventry Polytechnic*

6.1 INTRODUCTION

Following serious road accidents, the police wish to have
estimates of the speeds of the vehicles involved. Even if the
drivers are in a position to provide this information, the
police will want to have supportive evidence based on their
own observations.

Under suitable conditions, skid marks will be left on the
road. The appearance of these marks will give an indication
of the type of skid involved. Skid marks of a black, solid
appearance indicate a straight line skid, with the wheels
locked, while those of a "herring bone" appearance indicate
a skid around a curve, with the wheels revolving but slipping
sideways.

It is assumed that students have a knowledge of elementary
particle dynamics, to include motion in a straight line,
motion in a circle and friction.

6.2 ACCIDENT INVESTIGATION 1

STATEMENT OF PROBLEM

A car was driving towards some traffic lights which turned
red. The car screeched to a halt leaving some long skid marks
on the road. A policeman passing by heard the noise and when
he saw the skid marks he accused the driver of speeding.

Suggest a strategy for the police to enable them to calculate
the speed of the car just before it braked.

6.3   SIMPLE MODEL

A car driver braked fiercely and the car left skid marks on
the road. So the wheels were locked, ie. not revolving,
while the car slowed down. It was the friction between the
car tyres and the road, not the friction between the brakes
and the wheel, which stopped the car. The braking will not
have been as efficient as it would have been had the wheels
not locked up. Nevertheless, for a flat road in good, dry
conditions the stopping distances in the Highway Code give a
fair indication of the speed. Students should be able to
deduce that this data leads to a relationship between the
initial speed u, in m.p.h. and the braking distance s in feet,
given by

$$u^2 = 20s.$$

The length of the skid marks left by the car can be measured
and taken to be the braking distance. (In fact the car will
brake for a short time before the brakes lock up and there
will be a further short distance before the tyres leave skid
marks.) Hence

$$u = \sqrt{20s}.$$

Clearly this will not give a very good answer, but for long
skids in good conditions it will give an indication of the
speed involved. It has the benefit of being an easy model.

6.4   IMPROVED MODEL

The car was stopped by the friction between the tyres and the
road surface. Assume that this force was constant along the
whole length of the skid and take μ to be the coefficient of
friction. Newton's second law of motion can be used to show
that a, the car's deceleration during the skid, is given by

$$a = \mu g.$$

Since the deceleration is constant

$$v^2 = u^2 - 2as,$$

so that
$$u^2 = 2as;$$

i.e.
$$u^2 = ks,$$

where $k = 2a = 2\mu g$.

To determine the initial speed of the car it is necessary to
know a or μ. Some Police Forces print tables of values for
different types of road surfaces under different conditions;
see Table 6.1. However, it is preferable to measure a, or μ,
at the scene of the accident. One way of doing this is to
mount an accelerometer in a car and measure the deceleration
when the car brakes fiercely. However, a more popular method
is to skid a car to a halt from a known speed; the new skid
can then be measured and used to calculate a. This has the
advantage that it automatically allows for any slope in the
road. The police lay down two test skids and use the longer
to calculate the deceleration. It is difficult, usually, to
decide where a skid mark starts, so investigators need to be
careful when examining the scene of the accident. Further,
measurements cannot be taken exactly so it is usual to allow
an error of about 5% in the final answer, based on experience
gained in test runs by the police. A copy of an exhibit
produced by a Leicestershire policeman is given in Appendix 1
to illustrate how the calculations can be presented. (The
names have been changed!)

6.5 EXTENSIONS

1. Discuss the case of an incline and check that $u^2 = ks$.

2. What happens if part of the road has just been resurfaced
    and the car skidded from new tarmac onto old?

3. What happens if the slope of the road varies dramatically
    as would occur if a car skidded over the brow of a hill?

6.6 ACCIDENT INVESTIGATION 2

   STATEMENT OF PROBLEM

A car screeched round a corner and ended up in the ditch by
the side of the road. The police were called and when they
arrived they made detailed measurements of the skid marks left
on the road by the car. These measurements were used to draw
a plan of the scene of the accident, as shown in Figure 6.1.

When interviewed the driver said that the car's brakes failed
as he came into the bend and so he could not slow the car
down. He also said that he was driving at about 40 m.p.h.
(the speed limit for that road) when he entered the bend. An
examination of the car confirmed that the brakes were not
working at the time of the accident. But was the driver
telling the truth about his speed?

TABLE 6.1

Possible ranges of road drag factors for rubber tyres

Description of road surface	DRY				WET			
	Less than 30 mph		More than 30 mph		Less than 30 mph		More than 30 mph	
	From	To	From	To	From	To	From	To
CONCRETE								
New, Sharp,	.80	1.00	.70	.85	.50	.80	.40	.75
Travelled	.60	.80	.60	.75	.45	.70	.45	.65
Traffic Polish	.55	.75	.50	.65	.45	.65	.45	.60
ASPHALT or TAR								
New, Sharp,	.80	1.00	.65	.70	.50	.80	.45	.75
Travelled	.60	.80	.55	.70	.45	.70	.40	.65
Traffic Polish	.55	.75	.45	.65	.45	.65	.40	.60
Excess Tar	.50	.60	.35	.60	.30	.60	.25	.55
BRICK								
New, Sharp	.75	.95	.60	.85	.50	.75	.40	.70
Traffic Polish	.60	.80	.55	.75	.40	.70	.40	.60
STONE BLOCK								
New, Sharp	.75	1.00	.70	.90	.65	.90	.60	.85
Traffic Polish	.50	.70	.45	.65	.30	.50	.25	.50
GRAVEL								
Packed, oiled	.55	.85	.50	.80	.40	.80	.40	.60
Loose	.40	.70	.40	.70	.45	.75	.45	.75
CINDERS								
Packed	.50	.70	.50	.70	.65	.75	.65	.75
ROCK								
Crushed	.55	.75	.55	.75	.55	.75	.55	.75
ICE								
Smooth	.10	.25	.07	.20	.05	.10	.05	.10
SNOW								
Packed	.30	.55	.35	.55	.30	.60	.30	.60
Loose	.10	.25	.10	.20	.30	.60	.30	.60
METAL GRID								
Open	.70	.90	.55	.75	.25	.45	.20	.35

Suggest a strategy for the police to enable them to check the driver's estimate of his speed.

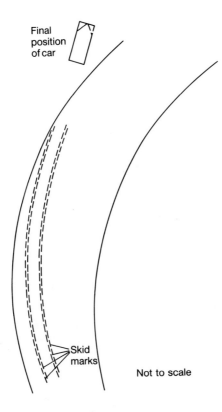

Figure 6.1 Plan of the scene of the accident

6.7 SKID MEASUREMENTS

Figure 6.2 Datum line to measure skid marks

A datum line was used to measure the skid marks. The distance
x was measured along the datum line and the distance y
perpendicular to it, (see Figure 6.2). For the outer skid
mark the values obtained are given in Table 6.2. (All
distances were measured in metres.)

TABLE 6.2

x	0	3	6	9	12	15	16.64
y	0	1.19	2.15	2.82	3.28	3.53	3.55

x	18	21	24	27	30	33.27
y	3.54	3.31	2.89	2.22	1.29	0

The police also measured the incline of the road and found
that this particular stretch was flat.

6.8 FURTHER INFORMATION FOR LECTURER

The plan should convey the information that the car did not
yaw as it moved round the curve, i.e. the car was always
pointing along the tangent. The skid marks left on the road
will be qualitatively different from those experienced in
Accident Investigations 1. When a car skids to a halt in a
straight line it produces thick, black skid marks. When a
tyre is rotating and slipping sideways at the same time, as
in Accident Investigation 2, it leaves thinner, lighter marks
on the road. Such marks contain striations, often in a
herring bone pattern. These types of skid marks are usually
called scuff marks or "critical speed" scuffs.

6.9 SIMPLE MODEL

The car moves round the curved path with its wheels rotating
but slipping sideways. It is assumed that the frictional
force acts in a direction normal to the car's velocity. Assume
that the car's speed, v, is constant and that its centre of
gravity moves in a circle with radius r. In this case friction
provides the centrifugal force. Using μ to denote the
coefficient of friction, then

$$\mu g = \frac{v^2}{r}$$

giving $\qquad v = \sqrt{\mu g r}.$

The measurement of μ has already been discussed in Accident
Investigation 1. For the test skid it is important to use a
car for which all four wheels lock up. The test will then
give the deceleration rate, a, where

$$a = \mu g.$$

In this case the result is conveniently written as

$$v = \sqrt{ar}.$$

6.10 CALCULATION OF RADIUS

The police in Leicestershire do not usually measure the
mid-point of a curve. [Thus they would normally omit the
point (16.64, 3.55), and possibly (33.27, 0), from their
measurements.] They are concerned to take accurate measurements in order to produce an accurate scale plane of the scene
of the accident. The plan can then be used to provide
additional data such as the co-ordinates of the mid-point.
However, the point has been included in the data to try and
nudge the students into using the first method given below
for calculating r.

Suppose the length of a chord, c, and the height of the circle
above its centre-point, m, are known (see Figure 6.3). Then
Pythagoras' theorem gives

$$r^2 = (r-m)^2 + (c/2)^2.$$

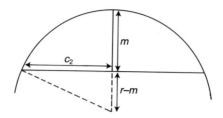

Figure 6.3   Determination of radius

This leads to

$$r = \frac{c^2}{8m} + \frac{m}{2}.$$

From the data

$$c = 33.27 \text{ and } m = 3.55,$$

giving

$$r = 40.75.$$

Once the value of a is known the velocity follows.

Alternatively, it is possible to fit a circle through the data (in this case it is perhaps best to remove the middle and last points). This involves estimating the centre of the circle too. One way to do this is to fit a circle through points 1, 2, and 3, then 2, 3 and 4, and so on. This gives a range of estimates for r from 34.6 to 48.3 and so is not very satisfactory. The large range arises because adjacent points were chosen. The students will probably now experiment with different choices of points. The range will decrease as the spacing increases. Choosing points separated by three others gives the values of

$$40.99, \ 40.47, \ 40.54$$

for r with an average value of 40.67. The students may examine the errors at each point to decide which is the best value for the radius. Again once a is known the velocity follows.

The problem of fitting a circle through the data points is suitable for first year students as a modelling problem in its own right. The use of a full least squares approach to fit the circle is not advisable. It contains hidden pitfalls and is far too hard for most undergraduates.

6.11 REAL ACCIDENT

As with Accident Investigation 1 a copy of an exhibit produced by a Leicestershire policeman is given in Appendix 2 to illustrate how the calculations can be presented. This contains a reference to a chalk gun. It is possible to mount an instrument on a car which fires a chalk pellet onto the road as soon as the brake pedal is pressed. The braking distance can thus be measured more accurately. A sketch of the plan of the accident scene is given in Figure 6.4.

6.12 EXTENSIONS

1. Discuss the case of a road with an incline.

2. Suppose the road is banked to help cornering. How will this affect the calculations?

3. What happens if the car is inclined to the tangent at a constant angle as it moves round the curve?

6.13 BIBLIOGRAPHY

Further information is contained in R. Byatt and R. Watts, Manual of Road Accident Investigation, Vol. 1 (1980) and 2 (1981), Pitman.

APPENDIX 1   Exhibit PP1

SERIOUS ACCIDENT ZYX STREET, LEICESTER, 30TH FEBRUARY, 1982

Involved

1. A Vauxhall Cavalier Saloon Motor Car registered number ACC 1 which was travelling along XYZ Street, Leicester towards ABC Road.

2. Pedestrian, Joe Smith, over 21, 1 ABC Road, Leicester.

Marks Found at Scene

Two skid marks, from front wheels of Vauxhall Cavalier.

         Front nearside   12 metres
         Front offside   2.3 metres.

Test Skids

I carried out test skids at the scene, using the same vehicle
involved. The test skids were carried out at 30 miles per
hour on the speedometer of the Vauxhall which was found to be
2 miles per hour out, therefore the test skids were actually
carried out at 28 miles per hour. The lengths of mark at
28 miles per hour (12.517 metres per second) were:

1.   Front nearside   10.6 metres
     Front offside   10.4 metres

2.   Front nearside   9.5 metres
     Front offside   11.0 metres.

The longest skid mark of the two tests, which are within 10%
of each other was, therefore, 11.0 metres.

Calculations

All calculations will be calculated to eight significant
figures, although in the exhibit they will only be shown to
one decimal place.

Deceleration of the Road

Using Newton's equation of motion

$$v^2 = u^2 - 2as,$$

where u = initial velocity, v = final velocity,
a = deceleration, and s = distance,

gives, on using the values u = 12.5 m/s, v = 0, and s = 11 m,
the result $a = \dfrac{u^2}{2s} = \dfrac{12.5 \times 12.5}{2 \times 11} = 7.1$ m/s/s.

Initial Velocity of Vehicle

From the end of the skid mark to the beginning is 12 metres,
so letting v = 0, a = 7.1 m/s/s and s = 12 m in the equation

of motion

$$v^2 = u^2 - 2as$$

leads to $u = \sqrt{2as} = \sqrt{2 \times 7.1 \times 12} = 13.1$ m/s $= 29.2$ m.p.h.

Conclusion

Taking into account all possible errors in measurements and speedometer, leads to an error of 5%, which in turn leads to a range of speed of:

27 to 31 miles per hour.

If all the errors were in favour of the car driver the lowest possible speed would be 27 miles per hour, but the most likely speed would be 29 miles per hour.

P. Brown, P.C.49.

APPENDIX 2   Exhibit PP2

MATHEMATICAL CALCULATIONS RE R.T.A.

P.C.49 P. Brown ABC Police Station

Available Data

Ford Escort saloon Regd. No. ACC 2B

Single vehicle only involved in the accident.

Vehicle extensively damaged to its front with a further area of damage towards the rear of its offside. This vehicle left a series of marks on the road surface. A scale plan of the scene was prepared. A sketch of this is shown in Figure 6.4. The marks shown on it are as follows:

i   At point A on the plan there are shown two scuff marks which cross the hazard centre lane marking.

ii Between points B and C on the plan there was a tyre mark on the road surface which showed the characteristics of a "critical speed" scuff. About midway between points B and C, the nearside wheels of the vehicle struck the nearside kerb.

iii Between points D and E on the plan there is a further "critical speed" scuff which forms the basis for my calculations.

iv   Between points F and G on the plan, the vehicle again
     struck and mounted the nearside kerb and verge, again
     laying "critical speed" scuffs.

 v   Between points H and K the vehicle mounted the offside
     kerb and crossed the footpath and verge.

vi   At point J, the offside bodywork of the vehicle collided
     with, and demolished, a concrete Fire Hydrant Post.

vii At point L the front of the vehicle collided with, and
     demolished a lamp post.

viii Point M shows the final position of the vehicle.

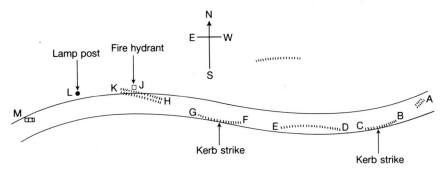

Vehicle travelling westward.

Figure 6.4   Sketch of accident scene

Test Skids

Test skids were conducted at the scene using a Ford Granada
(POL 1W) Police patrol car which produced a four-wheel lock-up
during skids. Two separate tests were conducted at 30 m.p.h.
(13.4112 m/sec). In each case a chalk gun was used to
determine the displacement of the vehicle during skidding, and
the results were as follows:

         1st Test: Displacement   s = 11.0m.
         2nd Test: Displacement   s = 10.85m.

The difference between these measurements, expressed as a
percentage is:

$$\frac{11.0 - 10.85}{10.85} \times 100 = 1.38\%$$

which indicates that the measurements are acceptably close.

In subsequent calculations the value of 11.0 metres is used for the displacement. (This is the largest value and thus it will produce the lowest possible value for "a" which will be in the favour of the accident vehicle).

Calculations

To calculate the drag factor a, for the road surface

Using

$$v^2 = u^2 - 2as,$$

where v = 0, u = 13.4112 m/s, and s = 11.0m leads to

$$a = \frac{13.4112^2}{2 \times 11} = 8.1754675 \text{ m/s/s.}$$

To calculate the radius of the path of centre of gravity for the vehicle (Between points D and E on the plan)

Chord to circle	c = 30 metres.
Mid-Ordinate	m = 1.05 metres.
Using	$r = \frac{c^2}{8m} + \frac{m}{2}$

Substituting known values, gives

$$r = \frac{900}{8.4} + 0.525 = \underline{107.66 \text{ metres}}$$

To calculate the "Critical speed" (Between points D and E)

An expression which will give the "critical speed" of the vehicle while leaving scuff marks may be written as

$$v = \sqrt{ra}.$$

Substituting the known values r = 107.66 metres, and a = 8.1754675 m/s, we obtain

$$v = \sqrt{107.66 \times 8.1754675}, = 29.667673 \text{ m/s}, = 66.36 \text{ m.p.h.}$$

Note that the policeman's statement would have quoted a speed
of 59 m.p.h., thus allowing a 10% error in the driver's favour.
A larger error is allowed here than in Accident Investigation
1 to allow for the errors involved in calculating the radius
of the circle.

7

Insulating a house

JOHN BERRY *Plymouth Polytechnic*

7.1 THE PROBLEM STATEMENT

Heating a house, or a flat, is an expensive part of the weekly
budget. In recent years the cost of heating fuels, that is,
coal, gas, electricity, oil, has increased in price quite
considerably.

It is important that as much of the heat as possible is
retained within the dwelling. Heat energy can escape through
the walls, windows, roofspace and floor, and there are several
products on the market to try to reduce this heat loss e.g.
(i) the cavity between the walls can be filled with various
materials; polystyrene balls and a chemical called urea
formaldehyde are just two such materials; (ii) the windows can
be double glazed forming a thin cavity of air between the two
panes of glass.

Figure 7.1 shows the relative proportions of heat loss for an
average sized detached house.

Clearly if some of escaping heat can be retained within the
house then less fuel is needed to heat the house to a certain
level and hence fuel bills will be lower. The heat loss can
be reduced by INSULATION.

New houses have a ten centimetre thickness of insulating
material in the loft reducing the heat loss through the
roofspace quite considerably. However the walls usually have
an unfilled air cavity between them and the windows consist of
a single pane of glass of about 4-6mm thickness.

A house owner wanting to reduce the fuel bills can invest in
"cavity-wall insulation" and/or "double glazing".

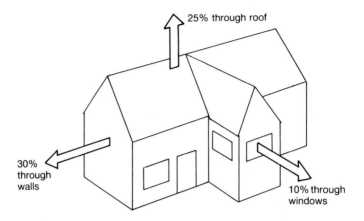

Figure 7.1   Heat losses from a house without roof or wall
             insulation or double glazing. The remaining 35%
             of heat loss goes through the floor, gaps round
             the windows and doors, etc.

Figures 7.2 and 7.3 show portions of two advertisements for
such forms of insulation.

Figure 7.2 suggests that cavity wall insulation could save
nearly five times the amount than double glazing. But that
sort of claim might be expected from a firm advertising the
installation of cavity wall insulation. How good are these
figures? This question is one that this modelling case study
sets out to answer. It is perhaps interesting to note that
the double glazing advertisement only compares competing
manufacturers and not other methods of insulation. Figure
7.3 introduces the term "U-value" which is one way in which
heat losses through material can be defined.

Compare the relative cost effectiveness of installing cavity-
wall insulation against double glazing. If you had to choose
one form of insulation, by comparing the return on the capital
investment, which would you choose? What factors that have
not be included in your mathematical model, might affect your
decision? Would this change your decision?

This case study is ideally suited to students who have studied
some basic physics of applied mathematics that has included
some models of heat transfer. It shows how a simple linear
model representing heat flow through a material can be used
to solve a problem of practical importance.

If students have not the background knowledge, then the relevant material is contained in this chapter.

DOUBLE GLAZE YOUR WALLS

Cavity walls, found in most houses built since 1920 were designed to keep damp from seeping in. Unfortunately, with today's central heating, they dont't stop costly heat from seeping out. 35% of all heat lost, in fact. Only 10% escapes through the windows.

Csavity wall insulation still keeps damp out, but also keeps that heat in.

HOW MUCH MONEY YOU CAN SAVE FOR EVERY POUND SPENT ON FUEL	
25p	WITH CAVITY WALL INSULATION
16p	WITH LOFT INSULATION
7p	WITH FLOOR INSULATION
5p	WITH DRAUGHT EXCLUDER
5p	WITH DOUBLE GLAZING

Figures from Department of Environment

It can actually save about a quarter of your heating bills (double glazing saves just 5%) and can pay for itself in about 5 years. So before you think about double-glazing, find out more about cavity wall insulation.

Surveys and quotations are FREE WITHOUT OBLIGATION. Phone, or Freepost the coupon, today for full details–Your've nothing to lose.

PRIORITY ADVICE SERVICES Ring (0342)123456

Figure 7.2 An advertisement for cavity wall insulation

The lower the U value the more efficient the insulation.
The test results, shown in the chart below, speak for
themselves.

	DOUBLE GLAZING AIR GAP	FRAME MATERIAL	U VALUE	INSULATION EFFICIENCY % INDEX 100
Single Glazed window		Aluminium	5.6	100%
Type A	20mm	Aluminium with plastic Thermal Break	2.2	254%
Type B	20mm	Aluminium with Plastic Thermal Break	2.9	193%
Type C	12mm	Aluminium with Plastic Thermal Break	3.0	187%
Type D	12mm	Aluminium with Plastic Thermal Break	3.2	175%
Type E	20mm	Aluminium with Plastic Thermal Break	3.3	170%
Type F*	9.5mm	Aluminium	3.7	151%
		Type F also manufacture a Thermaily Cad window		

The test reports may be inspected at our office by oppointment upon a written request.

Figure 7.3   An advertisement for double glazing

7.2   FORMULATING A MODEL

7.2.1 *Getting started*

It is very tempting for this problem, to rush in to the physics
of heat transfer and to start data collecting on the average
temperatures both inside and outside the house. However that
approach would soon lead to too much data and progress would
seem slow. At some stage the process of heat flow through the
walls and windows does need investigating but first it is a
good idea to stand back from the problem and see where we are
going.

The problem statement asks for a comparison of the costs of
installing two forms of insulation - double glazing and
cavity-wall insulation. So there are two aspects of the
problem to consider:

 (i)   the economics of the costs involved and
 (ii) the physics of heat transfer through materials.

Formulating a mathematical model for the first aspect does not
require any specialist knowledge of economics. However the
model for heat transfer may either be a familiar one to the
students or may require some investigation. In the description

of a possible solution to this problem a standard model is used.

The first stage is to write down a list of those features which we may need to take into account in the mathematical modelling process.

Perhaps the construction of a feature list would be a good place for the students to begin in a class discussion.

The following lists of features are relevant to the two different aspects of the problem already identified.

(i) Features affecting the 'economics'

     1. cost of installation
     2. cost of borrowing the money (i.e. interest paid)
     3. cost of fuel
     4. amount saved by insulating
     5. type of double glazing
     6. inflation

(ii) Features affecting the 'heat loss'

     7. temperature of room
     8. temperature of the outside
     9. convection
    10. conduction
    11. radiation
    12. area of walls
    13. area of windows
    14. thickness of glass
    15. thermal properties of glass
    16. thickness of walls
    17. thermal properties of walls
    18. heat saved by insulation

It is perhaps apparent that there are other features that do not seem to fit in the two categories given above. Two features that seem difficult to quantify are

(a)   comfort

i.e.   double glazed windows are more comfortable to sit by
         than single glazed windows;

(b)   attractiveness to the eye

i.e.   "replacement windows" are possibly nicer to have in
         the living area than "secondary double glazing".

The second one, (b), will affect the price of having the
house double glazed; so that if we choose double glazing by
installing replacement windows then, since this costs more
than secondary double glazing, a decision to have cavity-wall
insulation instead of double glazing may be because of the
concern for what it looks like.

7.2.2 Choosing variables and finding relations

The class could now be set the task of formulating a model
based on the feature lists given above. Each aspect, i.e.
the economics and the physics, can initially be investigated
separately although features 3 and 4 do provide a link.

With the list of 18 features given under headings (i) and (ii)
above, a model, which is based on the most important of them,
can now be formulated. Initially, for a simple model, we
will assume that the important economic features are

the cost of installing double glazing = C_G

the cost of installing cavity-wall insulation = C_B

Features 3 and 4 provide the link between the two aspects of
'economics' and 'heat transfer'. In fact

$$\frac{\text{Amount of money saved}}{\text{in unit time}} = \frac{\text{quantity of heat saved x}}{\text{cost of a unit amount of heat}} \qquad \text{I}$$

At this stage we will not worry about the 'type of double
glazing'. This feature affects the cost of installation so
that when a model to compare cost-effectiveness is formulated,
then, for different types of installation, different strategies
can be predicted.

Now consider the features that affect heat loss.

Figure 7.4 shows the physical processes involved with the
heat transfer through walls and windows. The variable T
represents the temperature (in $^\circ$C) and Q is the heat loss per
unit time (measured in watts).

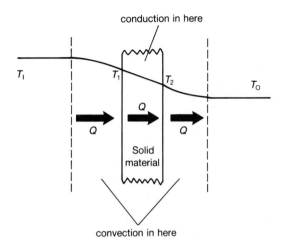

Figure 7.4

In Figure 7.4 the heat transfer due to radiation has not been
considered. It is assumed in this model that the heat loss
due to radiation is negligible in comparison with the heat loss due
to conduction and convection. Convection is due to the
movement of the air on either side of the material causing
temperature drops $T_I - T_1$ and $T_2 - T_O$. Conduction is due to
contact between the particles making up the material and there
is a temperature drop of $T_1 - T_2$ across its faces. The thermal
properties of materials are modelled by a simple expression
called the U-value. This is a coefficient that relates the
heat transfer per unit area to the total temperature difference
($T_I - T_O$ in the variables of Figure 7.4). The U-value can be
calculated experimentally for different substances so that it
takes into account convection and conduction. Figure 7.5
shows the U-values for walls and windows.

Material	U-value ($Wm^{-2}C^{-1}$)
Brick wall (no cavity)	1.92
Brick wall (with cavity not filled)	0.873
Brick wall (with filled cavity)	0.5
Single glass pane (6 mm)	6.41
Double glazed window	1.27

Figure 7.5 Typical U values for walls and windows

The basic heat transfer model is

> heat loss per unit area = U x (total temperature difference) II

  This formula can be deduced theoretically by combining
simple models for convection and conduction, in the following
way.

Consider again the slab of material of thickness a separating
two regions of temperature T_I and T_O shown in Figure 7.4.

Heating is conducted through the material because there is a
temperature difference $T_1 - T_2$ across its faces. The rate of
heat loss per unit area, Q, is related to $T_1 - T_2$ by the simple
linear model

$$Q = \frac{K}{a} (T_1 - T_2)$$

where K is the thermal conductivity and a is the thickness of
the material.

Convection occurs in thin boundary layers on each side of the
material. Simple linear models of convection for the inner
and outer boundary layers are given by

$$Q = h_1 (T_I - T_1)$$

$$Q = h_2 (T_2 - T_0)$$

where h_1 and h_2 are constants called convective heat transfer coefficients. Their values depend on (a) the type of boundary; (b) air speeds near the boundary. In each of the models for conduction and convection we are assuming that the temperature is independent of time, i.e. steady state conditions prevail.

Now we have three equations relating the temperatures T_I, T_1, T_2 and T_0. They are

$$Q = h_1 (T_I - T_1)$$

$$Q = \frac{K}{a} (T_1 - T_2)$$

$$Q = h_2 (T_2 - T_0)$$

Eliminating T_1 and T_2 between these three equations we have

$$\left[\frac{1}{h_1} + \frac{a}{K} + \frac{1}{h_2} \right] Q = T_I - T_0$$

or $$Q = U (T_I - T_0)$$

where $$U = \left[\frac{1}{h_1} + \frac{a}{K} + \frac{1}{h_2} \right]^{-1}$$

is the U-value introduced earlier.

Typical values for a single glazed window are

$$h_1 = 10 \text{ Wm}^{-2}\text{c}^{-1}, \ h_2 = 20 \text{ Wm}^{-2}\text{c}^{-1}, \ K = 1 \text{ Wm}^{-1}\text{c}^{-1} \text{ and } a = 0.006\text{m},$$

giving $U = \left[\frac{1}{10} + 0.006 + \frac{1}{20} \right]^{-1} = 6.41 \text{ Wm}^{-2}\text{c}^{-1}.$

Most of the features in list (ii) have been considered in this simple model of heat transfer. Feature 18 can be written in terms of the difference between the heat losses for non-insulated and insulated boundaries.

We have

| Heat saved by insulation | = | heat loss when uninsulated | − | heat loss when insulated | III |

In terms of variables, we define

Area of glass   = A_G (same for single and doubled glazed windows)

Area of external walls   = A_B (same for non-insulated and insulated walls)

Amount of money saved per unit time = $\begin{cases} S_G \text{ for glass} \\ S_B \text{ for walls} \end{cases}$

Heat saved by insulation per unit time = $\begin{cases} H_G \text{ for glass} \\ H_B \text{ for walls} \end{cases}$

Cost of heat per unit time   = c

Cost of double glazing = $\begin{cases} C_G \text{ for windows} \\ C_B \text{ for walls} \end{cases}$

Putting these variables into the three models I, II and III gives

For the windows:

II and III : $H_G = U_N A_G (T_I - T_O) - U_I A_G (T_I - T_O)$ (in Watts)

I : $S_G = c H_G$

where U_N and U_I are the U values for single and double glazed windows respectively.

For the walls:

II and III : $H_B = U_N' A_B (T_I - T_O) - U_I' A_B (T_I - T_O)$ (in watts)

I : $S_B = c H_B$

where U_N' and U_I' are the U values for unfilled and filled cavity walls respectively.

7.3   A STRATEGY FOR COST-EFFECTIVENESS

Now we must make a decision as to the cost-effectiveness of installing double glazing or cavity wall insulation. Defining the "payback period" P, for each type of insulation to be the ratio of the cost of the insulation to the money saved due to installing the insulation, then for the windows

$$P_G = \frac{C_G}{S_G}$$

and for the walls

$$P_B = \frac{C_B}{S_B}$$

A model for cost-effectiveness can then be formulated in the following way:

If $\dfrac{P_G}{P_B} > 1$ then install cavity wall insulation

If $\dfrac{P_G}{P_B} < 1$ then install double glazing

7.4   PUTTING IT ALL TOGETHER

We have

$$\frac{P_G}{P_B} = \frac{C_G}{S_G} \times \frac{S_B}{C_B}$$

$$= \frac{C_G \; c \; (U_N' - U_I') \; A_B \; (T_I - T_O)}{C_B \; c \; (U_N - U_I) \; A_G \; (T_I - T_O)}$$

$$= \frac{C_G \; A_B \; (U_N' - U_I')}{C_B \; A_G \; (U_N - U_I)} = 0.0726 \; \frac{C_G}{C_B} \; \frac{A_B}{A_G}$$

If we use the U-values given in Figure 7.5, we have reached an
equation that does not include the data on temperature
differences and the fuel costs. Hence the increase of the
price of fuel due to inflation and other factors do not affect
the decision. Furthermore, the strategy that we adopt will
hold for all types of heating fuel.

To proceed further, suppose the cost of installing double
glazing and cavity wall insulation are calculated at a basic
rate per square metre c_G and c_B respectively, then

$$C_G = c_G \; A_G$$

$$C_B = c_B \; A_B$$

so that

$$\frac{P_G}{P_B} = 0.0726 \; \frac{c_G}{c_B} = 0.0726 \; X$$

where

$$X = \frac{c_G}{c_B} \; .$$

Figure 7.6 shows a graph of $\dfrac{P_G}{P_B}$ against X

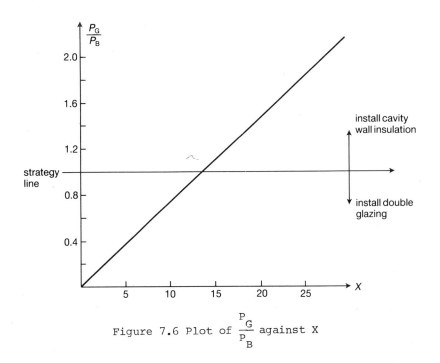

Figure 7.6 Plot of $\dfrac{P_G}{P_B}$ against X

From this graph we can make a decision whether to install cavity wall insulation or double glazing. The value of X will depend on the type of double glazing and cavity wall insulation, and probably the manufacturer.

7.5 MAKING A DECISION

Table 7.1 gives some example of the cost per square metre of cavity wall insulation and double glazing for the author's house.

TABLE 7.1

Type of insulation	Average cost per square metre in pounds (Winter 1981)
Professionally fitted sealed double glazed units replacement windows	181
Professionally fitted secondary units	28.9
Do-it-yourself secondary double glazing (frame and single pane)	16
Do-it-yourself sealed units	30
Cavity wall insulation	2

Using this data and the graph in Figure 7.5 we have the ratio $\frac{P_G}{P_B}$ for the four double glazing systems given by 6.57, 1.05, 0.58, 1.09 so that only for do-it-yourself secondary double glazing does the payback period become less than for cavity wall insulation.

7.6 TOWARDS A MORE COMPLICATED MODEL?

There are several features that may change the decision made on purely economic grounds. For instance it is more comfortable sitting by a window that has been double glazed.

If comfort is considered as important as cost then perhaps we should consider a model based on double glazing the "living" rooms only; or alternatively we could add a weighting so that for instance, we would install double glazing provided

$$\frac{P_G}{P_B} < 2 \text{ say instead of 1.}$$

We have not taken into account the heat saved by lining the curtains and drawing them more often. Curtains can save quite a lot of heat although there is still an uncomfortable draught under and around the edges of the curtains.

Installing cavity wall insulation and double glazing can increase the value of the house. An improved model could include an amount that takes this into account so that the true cost of the installation is reduced by a "recoverable amount".

Exercise 1

Which of the double glazing systems becomes cost effective (explaining what you mean by this) if we adopt a strategy of

(a) $\dfrac{P_G}{P_B} < 2$

(b) $\dfrac{P_G}{P_B} < 3$?

Exercise 2
Perfect double glazing

The following diagram shows ways in which heat is lost through a double glazed window and the convective and conduction coefficients.

Using the simple models of heat loss introduced in the text,

i.e. $Q = \dfrac{K}{a} (T_x - T_y)$ for conduction and $Q = h (T_x - T_y)$ for convection show that the theoretical formula for the U value of a double glazed window is

$$U = \left[\frac{1}{h_1} + \frac{2K}{a} + \frac{1}{h_c} + \frac{1}{h_2} \right]^{-1}$$

Using the values given in the diagram calculate a value for U.

INSULATING A HOUSE

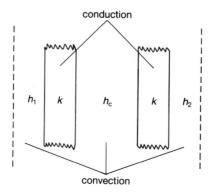

conduction

h_1 k h_c k h_2

convection

$h_1 = 10$ $h_2 = 20$ $h_c = 1.6$ (in $Wm^{-2}C^{-1}$)
$k = 1$ wc^{-1}
$a = 6$ mm

Diagram for Exercise 2

Exercise 3

The U value calculated in Exercise 2 is independent of the size of the double glazing air gap, b. However the advertisement shown in Figure 7.3 would suggest that the air gap size is important. Give reasons why this is so and how could the air gap size be taken into account?

Exercise 4

The calculation for perfect double glazing in Exercise 2 gives a U value much less than the quoted values in Figure 7.3. Can you give reasons to explain this apparent difference between the mathematical model and the experimental values?

8

Basketball shooting

STEWART TOWNEND *Liverpool Polytechnic*

8.1 THE PROBLEM

When a basketball player is fouled, he is awarded one, or
more, free shots. A free shot is akin to a soccer penalty in
that the player is not hindered in any way by his opponents.
The fouled player stands behind a particular line, called the
free throw line, drawn on the court and attempts to 'shoot'
the ball through a fixed circular horizontal hoop located some
distance away. The action of taking the shot is such that the
ball is essentially vertically above the free throw line when
released.

How accurately does the basket ball player need to throw the
ball in order to score from the free shot?

8.2 FURTHER INFORMATION

The students are told that further information is available
but that it will only be provided in answer to specific
questions.

8.3 TEACHING HINTS

The mathematical background required for the solution of this
problem is possessed by students preparing for the Advanced
Level examination in Mathematics and first year undergraduates
on Science and Engineering degrees in Universities and
Polytechnics.

It can be summarised under three headings

1. Equations of motion under constant acceleration.

2. Elementary differentiation and use of $\dfrac{dy}{dx} \doteqdot \dfrac{\delta y}{\delta x}$,

3. Coordinate geometry of the ellipse and circle, (optional, Section 8.6).

A minimum solution of the problem requires Sections 8.4 and 8.5, and possibly the construction component of Section 8.6. For those students with a knowledge of coordinate geometry, the latter part of Section 8.6 will be of interest. It is recommended that Section 8.7 should only be attempted by students with a good grasp of differential calculus. The following table showing the average time required for the various sections provides a guideline for lecturers.

Section Number	Time required to complete (hours)
8.3	1 - 2
8.4 and 8.5	2
8.6	1 if construction method used 2 if coordinate geometry used
8.7 and 8.8	1 - 2

It is suggested that the class is divided into small groups to which the problem statement is distributed. The groups are then left for perhaps thirty minutes to consider the problem by themselves. If members of staff eavesdrop on the groups they may well hear the following questions:

'Is this just the usual projectile problem?' - the answer, of course, is 'no' which should dismiss any 45° expectation the students may have!

'Which parameters are likely to be important to the problem?' - should produce suggestions of release height, release velocity and release angle.

'Are any of these more important than any others?'

'What happens when the basketball reaches the hoop?'

Additional information will probably need to be presented at
this stage. For example the rules of the game permit the ball
to be bounced off the rim of the hoop or off the backboard
(to which the hoop is attached) although this will introduce
additional complications due to the impact. For simplicity it
is assumed that the problem under consideration involves the
passage of the basketball through the hoop without any contact.
Experience has also shown that at this stage the students often
request details of the dimensions involved in a free throw:

'At what height above the ground is the ball released?'

'What is the release velocity?'

'What is the release angle?'

'How far is it from the free throw line to the hoop?'

Don't give any numerical data yet! It is far preferable for
the students to use algebraic symbols to represent the various
parameters and avoid the insertion of numerical values for as
long as possible. Generally they want to do exactly the
opposite! It should be emphasised to them that the algebraic
approach will give them a general, and far more useful, result.
By now the students should have identified the following
important features of the problem.

> 1. Release Velocity
>
> 2. Release Angle
>
> 3. Release Height

Experience of presenting this particular exercise to various
groups of students has shown that the provision of some
typical values helps to give them a clearer picture of the
problem.

$$\text{Typical values } V(ms^{-1}) \qquad 6 - 9$$

$$h(m) \qquad 2.0 - 2.75$$

Since the fouled player may be allowed more than one free shot,
the students should consider whether the players find it
easier to replicate the release velocity or the release angle
with each free throw.

Discussions with professional basketball players have revealed
that they consider it easier to replicate the release velocity.
Consequently the lecturer can suggest to the groups that they

develop their solution in terms of the release angle for a
fixed value of the release velocity, see next section.

8.4   'HALF' A SOLUTION

Once the important parameters of release height, and release
velocity have been identified and the relative positions of
the basketball and the hoop established, the groups invariably
launch into a projectile problem approach in which they attempt
to determine the angle of release necessary for the basketball
to pass through the hoop for a given release velocity.

From the knowledge they now possess about the diameters of the
ball and the hoop some students will realise that a certain
amount of offset is permitted, i.e. the ball will still pass
through the hoop even though their centres do not coincide.
It is recommended that, initially at least, a solution is
sought in which the basketball centre passes through the hoop
centre, but see also Section 8.6. If a set of Cartesian axes
is placed at the centre of the basketball's release position
and the ball is assumed to be released with velocity V at an
angle α to the horizontal then, neglecting air resistance, the
position of the ball centre at time t after release is given
by the equations

$$x = (V\cos\alpha)t$$

$$y = (V\sin\alpha)t - \frac{1}{2}gt^2, \quad \text{See Figure 8.1.}$$

The inclusion of air resistance in the model is discussed in
Section 8.9.

The equation of the trajectory can then be found by eliminating
t between these two equations to produce a parabola,

$$y = x\tan\alpha - \frac{gx^2}{2V^2}\sec^2\alpha \tag{1}$$

If the coordinates of the centre of the hoop are (x_1, y_1) then
the requirement that the ball centre passes through the hoop
centre gives

$$y_1 = x_1\tan\alpha - \frac{gx_1^2}{2V^2}\sec^2\alpha \tag{2}$$

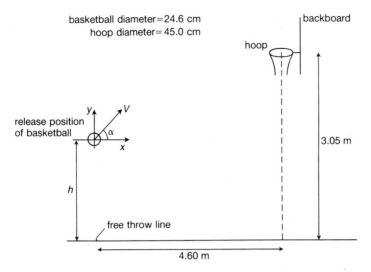

Figure 8.1   Dimensions involved in a free throw

Since $\sec^2\alpha = 1 + \tan^2\alpha$ this equation may be rewritten as a quadratic in $\tan\alpha$

$$\frac{gx_1^2}{2v^2} \tan^2\alpha - x_1 \tan\alpha + y_1 + \frac{gx_1^2}{2v^2} = 0 \qquad (3)$$

which can be solved for $\tan\alpha$ to give, after some manipulation,

$$\tan\alpha = \frac{v^2}{gx_1} \left[1 \pm \sqrt{1 - \frac{2g}{v^2}\left(y_1 + \frac{gx_1^2}{2v^2}\right)} \right] \qquad (4)$$

Measurements conducted by the author with some professional basketball players as subjects indicate that realistic values of V and h are, respectively, 8ms^{-1} and 2.15m. As a consequence of h = 2.15m it is found that y_1 = 0.90m; x_1 = 4.60m is a consequence of the geometry of the court.

When these values are substituted into equation (4) it is
found that

$$\tan\alpha = 2.0939 \text{ or } 0.7426$$

from which

$$\alpha = 64°28' \text{ or } 36°36' \tag{5}$$

This pair of answers invariably causes alarm within the groups!
The students are not accumstomed to a choice of answer.
Mathematics problems are always clear cut: do this, do that,
simplify your working and voila, the answer! Two answers
provoke all sorts of doubts:

'Are they both correct?'

'Is one invalid and, if so, why?'

In order to develop the student's solution further it may
be necessary for the lecturer to provide a clue, in the form
of a question:

'Don't forget that the basketball is not a point particle -
it has a finite size. Does this make a difference at any
time during the ball's trajectory?'

8.5 THE OTHER HALF OF THE SOLUTION

Experience of presenting this exercise to student groups has
shown that after some time thinking and perhaps experimenting
with the ball and the hoop they realised that as the ball
approaches the hoop, it 'sees' an ellipse. Dependent upon
the geometric ability of the student group this realisation
may need to be assisted by presenting the class with a circle
drawn on a sheet of card and then altering the inclination.
The length of the semi major axis (which is perpendicular to
the direction of travel of the ball) is equal to the diameter
of the circular hoop but the semi minor axis is shorter, say
length d cm. How much shorter depends on the angle at which
the ball approaches the hoop. If the angle of entry,
measured from the horizontal, is too small the ball will not
pass through the hoop. Figures 8.2 and 8.3 illustrate this
point.

Suppose the angle of entry is β then, assuming a hoop diameter
of 45 cm,

$$d = 45 \sin\beta$$

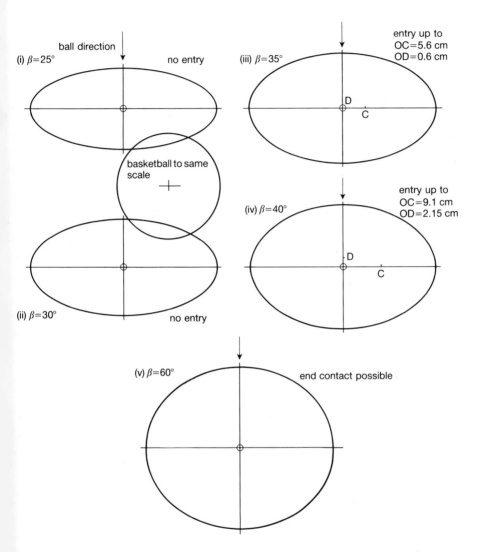

Figure 8.2   Apparent elliptic cross section of hoop - angle
of entry β

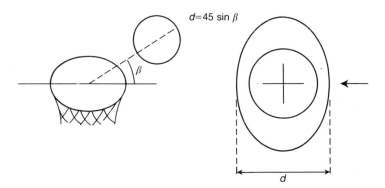

Figure 8.3   Entry to the hoop

It is evident that the ball will only pass through the hoop
provided that the length of the minor axis of the ellipse is
greater than or equal to the diameter of the ball (assumed to
be 24.6 cm, the midpoint of the permitted range)

$$45 \sin\beta \geq 24.6$$

i.e. $\beta \geq 33°8'$ (6)

The two values of α given in equation (4) must now be examined
in order to ascertain whether they are consistent with this
condition on β.

The angle of entry of the ball to the hoop is obtained from
the gradient of the trajectory at the point (x_1, y_1) or, in
terms of β, as $-\tan\beta$.

From equation (1)

$$\frac{dy}{dx} = \tan\alpha - \frac{gx}{v^2} \sec^2\alpha$$

Thus for passage through the hoop

$$-\tan\beta = \tan\alpha - \frac{gx_1}{v^2} \sec^2\alpha \tag{7}$$

The values of V and x_1, introduced earlier of 8ms^{-1} and 4.60m together with the values from equation (5) give

$\beta = 59°34'$ when $\alpha = 64°28'$ and

$\beta = 19°21'$ when $\alpha = 36°36'$.

In view of the condition determined for β, see (6), it is seen that in order for a free shot, released at a height of 2.15m with a velocity of 8 ms^{-1}, to score it must be released at an angle of $64°28'$ to the horizontal.

8.6 DISCUSSION AND EXTENSION

The above analysis satisfactorily explains the reason for the high release angles seen for basketball free shots. The solution presented this far has assumed that the centre of the basketball passes through the centre of the hoop. Consideration of the dimensions of the ball and the hoop indicates that a certain amount of overshoot of the ball centre relative to the hoop centre can be tolerated (see Figure 8.4). Assume, for simplicity, that the overshoot is measured along the minor axis of the ellipse 'seen' by the ball. How much overshoot can be tolerated?

The ellipse 'seen' by the basketball as it approaches the hoop at angle β to the horizontal has semi axes of length 22.5cm and $22.5 \sin\beta$ cm. Figure 8.2 shows this ellipse for a range of values of the entry angle together with a diagram of the circular cross section of the basketball, drawn to the same scale.

The amount of overshoot permitted can be investigated by placing a tracing of the ball over any of the ellipses (with the ball centre on the minor axis of the ellipse) to determine whether entry is possible, and if so, how much overshoot is permitted. Students could also draw their own ellipses for other values of β. The amount of overshoot permitted is shown as the distance OD in Figure 8.4 and is given in terms of β as

Overshoot, $OD = 22.5 \sin\beta - 12.3$ (8)

Alternatively the ball may yaw to one side or the other of its direction of travel. The yaw is measured along the major axis of the ellipse and is shown as OC in Figure 8.4. The value of OC can be investigated using the above idea of a tracing or it can be investigated rigorously using coordinate geometry. Referred to Cartesian axes (X,Y) with origin located at the centre of the ellipse, the equation of the ellipse is

$$\frac{X^2}{22.5^2} + \frac{Y^2}{(22.5 \sin\beta)^2} = 1 \tag{9}$$

With respect to the same axes the equation of the circular cross section of the ball having a yaw c from the centre of the ellipse measured along the major axis of the ellipse is

$$(X-c)^2 + Y^2 = 12.3^2 \tag{10}$$

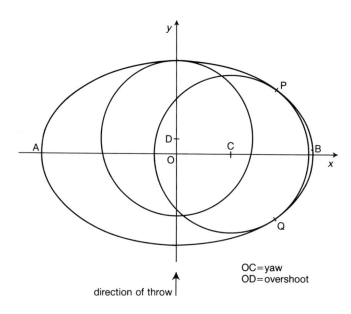

Figure 8.4 Permitted overshoot (+/-) and yaw (+/-)

Figure 8.4 shows an extreme case of the passage of the ball
through the hoop. Mathematically it is represented by the
simultaneous satisfaction of equations (9) and (10) at the
points P and Q. If the coordinates of the points of contact
are (X_1, Y_1) then

$$X_1^2 \sin^2\beta + Y_1^2 = 22.5^2 \sin^2\beta$$

and

$$(X_1-c)^2 + Y_1^2 = 12.3^2$$

Subtraction and subsequent rearrangement gives

$$X_1^2(1-\sin^2\beta) - 2cX_1 + (c^2 + (22.5\sin\beta)^2 - 12.3^2) = 0.$$

For equal roots of this quadratic, corresponding to contact at
P and Q only, we must have

$$4c^2 = 4(1-\sin^2\beta)(c^2 + (22.5\sin\beta)^2 - 12.3^2)$$

whence

$$c^2 = \frac{(1-\sin^2\beta)((22.5\sin\beta)^2 - 12.3^2)}{\sin^2\beta} \qquad (11)$$

This formula for the square of the yaw is only valid provided
that

$$22.5 \sin\beta \geq 12.3$$

i.e.

$$\beta \geq 33°8',$$

which agrees with the inequality (6).

Figure 8.2 shows the impossibility/possibility of the basketball passing through the hoop for a range of values of the
entry angle β. For example, if β = 35° then from equation
(11) the maximum permitted yaw is given by c = 5.58cm and from
equation (8) the maximum permitted overshoot is 0.60cm. These
agree with the measured values obtained by placing a tracing
of the basketball cross-section over the ellipse corresponding
to β = 35°.

For the higher values of β such as 60°, see Figure 8.2,
tangential end contact at A or B is possible. In this case
the value of the yaw is clearly

$$c = 22.5 - 12.3 = 10.2$$

The value of β above which end contact is possible can be
determined by solving equation (10) for sinβ with c = 10.2
to give

$$\sin\beta = \sqrt{\frac{12.3}{22.5}}$$

i.e. $\beta = 47°41'$ (12)

To summarise the results of this section

(i)   the basketball cannot pass through the hoop if the angle
       of entry β < 33°8';

(ii)   for values of β between 33°8' and 47°41' a certain
       amount of yaw c is permitted. The value of c can be
       determined from equation (11);

(iii) for the values of β > 47°41' the amount of yaw = 10.2cm
       which permits passage of the ball through the hoop even
       if internal contact is made at A and B;

(iv)   for the overshoot problem, the amount of overshoot
       measured from the centre of the apparent ellipse is
       given by

$$\text{overshoot} = 22.5 \sin\beta - 12.3.$$

Table 8.1 shows the effect on the permitted overshoot and yaw of varying the release velocity V ms^{-1} of a free throw, assumed to have been released with the basketball centre at a height of 2.15m above the ground.

TABLE 8.1

V (ms^{-1})	α(deg)	β(deg)	Successful shot?	Permitted Yaw (cm) +/-	Permitted Overshoot (cm) +/-
7.00	NONE*	-	-	-	-
7.25	NONE*	-	-	-	-
7.45	54°36'	45°27'	Yes	10.13	3.74
	46°28'	33°28'	Yes	2.49	0.11
7.50	56°22'	48° 2'	Yes	10.2	4.43
	44°42'	30°53'	No	-	-
8.00	64°28'	59°34'	Yes	10.2	7.10
	36°36'	19°21'	No	-	-
8.50	68°44'	56°20'	Yes	10.2	8.15
	32°20'	13°36'	No	-	-

      α values calculated from equation (4).

*tanα,   calculated from equation (4), was complex and hence
          no real α exists for these cases.

      β values calculated from equation (7).

Overshoot values calculated from equation (8).

Yaw values calculated from equations (11) or (12).

Notice that in each case, with the exception of V = 7.45ms^{-1}, only the larger of the two possible α values produces a valid angle of entry β, remember that for entry β ≥ 33°8'.

In the case of $V = 7.45\text{ms}^{-1}$ although both α values produce valid β values the lower value corresponds to such a small tolerance of yaw and overshoot that it does not represent a practical solution.

It is apparent from Table 8.1 that the free throw can remain successful despite varying amounts of yaw and/or overshoot. If we concentrate our attention on overshoot, since this is measured in the same direction as the free throw, then the students should realise that the velocity of projection and/or the angle of release can be varied slightly and yet the free throw will remain successful.

Students with a good background in differential calculus could be asked to investigate the extent to which V and α (separately!) can be varied consistent with the free throw remaining successful.

8.7   HOW SENSITIVE ARE THE RESULTS TO CHANGES IN V OR α?

A solution is presented based upon differentiation and the result that

$$\frac{dv}{dx} \doteqdot \frac{\delta v}{\delta x} \qquad (13)$$

where δx denotes a small change in x and δy denotes the corresponding change in y.

The effect on the trajectory of a small change $\delta\alpha$ in α (or δV in V) can thus be determined by differentiating the equation of the trajectory with respect to α (or V) and then using equation (13) to produce an expression for $\delta\alpha$ (or δV) in terms of δx (the amount of overshoot) and the various parameters of the free throw.

The equation of the trajectory of the basketball is given by (1) so that when the basketball centre reaches the level of the horizontal through the hoop we may write

$$y_1 = x\,\tan\alpha - \frac{gx^2}{2v^2}\,\sec^2\alpha,$$

i.e.

$$\frac{gx^2}{2v^2}\,\sec^2\alpha - x\,\tan\alpha + y_1 = 0 \qquad (14)$$

Differentiating this equation with respect to α gives

$$\frac{gx^2}{v^2} \sec^2\alpha \, \tan\alpha + \frac{gx}{v^2} \sec^2\alpha \, \frac{dx}{d\alpha} - \frac{dx}{d\alpha} \tan\alpha - x \sec^2\alpha = 0,$$

whence

$$\frac{dx}{d\alpha} = \frac{x \sec^2\alpha \, (gx \, \tan\alpha - v^2)}{(v^2 \tan\alpha - gx^2 \sec^2\alpha)}$$

Thus using equation (12)

$$\delta\alpha \doteqdot \frac{(v^2 \tan\alpha - gx_1 \sec^2\alpha)\delta x}{x_1 \sec^2\alpha \, (gx_1 \tan\alpha - v^2)}$$

where δx = the overshoot associated with release velocity V and release angle α.

Table 8.2 shows the change in angle, $\delta\alpha$, for a range of release velocities and release angles consistent with successful shots.

TABLE 8.2

V (ms^{-1})	(deg)	Overshoot δx (m)	$\delta\alpha$ (deg)	$\frac{\delta\alpha}{\alpha}$ x 100%
7.45	$46°36'$	$\pm$ 0.0011	$\pm\ 0°02'$	$\mp$ 0.06%
	$54°36'$	$\pm$ 0.0374	$\mp\ 1°06'$	$\mp$ 2%
7.50	$56°22'$	$\pm$ 0.043	$\mp\ 0°53'$	$\mp$ 1.6%
8.00	$64°28'$	$\pm$ 0.071	$\mp\ 0°35'$	$\mp$ 0.9%
8.50	$68°44'$	$\pm$ 0.082	$\mp\ 0°29'$	$\mp$ 0.7%

$(x_1 = 4.60\text{m})$

Figure 8.5 shows the successful trajectories corresponding to
$V = 8.00$ ms^{-1} with angles of release $\alpha \pm \delta\alpha$ as detailed in
Table 8.2.

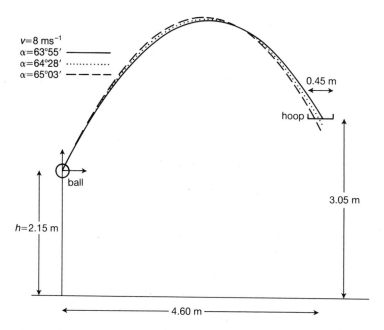

$v=8$ ms^{-1}
$\alpha=63°55'$ ———
$\alpha=64°28'$ ··········
$\alpha=65°03'$ — — —

0.45 m

hoop

3.05 m

ball

$h=2.15$ m

4.60 m

Figure 8.5   Effect of small changes in α on the overshoot
of a successful throw.

Alternatively equation (14) can be differentiated with respect
to V to produce an expression for δV in terms of the overshoot
δx and the various parameters of the free throw.

Differentiating equation (13) with respect to V gives

$$- \frac{gx^2}{V^3} \sec^2\alpha + \frac{gx}{V^2} \sec^2\alpha \frac{dx}{dV} - \frac{dx}{dV} \tan\alpha = 0,$$

whence

$$\frac{dx}{dV} = \frac{gx^2 \sec^2\alpha}{V(gx \sec^2\alpha - V^2 \tan\alpha)}$$

Thus using equation (12)

$$\delta v \doteq \frac{V}{gx_1^2} (gx_1 - \frac{V^2}{2} \sin 2\alpha) \delta x,$$

where δx = the overshoot associated with release velocity V and release angle α.

Table 8.3 shows the change in velocity, V, for a range of release velocities and release angles consistent with successful shots.

TABLE 8.3

V (ms^{-1})	α (deg)	Overshoot δx (m)	δv (ms^{-1})	$\frac{\delta v}{V}$ x 100%
7.45	$46°28'$	+ 0.0011	$\pm$ 0.0007	$\pm$ 0.01%
	$54°36'$	+ 0.0374	$\pm$ 0.0254	$\pm$ 0.34%
7.50	$56°22'$	+ 0.043	$\pm$ 0.0298	$\pm$ 0.40%
8.00	$64°28'$	+ 0.071	$\pm$ 0.0636	$\pm$ 0.80%
8.50	$68°44'$	+ 0.082	$\pm$ 0.695	$\pm$ 0.82%
			$(x_1 = 4.60m)$	

The results presented in Tables 8.2 and 8.3 indicate that the success of a throw is considerably more sensitive to the value of the release velocity than to that of the release angle (since the magnitude and range of relative errors in V are less than those for α). It is thus indeed fortunate that, as mentioned in Section 8.3, basketball players consider it easier to replicate the release velocity!

8.8   HOW HIGH DO THE FREE-THROWS REACH?

The height reached by a basketball is not limited in any way by the rules of the game, only by the ability of the players and any external constraints, such as beams and lights, imposed by the interior of the stadium used. Although these latter constraints are unlikely to be a problem in the stadia used by professional teams they may well pose a problem in the gymnasia used in schools and colleges.

The student groups could be asked to determine the maximum height reached, above ground level, by the successful shots detailed in Table 8.1.

Group discussion about the conditions prevailing when the ball reaches its zenith will produce the result that at its zenith the ball's vertical component of velocity is zero i.e.

$$\frac{dy}{dt} = 0$$

From Section 8.4 the equation for the vertical displacement of the ball is

$$y = (V \sin\alpha)t - \frac{1}{2}gt^2$$

so

$$\frac{dy}{dt} = V \sin\alpha - gt$$

Thus the basketball reaches its zenith when

$$t = \frac{V \sin\alpha}{g}$$

and at this time

$$y = \frac{V^2 \sin^2\alpha}{2g}$$

Since the basketball was released from a height of h = 2.15m above ground level then the maximum height reached is given by

$$\frac{V^2 \sin^2\alpha}{2g} + 2.15$$

Table 8.4 gives the value of this expression for the successful shots described in Table 8.1.

TABLE 8.4

$V(ms^{-1})$	(deg)	Maximum height reached above ground level (m)
7.45	$46°28'$	3.64
	$54°36'$	4.03
7.50	$56°22'$	4.14
8.00	$64°28'$	4.81
8.50	$68°44'$	5.35

8.9 THE EFFECT OF AIR RESISTANCE

For a sphere of diameter dm moving with the velocity of a basketball (v ms^{-1}) the air resistance force D is given by

$$D = 0.2 \ (dv)^2$$

$$= 0.121 \ v^2.$$

This force is oppositely directed to the motion of the ball and acts along the tangent to the trajectory of the ball. If $u = dx/dt$, $v = dy/dt$ and m denotes the mass of the basketball, 0.6-0.65 kg, the equations of motion applicable in the case of constant acceleration are modified to

$$m \frac{du}{dt} = -0.0121 \ u \ \sqrt{u^2 + v^2},$$

$$m \frac{dv}{dt} = -0.0121 \ v \ \sqrt{u^2 + v^2} - mg.$$

To solve this pair of simultaneous differential equations for the position (x,y) of the centre of the basketball requires the use of a computer program and a suitable numerical technique, such as the Runge Kutta method. Once the values of

the coordinates (x,y) have been output at different times,
the trajectory of the centre of the ball can be plotted and
compared with the parabolic trajectory obtained in the absence
of air resistance.

8.10 IS THERE ANYTHING ELSE WE COULD INCLUDE IN THE MODEL?

So far, the passage of the basketball through the hoop has not
involved contact with either the hoop or the backboard (the
vertical board to which the hoop is attached). The rules
governing free throws do allow the ball to contact either the
backboard or the rim of the hoop before entering the hoop.
Such contact makes the model much more complex and what happens
depends on many factors of which the most important are

1. The point at which contact between the ball and rim or
    backboard occurs.

2. The velocity of the ball at this instant.

3. The coefficient of restitution between the ball and the
    rim or backboard.

4. Any spin which may have been imparted to the ball at
    release.

It is obviously difficult to generalise in such complicated
cases although it is reasonable to suppose that if the ball
possessed some backspin its chances of rebounding through the
hoop from the backboard would be improved.

9

Putting the shot

JIM TABOR *Coventry Polytechnic*

9.1 INTRODUCTION

This variant of the maximum range problem is interesting,
because it can be approached on many levels, as we indicate
by giving different "answers" to the question posed in the
problem statement.

It also tempts the students not to question their pre-
conceptions too closely, because virtually all will be quite
familiar with the subject. The particular pre-conception we
refer to is that the speed of release of the shot can be
taken to be independent of the angle of release. This
assumption is so "reasonable" it will almost certainly not
even be mentioned, but it ignores simple mechanics, and the
structure of the human body. If an "answer" is to be had, it
will be concerned with fine tuning, and these sorts of
effects, though not of enormous importance cannot be ignored
without some justification.

Another possibility is that reasonable assumptions will not
be made. For a shot at the relatively slow speeds involved,
air resistance of the form kv^2 would be appropriate physically,
and analytic solution of the equations of motion in a useful
form is impossible. In any mathematical model, you must draw
the line between accuracy and simplicity somewhere. For an
object as compact and massive as a shot it should be clear
that air resistance will be completely inconsequential. This
point can be in any case readily checked using data from the
further information Section 9.3.

How the material is presented will depend on the duration of
the modelling exercise. If the exercise takes place over

an extended period, then it seems reasonable only to hand out the information contained in the problem statement. This does hint rather broadly that more information would be available in the real situation. If a group asked for such extra information they could be given the section on further information. If not the same, or similar, facts would be freely available elsewhere.

Quite a lot could be gained from this exercise over a single two or three hour session for small groups. In this case we feel that the further information should be provided even if not requested, though a group could be allowed to "stew" for twenty minutes or so. It is probably also more useful in the limited time situation, if the group is encouraged to regard the teacher as client - the coach in this case - since they should demand information more freely, which will mean that it is easier to prevent time wasted on dead ends. We feel it is necessary to be more directive over two hours than it would be over two weeks.

After the further information we present three "answers" of varying sophistication (or complexity), with a discussion of the appropriateness of the model and possible teacher input at the end of each.

9.2   PROBLEM STATEMENT

Putting the Shot

A local athletics coach specialises in shot put. Being progressive he makes videos of some of his athletes putting action. The purpose of this is mainly to criticise the balance and speed of movement across the circle.

However, on slow motion replay it becomes obvious that different athletes seem to release the shot at markedly different angles.

Further taping of world class putters reveals release angles usually in the range 38° - 45° with one as high as 55°.

With shot put events often being won by distances of a metre or less, our coach feels that release angle should be important, but at this moment does not know what advice he should give.

What do you think the coach should say to his athletes about release angle?

Supplementary Information

A shot for male adults is a solid sphere of iron weighing 16lb
(7.257 kg).

A shot putter makes his put from a putting circle as shown in
Figure 9.1.

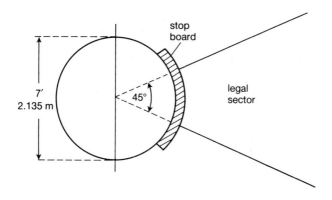

Figure 9.1   Plan view of putting circle

For a valid put, the shot must be carried in one hand; the
putter must leave the circle from the rear half, and the shot
must land within the legal sector.

A curved stop board is fixed to the ground in front of the
circle. Its section is square, about 4" (10 cm) on a side,
and the putter may touch (as hard as he likes) the vertical
face, but not the top face.

9.3   FURTHER INFORMATION

Figure 9.2 shows a sequence of photographs of Geoff Capes.
These photographs are reproduced by courtesy of Howard Payne
with whom copyright persists. Requests for copies of an A4
version of this figure for use with groups of students should
however be directed to the author.

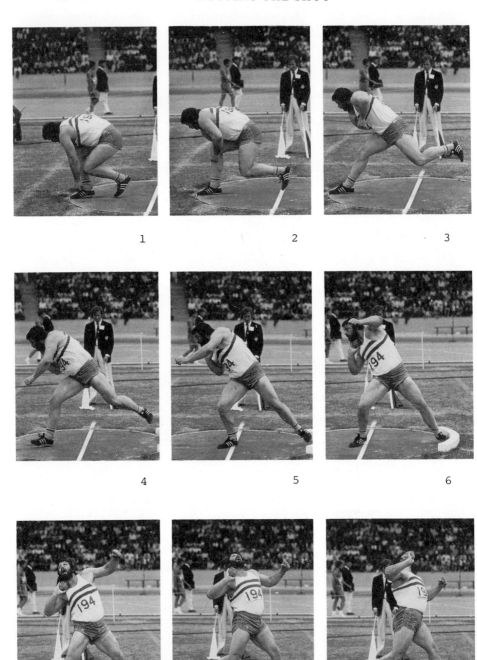

1

2

3

4

5

6

7

8

9

10   11   12

13   14

Figure 9.2   Shot technique: the sequence shows Geoff Capes
             Commonwealth record holder, winning a Europa Cup
             competition

Figure 9.3 is a schematic version of a similar throw. The dots give the position of the centre of the shot at equal time intervals. The point of release is marked with a cross. The data regarding this put are as follows:-

Height of release	1.98 m
Distance of point of release in front of circle	0.23 m
Angle of release	41°
Speed of release	12.5 ms^{-1}
Distance of put	18.11 m

(After Dyson, 1977, The Mechanics of Athletics, Hodder and Stoughton, London)

This put is about the same sort of distance as for the coach's putters - namely about 18 m.

As a point of interest, most world class putters appear to achieve their personal best distances at angles in the very narrow range 38° - 40°.

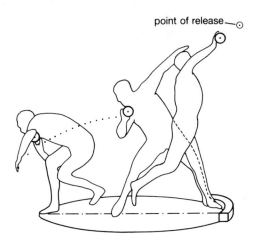

point of release

Figure 9.3   Schematic illustration of a throw

9.4   MODEL I

First consider a projectile having speed V projected from
ground level at an angle α to the horizontal.

Ignoring air resistance, Newton's 2nd law gives

$$m \frac{d^2x}{dt^2} = 0$$

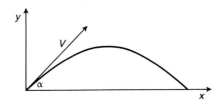

$$m \frac{d^2y}{dt^2} = -mg$$

so x = Vcosαt

$$y = -\tfrac{1}{2} gt^2 + V \sin\alpha t$$

Figure 9.4

on integrating and incorporating the initial conditions.
Substituting for time we have

$$y = - \frac{g}{2v^2 \cos^2\alpha} x^2 + \tan\alpha x$$

If y = 0 then either x = 0 or $x = \dfrac{2v^2 \sin\alpha \cos\alpha}{g}$.

Assuming that the speed of projection is independent of angle
of projection, for maximum range

$$\frac{dx}{d\alpha} = 0$$

i.e. $$\frac{d}{d\alpha} (\frac{v^2}{g} \sin2\alpha) = \frac{v^2}{g} 2\cos 2\alpha = 0$$

so $$2\alpha = \frac{\pi}{2}, \quad \alpha = \frac{\pi}{4}$$

If the shot were projected from ground level we could expect
maximum range for a projection angle of about 45°. However,
the world record for shot put is about 21 m, so a shot is
released at a distance above the ground, say 2.5 m, that is

significant with respect to the range, and this may affect
optimum release angles.

Considering this slightly more complicated problem where the
shot is released at height h we would have

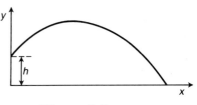

$$x = V \cos\alpha t$$

$$y = \tfrac{1}{2} gt^2 + V \sin\alpha t + h$$

So $$y = \frac{-g}{2V^2} \frac{x}{\cos^2\alpha} + \tan\alpha x + h$$

Figure 9.5

and to find the range we set $y = 0$ and solve the quadratic
equation

$$\frac{g}{2V^2 \cos^2\alpha} x^2 - \tan\alpha\, x - h = 0$$

At present we do not know the speed of projection, but we can
assume $x = 21$ m, $h = 2.5$ m and $\alpha = \dfrac{\pi}{4}$ to give some idea. This
yields, for a value of $g = 9.81$ ms^{-2},

$$\frac{9.81}{V^2} \; 21^2 - 21 - 2.5 = 0$$

$$V^2 = 184.094$$

or $$V = 13.57 \text{ ms}^{-1}$$

We can expect that the optimum release angle will be about $45°$,
so we can use the usual quadratic formula

$$x = \frac{\tan\alpha + \sqrt{\tan^2\alpha + 2gh/(V^2\cos^2\alpha)}}{g/V^2\cos^2\alpha}$$

to draw up a table of ranges for the release speed given above. The angles covered should cover the band 38° - 45°, since these are the angles used by putters, and are probably close to the optimum angle.

Rearranging the formula slightly we have

$$x = \frac{v^2}{g^2} \sin 2\alpha + \sqrt{(\frac{v^2}{2g} \sin 2\alpha)^2 + 2h \frac{v^2}{2g} \cos^2 \alpha}$$

The table of ranges is given in Table 9.1 . The conclusions that can be drawn from this table are clear.

TABLE 9.1

Table of ranges

V (ms^{-1})	$v^2/2g$ (m)	Angle ($^\circ$)	Range (m)
13.57	9.383	55	19.24
"	"	47.5	20.76
"	"	45	21.00
"	"	42.5	21.11
"	"	40	21.09
"	"	38	20.99
"	"	36	20.80
"	"	41.2	21.12
13.0	8.614	41.2	19.57
14.0	9.990	41.2	22.34

For a constant speed of projection, an angle of projection anywhere between 38° and 45° produces minimal variation in range - only 13cm, or 0.6%, with the optimum occurring around 41.2°. However a small variation in speed, from 13ms^{-1} to 14ms^{-1} - an 8% increase - produces a larger

variation in the range, from 19.57 m to 22.34 m - a 14%
increase.

The advice from the coach should be not to worry too much about
angle, since the range is quite insensitive, but should
concentrate on increasing the speed, since the range is much
more sensitive to this.

9.5 DISCUSSION OF MODEL I

The major failing of this model lies in the fact that the
further information was clearly not asked for, and only the
information given in the problem statement used.

This is quite a serious defect. In our experience the most
difficult task in a mathematical modelling or operations
research project is to find out what the problem is. The
client may have only a very sketchy idea of the things that
are relevant to the modeller, and the modeller will not have
the wealth of background knowledge of the client.

During a fairly lengthy initial phase, modeller and client
should be involved in discussions that range well around the
narrow limits of the problem, during which the modeller has to
find out (a) what the client wants and (b) what the client
needs - they are not always the same.

The further information section is meant to simulate this
initial phase - if only symbolically - you will not get it
unless you ask for it.

Because of this, the model solves the wrong problem - if only
marginally. The model considers a "world record" put of
about 21 m, whereas the coach is interested in an 18 m put,
made clear in the further information. In this case,
differences would be slight and the conclusions are almost
certainly still valid.

However, its a common sight to see an unwary modeller weeping
silently in a corner. After only brief contact, or possibly
none at all, with the client, the modeller gets his problem
specification and then gets his head down and beavers away
and comes up with a model or problem solved. Only then,
trying to implement the model or solution does he find out
that something crucial has been missed, and that the work is
useless. It may be that assumptions have been made that
appear reasonable, but cannot be justified for this particular
problem, or that the problem specification was vague, or just
plain wrong.

Having issued these tirades, we have to go on to say that,
apart from these defects it is not a bad model. It is "quick
and dirty", but does state the two major assumptions, ignoring
air resistance and taking speed independent of angle, even if
no attempt at justification is made. The mathematics is
unsophisticated, with the maximum range found just by putting
a few different angles into the formula derived, but that is
consistent with the level of crudity of the assumptions.
Finally the model does yield enough information to draw a
sensible conclusion, namely that projection speed is much more
important than angle, and in that sense, does answer the
coach's question, but in the rather negative way - "do not
bother with angle, concentrate on speed". It does not provide
any insight as to how projection speed is acquired, and might
be improved.

9.6   MODEL II

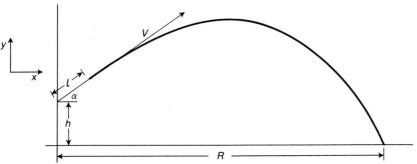

Figure 9.6   Illustration of Model II

$$m \frac{d^2x}{dt^2} = 0$$

$$m \frac{d^2y}{dt^2} = -mg$$

$$x = \ell\cos\alpha + V\cos\alpha t \qquad\qquad (1)$$

$$y = -\tfrac{1}{2} gt^2 + V\sin\alpha t + h + \ell\sin\alpha \qquad\qquad (2)$$

$$t = \frac{x}{V\cos\alpha} - \frac{\ell}{V} \qquad\qquad (3)$$

Substitute back into (2)

$$y = -\tfrac{1}{2} g \left(\frac{x}{V\cos\alpha} - \frac{\ell}{V}\right)^2 + V\sin\alpha \left(\frac{x}{V\cos\alpha} - \frac{\ell}{V}\right) + h + \ell\sin\alpha$$

$$y = 0 \rightarrow x = R$$

$$\therefore \ 0 = -\tfrac{1}{2} g \left(\frac{R}{V\cos\alpha} - \frac{\ell}{V}\right)^2 + V\sin\alpha \left(\frac{R}{V\cos\alpha} - \frac{\ell}{V}\right) + h + \ell\sin\alpha \quad (4)$$

Differentiating

$$0 = -\tfrac{1}{2} g \cdot 2 \left(\frac{R}{V\cos\alpha} - \frac{\ell}{V}\right) \frac{d}{d\alpha} \left(\frac{R}{V\cos\alpha}\right) + \frac{d}{d\alpha} (R\tan\alpha - \ell\sin\alpha)$$

$$+ \frac{d}{d\alpha} (\ell\sin\alpha)$$

$$0 = -g \left(\frac{R}{V\cos\alpha} - \frac{\ell}{V}\right) \left[\frac{dR}{d\alpha} \frac{1}{V\cos\alpha} + \frac{R}{V} \frac{\sin\alpha}{\cos^2\alpha}\right] + \frac{dR}{d\alpha} \tan\alpha + R\sec^2\alpha$$

At optimum α, $\dfrac{dR}{d\alpha} = 0$ so that

$$0 = -g \left(\frac{Rmax}{V\cos\alpha} - \frac{\ell}{V}\right) \frac{Rmax}{V} \frac{\sin\alpha}{\cos^2\alpha} + \frac{Rmax}{\cos^2\alpha}$$

i.e. $$\left(\frac{Rmax}{V\cos\alpha} - \frac{\ell}{V}\right) = \frac{V}{g\sin\alpha} \quad (5)$$

Now $$\frac{Rmax}{V\cos\alpha} - \frac{\ell}{V} = \frac{-V\sin\alpha \pm \sqrt{V^2\sin^2\alpha + 2g\,(\ell\sin\alpha + h)}}{-g}$$

from (4) so substituting (5) into this

$$\frac{V}{g\sin\alpha} = \frac{V\sin\alpha \pm \sqrt{V^2\sin^2\alpha + 2g\,(\ell\sin\alpha + h)}}{g}$$

Choosing the + sign gives

$$\frac{V}{\sin\alpha} = V\sin\alpha + \sqrt{V^2\sin^2\alpha + 2g\ (\ell\sin\alpha + h)}$$

$$V^2(\frac{1}{\sin^2\alpha} - 2 + \sin^2\alpha) = V^2\sin^2\alpha + 2g\ (\ell\sin\alpha + h)$$

yielding finally

$$\frac{V^2}{\sin^2\alpha} - 2g\ell\sin\alpha = 2V^2 + 2gh \qquad\qquad (6)$$

Setting ℓ and h to zero

$$\frac{1}{\sin^2\alpha} = 2 \qquad\text{i.e. } \alpha = \frac{\pi}{4} \text{ as required}$$

Using V = 14ms^{-1}

h = 1.6 m

ℓ = 0.6 m

g = 9.81ms^{-2}

we have $\frac{196}{\sin^2\alpha} - 11.77\sin\alpha - 423.39 = 0$ \qquad (7)

Using a Reguli Falsi method to solve this equation with end
points of 40° and 45°.

α	$f(\alpha)$
45°	−39.71
40°	43.42
42.73°	− 5.68
42.42°	− 0.59

Therefore, the answer is 42.4° and this is the optimum shot put angle for the above data.

9.7 DISCUSSION OF MODEL II

This is a real "head down" model. Never mind the facts, lets get on with the mathematics. In fact the way the solution is worked out is quite neat, but is absolutely senseless.

All the criticisms of model I apply here in full force, plus many others. There is absolutely no explanation given to any aspect of this model, and possibly more importantly none of the assumptions is stated. The "achievement" of the model is the production of the non-linear equation (6) for the optimal α, but for the same amount of computational effort, the quadratic in R given in equation (4) could have been solved several times and more information would have been gained, since the sensitivity of the range to angle would have been found.

Worse than this, a (fairly) sophisticated model is built on crude assumptions, namely that projection speed is independent of angle. All in all, model II is a total waste of time.

9.8 MODEL III

Introduction

Having examined the problem statement and further information, especially figures 9.2 and 9.3, we feel there are two questions to be answered:

(i) What range of angles should a shot putter putting about 18 m aim for?

This question is answered in part by the casual observation that most world class putters achieve their best puts between 38° and 40°. So the second question is:

(ii) Can we justify quantitatively the selection of angles in the range 38° - 40° as optimum?

We cannot expect what will be a fairly simple mathematical model to overturn custom and practice, that should have "shaken down" to the optimum technique, but we can give some insight as to why this technique comes about.

Assumptions and Models

In order to answer the question posed in the introduction we
have to construct a mathematical model of a shot put. This
clearly divides into two phases:

(i)   Putting phase before release

(ii) Flight of shot after release

The second phase appears easiest to model. The shot is
spherical, very dense and moving relatively slowly through the
air, so there is no hesitation in using Newtonian particle
dynamics.

It also seems clear that air resistance should not be important
during the flight for similar reasons. This is easily checked
using the figures for the put depicted in Figure 9.3, and the
formulae derived in Appendix 9.8.1 which ignore air resistance.
The predicted range, ignoring air resistance, is, in fact,
less than the stated range, but within the possible numerical
error, rather than more, as would be the case if air
resistance was important.

Before we give models for the putting action we consider
Figure 9.2 in more detail. From this we can divide a shot put
into five phases, which obviously still blend into one
another.

(i)   Frames 1 - 4   - glide across the circle

(ii)   Frames 5 - 8   - body rotation which continues during
                         arm explosion

(iii) Frames 9 - 10   - arm explosion

(iv)   Frame 11   - wrist flick

(v)   Frames 12 - 14 - follows through and recovery

We do not need to model accurately phases (i) (ii) and (v) as
long as we can make the following assumptions

(i)   the shot putter's shoulder will occupy the same position
       at the time of release whatever the angle of release.

(ii)   just before the arm explosion the shot is travelling in
       the same direction that it is finally released into

(iii) the speed of the shot just before this arm explosion is
       independent of the angle of release.

Figure 9.2 frame 11 justifies assumption (i). The putter's body would probably take up this attitude whatever the arm angle. The other two assumptions are probably close but not quite right. Given the amount of information we have, they are the best we can come up with.

We now have to model the arm explosion and wrist flick, which are the most important phases of the shot put, but are again slightly hampered by lack of information. We will therefore have to keep it simple. Bearing this in mind we make the following assumptions.

(iv)   the shot moves in a straight line from beginning of "explosion" to release.

Figure 9.3 appears to confirm this, although it would be possible for the wrist flick to change the direction at the last moment.

The above assumptions can be argued for by examining Figures 9.2 and 9.3, but we now have to decide on a prediction for the speed of the shot at the point of release. Here we make conflicting assumptions, giving the results for each resulting model.

(a)   the speed of projection is independent of the angle of release (model (a))

This assumption is simple, but it is counter-intuitive to expect a human to project the shot at the same speed say vertically as horizontally, so the speed should have some dependence on angle.

(b)   the putter can exert a force on the shot that is both constant over the explosion and independent of angle (model (b))

If this force is F, the mass of the shot M, the angle of projection α, and the acceleration produced f, then from Appendix 9.8.2 we have:

$$f = \frac{F}{M} - g\sin\alpha \quad \text{(model b)} \qquad (8)$$

so that

$$v^2 = u^2 + 2S \left(\frac{F}{M} - g\sin\alpha\right) \qquad (9)$$

where U is the speed of the shot just before the "explosion" and S the distance over which it takes place. V is the projection speed, and clearly depends on α in this model.

It is true that the muscles of the putter's arm are having to lift the arm itself as well as the shot. We can include some dependence on this by using the formula:

$$f = \frac{F}{M} - r_m \, g\sin\alpha \qquad \text{(model (c))} \qquad (10)$$

where $r_m > 1$ to allow for having to lift the arm. If we say that the centre of mass of the arm is $\frac{1}{3}$ out from the shoulder, and a shot putter's arm weighs about $1\frac{1}{2}$ times that of a shot - about $10\frac{1}{2}$ kg or 24 lb this gives

$$r_m = 1.5 \qquad (11)$$

and this is the value used in model c.

Results

Appendix 9.8.3 shows how values for the various quantities required to calculate ranges may be obtained.

The single formula (see A2.3 and A2.4 of Appendix 9.2)

$$\text{Range} = \frac{(U^2 + 2(\frac{F}{M} - r_m \, g\sin\alpha) \, \ell_2)}{2g} \sin 2\alpha$$

$$\times \left\{ 1 + \sqrt{1 + \frac{2g(h + \ell_1\sin\alpha)}{(U^2 + 2(\frac{F}{M} - r_m \, g\sin\alpha))\sin^2\alpha}} \right\} + \ell_1\cos\alpha - \ell_3$$

$$(12)$$

can be used for all three models.

The meanings of the terms are as follows:-

ℓ_1 - length of the putter's arm

ℓ_2 - distance over which arm explosion takes place

ℓ_3 - distance behind stop board of shoulder

h - height of shoulder above ground

g - gravitational acceleration

α - angle of projection to the horizontal

$\frac{F}{M}$ - force exerted by arm

r_m - fudge factor to allow for arm mass

U - speed of shot just before arm explosion

Values for these quantities are given in Table 9.2 for each model. Table 9.3 gives the put distance for each model for varying angles of projection. All three models give the distance 18.02 m for $\alpha = 41^\circ$ since a projection speed of 12.5 ms^{-1} was assumed at this angle. The distance quoted in the further information i.e. 18.11 m is attained at 12.53 ms^{-1} (see Appendix 9.1).

Figure 9.7 is a graph of range against angle for the three models. The dashed line is for model (a) where projection speed is independent of angle: the dash dot line in model (b) where the force applied to the shot is independent of angle: the solid line in model (c) where some ad hoc attempt is made to allow for the mass of the arm.

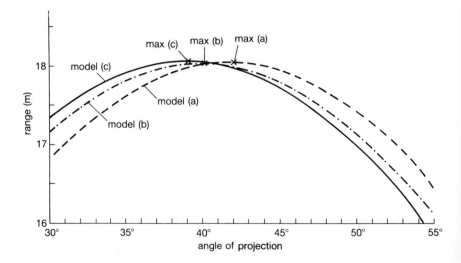

Figure 9.7

Conclusions

It is easiest to argue from Figure 9.7. The first point that is evident is that whatever model is used, the put is longer than 17.9 m for angles between $37\frac{1}{2}°$ and $43°$. If we look more closely at model (c), this has its optimum release angle at $39°$ - in the middle of the band of angles quoted in the further information. But the put is longer than 18.0 m for any angle between $36\frac{1}{2}°$ and $41\frac{1}{2}°$. This is only 6 cm less than the maximum of 18.06 m so that the recommendation to the shot putter would be to aim for somewhere in the range $37°$ - $41°$, but not worry since range is relatively insensitive to angle: by far the more important factor is release speed.

Shortcomings of the Models

Model (a) is very much a first approximation, and since Model (b) is a subset of Model (c) we must consider this model most fully.

The major criticisms of this model are:

(i)   choice of r_m = 1.5

(ii) wrist flip ignored.

To assume that a shot putter's arm weighs $10\frac{1}{2}$ kg i.e. 10% of a bodyweight of 105 kg (16st. 7lb) or 8% of a bodyweight of 130 kg (20st. 7lb) might seem a little excessive. It could be argued that if the movement of the arm was dealt with in detail it would have a greater retarding effect on the shot than the extremely crude way it is taken into account. Further, the large pectoral muscle must be capable of being used to greater effect if the shot is put horizontally rather than vertically (see frame 9 of Figure 9.2), and this factor is not taken into account at all. We must regard r_m as a parameter, to some extent, and the model "fits" the observed situation with a value r_m = 1.5, which is by no means unreasonable.

The second criticism is much more damaging. If we look at frame 11 of Figure 9.2 the angle of the arm is about $36°$, and while we do not know at what angle this shot is released in this instance it would probably be $39°$ or so.

It may be that the arm has moved down (or been "pushed" by
the shot) but this seems a little unlikely considering the
position of the hand in the frame. It seems likely that the
wrist flip can change the direction of the shot rather than
give it an extra boost in the direction in which it is already
travelling.

It is also clear from frames 10 and 11 that the arm is pushed
out below the shot, which may have some effect. However, we
can draw no conclusions concerning speeds and accelerations
during the flip from the information we have, and in any case
it seems unlikely that significant changes would be made to
curve (c) in Figure 9.7 even if we could take the wrist flip
into account.

TABLE 9.2

Values for quantities given in equation 5

Quantity	Model (a)	Model (b)	Model (c)
ℓ_1 (m)	0.7	0.7	0.7
ℓ_2 (m)	0	1.3	1.3
ℓ_3 (m)	0.3	0.3	0.3
h (m)	1.52	1.52	1.52
g (ms^{-2})	9.81	9.81	9.81
α (deg)	Various	Various	Various
$\frac{F}{M}$ (ms^{-2})	0	62.146	65.345
r_m	0	1	1.5
U (ms^{-1})	12.5	3.38	3.38

TABLE 9.3

Range versus Angle for the three models

Angle of projection (degrees)	Range with speed independent of angle	Range with speed dependent on angle	Range with allowance for arm mass
30	16.81	17.17	17.35
35	17.61	17.82	17.92
36	17.72	17.90	17.98
37	17.826	17.96	18.03
38	17.89	18.00	18.05
39	17.95	18.03	18.06
40	18.00	18.03	18.05
41	18.02	18.02	18.02
42	18.03	17.99	17.98
43	18.01	17.95	17.91
44	17.98	17.88	17.83
45	17.93	17.80	17.73
50	17.40	17.12	16.98
55	16.41	16.01	15.81
41.8	18.026		
39.9		18.032	
39.0			18.059

APPENDIX 9.8.1 - Range formula

Given the initial position and velocity for a trajectory as shown in figure A1.1, we wish to calculate the range R, neglecting air resistance.

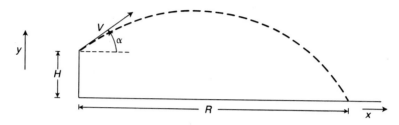

Figure A1.1   Sketch of trajectory

Resolving Newton's 2nd law horizontally and vertically

$$m \frac{d^2x}{dt^2} = 0$$

$$m \frac{d^2y}{dt^2} = -mg$$

so $x = at + b$, and taking $x(0) = 0$

$$\left. \frac{dx}{dt} \right|_{t=0} = V\cos\alpha$$

$$x = V\cos\alpha t$$

and $y = -\frac{1}{2} gt^2 + ct + d$, and taking $y(0) = h$

$$\left. \frac{dy}{dt} \right|_{t=0} = V\sin\alpha$$

$$y = -\frac{1}{2} gt^2 + V\sin\alpha t + H$$

Eliminating t we have

$$y = \frac{-gx^2}{2v^2\cos^2\alpha} + \tan\alpha\ x + H$$

x is equal to the range when the shot hits the ground - i.e. y = 0, so R satisfies the quadratic

$$\frac{gR^2}{2v^2\cos^2\alpha} - \tan\alpha\ R - H = 0 \qquad\qquad A1.1$$

or

$$R^2 - \frac{v^2}{g}\sin2\alpha\ R - 2\frac{HV^2}{g}\cos^2\alpha = 0$$

i.e.

$$R = \frac{v^2}{2g}\sin2\alpha + \sqrt{\frac{v^4}{4g^2}\sin^2 2\alpha + \frac{HV^2}{2g}\cos^2\alpha}$$

$$= \frac{v^2}{2g}\sin2\alpha\ (1 + \sqrt{1 + \frac{2gH}{v^2\sin^2\alpha}}) \qquad\qquad A1.2$$

For the put given as Figure 9.3 of the further information we have:

$$V = 12.5\ ms^{-1}$$

$$H = 1.98\ m$$

$$\alpha = 41^\circ$$

$$g = 9.81\ ms^{-2}$$

So   R = 17.79 m.

Adding on 0.23 m since the position of release was in front of the board we have put distance should be 18.02 m.

If air resistance was in any way important the measured distance should be less than this figure, whereas, at 18.11 m it is 9 cm more. This is not inconsistent, since the speed of release is not quoted accurately.

Rearranging equation A1.1 to make v^2 the subject we have:

$$v^2 = \frac{gR^2}{2\cos^2\alpha(\tan\alpha R + H)}$$

A1.3

So using $g = 9.81 \text{ ms}^{-2}$

$R = 18.11 - 0.23 = 17.88 \text{ m}$

$\alpha = 41^{\circ}$

$h = 1.98 \text{ m}$

we find $V = 12.53 \text{ ms}^{-1}$ which is within the implicit error of the quoted figure.

So the figures quoted for a put in the further information section are consistent with neglecting air resistance.

APPENDIX 9.8.2 - The Mechanics of Shot Release

We now consider how the shot is accelerated up to the point of release, and use the result of Appendix 9.1 to give a put distance.

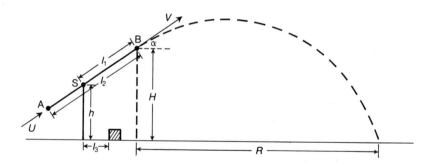

Figure A2.1   Illustration of shot release

S is the shoulder and this point is taken as fixed even though α varies.

A is the point where the arm explosion starts and B is the point of release. So ℓ_1 is the actual arm length, and ℓ_2 is the distance over which the shot is accelerated during the arm explosion - it is longer than ℓ_1 because of body rotations.

V is the speed of the shot before the explosion, and we assume a constant acceleration f during it.

Using the formulae for constant acceleration we have:

$$v^2 = u^2 + 2f\ell_2 \qquad\qquad A2.1$$

We also have $H = h + \ell_1\sin\alpha$, where h is the height to the shoulder which is fixed.

Substituting these quantities into equation A1.2 we have:

$$R = \frac{(u^2 + 2f\ell_2)}{2g}\sin2\alpha \left[1 + \sqrt{1 + \frac{2g\,(h + \ell_1\sin\alpha)}{(u^2 + 2f\ell_2)\sin^2\alpha}}\right] \qquad A2.2$$

The final put distance is therefore:

$$D = R + \ell_1\cos\alpha - \ell_3 \qquad\qquad A2.3$$

where ℓ_3 is the distance of the shoulder behind the throw line, and this is assumed to be independent of α.

We would also expect the acceleration f to depend on α. We assume that the putter's arm is capable of exerting a constant force on the shot throughout the "explosion" and this has to accelerate the shot, and lift it against gravity.

Using Newton's 2nd law

$$Mf = F - mg\sin\alpha$$

$$A2.4$$

or $$f = \frac{F}{M} - g\sin\alpha$$

where $\frac{F}{M}$ is taken as independent of α

This is not quite the whole story, since the arm muscles must
also accelerate and lift the arm itself, and we can make some
allowance for this by writing:

$$f = \frac{F}{M} - rgsin\alpha \qquad\qquad A2.5$$

where $r \geq 1$ can really only be guessed at.

APPENDIX 9.3.3 - Determining Constants

To use the formulae of Appendix 9.2 we must determine sensible
values for the quantities

$$\ell_1, \; \ell_2', \; \ell_3, \; h, \; U, \; \frac{F}{M};$$

For this we use Figure 9.3 predominantly. With various
distances marked on it, it is reproduced in Figure A3.1

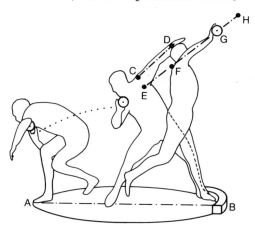

Figure A3.1

The distance AB must be 2.135 m since it is the width of the
circle, and this gives us a length scale.

The lengths on the diagram and in metres are given in Table A3.1.

TABLE A3.1

Measured Lengths

	Name	Length on diagram (mm)	Actual length (m)
AB	–	59	2.135
CD	ℓ_1	19	0.7
EH	ℓ_2	36	1.3
EF	s_1	10.25	0.371
EG	s_2	28	1.013

We have taken the arm explosion to start at the point E rather than the dot before it, since Figure 9.2 frame 7 seems to indicate that it is at about this position that the shot leaves the neck.

We now use the two constant acceleration formulae:

$$s = ut + \tfrac{1}{2} ft^2$$

$$v^2 = u^2 + 2fs$$

and the final speed of the shot of 12.5 ms^{-1} to determine U and $\frac{F}{M}$.

Since the time interval between positions E and F is the same as that between F and G we can say:

$$s_1 = U\delta t + \tfrac{1}{2}f\delta t^2$$

$$s_2 = 2U\delta t + 2f\delta t^2$$

So

$$U = (4s_1 - s_2)/2\delta t = \frac{0.2355}{\delta t}$$

$$f = (s_2 - 2s_1)/\delta t^2 = \frac{0.271}{\delta t^2}$$

Using $\quad v^2 = (12.5)^2$ we have

$$(12.5)^2 = \{\frac{(4s_1 - s_2)^2}{4} + 2\ (s_2 - 2s_1)\ell_2\}/\delta t^2$$

with $s_1 = 0.371$ m, $s_2 = 1.013$ m we have

$$\delta t = 0.06975 \text{ s}$$

$$U = 3.38 \text{ ms}^{-1}$$

$$f = 55.71 \text{ ms}^{-2}$$

This would mean that the force applied would be given by:

$$F = M(55.71 + g\sin41^{\circ})$$

so that $\qquad \frac{F}{M} = 62.146$

If we wished to take account of the mass of the putter's arm we might say

$$F = M(55.71 + 1.5\ g\sin41^{\circ})$$

so that $\qquad \frac{F}{M} = 65.364$

In order to find ℓ_3 we note that the shot was released 0.23 m in front of the board, so

$$\ell_3 = \ell_1 \cos41^\circ - 0.23$$

$$= 0.30 \text{ m}$$

For h we note that $H = h + \ell_1 \sin41^\circ$ is quoted as 1.98 so

$$h = 1.52 \text{ m}$$

It is these figures that are used for the calculations leading to Figure 9.7 and Table 9.3.

9.9 DISCUSSION OF MODEL III

This model is clearly meant to be the "model" model, and is in a good format where the objectives are clearly stated at the outset. Then the information available and assumptions made are discussed in some detail. None of the mathematics appears in the main body of the write up so, for a first read through, or for a non-technical reader, there is no need to wade through pages of equations to get to the conclusions. The results are clearly presented in tabular and graphical form, and the conclusions are succinct. We are left in no doubt that the release angle is not of paramount importance, but if we are interested there are good reasons to believe the

optimum is around 39°.

Given that the presentation is reasonable the main question to ask is whether the assumptions are consistent both with the data given, and with the expected "benefit" to be derived from the model. In other words, is Model III too long and complicated?

Now this last model contains Model II in the guise of assuming a constant projection speed, and this portion would be very much shorter to write out on its own. The main amount of work arises in trying to decide a reasonably physical form for the dependence of projection speed on angle. We could not think of a simpler formulation that had any connection with the physical situation outlined in the further information.

The main alternative would be to assume that the amount of energy that could be imparted to the shot was independent of angle.

It is then very easy to write down the dependence of V on α
since

$$\tfrac{1}{2}v^2 + g\ell_1 \sin\alpha = C$$

or
$$v^2 = C - 2g\ell_1 \sin\alpha$$

as opposed to (see A2.1 and A2.4)

$$v^2 = (U^2 + 2\frac{F}{M}\ell_2) - 2g\ell_2 \sin\alpha$$

Since, in the case given, $\ell_2/\ell_1 \simeq 1.9$, the model used gives v^2
a stronger dependence on α.

The constant energy assumption is so much simpler and has many
fewer quantities that must be estimated from limited and poor
data.   However, a shot putter has very little to do with a
system that conserves energy.   The constant force assumption
seems to have much more relevance to what is actually going on.

This perhaps illustrates one of the underlying principles of
modelling: Simplicity, but not at all costs.

10

Epidemics and the spread of diseases

GLYN JAMES and NIGEL STEELE
Coventry Polytechnic

10.1 STATEMENT OF THE PROBLEM

Two dictionary definitions of the word epidemic are:

- it is a disease that attacks great numbers in one place, at one time, and itself travels from place to place.

- it is a disease that is temporarily prevalent in a society.

If a disease is constantly or generally present in a society then it is said to be endemic.

Many of the epidemics experienced in developed countries, such as common colds or influenza, cause only inconvenience to most sufferers, although economically (in terms of lost employment and so on) their effects may be substantial. In underdeveloped countries, however, epidemics occur involving diseases such as cholera, and cause serious illness and sometimes large numbers of deaths, especially if treatment is not made available.

Thus, when considering epidemics, the concern is with diseases which are infectious (or contagious) - in the sense of being capable of transmission, at some stage in the life cycle of the appropriate organism, from an infected host to an uninfected susceptible. The transmission may be by contact as, for example, in the case of measles; alternatively, as in the case of parasitic diseases, it may involve an intermediate host, such as the mosquito in the case of malaria. Another possibility is that the virus causing the disease is free in the environment, as is the case with an air or water borne virus. In the case of transmission by contact the existence

of 'carriers' further complicates the situation – these are
individuals who, apparently healthy themselves, harbour
infection that can be transmitted to others. Also, some
diseases, such as measles, usually confer life long immunity
from further attack.

It is clear that the need to understand the nature of epidemic
processes needs no special justification in that such knowledge
will assist researchers to develop preventive measures for the
spread of such diseases. It is also desirable to know more
about the endemic level and how it is related to factors which
can be controlled by public health intervention.

Typical questions which the public health authorities are
likely to need answers to are:

   (i)   If an infection is introduced into a society at what
         rate will it spread?

  (ii)   How many initial infections are required to cause an
         eventual epidemic?

 (iii)   When will an epidemic be at its worst?

  (iv)   Does the number of individuals who contact the disease
         settle down to some fixed value (i.e. a 'steady state
         or equilibrium value')? If so, is this a stable
         situation?

   (v)   How quickly must infectives be removed from society,
         by say isolation, if one is to prevent an epidemic
         developing?

  (vi)   Does the number of infectives follow any specific
         pattern?

No doubt you can think of many other likely questions.

The problem is to construct mathematical models to describe
the spread of an infectious disease through a society. In
particular we can restrict consideration to the spread of a
disease, transmitted by case to case contact, through a large
society in which the population mixes reasonably homogeneously .
Data on the annual number of reported cases for both measles
and whooping cough given are in Figures 10.1 and 10.2.

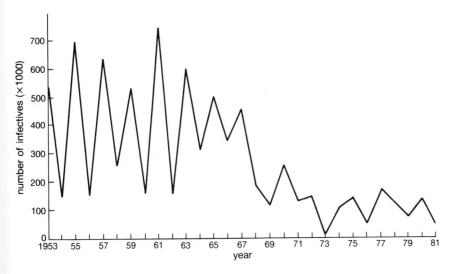

Figure 10.1   Incidence of Measles in England and Wales

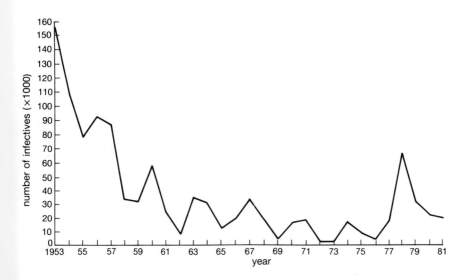

Figure 10.2   Incidence of Whooping Cough in England and
              Wales

10.2 NOTE TO LECTURER

This problem may be handled in many different ways involving various degrees of mathematical analysis and the textbook by Bailey (1975) provides excellent extended reading. The type of model that is suitable and valid in practice depends on circumstances. If the number of susceptibles and infectives are both large, and mixing is reasonably homogeneous, then a deterministic approach is likely to be fairly satisfactory as a first approximation and is the one suggested here. For small communities however, this is not a realistic approach and one would need to consider stochastic effects.

As the investigation proceeds it becomes necessary to incorporate new ideas, often developed as a result of the insight gained by the mathematical formulation already adopted. Inevitably, such a process yields, at each stage, a more complicated model and, more problems in determining an analytical solution. It is the opinion of the authors that the material presented here may be used in different ways depending on the ability of the students in the group and upon the wishes of the lecturer. As a major piece of work, the problem of setting up a description of the epidemic process to incorporate certain desirable features is one possibility. On the other hand, operating within a framework laid down by the lecturer, small groups of students might be asked to enhance a given model by investigating the inclusion of recovery, replenishment or perhaps incubation time effects.

Indeed, the material would seem suitable as follow-up work to a first course in differential equations, with the emphasis very much on obtaining qualitative data from the equation before actually solving it. The information gleaned in this way should serve to convince the student of the value of such an approach, even when it is clear that numerical methods will eventually be required. Also on this theme, following a fairly detailed investigation using differential equation models, attention is drawn to an alternative discrete time formulation in terms of difference equations. Thus a further strategy would be to use the material in the ways suggested above, but with some students being encouraged to develop a continuous time differential equation model with others adopting a discrete time formulation.

10.3 ONE APPROACH TO THE PROBLEM

Before embarking on the modelling exercise some time should be spent discussing the information contained in Figures 10.1 and 10.2.

There is clearly periodicity in the measles data for the
earlier years but, what about the later years? It appears
that following the removal of the transient effects, due to
sudden changes in the late sixties, a periodic pattern, having
a two year cycle, is again emerging but this time about a
lower base level. It is also interesting, at this stage, to
speculate about factor(s) that were responsible for the drop
in the number of reported cases in the late sixties. Here,
such factors as changes in living conditions, and the introduction of vaccination should be discussed (measles vaccination
was first recommended for children in the late sixties).

The whooping cough data seems to indicate an underlying downward trend for most of the time but again there is clearly a
four year cycle periodic pattern present. Again, such matters
as living conditions, and the introduction of vaccination
should be considered as possible factor(s) causing the downward
trend. Whooping cough vaccination was first recommended for
children in 1957. In 1974 some doctors produced a report
which showed that following whooping cough vaccine, some
children had convulsions or encephalitis and developed
permanent brain damage. As a result of media publicity there
was a vaccine scare which is probably the cause for the
upsurge in the late seventies.

Initial student reaction to the problem statement will usually
be chaotic but following a group discussion an idea which
should emerge is that, for the purposes of describing the
epidemic, the population has to be categorised by reference
to the effects of the illness-sick, healthy, recovered and
so on.

At this stage the students should be given an opportunity to
consider possible divisions of members of a population whilst
an epidemic is prevalent.

After discussion this should lead to a categorisation somewhat
along the lines listed in Figure 10.3. This is obviously a
simplified subdivision of the population and additional
categories could be introduced to complicate the situation
further.

The next stage is the realisation that the evolution of the
epidemic can be thought of as a movement of individuals from
one category to another. Again students should, at this
stage, be given an opportunity to consider the inter-
relationships between the various categories.

CLASS	SUB-CLASSES
HEALTHY	H1 Healthy and susceptible H2 Healthy and immunised artificially H3 Healthy and immunised by recovery
INFECTED	I1 Infected and undetected I2 Infected and detected
NEW ENTRANTS	E1 New entrants to healthy class E2 New entrants to infected class
DEATHS	M1 Deaths from healthy class M2 Deaths from infected class

Figure 10.3   Categories within a Society

A possible way of representing the inter-relationships is
shown diagramatically by the flow chart of Figure 10.4.   On
reaching this conceptual stage a large part of the formulation
stage of the modelling process has been completed.   It remains
to translate the flow chart into mathematical equations.

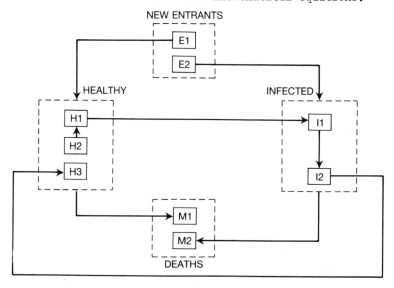

Figure 10.4   Flow between categories of the population

An initial attempt to model the complete situation, as
represented by the flowchart of Figure 10.4 would lead to a
complex mathematical model which would be difficult to analyse
and interpret. An alternative approach, adopted here, is to
consider first a simplified version and then gradually build
up the model to accommodate all the desirable complexities.
Although, initially, this approach may lead to an over-
simplification of the problem, it is reasonable to consider
such problems first, in the expectation that the knowledge
gained will prove to be capable of extension to complicated,
but more realistic, models at a later stage.

10.4 A SIMPLE MODEL

In the first instance, consider the spread of a non-fatal
disease, to which no-one is naturally immune, in a homogeneously
mixed population which is assumed to have a constant size N
over the period of the epidemic. Assume also that the period
of the epidemic is such that no-one is immuned by recovery,
that there is no isolation of infectives, and that all infectives
are assumed to be infectious.

In this particular case we can subdivide the community into
two categories as illustrated in Figure 10.5.

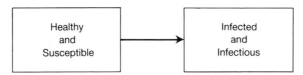

Figure 10.5 A Simple Model

Assume that at a general time t:

   x(t) = Number of susceptibles

   y(t) = Number of infectives

   with x(t) + y(t) = N.

The problem now is to model the spread of the disease. In the
opening section three possible types of disease transmissions
were identified, direct contact, contact via an intermediate
host, or contact by the ingestion of a 'free' virus. Although
a decision was taken to model only epidemics transmitted by the
contact process it would be worthwhile at this stage to
encourage discussion on how all these processes could be
modelled. In particular, the concepts of events occurring in an

interval of time should emerge, leading to detailed thoughts
about what actually happens in that interval.

If the infection is transmitted by contact, then when an
individual who is susceptible comes into contact with an
infected individual the susceptive individuals may become
infected. Thus, during the time interval $[t, t+\delta t]$ each
person who is infected at the start of the interval will be
responsible for a certain number of new infectives during the
interval. This number of new infectives will depend on the
number of susceptibles with whom the infected individual comes
into contact during the interval, which in turn depends on the
number of susceptibles $x(t)$ present at the beginning of the
interval. In the absence of any reason for acting otherwise,
it is sensible to seek the simplest possible relationship for
this dependence. This is a direct proportionality with the
number of susceptibles, so that during the specified time
interval an infected individual will be responsible for

$$\beta_1 \beta_2 \delta t \ x(t),$$

new infectives. Here β_1, β_2 ε $[0,1]$ and $\beta_2 \delta t$ is the fraction
of susceptibles that come into contact with an infected
individual during the time interval, and β_1 is the fraction
of these that become infected. For simplicity we define
$\beta = \beta_1 \beta_2$ as a composite proportionality constant known as the
contact rate or transmission rate.

Since each infected individual will be responsible for a number
of new infectives, and there are $y(t)$ infected individuals
present at the beginning of the interval it follows that the
number of new infectives δy during the time interval $[t, t+\delta t]$
is

$$\delta y = \beta x(t) \ y(t) \ \delta t.$$

Proceeding to the limit $\delta t \to 0$ the number of infectives at time
t is given by the differential equation

$$\frac{dy}{dt} = \beta \ xy,$$

or $$\frac{dy}{dt} = \beta y \ (N-y) \qquad\qquad (1)$$

since $x + y = N$. This is a very famous result, and is known as the logistic equation.

Assuming that initially, when $t = 0$, there are y_0 infected individuals, then differential equation (1) may be written

$$\int_{y_0}^{y} \frac{dy}{y(N-y)} = \int_{0}^{t} \beta dt$$

which, on using partial fractions, may be readily integrated to give

$$y(t) = \frac{N\,y_0}{y_0 + (N-y_0)e^{-\beta Nt}} \tag{2}$$

A plot of (2) is given in Figure 10.6 and it is seen that this model predicts that the disease will eventually spread throughout the population. This type of behaviour is not apparent from the graphs given in Figures 10.1 and 10.2. However, the model may well be a suitable representation of a highly contagious disease that spreads rapidly through a closed community.

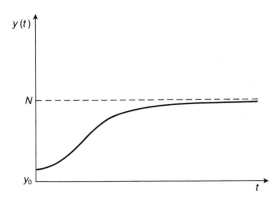

Figure 10.6   Spread of Disease for Simple Model

It was fortunate in this case that the nonlinear differential
equation (1) was soluble. It is pertinent to ask whether the
same information, regarding the spread of the disease be
deduced without actually solving the differential equation.
In many applications it would be satisfactory to have
information about the main features of the solution, without
actually having an explicit solution. The approach adopted
is widely used in the study of nonlinear differential
equations (see Jordan and Smith (1977)) and proceeds as
follows,

First determine the value(s) of y corresponding to situations
when the number of infectives is in a state of equilibrium,
which occurs when $\dot{y}=0$. From equation (1) it follows that in
this case there are two states of equilibrium corresponding
respectively to

$$y(t) = 0 \text{ and } y(t) = N.$$

Next a graph of $\dot{y}(t)$ against $y(t)$, as illustrated in Figure
10.7, is plotted from equation (1). Such a graph is normally
referred to as a phase plane plot or as a state space plot.

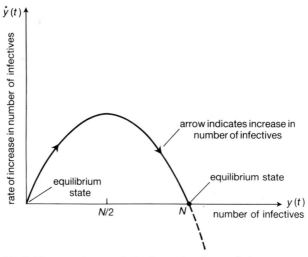

Figure 10.7 Phase plane plot for simple model

The concern is only with values of y in the interval [0,N].
In this interval the graph lies above the horizontal axis,
indicating that $\dot{y}(t) > 0$ which means that the number of
infectives is increasing. Such information is indicated in

the graph by an arrow moving along the graph in the increasing
y(t) direction.

By inspection of the completed Figure 10.7 it is seen that the
arrow approaches the equilibrium state y = N for all permissible
values of y. This means that the number of infectives will
tend to the equilibrium state N, no matter how many infectives
(provided non-zero) are initially present. Remember that this
was the conclusion arrived at after obtaining the explicit
solution of the differential equation; such an equilibrium
state is referred to as a stable equilibrium state.

Inspection of Figure 10.7 also indicates that the arrow moves
away from the equilibrium state y(t) = 0, meaning that once
one member of the population becomes infective then the
number of infectives will increase. Thus y(t) = 0 is referred
to as an unstable equilibrium state.

In practice one is interested in the rate of spread of the
epidemic, as this indicates the rate at which new infectives
occur, i.e. it is a measure of the intensity of the epidemic.
Consequently, it is customary to plot a graph of the
number of new infectives reported against time. In this case
this is simply $\dot{y}(t)$, obtained by differentiating (2), and is
plotted against time in Figure 10.8.

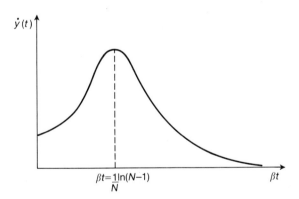

Figure 10.8 Epidemic curve

This plot is known as the epidemic curve and it can be shown
that maximum activity occurs when $\beta t = \dfrac{1}{N} \ln(N-1)$ corresponding
to the situation when half the population is infected. Note

that this latter piece of information is readily obtained from
Figure 10.7.

It is thus clear that by drawing the phase-plane plot of
Figure 10.7 it has been possible to deduce much of the
information needed without actually solving the differential
equation.

The phase-plane plot has yielded useful information without
having actually to solve the differential equation. Whilst
such an approach is worthwhile there is, of course, great
value in solving the differential equation, for it is only
by doing this that complete quantitative information can be
obtained.

10.5 PUTTING IN RECOVERY

It was concluded in the previous section that the model
developed may well be a suitable representation of a highly
contagious disease that spreads rapidly through a closed
community, when it is reasonable to assume that there are no
recoveries during the period of the epidemic; that is, it
models the situation in the short term whilst the epidemic
is prevalent. However, in most circumstances such an
assumption is not valid. Thus a reasonable development is to
extend the model by allowing the possibility of recovery during
the period of the epidemic.

Discussion with the students could lead to two possible
situations, depending on the nature of the disease. Following
recovery, an individual either becomes immune to the disease
or again becomes susceptible to it. Initially the latter
case, which may be represented by the flowchart of Figure 10.9,
is considered.

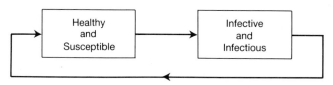

Figure 10.9 Model incorporating recovery

Having discussed the situation of the previous section fully
students should, at this stage, be given an opportunity to
investigate for themselves the effects of introducing the
recovery term.

Again taking $x(t)$, $y(t)$, (with $x(t) + y(t) = N$) to represent the number of susceptibles and infectives at general time t, then in this case during the time interval $[t,t + \delta t]$ the increase δy in the number of infectives is given by

$$\delta y = \begin{bmatrix} \text{Number of susceptibles becoming} \\ \text{infective during the interval} \end{bmatrix} - \begin{bmatrix} \text{Number of infectives} \\ \text{recovering during the} \\ \text{interval} \end{bmatrix}$$

(3)

Looking at the recovery term, the number of people recovering in unit time is obviously dependent on the number of infectives. Again, in the absence of any other information, the simplest possibility is a proportional relationship when the number of people recovering during the time interval $[t,t+\delta t]$ becomes

$$\gamma\, y(t)\, \delta t,$$

where γ is the constant proportionality term called the recovery rate.

Taking the contact rate to be β, as before, equation (3) becomes

$$\delta y = \beta\, xy\, \delta t - \gamma y\, \delta t$$

which, on proceeding to the limit $\delta t \to 0$, gives

$$\frac{dy}{dt} = \beta\, x\, y - \gamma y$$

ie
$$\frac{dy}{dt} = y\, (N\beta - \gamma - \beta y),$$
(4)

since $x(t) + y(t) = N$.

Again equation (4) may readily be solved to give an explicit expression for $y(t)$. This could readily be achieved by comparing equation (4) with (1). However, since the concern is with trends, a graphical procedure as outlined above is used.

Equilibrium states of equation (4) occur when $\dot{y} = 0$, so that

$$y(t) = 0 \text{ and } y(t) = \frac{N\beta - \gamma}{\beta} = N - \frac{\gamma}{\beta}.$$

Three different cases arise dependent on the sign of $N - \frac{\gamma}{\beta}$. These are

Case   (i) $\frac{\gamma}{\beta} < N$,

Case   (ii) $\frac{\gamma}{\beta} > N$,

Case   (iii) $\frac{\gamma}{\beta} = N$,

and the corresponding phase plane plots are given in Figure 10.10.

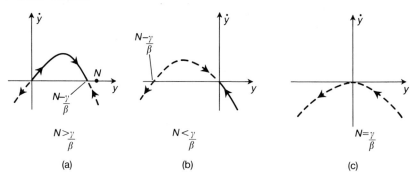

Figure 10.10   Phase plane plots for model incorporating recovery

Inspection of Figure 10.10(a) clearly indicates that $y = N - \frac{\gamma}{\beta}$ corresponds to a stable equilibrium state whilst $y = 0$ corresponds to an unstable equilibrium state. Thus, if the disease is introduced into the society then, if $\frac{\gamma}{\beta} < N$, it will always remain in the society reaching a stable situation when $N - \frac{\gamma}{\beta}$ of its members are infected and the other $\frac{\gamma}{\beta}$ healthy. The disease is, therefore, endemic within the society with the equilibrium state

$$x(t) = \frac{\gamma}{\beta}, \qquad y(t) = N - \frac{\gamma}{\beta},$$

being the endemic state.

By solving equation (4) to obtain the closed form solution for the number of infectives

$$y(t) = \frac{(N - \frac{\gamma}{\beta})y_0}{y_0 + (N - \frac{\gamma}{\beta} - y_0)e^{-\alpha(N\beta-\gamma)t}}, \qquad (5)$$

it is seen that the epidemic converges exponentially to the stable endemic state.

Inspection of Figures 10.10(b), (c) indicates that, when $\frac{\gamma}{\beta} \geqslant N$, the origin y=0 is a stable equilibrium state for permissible values of y(t). Thus, in both cases, $y(t) \to 0$ as $t \to \infty$, so that the disease dies out independent of the number who are infected initially. In a sizeable population, this case corresponds to the situation when the recovery rate γ is much greater than the contact rate β. The original infected group recover quickly infecting only a small number of susceptibles, who themselves quickly recover with even smaller further infection so that the disease quickly leaves the population.

The graphs of Figures 10.1 and 10.2 may indicate an endemic level within the population for both measles and whooping cough, with oscillations imposed upon this base level. In the case of measles there is a clear change in the endemic level during the sixties. The model, however, does not predict the periodic oscillations exhibited by the graphs. At this stage the students should be encouraged to investigate the connection between the endemic level and the parameters used.

10.6 INTRODUCTION OF IMMUNISATION AND ISOLATION

The previous model assumes that the disease is continuously contracted even after recovery. This is unlikely to be the case, as the majority of diseases confer some form of immunity

whilst many confer life long immunity. Also, the model does
not take into account the fact that infectives, once detected,
may be isolated from the community at large.

As the next stage in the development of a suitable model we
assume that all infectives, once detected, are isolated, and
that once recovered life long immunity is conferred. It will
be assumed that all infectives are isolated prior to recovery.

Again, at this stage, give the students an opportunity to
develop a suitable model prior to a group discussion.
Diagrammatically, the situation is now illustrated by the flow
diagram of Figure 10.11. Discussion regarding the pattern of
events following isolation should lead to the conclusion that
they are not immediately relevant to the transmission of the
disease, and consequently they may all be accounted for by the
introduction of a single removal term.

Thus, at general time t, we have the three variables

$x(t)$ = number of healthy susceptibles

$y(t)$ = number of infectives free in the society

$z(t)$ = number of removals

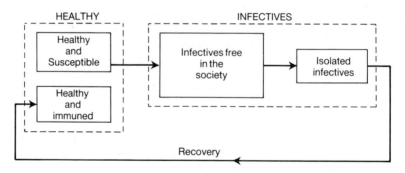

Figure 10.11 Model including immunisation and isolation

The number of infectives removed obviously depends on the
number of infectives present. Assuming a direct proportional
relationship, the number of new removals δz during the time
interval $(t, t+\delta t)$ is taken to be

$$\delta z = \alpha \, y \, \delta t,$$

where α is the proportionality constant called the removal rate.

Assuming, as before, that the infectives free within the
society mix homogeneously with the healthy susceptibles, the
increase δy in the number of free infectives during the time
interval $[t, t + \delta t]$, is given by

$$\delta y = \text{number of new infectives} - \text{number removed}$$

$$= \beta \, xy \, \delta t - \alpha \, y \, \delta t,$$

whilst the increase δx in the number of healthy susceptibles
during the same time interval is given by

$$\delta x = -\beta xy \, \delta t.$$

Proceeding to the limit $\delta t \to 0$, the situation is modelled by
the system of differential equations

$$\frac{dx}{dt} = -\beta \, xy \qquad\qquad \text{susceptibles} \quad \text{(i)}$$

$$\frac{dy}{dt} = \beta \, xy - \alpha y \qquad\qquad \text{infectives} \quad \text{(ii)} \quad \text{(6)}$$

$$\frac{dz}{dt} = \alpha y \qquad\qquad \text{removals} \quad \text{(iii)}$$

with $x(t) + y(t) + z(t) = N$, under the assumption of a closed
community.

The only equilibrium state predicted by (6) is when $y = 0$,
corresponding to no infectives free in the society. The
students should now be given an opportunity to consider the
nature of this equilibrium state. To do this they need to
consider the effects, as predicted by the model, of disturbing
the state of equilibrium by allowing some of the inhabitants
to become infective. In particular, will an epidemic develop?
As in the phase plane approach they should be encouraged to
consider the sign of $\frac{dy}{dt}$, although a plot of $\frac{dy}{dt}$ against y is
not readily drawn in this case.

Suppose initially, at time $t = 0$, the number of susceptibles
and free infectives are respectively x_0 and y_0, with

$$x_0 + y_0 = N$$

since initially there are no removals. From equation 6 (ii)

$$\left[\frac{dy}{dt}\right]_{t=0} = y_0(\beta x_0 - \alpha)$$

so that no epidemic can start to build up unless

$$\beta x_0 - \alpha > 0,$$

that is, $$x_0 > \frac{\alpha}{\beta} = \rho,$$

where ρ is termed the relative removal rate.

In particular, if y_0 is small then $x_0 \simeq N$ in which case ρ may
be regarded as representing a threshold level of number of
susceptibles. Provided there are infectives and susceptibles
free in the society it follows from 6(i) that $\frac{dx}{dt} < 0$, implying
that the number of susceptibles $x(t)$ decreases with time,
so that

$$x(t) < x_0 \text{ for } t > 0.$$

Thus if $x_0 > \rho$ an epidemic will develop; the number of free
infectives $y(t)$ will increase until the number of healthy
susceptibles $x(t)$ is reduced to ρ, thereafter there will be a
decrease in the number of infectives. If $x_0 < \rho$ an epidemic
will not develop; rather the infectives present initially will
be removed before they can inflict the disease on healthy
susceptibles.

The conclusion in this case is that this model does not predict
a stable equilibrium state corresponding to a possible endemic
state. Rather the model predicts that, provided the initial
number of susceptibles x_0 is greater than the relative removal
rate ρ, the epidemic will build up to a peak of activity and

then eventually die out, which corresponds to observations for
many diseases.

In order to discuss the predicted build up and the eventual
size of the epidemic it is desirable to solve equations (6)
to obtain an explicit solution for y(t).

There are various possible ways of proceeding at this stage
and a disucssion with students regarding possible strategies
would be advantageous.

One possibility is to divide (ii) by (i) in (6) giving

$$\frac{dy}{dx} = \frac{\rho}{x} - 1,$$ (7)

which may be readily solved to give a functional relationship
between x(t) and y(t). A state-space diagram of y(t) against
x(t) may then be plotted from which some conclusions could be
drawn. Unfortunately, this approach provides no further
information over that already obtained. Also, having obtained
the functional relationship between x(t) and y(t) it is still
difficult to use it to obtain an explicit solution for y(t).

Since z(t) is actually a measurable quantity in practice there
is merit in seeking a solution for z(t) rather than y(t) as
given "real life" data it would then be possible to validate
the conclusions. Initially, students should be asked to
undertake this exercise for themselves.

Eliminating y, by division, between (i) and (iii) in equation
(6) gives

$$\frac{dx}{dz} = \frac{-x}{\rho},$$

which is readily integrated giving

$$x = x_0 e^{-z/\rho}.$$ (8)

Substituting (8) in 6(iii) gives

$$\frac{dz}{dt} = \alpha(N-z-x_0 e^{-z/\rho}).$$ (9)

In order to obtain the time predicted epidemic curve it is
required to solve the differential equation (9). The
existence of both a linear and exponential term makes it very
difficult, if not impossible, to solve (9) for an analytic
expression for z(t). Consequently, it seems sensible to seek
an approximate solution by approximating the exponential term
by its truncated series expansion.

On the assumption that $\frac{z}{\rho}$ is small, $e^{-z/\rho}$ may be approximated
by

$$e^{-z/\rho} = 1 - \frac{z}{\rho} + \frac{z^2}{2\rho^2}$$

so that (9) becomes

$$\frac{dz}{dt} = \alpha[(N-x_O) + (\frac{x_O}{\rho} - 1)z - \frac{x_O}{2\rho^2}z^2] , \tag{10}$$

Using standard tables of integrals, this may be integrated
to give

$$z = \frac{\rho^2}{x_O}[(\frac{x_O}{\rho} - 1) + \mu\tanh(\frac{1}{2}\mu\alpha t - \theta)], \tag{11}$$

where the constants μ and θ are given by

$$\mu = [(\frac{x_O}{\rho} - 1)^2 + \frac{2x_O y_O}{\rho^2}]^{\frac{1}{2}}, \quad \theta = \tanh^{-1}\frac{1}{\mu}(\frac{x_O}{\rho} - 1)$$

Differentiating equation (11) then gives the rate of removals
with time as

$$\frac{dz}{dt} = \frac{\mu^2\rho^2}{2x_O}\alpha \operatorname{sech}^2(\frac{\mu\alpha t}{2} - \theta) \tag{12}$$

A plot of this is shown in Figure 10.12 and, assuming that
the period an individual is sick is constant, this may be
taken to be the general form of the epidemic curve confirming
that the epidemic builds up to a peak and then dies away.

Differentiating (9) gives

$$\frac{d}{dt}\left(\frac{dz}{dt}\right) = \alpha(-\dot{z} + \frac{x_o z}{\rho} e^{-z/\rho}) = \alpha^2 y(\frac{x}{\rho} - 1)$$

so that the peak of the epidemic curve occurs when $x = \rho$.

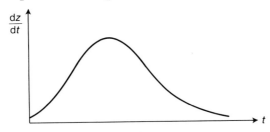

Figure 10.12   Plot of $\dot{z}$ versus t

From equation (11) a plot of z versus t may be drawn as shown
in Figure 10.13.   To determine the size of the epidemic the
eventual number of removals z* has to be determined.   Again,
students should be encouraged to determine this for themselves.

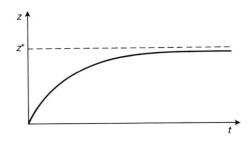

Figure 10.13   Number of Removals

To determine z* allow $t \rightarrow \infty$ in (ii) giving

$$z^* = \frac{\rho^2}{x_o}\left[(\frac{x_o}{\rho} - 1) + \mu\right].$$

Alternatively z^* may be obtained by taking it to be the solution of (10) when $\frac{dz}{dt} = 0$.

If μ is approximated by $\mu = (\frac{x_0}{\rho} - 1)$, the first term in its series expansion, then z^* may be estimated by

$$z^* \simeq 2\rho \ (1 - \frac{\rho}{x_0}) \tag{13}$$

It was shown earlier that no epidemic will develop unless $x_0 > \rho$ so taking $x_0 = \rho + \xi$ in (13) gives

$$z^* \simeq 2\rho \left[1-(1 + \frac{\xi}{\rho})^{-1} \right] \simeq 2\rho \ (1-1+ \frac{\xi}{\rho}) \simeq 2\xi.$$

This predicts that sooner or later the number of persons infected, and consequently removed, will be 2ξ, where ξ is the amount by which the relative removal rate ρ falls short of its threshold value x_0.

In conclusion this model predicts that in order for an epidemic to build up the initial number of susceptibles must be greater than the relative removal rate, $x_0 \simeq N > \rho$. When this occurs, the number of susceptibles first falls to the threshold value ρ, when the rate of cases identified is at its peak, and then continues to drop until it reaches the ultimate value $2\rho-N$ corresponding to $2(N-\rho)$ individuals having ultimately contacted the disease.

In reaching these conclusions certain approximations were made regarding the relative sizes of variables and parameters. Students should be asked, as an extended exercise, to investigate the accuracy of these approximations and show that they are tolerable in the case of a mild epidemic (that is, one in which the removal rate is very near its threshold value).

10.7   ALLOWING FOR REPLENISHMENT

Over a short period of time it may be realistic, as in the previous model, to assume that the number of healthy susceptibles is not added to. Over a longer period of time, particularly in large communities, this assumption is not realistic and the model should be further developed so as

to incorporate the possibility of replenishment in the
number of healthy susceptibles. This may be in the form of
new births, immigration, or by the loss of immunity of some of
those who have previously had the disease and recovered.

An easy way of accommodating this is simply to extend the
previous model on the basis that the number of healthy
susceptibles x(t) is being added to at a constant rate. In
order to balance the population in the simplest way, it is
assumed that deaths occur only amongst the removals z(t).
Such a model could, for example, be regarded as representing
a childhood disease, such as measles, in the absence of
vaccination; the replenishment is in the form of fresh births,
and the deaths occur naturally amongst the immune older
people, most of whom have had the disease.

This is another stage in the development where students
should be given an opportunity to proceed by themselves. On
the basis of a constant replenishment rate μ per unit time
we know that the increase δx in the number of healthy
susceptibles, during the time interval (t, t+δt) is given by

$$\delta x = -\beta xy \; \delta t + \mu \; \delta t$$

which, on proceeding to the limit δt → 0 gives

$$\frac{dx}{dt} = -\beta xy + \mu.$$

Since we are assuming a constant population, size N, over the
period of the epidemic we balance it by appropriate death rate
amongst the removals, the model of equation (6) may be updated
to the following form

$$\frac{dx}{dt} = -\beta xy + \mu \qquad \text{susceptibles} \quad \text{(i)}$$

$$\frac{dy}{dt} = \beta xy - \alpha y \qquad \text{infectives} \quad \text{(ii)} \qquad \text{(14)}$$

$$\frac{dz}{dt} = \alpha y - \mu \qquad \text{removals} \quad \text{(iii)}$$

It is readily seen that

$$x(t) = \frac{\alpha}{\beta} , \ y(t) = \frac{\mu}{\alpha}$$

is an equilibrium state corresponding to (14). To investigate
the nature of this equilibrium state the variations in the
variables $x(t)$ and $y(t)$, corresponding to the 'active'
inhabitants of the society must be investigated. This is done
by considering equations (i) and (ii) of (14).

Again there are various ways of proceeding and a discussion
with students on various possibilities would be worthwhile.
It is clear that there is no simple way of proceeding to
obtain analytic solutions for $x(t)$ and $y(t)$. Also, in this
case $z(t)$ is not accessible, since it is not possible to
eliminate y between (i) and (iii). Another possibility is
to make use of the state-space, with $x(t)$ and $y(t)$ as
co-ordinate axes; as t increases, the point $(x(t), y(t))$ will
trace out the state trajectory, from which the nature of the
equilibrium state can be interpreted. Dividing (ii) by (i)
in (14) gives

$$\frac{dy}{dx} = \frac{\beta xy - \alpha y}{\mu - \beta xy}$$

Unfortunately, this differential equation is not readily
integrable to give a functional relationship between y and x
which represents the equation of the trajectory in state
space. In such cases a technique often used is perturbation
analysis, which essentially involves investigating the nature
of the trajectory in a small region surrounding the equilibrium
state. Near the equilibrium state put

$$x(t) = \frac{\alpha}{\beta} + \xi(t) ,$$

$$y(t) = \frac{\mu}{\alpha} + \eta(t) ,$$

(15)

where $\xi(t)$ and $\eta(t)$ are small variations in $x(t)$ and $y(t)$
respectively.

Substituting (15) in (i) and (ii) of (14) and retaining only linear terms in $\xi(t)$ and $\eta(t)$ gives

$$\dot{\xi}(t) = \frac{-\beta\mu}{\alpha} \xi - \alpha\eta$$

$$\dot{\eta}(t) = \frac{\beta\mu}{\alpha} \xi$$

which, on eliminating $\xi(t)$ gives

$$\alpha \ddot{\eta}(t) + \beta\mu \dot{\eta}(t) + (\beta\mu\alpha) \eta = 0 \qquad (16)$$

This is a second order differential equation with constant coefficients which approximately describes the behaviour of the solution of (14) in a small region surrounding the equilibrium state. The exact nature of the solution of (16) depends on the values of the parameters α, β, and μ (see James (1981)) but, since all are positive real quantities, it follows that both $\eta(t) \to 0$ and $\xi(t) \to 0$ as $t \to \infty$. This indicates that the equilibrium state is a stable one, corresponding to an endemic state of the disease.

In the particular case when $\beta\mu < 4\alpha^2$, the solution of (16) will be a damped harmonic oscillation with period $4\pi\alpha/\sqrt{(4\alpha^2-\beta\mu)\beta\mu}$. Thus, an important consequence of the inclusion of replenishment into the model is to account for periodic epidemic waves. However, the "damping down" or attenuation of these waves to a stable endemic state is at variance with our observations from Figures 10.1 and 10.2. In noting the discrepancy, it is pertinent to observe that the model has not included any consideration of the geographical distribution of the population. In order to include such effects, it would be necessary to reformulate the model as a so-called spatial model, where attention is focussed on the location of infected individuals as well as the total number. Also the models above do not take into account any time delays between various stages, notably incubation of the disease.

10.8 DISCRETE-TIME MODELS

So far only continuous time models have been considered. At least in theory, these are more readily analysed, although not

without difficulties, particularly as more factors are built
into the model. It may, therefore, seem a little drastic to
make major changes in formulation at this stage. There is,
however, value in doing this from two distinct standpoints,

(i)   In practice, data on an epidemic (number of infections
       and so on) would not be presented as a continuous
       variable. Rather, such data would be available on a
       daily or perhaps a weekly basis.

(ii)   From the purely mathematical viewpoint the differential
       equations have become less tractable as the model has
       become more complicated. If the model is to be
       complicated further by, for example, introducing time
       delays to allow for an incubation period, then a
       computer will be needed to seek a numerical solution.

In this section, therefore, a discrete-time formulation of the
models is considered, in which differential equations are
replaced by difference equations. It will soon become apparent
that such a formulation is most appropriate for use in
conjunction with a digital computer and that the introduction
of complications, such as time delays, cause little further
problems.

Initially, it is suggested that the lecturer illustrates the
approach by reconsidering the replenishing model discussed in
the previous section. The variables x,y and z retain their
associations with the numbers of healthy susceptibles,
infectives and removals respectively; however, it is now
appropriate to write $x(n)$, $y(n)$, $z(n)$, where n is an integer
measuring the number of days (or weeks) from some starting
day when records began. Specifically, $x(n)$ is defined to be
the number of healthy susceptibles at the start of day n, and
with this definition relationships relating conditions at the
start of day (n+1) with the events of day n can be written
down. Considering first the healthy susceptible element of
the population it is clear that

$$
\begin{bmatrix} \text{Number of healthy susceptibles} \\ \text{at the start of day (n+1)} \end{bmatrix} = \begin{bmatrix} \text{Number of healthy} \\ \text{susceptibles at the start} \\ \text{of day n} \end{bmatrix}
$$

$$
- \begin{bmatrix} \text{Number becoming sick} \\ \text{during day n} \end{bmatrix}
$$

$$
+ \begin{bmatrix} \text{Replenishment on day n} \end{bmatrix}
$$

Adopting the same model as before for the spread of the
disease, namely that the number of new cases during day n is
proportional to both the current numbers of healthy susceptibles
and the number of infectives, then

$$x(n+1) = x(n) - \beta\, x(n)y(n) + \mu$$

This is the discrete time analogue of the first differential
equation in (14); β and μ retain their meanings as contact
(or sickness) and replenishment rates, but are now rates per
day. Similarly, the discrete analogues of the other two
equations in (14) are

$$y(n+1) = y(n) + \beta x(n)\ y(n) - \alpha y(n)$$

and
$$z(n+1) = z(n) + \alpha y(n) - \mu,$$

where α is the daily removal rate and μ the daily death rate
amongst the immuned population which again, for simplicity,
is assumed to balance the replenishment rate.

The major advantage of this formulation is now apparent. The
model is described by the set of three simultaneous difference
equations

$$x(n+1) = x(n) - \beta x(n)y(n) + \mu \qquad \text{susceptibles}$$

$$y(n+1) = y(n) + \beta x(n)y(n) - \alpha y(n) \qquad \text{infectives} \qquad (17)$$

$$z(n+1) = z(n) + \alpha y(n) - \mu \qquad \text{removals}$$

and it is easy to see that a very simple computer program
can be written to evaluate the values of $x(n)$, $y(n)$ and $z(n)$
from some starting values. Also, additional complications are
readily introduced.

The results of a typical run for a population of 1000, with
20 individuals initially immune from the disease, and one
inhabitant initially infected (at day zero), are shown
graphically in Figure 10.14. The parameter values used were
$\beta = 0.0005$, $\alpha = 0.05$ and $\mu = 0$.

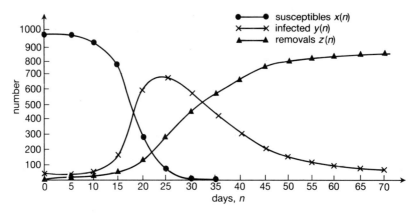

Figure 10.14   Simulated results of discrete model

Most diseases have an incubation period, during which time a
person appears healthy but is in fact sick, but undetected as
yet.   If such an individual can transmit the disease during
this period, it will be necessary to split the class of
infectives into two groups, as in Figure 10.4.   Again no
major problem is involved in producing a computer solution.
On the other hand, if it may be assumed that an individual
does not communicate the disease during the incubation period,
a so-called latent period, then the effects of an incubation
period on the spread of disease can be modelled by altering
the term governing disease transmission.   As an example,
suppose that the incubation period for a certain disease is
one day.   This means that an individual exhibiting symptoms
during day (n) actually caught the infection on day (n-1), and
since this was brought about by conditions as they were on
day (n-1) then the sickness transmission term becomes
$x(n-1) \, y(n-1)$.   Now, however, the modeller must take care to
ensure that his program avoids problems with negative array
subscripts and with negative populations (see Haberman (1977)).

10.9   FURTHER PROBLEMS

An obvious extension at each stage in the development is to
ask the students to develop and investigate, possibly using a
microcomputer, a corresponding discrete time model.

In order to give the lecturer maximum flexibility in the use
of the case study   further problems are categorised in
accordance with the various stages in its development.

10.9.1 Extensions to the Simple Model of Section 10.4

1.   The epidemic curve of Figure 10.6 gives the rate at which
     new infectives accrue. Show that

$$y = \beta N^2 (n-y_0) \ e^{-\beta Nt}/[y_0 + (N-y_0)e^{-\beta Nt}]^2$$

Normalising, by considering $W = y/N$, the curve may be
interpreted as the frequency function of the time of
occurrence of a new infective. With this interpretation
show that the mean value of the time variable t is

$$\bar{t} = \frac{1}{\beta N} \ ln \ \frac{N}{y_0} \ .$$

Conclude what the model predicts about the rate at which
the epidemic spreads through a highly populated society.
Can you suggest an alternative expression for β taking
account of the size of the population?

2.   The model developed in the text assumes a constant
     infection rate β. An obvious extension is to consider
     the effects of making β time varying. As an example, one
     could argue that β varies in direct proportion to the
     number of healthy susceptibles present. Develop and
     discuss the model corresponding to this possibility, and
     show that maximum activity occurs when a third of the
     population is infected.

3.   Consider the introduction of carriers into the simple
     model. For simplicity assume that the infection is only
     spread by carriers free in the society. When a healthy
     susceptible becomes infected it is assumed that he exhibits
     symptoms sufficiently quickly to be removed from society
     prior to infecting others. Carriers once detected are
     removed from the society. If initially, at time t = 0,
     the number of susceptibles and carriers free in the
     society are x_0 and c_0 respectively show that if it is
     assumed that carriers are removed at a constant rate η
     then the eventual total size of the observed epidemic will
     be

$$x_0[1 - \exp(-\beta c_0/\eta)],$$

when, as before, β is the infection rate.

4. Update the model of Q3 to allow for replenishment in the number of healthy susceptibles and carriers. These can be generated from within the society by, for example, new births or arise due to immigration. For simplicity assume that new susceptibles and carriers appear at constant rates μ and λ respectively. Determine the equilibrium state and discuss its nature.

10.9.2 Extensions to the Recovery Model of Section 10.5

5. Update the model allowing the constant rate β to vary as in Q2 above. Show that the equilibrium states of interest occur when $y(t) = 0$ and $y(t) = N - \sqrt{\frac{\gamma}{\beta}}$. Discuss their nature and develop conclusions regarding the spread of the epidemic as predicted by the model.

6. Consider the introduction of carriers. In particular, investigate the following two different possibilities.

   (i) There are a fixed number of carriers free in the society and they are undetectable. Infection is transmitted by both the carriers and free infectives. Develop an appropriate model; discuss the equilibrium point and the extent of the epidemic.

   (ii) Assume the situation of Q3 above where only carriers are responsible for spreading the disease. They are, however, detectable and are removed on detection. Develop and discuss a suitable model.

7. The model assumes that an infective once recovered immediately becomes susceptible again. However, it is likely that the majority of diseases confer some element of immunity. To account for this, assume that an individual recovering at time t becomes susceptible again at time $t + \lambda$, where λ is a fixed constant. How would the introduction of such a delay affect your model and conclusions?

10.9.3 Extensions to the Isolation Model of Section 10.6

8. Update the model allowing the contact rate β to vary as in Q2 above. Show that the threshold level of susceptibles now becomes $\rho^{\frac{1}{2}}$. Develop an approximate solution for z as in section 10.6. Show that the peak of the epidemic curve occurs when $z = \rho^{\frac{1}{2}} - \frac{\rho}{x_0}$ and that if x_0 is taken to be

$\rho^{\frac{1}{2}} + \xi$ then the total epidemic size will be given approximately by 2ξ.

9. Suppose the healthy susceptible persons are immunised artificially by vaccination and vaccination is performed at a constant rate σ. Extend the model to incorporate this feature and discuss.

10. Suppose that there is a constant latent period of length τ from the time an individual becomes infected to the time he becomes infective. In this case the infectives fall into two categories; (1) those who are infected but not yet infectious; (2) those who are both infected and infectious. Introduce this condition into the model and discuss its consequences. A detailed investigation is more readily carried out using a discrete time model.

Another possible extension along the same lines is to allow for a time lapse between the time an individual becomes infective and when he recovers; that is, assume that an individual that becomes infective at time t recovers at time $t + \sigma_1$ for some constant σ_1.

10.9.4 Extensions to the replenishment of section 10.7

11. Again update the model to allow the contact rate β to vary as in Q2 above. Show that the equilibrium state becomes $(\sqrt{\frac{\alpha}{\beta}}, \frac{\mu}{\alpha})$. Obtain the differential equations for small variations about this equilibrium state and discuss the solution. Show that damped harmonic waves will occur if $\mu < 2\sqrt{\alpha^2/\beta}$. What is their period?

12. The model developed in section 10.7 explained the existence of epidemic waves in terms of oscillations about an endemic state. These waves are damped and appear therefore, to be at variance with observed facts, as the observed level of many of the commoner diseases tend to be oscillatory. For example, we noted earlier that whooping cough in the U.K. has approximately a four year cycle. Many attempts have been made to develop models to exhibit this characteristic.

Consider a disease which is lethal to all those contacting it, so that all removals are, in fact, deaths. Suppose also the disease is sufficiently virulent to suppress any live births amongst the infectives, so that new births only arise from the healthy susceptible group.

Assuming that the number of births is proportional to the number of healthy susceptibles present in the society, develop a model along the lines of section 10.7. By carrying out a perturbation analysis about the appropriate equilibrium state show that the model predicts undamped oscillations.

13. Many diseases, such as measles, show a seasonal variation. The precise reason for this is unknown, but in the case of measles it could, for example, correspond to school and holiday periods. In an attempt to account for this, try replacing the contact rate β by $\beta^1 = \beta + \beta_1 \cos wt$, where $2\pi/w = 52$ weeks.

14. Again consider the introduction of a latent time τ, as in Q10, to allow for an incubation period. If this is done to the model of this section show that an effect is to halve the damping coefficient. A discrete version of this question is given in Q16.

10.9.5 Extensions to the discrete model of section 10.8

Further discrete time models have already been suggested. Extension problems specific to the model of section 10.8 are as follows:

15. Consider the system of difference equations (14). Show that in the absence of an incubation period and with zero replenishment, then if the equilibrium values of $X(n)$, $Y(n)$ and $Z(n)$ are $\overline{X}, \overline{Y}, \overline{Z}$ then

$$\overline{X} = \overline{Y} = 0, \quad \overline{Z} = N$$

If there is a constant value for the replenishment term U, show that

$$\overline{X} = U/\alpha, \quad \overline{Y} = \alpha/\beta$$

Confirm these results for your computer calculations. Would an incubation period affect these values?

16. Suppose that, for a certain disease, an infected individual is contagious for a short period before himself exhibiting symptoms. Set up a discrete time model for this epidemic when:

(1) the disease can be communicated only during the latent period,

(2) the disease can be communicated during the latent period and the subsequent period of illness.

17. (a) Data are given below for a measles outbreak in 1980 for a large city with a population of about 300,000. The data take the form of the number of new cases reported in each week i. Plot these figures on a graph against i, the week number and comment on the resulting picture. Argue that the exact date for the report of a case is somewhat susceptible to unpredictable variation and filter the data as follows.

Let the number of new cases reported in week i be x(i), i = 0,1,.... and form the filtered data sequence

$$y(i) = \frac{1}{3} \sum_{j=0}^{2} x_{i-j} \qquad i = 2,3........$$

Now plot y(i), i = 2,3,.... against the week number i and comment on the resulting curve.

Write a computer program to predict the number of new cases per week and after making appropriate assumptions on the size of population at risk, endeavour to find parameter values to fit this outbreak.

(b) Obtain data on population in your own health authority area and using the parameter values found in (a) above, predict the effects of a measles outbreak.

(c) Compare your predictions with the most recent outbreak in your area, and publish your results!

i	x(i)	i	x(i)	i	x(i)	i	x(i)
0	6	10	46	20	67	30	26
1	7	11	45	21	28	31	36
2	13	12	66	22	41	32	35
3	13	13	60	23	42	33	21
4	17	14	82	24	34	34	12
5	32	15	130	25	55	35	9
6	21	16	98	26	27	36	8
7	26	17	82	27	40	37	7
8	29	18	54	28	33	38	1
9	27	19	93	29	15	39	1

REFERENCES

Bailey, N.T.J., 1975   The Mathematical Theory of Infectious
   Diseases and its Applications. Charles Griffin, London.

Haberman, R., 1977   Mathematical Models, Prentice Hall, Inc.,
   Englewood Cliffe, p. 178-185.

James, D.J.G., 1981   Appendix to Hydroelectric Power
   Generation System, Case Studies in Mathematical Modelling,
   Eds. James, D.J.G. and McDonald, J.J., Stanley Thornes
   (Publishers) Limited, Cheltenham, England.

Jordan, D.W. and Smith P., 1977   Nonlinear Differential
   Equations, Clarendon Press, Oxford.

11

Pollution of the Great Lakes

DAVID LE MASURIER *Brighton Polytechnic*

11.1 STATEMENT OF THE PROBLEM

It is estimated that the Great Lakes of America provide the
main water supply for at least 30 million inhabitants. They
are also commercially fished, provide economic transportation
and a source of recreational facilities. Unfortunately, the
same inhabitants dump much of their waste and sewage into these
same lakes. This waste includes a massive overdose of
phosphates which have been traced to expended detergents,
insecticides and other chemicals, such as DDT and mercury.
Extensive pollution of this form is liable to kill off the
fish and other forms of animal and plant life. Excess of
phosphates leads to eutrophication, which is likely, amongst
other things, to cause an obnoxious smell.

Due to their immense size, it is extremely difficult to locate
all the causes of pollution. It has been frequently
demonstrated that its control cannot be practised without
consideration of the economics and politics allied to the
situation. The detergent industry, for example, has spent
vast sums changing over to biodegradable detergents, with
little apparent affect on the degree of pollution. Thus it
seems that the only feasible solution is to rely on natural
processes. Rivers will usually clean themselves up quickly
once pollution is stopped, but large lakes are less readily
decontaminated because of the amount of polluted water already
present. The average retention time of water in Lake Michigan
(see Figure 11.1 and the appendix) is over 30 years, and for
Lake Superior is as high as 189 years. So how long will it
take to make a significant improvement to the cleanliness of
the Great Lakes, even if all pollution ceased?

Figure 11.1   The Great Lakes

The figures indicate the number of years, τ, required to
drain the lakes if outflow is unchanged and inflow stops.

Should the lakes be used as a dump? It would be interesting
to make some attempt to investigate the costs involved in
pollution reduction, and what might be gained as a result.
How could we possibly quantify the benefits to the local
inhabitants? One would need to balance the cost of pollution
reduction (either by natural processes or by artificial means
e.g. chemicals) against the cost of storing or dumping waste
elsewhere. Such a complicated model is beyond our scope, but
some of the political and social aspects could be taken up at
greater length (see Section 11.10).

11.2   INITIAL STUDENT REACTION

Students will need plenty of time to assimilate the problem.
First, they need to appreciate that there must be a process
whereby pollutants are transported into, and out of, the lakes,
and that should lead to the assumption that the pollution in
the lake is a function of time. Somehow the balancing
principle

$$\text{Change} \quad = \quad \text{Input} \quad - \quad \text{Output}$$

must be introduced whereby important variables are related.
Perhaps students should be reminded that it may be helpful to
include dimensions, and sensible units of measurement, wherever
new variables are introduced.

11.3 APPROACH TO THE PROBLEM

Before we start to construct a model, we must attempt to
identify the features which are likely to be of major
importance, and make some assumptions about them. If we ignore
variations due to different types of pollutant, it is fair
to assume that contaminants are either dumped directly in the
lake, or they flow in mainly via rivers (inputs). How are
pollution levels measured? It is common for such quantities
to be recorded in parts/unit volume, so it will be convenient
to measure input pollution density, $P_I(t)$, in terms of

mass/volume. Hence, to determine the amount of pollution
deposited in the lake we need also to know the input volume
of water. We must examine the form of our data (in essence,
volume/time - see the appendix) so we will assume an input
flow rate $r_I(t)$, yielding a pollutant mass $r_I(t)P_I(t)$ per unit

time. This process can be repeated for any pollution output
$r_O(t)P_O(t)$ from the lake, where $r_O(t)$, $P_O(t)$ are the outflow
rate and output pollution density respectively.

We can now write down one side of our balance equation - viz:

$$\text{Input} \quad - \quad \text{Output} \quad = \quad r_I(t)P_I(t) - r_O(t)P_O(t) \qquad (1)$$

The major assumption underlying this result is a simple
input-output model as depicted in Figure 11.2.

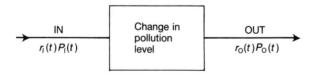

Figure 11.2   Input - output model

11.4 STUDENT REACTION

Most students should not have found the first stage too difficult to follow, although it will probably be necessary to sort out such apparent trivia as dimensions and units e.g. which unit should be used to measure time? Deriving the pollution change in the lake in appropriate mathematical terms, and then converting the balance equation to a first order differential equation - if this is the approach to be adopted - is likely to prove more demanding. As a basis we introduce the concept of a (small) discrete time interval over which the change is assumed to take place, and then follow the standard limiting procedure, transforming from a discrete to a continuous variable. Even following a course on differential equations, this is not likely to be a simple task for the student. This is the stage at which the mathematical model is being constructed, and its formulation can be a slow and painful process, and it will not be obtained in such a logical and coherent order.

11.5 MODEL FORMULATION

The change in the pollution mass in the lake in the time interval $[t, t + \delta t]$ may be determined by:

Pollution mass at time $(t + \delta t)$ - Pollution mass at time t.

If $V(t)$ and $P(t)$ are the volume and pollution density of the lake at time t, then the pollution mass is $P(t) V(t)$, and so the change in pollution in the time interval is

$$\frac{P(t + \delta t)V(t + \delta t) - P(t)V(t)}{\delta t}$$

so that our balance equation (1) becomes

$$\frac{P(t + \delta t)V(t + \delta t) - P(t)V(t)}{\delta t} = r_I(t)P_I(t) - r_O(t)P_O(t) \qquad (2)$$

11.6 ASSUMPTIONS

11.6.1 Perfect mixing

The lake pollution density P(t) does not depend on position
in the lake. This avoids the introduction of partial
differential equations, and also implies that the pollution
density at the lake output is the same as that throughout the
lake, i.e.

$$P_O(t) = P(t)$$

11.6.2 Single inflow, single outflow

A large number of inputs and outputs - rivers - would tend
to improve the validity of our perfect mixing assumption.
However, unless we are interested in pollution from a
particular source, in the first instance it seems reasonable
only to concern ourselves with the net pollution volume and
mass flows, in and out.

11.6.3 Continuity of variables

In practice, measurements of the variables (V, P, r) could
only be taken at discrete intervals of time. However, these
variables are likely to be reasonably smooth "functions" of
time, t, so that the limiting process of letting $\delta t \to O$ in
Equation (2) is valid. (See, also, Section 11.11.3).

Equation (2) thus becomes

$$\frac{d}{dt}(PV) = r_I P_I - r_O P \qquad (3)$$

dropping the argument t, for clarity.

However,

$$\frac{d}{dt}(PV) = P\frac{dV}{dt} + V\frac{dP}{dt}, \qquad (4)$$

and since

$$\frac{dV}{dt} = \lim_{\delta t \to 0} \frac{V(t + \delta t) - V(t)}{\delta t} = r_I(t) - r_O(t) \qquad (5)$$

we may combine equations (4) and (5) so that equation (3) becomes

$$P(r_I - r_O) + V\frac{dP}{dt} = r_I P_I - r_O P.$$

On rearranging this yields

$$V\frac{dP}{dt} = r_I(P_I - P) \qquad (6)$$

It is worth noting that this is independent of the outflow rate r_O, other than through the volume equation (5).

11.6.4 Volume of the lake is constant

One of the major problems for students is to constrain the model to the data available, or which may be collected, and then to make the best use of them. Assuming the volume of the lake is constant clearly implies that $r_I = r_O$, so that inflow rate due to precipitation, etc. is balanced by outflow due, amongst other things, to evaporation and seepage. In effect this would mean ignoring seasonal variations, so that it seems justifiable to make the further assumption that r_I, and therefore r_O, is also constant.

Hence, $\dfrac{V}{r_I} = \dfrac{V}{r_O} = \tau$, say, where τ is a constant, which may be regarded as the time required to drain the lake assuming

(i) input of water is stopped,

(ii) output rate maintained.

Values of τ are available for four of the Great Lakes. (See table in the appendix.)

Equation (6) now becomes

$$\tau \frac{dP}{dt} = P_I - P \ ,$$

which on rearranging gives

$$\frac{dP}{dt} + \frac{1}{\tau} P = \frac{1}{\tau} P_I \tag{7}$$

11.7 CASE 1

The analysis of equation (7) needs information about the input function P_I. The simplest would seem to be $P_I = K$, a constant, so that equation (7) becomes

$$\frac{dP}{dt} = \frac{1}{\tau} (K - P)$$

which has a general solution

$$P(t) = Ce^{-t/\tau} + K \tag{8}$$

where C is an arbitrary constant.

For a particular solution, we need additional information in order to determine C. We suppose a starting pollution level, $P(0) = P_s$ so that $C = P_s - K$ and

$$P(t) = (P_s - K)e^{-t/\tau} + K \tag{9}$$

Since $P(t) \to K$ in infinite time it is probably more instructive to ask how long it would take for $P(t)$ to get down to some desired level P_1 which lies between P and K, so that

$$P_s > P_1 > K$$

Rearranging equation (9) gives

$$\frac{P}{P_s} = \frac{K}{P_s} + \left[1 - \frac{K}{P_s}\right] e^{-t/\tau} \tag{10}$$

For given values of $\frac{K}{P_s}$ (say 0, 0.25, 0.5, 0.75) graphs of

$\frac{P}{P_s}$ against t are shown in Figure 11.3

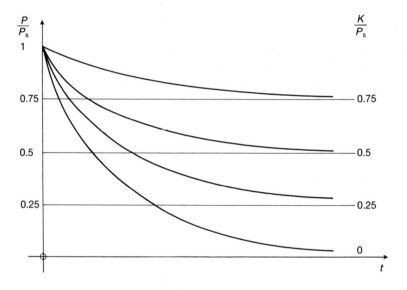

Figure 11.3

Note that $\frac{P}{P_s} \rightarrow \frac{K}{P_s}$ thereby confirming the obvious requirement
that K must be less than P_s for any "clean up" to be achieved.

The difficulty which students experience in knowing what to
do with their "solutions", and how to display their results,
should not be overlooked. It is a common assumption that an
endless jumble of numbers is sufficient to demonstrate that
the task has been completed. Tables of selected results, and
comprehensible graphs with sensible scales do not always come
readily to mind. What is a parameter, and what is its
significance to the problem in hand?

11.8 CASE 2

It is unlikely that a sudden discontinuous reduction in
pollution rate inflow to K could be made, owing to economic
and political constraints. In practice it is much more likely
to be a gradual process, with a "planned" decrease over several
years. This could be modelled by taking $P_I(t) = K_0 e^{-\alpha t}$, where
the parameter $\alpha (> 0)$ governs the rate at which the inflow is
reduced. What is a realistic level of reduction to aim for,
and over how many years? For $\alpha = 0.14$, the reduction is
approximately 50% over each period of 5 years.

Equation (7) becomes

$$\frac{dP}{dt} + \frac{1}{\tau} P = \frac{1}{\tau} K_0 e^{-\alpha t} \tag{11}$$

The solution of (11) with initial condition $P(0) = K_0$ is

$$\frac{P(t)}{K_0} = e^{-t/\tau} - \frac{e^{-t/\tau}}{(1 - \alpha\tau)} \left[1 - e^{(1/\tau - \alpha)t} \right] \tag{12}$$

As in Case 1, graphs of $\dfrac{P}{K_0}$ against t can be drawn for various
α, and the respective effects compared.

11.9 VALIDATION

It is not difficult to check that the results obtained are
sensible for the model used. Is the model a good one? How
much faith can we put in the times obtained? Of the
assumptions made, that of perfect mixing may be far off. This
error is not likely to allow clean-up times less than τ, and
they will probably be significantly greater.

Other assumptions have been made concerning the nature of
the pollution, as described in the statement of the problem.
For persistent pollutants, such as DDT, the estimated clean-up
times may well be too low.

11.10   PRESENTATION OF RESULTS

One of the features of this study is the way in which the
problem can be varied, depending upon the "client". What is
the purpose of the analysis, and who is going to read and
possibly act on the report? Is it an ecologist, a politician
or a manufacturer accused of causing a significant proportion
of the pollution? Discussion upon this point can be most
rewarding, particularly with reference to the manner in which
results are presented, e.g. choice of different scales for
graphs of the same relationships. With a group of students it
is fruitful to give subgroups the different roles to perform.

11.11   EXTENSIONS AND DEVELOPMENTS

11.11.1   Initial build-up

The analysis of equation (7) needs two pieces of information,
(i) the initial level of pollution, (ii) the input function
$P_I(t)$. One might suggest discussing the initial build up of
pollution from a "clean" lake at time zero, $P(0) = 0$ under an
uncontrolled "dumping" policy, say taking $P_I(t) = K_1$ (constant)
for simplicity.   Then

$$P(t) = C_1 e^{-t/\tau} + K_1,$$

where C, is an arbitrary constant, and for $P(0) = 0$, $C_1 = -K_1$
so that $P(t) = K_1(1 - e^{-t/\tau})$ as shown in Figure 11.4.

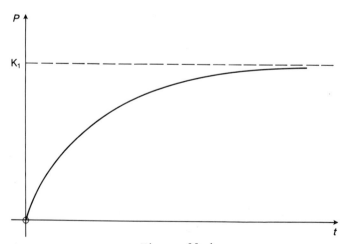

Figure 11.4

The "half-life" of the growth curve is that time, T_H, for which $P(T_H) = \dfrac{K_1}{2}$. Thus

$$\frac{K_1}{2} = K_1(1 - e^{-T_H/\tau})$$

giving $e^{-T_H/\tau} = \dfrac{1}{2}$ or $T_H = \tau \log_e 2 \approx 0.7\tau$

The pollution in the lake will tend exponentially towards the pollution level of the input with a half-life of 0.7τ. This has interesting repercussions. For example, if a lake has $\tau = 100$ years and we have been polluting it at the same level as at present (the worst assumption) for 50 years then we are not yet half way to maximum pollution, K_1. (Half-life is 70 years.) Thus if we now cut pollution input by 50%, the lake pollution will still continue to increase, but at a slower pace, and to a lower level, $\dfrac{K_1}{2}$.

Owing to the time scale of industrial development, and its consequences on pollution of lakes, because that pollution is likely to have been increasing since the start, and because τ will be of the order of the above mentioned timescale, it is likely, more than likely, that $P(t)$ now is far short of K_1.

Further work could therefore include estimates of K_1 and $P(t)$, and answer the question - what percentage cut in K_1 is now required merely to see that P stops increasing?

In the "clean-up" phase we supposed a starting pollution level P_s, and a pollution input K which must be less than P_s (Section 11.6). If one examines build-up and clean-up of the lake as a two-phase process, with a time T, then

$$P_s = K_1(1 - e^{-T/\tau})$$

and the clock is restarted at T.

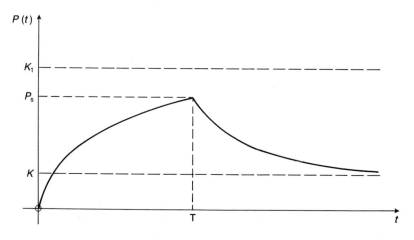

Figure 11.5

11.11.2 Evaporation and seepage

The constraint that $r_I = r_O$ could be relaxed. For example some interplay between r_O and V could be examined, say $r_O(t) = kV(t)$. However this is probably of less significance than, say, the assumption of perfect mixing. Alternatively, some account could be taken of evaporation or seepage loss. This would create an additional output term in the first part of the balance equation (1)

$$A \; P(t) \; V(t)$$

It must be admitted that the estimation of the value of A (which would have dimensions of l/time) would be no easy matter.

11.11.3 Discrete variables

The question of introducing continuous variables has already been raised. Clearly, measurements of pollution levels, flow rates, etc. can only be made at discrete intervals. It is instructive to replace equation (7) by a first order difference equation of the form

$$P_{t+1} = (1 - \frac{1}{\tau}) \; P_t + \frac{1}{\tau} \; P_I$$

It may be that information relating to the problem is available only in this form, which implies a numerical solution which itself calls for a discrete model.

11.11.4 Pollutants

It is tempting to consider a model for the more persistent pollutants, such as DDT or mercury. As DDT is very soluble in fat, it is normally retained within the body of prey and predators, and tends to be transferred up the food chain. It would be necessary to investigate the way in which predator and prey inter-relate - a familiar and more complex problem than the one considered so far.

FURTHER READING

Bender, E.A., 1978 An introduction to mathematical modelling. Wiley.

Rainey, R.H., 1967 Natural Displacement of Pollution from the Great Lakes. (*Science,* Vol. 155, pp. 1242 - 1243).

Sperry, K., 1967   The Battle of Lake Erie: Eutrophication and Political Fragmentation. (*Science*, Vol. 158, pp. 351-355).

APPENDIX

DATA ON THE GREAT LAKES SYSTEM

Characteristic	Lake Superior	Lake Michigan	Lake Erie	Lake Ontario
Length (km)	560	490	385	309
Breadth (km)	256	188	91	85
Area (km^2)				
Water surface, United States	53,618	58,016	12,898	9,324
Water surface, Canada	28,749		12,768	10,360
Drainage basin land, United States	43,253	117,845	46,620	39,370
Drainage basin land, Canada	81,585		12,224	31,080
Drainage basin land, total	124,838	117,845	58,793	70,448
Drainage basin (land and water), total	207,200	175,860	87,434	90,132
Maximum depth (m)	406	281	60	244
Average depth (m)	148	84	17	86
Volume of water (km^3)	12,221	4,871	458	1,636
Average annual precipitation (mm)	736	787	863	863
Mean outflow (litre/sec)	2,067,360	5,012,640	5,550,720	6,626,880
Average retention time of water (yr) (τ)	189	30.8	2.6	7.8

12

Quarrying for sand

LEON WALKER *Paisley College*

12.1 BACKGROUND

Sand is one of the most important materials used in the
building industry and it is in constant demand. It is usually
formed at the coast, in a bay, where the weather and waves
crack and break the rocks into fragments which gradually become
small enough to be called sand, and a beach is formed. As
time passes, the land may be raised up, or the sea level
recede, and a large inland deposit of sand is formed. This
becomes covered in other material and sandstone is formed if
enough pressure and heat is applied. Where this covering
material, called the overburden, is thin, the sand stays fairly
loose and does not change its form. This sort of deposit is
the type exploited by companies producing raw materials for
industry.

It is not possible to mine sand because of the loose nature of
the overburden. Quarrying is used instead. The overburden is
removed and dumped elsewhere, and the sand is simply dug up
from the surface. One of the largest fixed costs of this
operation is the removal of the overburden.

In order to determine the future profitability of a possible
quarry site, it is necessary to estimate the amount of sand
and overburden present. To do this samples are taken at the
site over a regular rectangular grid. A tube is drilled
vertically into the ground and the resulting core pulled out
and examined. The surface is well surveyed and by measuring
the sample carefully it is possible to determine the height,
relative to some fixed level, of each interface. Thus, at
regular mesh points over the site, the thickness of the various
layers may be determined. From these an estimate of the
volumes of sand and overburden may be made.

12.1.1 Map of the site

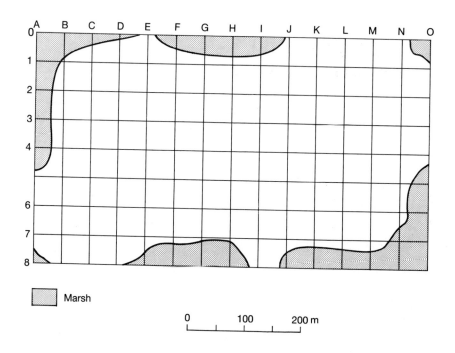

Marsh

0   100   200 m

12.1.2 Survey

Core samples have been taken at each accessible grid point.
Table 12.1 gives three readings at each point, except those
covered by marsh. All refer to an absolute height. The
first entry is the height of the surface, the second entry is
the height of the top of the sandy layer, and the third entry
corresponds to the bottom of the sandy layer. All heights
are in metres.

12.2 POSSIBLE STATEMENTS OF THE PROBLEM

(i) Blue Tunnel Industries (B.T.I) produce raw materials
for the building industry. Amongst the products in greatest
demand is sand, for which there is always a steady market.
A team of geologists surveying an estate in the Midlands, has
sent B.T.I. details of an area containing a large deposit of
sand. The estate managers have also given details of the
payments they expect. B.T.I. have sent the package to you
along with details of their costs. They want you to decide

	A	B	C	D	E	F	G	H	I	J	K	L	M	N	O
0	**** / **** / ****	**** / **** / ****	**** / **** / ****	**** / **** / ****	22.4 / 20.0 / 5.8	**** / **** / ****	**** / **** / ****	**** / **** / ****	**** / **** / ****	22.5 / 18.4 / 0.5	23.0 / 17.8 / 0.4	23.2 / 18.0 / 0.4	23.2 / 19.0 / 0.2	22.6 / 19.0 / 0.2	**** / **** / ****
1	**** / **** / ****	22.4 / 19.5 / 10.6	22.5 / 19.6 / 8.4	22.6 / 19.7 / 6.	23.0 / 19.9 / 6.0	23.1 / 20.0 / 3.2	23.2 / 19.8 / 1.6	23.4 / 19.8 / 1.0	23.5 / 19.9 / 1.1	24.0 / 20.0 / 1.0	24.0 / 19.8 / 0.8	24.0 / 19.6 / 0.9	23.8 / 19.5 / 0.8	23.0 / 19.3 / 0.3	22.5 / 19.1 / 6.0
2	**** / **** / ****	22.6 / 20.2 / 8.2	22.7 / 19.6 / 8.4	22.8 / 19.8 / 2.1	23.1 / 20.0 / 2.2	23.3 / 19.7 / 1.4	23.4 / 19.8 / 0.6	23.4 / 20.0 / 0.5	23.5 / 20.1 / 0.3	24.0 / 20.3 / -0.2	24.1 / 20.4 / -0.1	24.1 / 20.4 / -0.1	24.0 / 20.7 / 0.7	23.0 / 20.6 / 0.4	22.5 / 19.6 / 5.0
3	**** / **** / ****	22.6 / 20.4 / 6.1	22.9 / 20.0 / 4.3	23.0 / 20.1 / 1.8	23.1 / 20.0 / 1.8	23.5 / 19.5 / 1.4	23.6 / 19.5 / 0.7	23.4 / 19.8 / 0.6	23.6 / 20.2 / 0.4	23.8 / 20.4 / 0.1	23.9 / 20.6 / 0.1	23.8 / 20.8 / 0.1	23.7 / 20.7 / 0.9	23.4 / 20.6 / 1.3	22.6 / 20.6 / 6.2
4	**** / **** / ****	22.8 / 20.3 / 4.2	23.0 / 20.0 / 3.0	23.1 / 20.2 / 1.6	23.2 / 20.5 / 1.4	23.4 / 20.6 / 1.2	23.8 / 20.6 / 1.0	24.0 / 20.4 / 0.8	24.0 / 20.4 / 0.8	24.0 / 20.5 / 0.3	23.9 / 20.6 / 0.5	23.8 / 20.8 / 0.6	23.7 / 20.7 / 1.4	23.4 / 20.5 / 5.0	22.6 / 20.6 / 6.2
5	22.2 / 19.8 / 3.6	23.0 / 20.0 / 3.6	23.2 / 20.1 / 3.0	23.3 / 20.3 / 2.0	23.4 / 20.4 / 1.5	23.6 / 20.7 / 1.1	23.8 / 20.9 / 1.0	23.9 / 21.0 / 0.9	23.9 / 20.9 / 0.6	24.0 / 20.8 / 0.6	24.1 / 20.8 / 0.9	24.2 / 20.7 / 7.1	24.0 / 20.3 / 8.3	23.0 / 20.3 / 5.0	22.5 / 19.8 / 6.0
6	23.0 / 19.3 / 2.8	24.0 / 19.5 / 2.6	24.0 / 20.2 / 2.0	23.0 / 20.3 / 1.5	23.5 / 20.6 / 1.4	23.4 / 20.8 / 1.2	23.3 / 21.0 / 1.0	23.2 / 20.8 / 0.9	23.1 / 20.6 / 0.6	23.0 / 20.4 / 1.2	22.9 / 20.2 / 4.1	22.8 / 20.0 / 8.0	22.7 / 19.6 / 8.3	22.5 / 19.4 / 8.9	22.6 / 20.6 / 6.2
7	18.8 / 19.0 / 1.0	19.0 / 19.0 / 0.8	20.2 / 20.2 / 0.7	20.3 / 20.3 / 0.7	20.7 / 20.7 / 1.2	20.9 / 20.9 / 1.2	21.0 / 21.0 / 1.5	20.6 / 20.6 / 2.3	20.4 / 20.4 / 2.4	20.0 / 20.0 / 3.0	19.4 / 19.4 / 7.0	20.0 / 20.0 / 10.2	19.0 / 19.0 / 14.0	19.4 / 19.4 / 5.0	**** / **** / ****
8	22.8 / 18.8 / 1.0	25.0 / 19.5 / 0.9	24.0 / 20.1 / 0.9	23.0 / 20.2 / 1.2	**** / **** / ****	**** / **** / ****	**** / **** / ****	**** / **** / ****	22.0 / 19.8 / 4.7	**** / **** / ****	**** / **** / ****	**** / **** / ****	**** / **** / ****	**** / **** / ****	**** / **** / ****

whether they should invest in the project.   (Here the student
should be given the map, Table 12.1 and a sheet containing all
the information on costs.)

(ii)   The problem could be set in two parts, possibly as
successive courseworks.

(a)   Blue Tunnel Industries (B.T.I.) produce raw materials for
the building industry. Amongst the products in greatest demand
is sand, for which there is always a steady market. A team of
geologists surveying an estate in the Borders has sent B.T.I.
details of an area containing a large deposit of sand. B.T.I.
have sent the package to you, saying that the quarry can be
profitable only if there is over 4 million tonnes of sand and
the volume of the overburden is less than 19% of the volume
of the sand. They wish to know whether they should invest or
not. (The student would require the map and Table 12.1 at
this point.)

(b)   B.T.I. have considered your report, and now require you to
provide an economic analysis of the project.

Their engineers have studied the contour maps contained in the
report, and conclude that it is possible to extract 100,000
tonnes of sand each month. Preliminary discussions have taken
place with contractors in the nearby new town, and it appears
likely that a contract for this amount monthly can be agreed.
(The information sheet can now be distributed.)

12.2.1 Some relevant data

Average density of overburden $= 1350 \text{ kg/m}^3$

Average density of sand $= 1620 \text{ kg/m}^3$

Monthly discount rate $= 1\%$

Maximum extraction rate of the sand $= 100,000$ tonnes/month

12.2.2 Charges made by the estate

   (i)   To cover disruption of existing farming, housing etc.
          an initial payment of £200,000.

  (ii)   A royalty of 54.72p per tonne of sand removed.

 (iii)   The overburden may be dumped in a nearby quarry, which
          is exhausted, but a charge of 12.1p per tonne dumped
          will be made.

(iv) Charge for landscaping of the area after the sand has
      been removed £1,000,000.

12.2.3 Costs incurred by B.T.I.

(i)   For digging and transporting overburden to nearby
      quarry 36.72p per tonne.

(ii) For extracting sand and transporting to market area
      45.93p per tonne.

12.2.4 Profits to be made to B.T.I.

Sale price of sand = £2.96 per tonne.

12.3 USES OF THE PROBLEM

The answer to the problem as posed is made up of two steps:

(i)   Calculate the volumes and hence masses, of the overburden
      and sand.

(ii) Find the total expenditure and income and thus the
      profitability of the project.

We will discuss the two sections separately.

(i)   The presence of the marsh on the site precludes
      sampling at some grid points. Some form of extrapolation
      has to be used to find the thickness of the layers. If
      this is too advanced for the students then Table 12.2
      may be distributed and the marsh removed from the map.
      To introduce interpolation into the problem an area of
      marsh could be placed in the middle of the site and the
      corresponding entries removed from the table. One
      protest the students are likely to bring up is that if
      there is marsh around, then there is water around and
      quarrying will be difficult if not impossible.

      One solution is to explain that the costs for removing
      the overburden and extracting the sand include the costs
      for pumping the water away. Another is that the sand
      will be dredged up from the bottom of the pond that will
      form as soon as the digging commences.

      With the figures given there is sand beneath the entire
      rectangular area. If a model which needs careful
      numerical techniques is required, then the area of the
      deposit can be changed to a less amenable shape.

(ii)   The cost analysis section can be quite tricky to
       students who have no experience of cash discounting.
       Perhaps, a more simple example involving net present
       value should be given as a pointer in the right direction.

       We have given an extraction rate of 100,000 tonnes of
       sand per month, based on the expected capacity for
       lorries of the site. Perhaps, this extraction rate
       could be left as an unknown, and the student required
       to find a sensible figure.

12.4 POSSIBLE SOLUTIONS

12.4.1 Filling the blanks in the table

There exist very complicated methods for extrapolating
functions of two variables, but we present two simple approaches
and assume that the error introduced is small and hence does
not affect the final volume appreciably. As a typical example,
we will give the details of filling the blanks at grid point
OI.

As a first approach, we will use linear extrapolation from
adjacent grid points. From the entries in OJ and OK we have
the result

$$22.0$$
$$19.0$$
$$0.6$$

However, we may also use the entries for grid points 1I and
2I. These give the result

$$23.5$$
$$19.7$$
$$1.9$$

Of course, we now have two equally valid results, and we must
do something about it. A sensible approach is to take the
average of these two, to give a final result

$$22.75$$
$$19.35$$
$$1.25$$

These are good enough, but one could also use the result
obtained from grid points 1J and 2K, or grid points 2G and IH,
and so on. This is perhaps carrying things a bit far and we
should look for another method.

The second approach is to put a plane through the three adjacent points as illustrated in Figure 12.1. Of course, this is not possible for point OA until the entries for points 1A and OB have been calculated. The formula we require will give the height of the fourth edge of a box with a square base, vertical sides, with a plane top which is not necessarily parallel to the base. Let h_1, h_2, h_3 be the heights of the known corners. Then, by symmetry,

$$h_1 + h_4 = h_2 + h_3$$

so that
$$h_4 = h_2 + h_3 - h_1$$

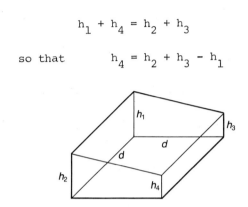

Figure 12.1   Plane through four points

This proof may seem a bit glib but the formula is easily obtained using three dimensional coordinate geometry. Using the entries for points OJ, 1I and 1J, and the above formula, we find the result for OI is

$$
\begin{aligned}
&22.0 \\
&18.3 \\
&0.6
\end{aligned}
$$

These figures compare fairly well with those obtained by the first method.

Both these methods use straight lines to extrapolate, and this seems sensible if we propose to use the trapezoidal rule to find the volume; however, the use of Simpson's rule would seem to demand that we use quadratic extrapolation. This is possible, but the increased accuracy will be swamped by other approximations used in the solution.

Table 12.2 was completed by using the second method of extrapolation, with averaging where necessary.

	A	B	C	D	E	F	G	H	I	J	K	L	M	N	O
0	21.0, 19.4, 10.4	21.8, 19.6, 10.4	21.9, 19.7, 8.2	22.0, 19.8, 6.0	22.4, 20.0, 5.8	22.0, 19.5, 2.9	21.7, 18.0, 1.1	21.9, 18.2, 0.5	22.0, 18.3, 0.6	22.5, 18.4, 0.5	23.0, 17.8, 0.4	23.2, 18.0, 0.4	23.2, 19.0, 0.2	23.0, 19.0, 0.2	21.8, 18.8, 5.9
1	21.6, 19.3, 10.6	22.4, 19.5, 10.6	22.5, 19.6, 8.4	22.6, 19.7, 6.2	23.0, 19.9, 6.0	23.1, 20.0, 3.2	23.2, 19.8, 1.6	23.4, 19.8, 1.0	23.5, 19.9, 1.1	24.0, 20.0, 0.5	24.0, 19.8, 0.8	24.0, 20.0, 0.9	23.8, 19.5, 0.8	23.0, 19.3, 0.3	22.2, 19.1, 6.0
2	21.8, 20.0, 8.2	22.6, 20.4, 8.2	22.9, 20.0, 4.3	23.0, 20.1, 1.8	23.1, 20.0, 1.8	23.5, 19.5, 1.4	23.6, 19.5, 0.6	23.4, 20.0, 0.5	23.6, 20.2, 0.4	23.8, 20.4, 0.1	24.0, 20.6, 0.1	24.0, 20.7, 0.1	24.0, 20.8, 0.7	23.0, 20.0, 0.4	22.5, 19.8, 5.0
3	21.8, 20.2, 6.1	22.8, 20.3, 6.1	23.0, 20.2, 3.6	23.1, 20.3, 2.0	23.2, 20.5, 1.5	23.4, 20.6, 1.4	23.8, 20.6, 0.7	24.0, 20.4, 0.6	24.0, 20.4, 0.6	24.0, 20.5, 0.3	23.9, 20.6, 0.1	23.8, 20.8, 0.1	23.7, 20.7, 0.9	23.4, 20.5, 1.3	22.6, 20.6, 6.0
4	22.0, 20.1, 4.2	22.8, 20.3, 4.2	23.0, 20.0, 3.0	23.3, 20.3, 1.6	23.5, 20.4, 1.4	23.6, 20.7, 1.2	23.8, 20.6, 1.0	23.9, 21.0, 0.8	23.9, 20.9, 0.8	24.0, 20.8, 0.6	24.1, 20.8, 0.6	24.2, 20.7, 0.6	24.0, 20.3, 1.4	23.0, 20.3, 8.9	22.2, 20.4, 6.2
5	22.2, 19.8, 3.6	23.0, 20.2, 3.6	23.2, 20.1, 3.0	23.3, 20.3, 2.0	23.4, 20.4, 1.5	23.6, 20.7, 1.1	23.8, 21.0, 1.0	23.9, 21.0, 0.9	23.9, 20.9, 0.6	24.0, 20.8, 0.6	24.1, 20.8, 0.5	24.2, 20.8, 0.6	24.0, 20.7, 0.7	23.0, 20.3, 6.0	22.2, 20.4, 6.0
6	23.0, 19.3, 2.8	23.0, 19.5, 2.8	23.3, 20.2, 3.0	23.0, 20.3, 1.5	23.5, 20.6, 1.4	23.4, 20.8, 1.2	23.3, 21.0, 1.0	23.2, 21.0, 0.8	23.1, 21.0, 0.7	23.0, 20.8, 0.9	22.9, 20.8, 0.9	22.8, 20.0, 7.1	22.7, 20.3, 8.3	22.5, 20.5, 8.9	22.6, 20.6, 9.1
7	19.3, 18.8, 1.0	19.5, 19.0, 0.8	20.1, 20.2, 0.7	20.2, 20.3, 0.7	20.7, 20.7, 1.2	20.8, 20.9, 1.2	20.6, 21.0, 1.5	20.0, 20.6, 2.3	19.8, 20.4, 2.4	19.4, 20.0, 3.0	18.8, 19.4, 7.0	18.6, 19.2, 10.2	18.4, 19.0, 10.2	18.2, 19.4, 11.4	18.3, 19.5, 11.6
8	23.3, 19.3, 1.1	25.0, 19.5, 0.9	24.0, 20.1, 0.9	23.0, 20.2, 1.2	23.0, 20.6, 1.5	22.4, 20.8, 1.5	22.3, 20.6, 2.5	22.1, 20.0, 4.6	22.0, 19.8, 4.7	22.0, 19.4, 5.3	22.1, 18.8, 9.3	22.1, 18.6, 12.5	22.2, 18.4, 16.3	22.0, 18.2, 17.9	21.2, 18.3, 18.1

Table 12.2

12.4.2 *Calculating the volumes*

We require a method of calculating the volume between two
surfaces. For the more advanced student double integration
and its numerical equivalents should spring to mind, but we
will look at simpler approaches first. These will give an
order of magnitude against which we can check the results from
the more complicated procedures.

The most elementary formula is that the volume is given by

Area x Average thickness of layer

From Table 12.2 we can obtain the thickness of the layers at
each grid point by subtracting the bottom height from the top.
These thicknesses are given in Table 12.3. At each point,
the top entry is the depth of overburden and the bottom is the
depth of sand. An immediate rough and ready approach is to
find the average depth by making a good guess. From Table
12.3, we see that the average thickness of the overburden is
about 3 metres and that of the sand is 15 metres. Hence, the
volume of overburden is approximately

$$400 \times 700 \times 3 = 8.4 \times 10^5 \text{ m}^3$$

whilst that of the sand is

$$400 \times 700 \times 15 = 4.2 \times 10^6 \text{ m}^3$$

A better average thickness is obtained by taking the thickness
at each grid point into account. Adding the top figures at
all the grid points and dividing by the number of grid points
(135) gives the approximate average depth of overburden. Then,
using this method, the volume of overburden is

$$400 \times 700 \times 415.9 / 135 = 8.626 \times 10^5 \text{ m}^3$$

and the volume of the sand is

$$400 \times 700 \times 2187.8 / 135 = 4.538 \times 10^6 \text{ m}^3$$

	A	B	C	D	E	F	G	H	I	J	K	L	M	N	O
0	1.6 / 9.0	2.2 / 9.2	2.2 / 11.5	2.2 / 13.6	2.4 / 14.2	2.5 / 16.6	3.7 / 16.9	3.7 / 17.7	3.7 / 17.7	4.1 / 17.9	5.2 / 17.4	5.2 / 17.6	4.2 / 18.8	3.6 / 18.8	3.0 / 12.9
1	2.3 / 8.7	2.9 / 8.9	2.9 / 11.2	2.9 / 13.5	3.1 / 13.9	3.1 / 16.8	3.2 / 17.7	3.6 / 18.8	3.6 / 18.8	4.0 / 19.0	4.2 / 19.0	4.4 / 18.7	4.3 / 18.7	3.7 / 19.0	3.1 / 13.1
2	1.8 / 11.8	2.4 / 12.0	3.1 / 15.3	3.0 / 17.7	3.3 / 17.6	3.6 / 18.4	3.6 / 18.4	3.4 / 18.8	3.4 / 18.8	3.9 / 20.5	3.7 / 20.5	3.6 / 20.5	4.0 / 19.3	3.4 / 19.2	2.9 / 14.6
3	1.6 / 14.1	2.2 / 14.3	2.9 / 16.4	2.9 / 18.3	3.1 / 17.6	3.6 / 18.3	3.6 / 19.2	3.6 / 19.5	3.4 / 19.8	3.4 / 20.3	3.4 / 20.5	3.5 / 20.6	3.2 / 19.3	3.0 / 19.2	2.7 / 13.3
4	1.9 / 15.9	2.5 / 16.1	3.0 / 17.0	2.9 / 18.6	2.7 / 19.1	2.8 / 19.4	3.2 / 18.8	3.6 / 19.6	3.6 / 19.6	3.5 / 20.2	3.3 / 20.1	3.0 / 20.2	3.0 / 19.3	2.9 / 14.5	2.0 / 14.4
5	2.4 / 16.2	3.0 / 16.4	3.1 / 17.1	3.0 / 18.3	3.0 / 18.9	2.9 / 19.6	2.9 / 19.9	2.9 / 20.1	3.0 / 20.3	3.2 / 20.2	3.3 / 19.9	3.5 / 13.6	3.7 / 12.0	2.7 / 11.4	1.8 / 11.3
6	3.7 / 16.2	4.5 / 16.9	3.8 / 18.2	2.8 / 18.8	2.9 / 19.2	2.6 / 19.6	2.3 / 19.9	2.4 / 20.0	2.5 / 19.9	2.6 / 19.2	2.7 / 16.1	2.8 / 12.0	3.1 / 9.4	3.1 / 8.0	2.2 / 7.9
7	4.0 / 17.8	5.5 / 18.2	3.8 / 19.5	2.7 / 19.6	2.3 / 19.5	1.5 / 19.7	1.3 / 19.5	1.6 / 18.3	1.7 / 18.0	2.1 / 17.0	2.8 / 12.4	3.0 / 9.0	3.3 / 5.0	3.3 / 3.2	2.4 / 3.1
8	4.0 / 18.2	5.5 / 18.6	3.9 / 19.2	2.8 / 19.0	2.4 / 19.1	1.6 / 19.3	1.7 / 18.1	2.1 / 15.4	2.2 / 15.1	2.6 / 14.1	3.3 / 9.5	3.5 / 6.1	3.8 / 2.1	3.8 / 0.3	2.9 / 0.2

Table 12.3

With a little more thought we can obtain a closer approximation
to the volume by considering the shape of the surfaces between
the grid points. If we join the grid points by straight lines,
the volume is made up of boxes, each of square cross-section,
with vertical sides, with the top and bottom curved surfaces
passing through four points (see Figure 12.2). The volume of
such a box is given by

$$V = A \bar{h}$$

where $\bar{h}$ is the average height of the box and A the cross-
sectional area.

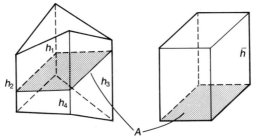

Figure 12.2   Averaging the heights

A good approximation for $\bar{h}$ is

$$\bar{h} = (h_1 + h_2 + h_3 + h_4)/4$$

where the h_i (i = 1,4) are the lengths of the four vertical
edges of the box.   Then

$$V = A(h_1 + h_2 + h_3 + h_4)/4$$

Applying this formula to all the boxes and adding up we obtain

$$V = A(\Sigma \text{ Thicknesses at corner grid points}$$
$$+ 2\ \Sigma \text{ Thickness at edge of grid points}$$
$$+ 4\ \Sigma \text{ Thickness at internal grid points})/4$$

Then, using this formula and Table 12.3, we find

$$\text{Volume of overburden} = 8.696 \times 10^5 \text{ m}^3$$

$$\text{Volume of sand} = 4.690 \times 10^6 \text{ m}^3$$

This second method is, of course, the trapezium rule extended for a double integral, but we can see that is unnecessary for the student to know this advanced concept in order to get a fairly accurate solution. We now arrive at the most sophisticated methods using the trapezium and Simpson's rule. The student may not understand that the two dimensional extension to Simpson's rule approximates a surface by a series of paraboloids, but he may obtain the correct solution, if he knows the one dimensional formula.

We will not reproduce the formulae and reasoning behind the trapezium and Simpson's rules, since this material is available from elementary textbooks on numerical analysis (e.g. Watson, W.A. et al. (1981)). We use the one dimensional formulae to integrate across the rows, giving columns of figures, then integrate these figures using the same formula.

The trapezium rule gives

$$\text{Volume of overburden} = 8.696 \times 10^5 \text{ m}^3$$

$$\text{Volume of sand} = 4.690 \times 10^6 \text{ m}^3$$

and Simpson's rule gives

$$\text{Volume of overburden} = 8.732 \times 10^5 \text{ m}^3$$

$$\text{Volume of sand} = 4.689 \times 10^6 \text{ m}^3$$

(Of course, the same results could be obtained by integrating down the columns, then across the resultant row.)

For completness we include contour maps of the three surfaces. (See Figures 12.3, 12.4, 12.5.) These may assist B.T.I. in planning the extraction of the sand.

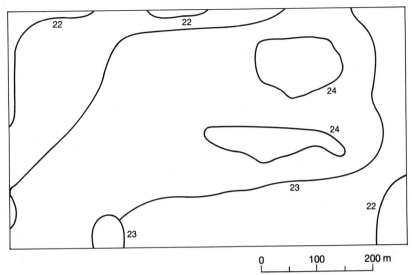

Figure 12.3   Contours of top surface
(Heights in metres)

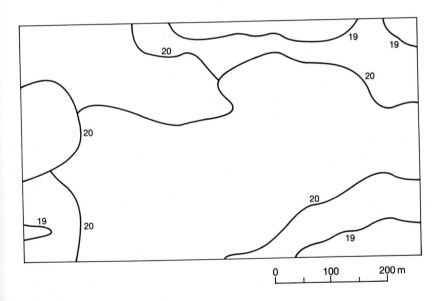

Figure 12.4   Contours of overburden-sand interface
(Heights in metres)

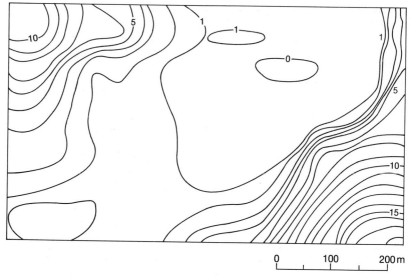

Figure 12.5   Contours of bottom surface of sand
(Heights in metres)

12.4.3 Cost analysis

As a first step we require the mass of overburden and sand,
and we will use the results given by Simpson's rule. We
have

$$\text{Mass} = \text{Volume} \times \text{Density}$$

Hence, mass of overburden $= 8.732 \times 10^5 \times 1.350 \times 10^3$ kg

$$= 1.179 \times 10^6 \text{ tonne}$$

Mass of sand $= 4.689 \times 10^6 \times 1.620 \times 10^3$ kg

$$= 7.596 \times 10^6 \text{ tonne}$$

Since the sand can be sold at a rate of 100,000 tonnes a month
the project will last $7.596 \times 10^6/10^5$ months or 76 months. We
must make a decision about the removal of the overburden. We
could remove it all at once, though this is obviously an
expensive strategy. It is not possible to remove any sand
without first removing its covering of overburden. It seems
logical that to remove a portion of the sand we must on average
remove the same proportion of overburden. Thus, the extraction
of 100,000 tonnes of sand a month requires the removal of

$$1.179 \times 10^6 \times 10^5 / (7.596 \times 10^6) = 1.55 \times 10^4$$

tonnes of overburden per month.

Now, since the contract for sand is paid monthly we will assume that all costs are to be paid monthly. Thus, we have the following monthly outgoings:

Royalties : $10^5 \times .5472$ = £54,720.00

Dumping charge for overburden:

$1.55 \times 10^4 \times .121$ = £1875.50

Digging and transporting overburden:

$1.55 \times 10^4 \times .3672$ = £5691.60

Extracting and transporting sand:

$10^5 \times .4593$ = £45,930.00

Total = £108,216.66

The monthly income from sales of sand is

$$10^5 \times 2.96 = £296,000.00$$

Hence the monthly profit is

$$296,000.00 - 108,216.66 = £187,783.34$$

We now total the profits for each month to find the total profit, but each profit must first be reduced to its net present value. Thus if we make a profit of £P n months from now, the net present value of £P is

$$£P / (1 + i)^n$$

where i is the monthly discount rate. Thus, the total of the discounted monthly profits is given by

$$£P/(1+i) + £P/(1+i)^2 + £P/(1+i)^3 + \ldots + £P/(1+i)^{76}$$

$$= \sum_{r=1}^{76} £P/(1+i)^r$$

The student with little insight may have to evaluate this using
a small computer program, but for the more able, the formula
for a geometric series should spring to mind

$$\sum_{r=1}^{76} P/(1+i)^r = \frac{P}{1+i} \left(\frac{1 - (1+i)^{-75}}{1 - (i+i)^{-1}} \right)$$

In our case P = £187,783.34 and i = 0.01. Applying the above
formula we find that the total discounted profits are
£9,874,746.50.

From this sum we must deduct the initial payment and the
landscaping charge. The £100,000 for landscaping is not
payable until the end of the project. Hence we discount this
sum to

$$1,000,000/1.01^{76} = £469,447.00$$

Hence the total profit is

$$9,874,764.5 - 200,000 - 469,447.00$$

$$= £9,205,299.5$$

We must now decide whether or not this is a healthy profit.
We cannot just compare it with the obvious capital expenditure
of £200,000 and £469,447. There are three obvious criteria.
The first that the profit should be positive and the second
that the initial capital outlay should, in some sense, be
small. The third is more subtle: the profit must be a fair
percentage of turnover. In this case, of the turnover of
£296,000 about 60% of it is profit. For these reasons we can
say that the project will be profitable.

12.5 NOTES

1. We should really make allowances for the fact that the
sand at the sand/overburden interface will be of low quality.
Perhaps we should say that this interfacial layer is of
thickness 15 cm. The volume of this layer is

$$400 \times 700 \times .15 = 4.2 \times 10^4 \ m^3$$

Assuming this volume to be lost from the sand the density of this layer may be assumed to be 1620 kg/m^3. Hence, we have a quantity of

$$4.2 \times 10^4 \times 1.62 = 6.8 \times 10^4 \quad \text{tonnes}$$

of low quality sand. The mass of good quality sand is thus reduced to 7.52×10^6 tonnes. The monthly costs must now be adjusted accordingly. One can adopt one of two strategies. Either assume that this low quality sand is saleable at a price approximately half of that of the pure sand or assume that it is of such poor quality that it must be dumped along with the overburden.

2. By inspection of the contour plots given in Section 12.4.2, the sand in the lower right hand corner of the site is very thin. It may be worthwhile investigating whether this area should be quarried at all. I suspect the cost of dumping the overburden far outweighs the income to be expected from the sand.

REFERENCES

Watson, W.A. et al., 1981 Numerical Analysis. Edward Arnold.

13

The Ruritanian Sports and Social Club

IAN HUNTLEY   *Sheffield City Polytechnic*

13.1   COMMENT TO LECTURER

The case study which follows is strongly based on material
from "Computer Models in the Social Sciences" by R.B. Coats
and A. Parkin (Arnold, 1977). The study has been extended,
however, to show how this sort of example can provide a
useful modelling exercise at many different levels of
maturity. As written, the example is probably best suited
to numerate undergraduates, but with only minor changes
(such as changing "Ruritanian" to "Glasgow Rangers"!) it
has already been tried out with mathematics students in
the third year and modern studies/geography students in
the fourth year at secondary school. In fact, the ability
to use the same modelling exercise across the ability
spectrum seems to be one of the features of a good example:
the approaches used and answers received will vary
enormously, but - no matter what their ability - students will
be able to display their full potential.

13.2   BACKGROUND

The Ruritanian Sports and Social Club Committee was
discussing its expenditure for the coming year. The debate
was particularly pointed because, in the season just ended,
the two annual fundraising events (the Gala Day and the
Barbecue Dance) had not proved very profitable.

'Look', said the Membership Secretary, 'we can't possibly
afford another year like the last - the members won't stand
for it. We started the year with £25000 ; we authorised
expenditure on new buildings and equipment to the tune of
£20000;   yet the Gala and Barbecue were such a washout that
we only netted £5000,   leaving us with a credit balance of a

mere £10000. We must make quite sure we don't overspend
this coming year, so that we can build up our reserves again'.

The Treasurer looked doubtful. 'What do you mean by quite
sure? If you mean that there must be absolutely no risk of
a loss, then there is only one course of action open to
us - we should not spend anything on new facilities next
year. Indeed, to be strictly accurate, we should not even
authorise the preliminary expenditure on the Gala and
Barbecue - after all, it's on the cards that we could make
a loss on both events. Look what happened this year at the
Gala'.

'That's a bit thick, isn't it?', interposed the Events
Organiser. 'The only reason that we did so badly this year
is that it poured with rain on both days. The chance of that
happening two years running is so remote that we can ignore
it'.

The Treasurer thought to himself, 'There's something wrong
there. I don't see how this year's weather can affect next
year's. The chances of bad weather next year must be the
same, irrespective of what weather we had this year'. He
opened his mouth to make this point but hesitated, wondering
if the Events Organiser would understand him. Then he had a
vision of an ensuing argument, a considerable detour from
the matter in hand, and an even more protracted meeting. He
shut his mouth again.

The Membership Secretary ended the hiatus with a bland
inconsistency. 'We can't have no expenditure next year - there
would be uproar from the members if we failed to provide any
new equipment at all. Then there's the repairs to the
pavilion roof, a new filtration system for the swimming
pool,....' He went on with a long list which made it evident
that there were ample outstanding projects to soak up
whatever funds were made available.

'Then what you must decide', declared the Treasurer, 'is
this: exactly what risk of loss is the club prepared to
accept?'

There was silence for a moment, as nobody knew how to answer
this question. 'I should have thought', said the Chairman
tentatively, 'that we want to be about 90% sure that we will
more than break even'.

'And accept a 10% risk of loss?', queried the Events Organiser
doubtfully. 'I suppose we could afford a small overdraft,
but I don't think we want more than, say, a 1% risk of one of

more than about £5000'.

'And I don't think we should accept any risk of a deficit as
large as £20000', added the Treasurer, 'since we would never
find large enough overdraft facilities to cover it and that
would mean we would have to fold up completely. Now let me
get this straight: the feeling of the Committee is that the
planned expenditure for next year should aim to give us 90%
chance of balancing the books. We are prepared to accept a
small risk, 1%, of a deficit of £5000 and no risk of one greater
than £20000 ?' There were murmurs of assent. 'Of course',
continued the Treasurer, 'the last constraint means we cannot
contemplate more that £30000 expenditure, for if we are
avoiding any risk at all of a greater loss we must consider
the worst case - with no receipts'.

The Membership Secretary looked glum, but no one was prepared
to counter this argument. The Committee members fidgeted,
many eyes on the clock. 'Give me until the next meeting to
think about it, and I shall try to find the figure which
meets these criteria', concluded the Treasurer.

The Chairman closed the meeting.

Considering the problem in the comfort of his study, the
Treasurer was beginning to realise that his problem was not
an easy one. He was not worried much by what was meant by
'a 90% chance' of being all right. His concept was that
there was a certain level of expenditure which (if the same
policy were applied each year and other circumstances did
not change significantly) would tend, in the long run, to
produce receipts exceeding payments in 90% of the years.
It did strike him that a very large number of years - perhaps
more that his remaining years as Treasurer - might be needed
before anyone could say whether his recommended figure had
been right or wrong, but he found this more of an
encouragement to continue than a philosophical obstacle.

No, his real problem was that the club had been running only
five years and he did not have much past data to work on.
He was fully aware that Ruritania enjoyed an extraordinarily
stable economy, currency and population, and that Ruritanians
were famous for their consistent habits. 'The only thing',
he mused to himself, 'that can be effecting receipts from our
annual events is the weather'. To test this hypothesis, he
rang the Weather Bureau and asked for the rainfall figures
during the time of the Gala (10 am to 5 pm) and the Barbecue
(8 pm to 1 am) on the relevant dates in previous years.

Year	Gala		Barbecue	
	profit(£)	rain(mm)	profit(£)	rain(mm)
1	20 000	1	5 000	5
2	3 000	12	7 000	1
3	28 000	0	1 000	21
4	17 000	2	8 000	0
5	1 000	17	4 000	8

TABLE 13.1

The Treasurer found the consistent correlation between
rainfall and receipts, as shown in Table 13.1, an encouragement
to his hypothesis. He noticed that the Gala seemed to be
effected by poor weather more than the Barbecue and found
this encouraging, for he knew that the Gala was entirely
open air while the Barbecue was partly covered, and so he
would not expect the Barbecue to suffer as badly when it
rained. He decided to make the pragmatic assumption that the
relationships were reliable and described what could be
expected in the coming year.

It was now becoming clear that if he could predict the
rainfall on the days of the Gala and Barbecue in the
coming year, he would be able to make a prediction of the
total receipts. The Gala was scheduled for 1st July and
the Barbecue for 27th August, so he again contacted the
Weather Bureau and asked them for the rainfall figures for
the relevant periods. The Bureau's figures went back 50 years,
and he was able to construct the histogram of Figure 13.1 from
the data they supplied.

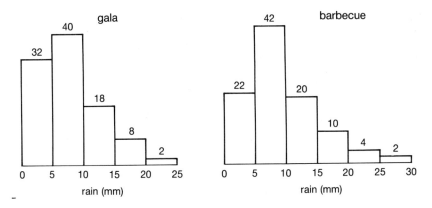

Figure 13.1 % occurrence of rain

Armed with all this information, the Treasurer felt sure
that he could work towards an answer to his problem. He
thought that at least he would be able to make statements
like 'There's only a 5% chance of a deficit if we
authorise capital expenditure of £15 000 next year', which
would go some way to meeting the Committee's requirements.
What would you do in his place?

13.3   FIRST THOUGHTS

When presented with a table of data it is often a good
idea to draw a rough graph, since the eye is very quick
to spot a trend. The plot of receipts (ie. profit) against
rainfall for each event is shown in Figure 13.2, and
immediately confirms the expected relationship. (The linear
portions between data points have been inserted merely to
aid the eye).

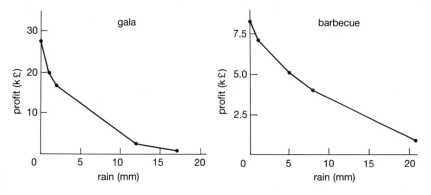

Figure 13.2   Plots of profit against rainfall

We notice from the histograms, however, that the information
on expected rainfall is grouped into very coarse bands
(each of width 5mm). As a first step, we wish to make the two
sources of information compatible, and so we read off from
the graphs above the receipts corresponding to the midpoint
of the range. This leads to Table 13.2

	Gala		Barbecue
rain(mm)	profit(£)	rain(mm)	profit(£)
0 - 5	16 000	0 - 5	6 000
5 - 10	9 000	5 - 10	4 000
10 - 15	3 000	10 - 15	3 000
15 - 20	1 000	15 - 20	2 000
20 - 25	0	20 - 25	1 000
		25 - 30	0

TABLE 13.2

We have now simplified the situation tremendously: we have
5 possible outcomes of the Gala and 6 of the Barbecue, 30
in all. For instance, we might have 3mm of rain on the day
of the Gala and 7mm on that of the Barbecue. Using the
table above, we could now predict about £20 000 net profit
from the two events.

In fact we can go further than this, since we know that a
Gala rainfall such as 3mm (ie. between 0 and 5) occurs 32%
of the time and similarly the Barbecue rainfall occurs 42%
of the time. Thus we would expect our £20 000 profit at
least 13.4% (ie. 0.32 x 0.42) of the time.

All 30 possible outcomes are displayed in Figure 13.3,
where the numbers x(y) in each box signify a profit of £x 000
for y% of the time and the size of the box also indicates
the relative frequency y.

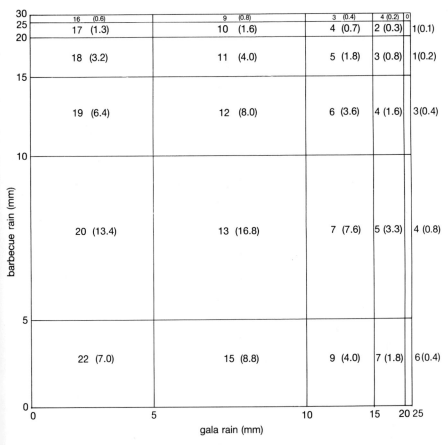

Figure 13.3

This same information is sorted in the Table 13.3 and
displayed in the graph of Figure 13.4.

Profit (K£)	% of times	Cumulative%
22	7.0	7.0
20	13.4	20.4
19	6.4	26.8
18	3.2	30.0
17	1.3	31.3
16	0.6	31.9
15	8.8	40.7
13	16.8	57.5
12	8.0	65.5
11	4.0	69.5
10	1.6	71.1
9	4.8	75.9
7	9.4	85.3
6	4.0	89.3
5	5.1	94.4
4	3.1	97.5
3	1.6	99.1
2	0.5	99.6
1	0.3	99.9
0	0.1	100

TABLE 13.3

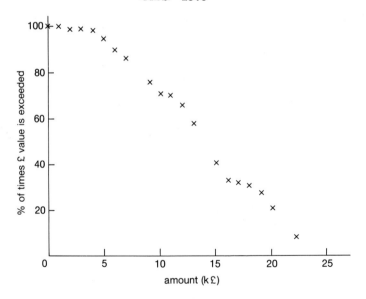

Figure 13.4

As a quick check on the calculations above, we note that the
graph implies an average profit (ie. that occurring 50% of the
time) of about £14 000. On the other hand, the histograms tell
us that the average Gala rainfall was 7.9 mm and the average
Barbecue rainfall was 9.4 mm. Reading off the appropriate
profits yields an average of £13 000 - in good agreement with
the figure above.

13.4 ALTERNATIVE MODEL

Although the solution above is easy to obtain in this
instance, this is due to the fact that the rainfall histogram
is quite coarse. With better data the method would become
very tedious. We can, however, extend the idea quite
simply, so that the situation may be simulated on a computer.

The essential idea above was that if we knew the rainfall
on the days of the Gala and Barbecue we could make a good
estimate of the resulting profit. The information we have
is that each rainfall occurs a certain proportion of the time.

To begin to code this for a computer simulation we consider
the Gala rainfall, and a random number G in the range [0,1).
We recall from the work above that we expect the rainfall on
the day of the Gala to be in the range 0-5mm 32% of the
time, and to result in £16 000 profit. We simulate this
by saying that if the random number G is less than 0.32
(which it will be 32% of the time) then the Gala profit GG
will be £16 000. Similarly, the rainfall is in the range
5-10 mm 40% of the time, and results in £9 000 profit. Thus
G ε [0.32, 0.72) gives profit GG of £9 000.

The above simulation is very simply coded for the computer.
In BASIC on an Apple, for instance, we would have the
following:

```
50    G = RND(1)

60    IF G < 0.32 THEN GG = 16000: GOTO 110

70    IF G < 0.72 THEN GG =  9000: GOTO 110

80    IF G < 0.90 THEN GG =  3000: GOTO 110

90    IF G < 0.98 THEN GG =  1000: GOTO 110

100   GG = 0

110
```

Doing exactly the same for the Barbecue leads to the
following code.

```
110    B = RND(1)

120    IF B < 0.22 THEN BB = 6000: GOTO 180

130    IF B < 0.64 THEN BB = 4000: GOTO 180

140    IF B < 0.84 THEN BB = 3000: GOTO 180

150    IF B < 0.94 THEN BB = 2000: GOTO 180

160    IF B < 0.98 THEN BB = 1000: GOTO 180

170    BB = 0

180
```

Finally, the total profit is given by the sum of the Gala
and Barbecue profits

$$180 \ REC = GG + BB,$$

and we now merely repeat the whole exercise many times in
order to average out the random variation and obtain sensible
statistics.

The complete program is shown in Figure 13.5(a) together
with a typical graphical output in Figure 13.5(b).

(Lecturers unfamiliar with computer-generated pseudorandom
numbers should note the use of a seed to initiate the
sequence. With a fixed seed (as in line 20), the same random
numbers are generated each time the program is run. Thus
one run of 50 replications is not the same as 5 runs of 10
replications).

The graph is seen to be very similar to that obtained
previously, but we note that it is now trivial to repeat
the simulation when a less coarse histogram is provided.

```
5        DIM L(23)
10       FOR J = 0 TO 23
12       L(J) = 0
14       NEXT J
20       SEED = RND ( - 1)
30       INPUT "NUMBER OF REPLICATIONS?    ";NMAX
40       FOR N = 1 TO NMAX
50       G = RND (1)
60       IF G < 0.32 THEN GG = 16000: GOTO 110
70       IF G < 0.72 THEN GG = 8000: GOTO 110
80       IF G < 0.90 THEN GG = 3000: GOTO 110
90       IF G < 0.98 THEN GG = 1000: GOTO 110
100      GG = 0
110      B = RND (1)
120      IF B < 0.22 THEN BB = 6500: GOTO 180
130      IF B < 0.64 THEN BB = 4000: GOTO 180
140      IF B < 0.84 THEN BB = 2500: GOTO 180
150      IF B < 0.94 THEN BB = 1500: GOTO 180
160      IF B < 0.98 THEN BB = 500: GOTO 180
170      BB = 0
180      REC = GG + BB
190      REC = REC / 1000
200      FOR J = 0 TO 23
210      IF J < REC THEN L(J) = L(J) + 1
220      NEXT J
230      NEXT N
240      HGR
250      HCOLOR= 2
260      HPLOT 0,0 TO 230,0 TO 230,159 TO 0,159 TO 0,0
270      FOR J = 0 TO 23
280      L(J) = L(J) / NMAX
290      X = 10 * J
300      Y = 159 * (1 - L(J))
310      HPLOT TO X,Y
320      NEXT J
330      END
```

Figure 13.5(a)   Computer Program written in Apple BASIC

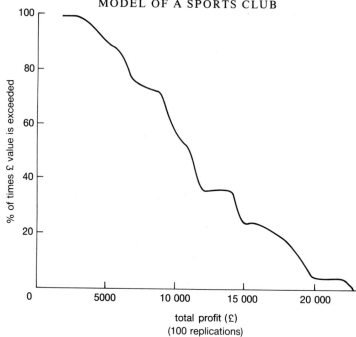

Figure 13.5(b)   100 replications

13.5   FURTHER THOUGHTS

We could improve the previous approach by using all the
information in the rainfall v. profit curves rather than
just selected points.

Probably the easiest way to do this is to use a least-squares
method to find the equations of the rainfall v. profit curves.
The following shows the results of such an approach,
where the Gala data have been fitted with

$$p = 25.91e^{-0.188\ r}$$

and the Barbecue data with

$$p = 7.789 - 0.5957\ r + 0.01300\ r^2,$$

using p = profit (K£) and r = rainfall (mm).

(These representations have been chosen to ensure that the
graph of p(r) looks sensible even outside the range of
interest of r.)

This extra information is easily added into the previous
program, and the new program with output are shown in Figures
13.6 (a) and (b) respectively.

As might be expected, the results are still very similar to
those in the previous section. In fact, the accuracy of the
method is being limited by the coarseness of the histograms
supplied.

```
5     DIM L(23)
10    FOR J = O TO 23
12    L(J) = O
14    NEXT J
20    SEED = RND ( - 1)
22    DEF FN GP(R)  =  25.91 * EXP ( - O.188 * R)
24    DEF FN BP(R)= 7.789 - O.5957 * R + O.O13 * R * R
30    INPUT "NUMBER OF REPLICATIONS?" ;NMAX
40    FOR N = 1 TO NMAX
50    G = RND (1)
60    IF G < O.32 THEN GP = FN GP(2.5): GOTO 110
70    IF G < O.72 THEN GP = FN GP(7.5): GOTO 110
80    IF G < O.90 THEN GP = FN GP (12.5): GOTO 110
90    IF G < O.98 THEN GP = GN GP (17.5): GOTO 110
100   GP = FN GP (22.5)
110   B = RND (1)
120   IF B < O.22 THEN BP = FN BP(2.5): GOTO 180
130   IF B < O.64 THEN BP = FN BP(7.5): GOTO 180
140   IF B < O.84 THEN BP = FN BP(12.5): GOTO 180
150   IF B < O.94 THEN BP = FN BP(17.5): GOTO 180
160   IF B < O.98 THEN BP = FN BP(22.5): GOTO 180
170   BP = FN BP (27.5)
180   PROFIT = GP + BP
200   FOR J = O TO 23
210   IF J < PROFIT THEN L(J) = L(J) + 1
220   NEXT J
230   NEXT N
240   HGR
250   HCOLOR= 2
260   HPLOT O,O TO 230,O TO 230,159 TO O,159 TO O,O
270   FOR J = O TO 23
280   L(J) = L(J) / NMAX
290   X = 10 * J
300   Y = 159 * (1 - L(J))
310   HPLOT TO X,Y
320   NEXT J
330   END
```

Figure 13.6(a)

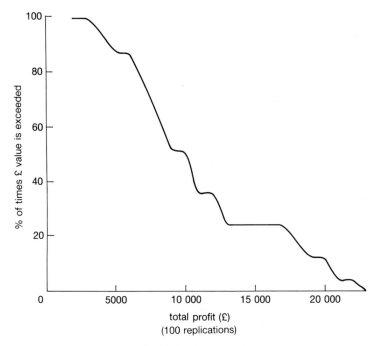

Figure 13.6(b)   100 replications

13.6   PROBABILITY THEORY

The final approach above still retained the histograms
(i.e. discrete probability density functions) of the
question. Clearly, if more data were available, it would
be sensible to use a continuous curve rather than a series
of many discrete steps.

To illustrate the essential ideas, but to avoid losing sight
of our goal in the details of hypergeometric distributions
and the like, we here fit the histograms given in the
question with a negative exponential distribution. This is
certainly not statistically correct, but should help to
illustrate the method.

The negative exponential distribution has probability
density function $f(t) = \lambda e^{-\lambda t}$, with

$$\text{mean} \quad E(t) \quad = \quad \int_{0}^{\infty} t \; f(t) \; dt \quad = \quad {}^{1}\!/_{\lambda} \; ,$$

variance $E(t^2) - E^2(t) = 1/\lambda^2$,

and   standard deviation $1/\lambda$

We here choose to fit our data using the mean (although appreciating that mean and standard deviation are not equal in fact), and obtain the following.

Gala: $\lambda = 0.127$

Barbecue: $\lambda = 0.106$

Graphs of these distributions are shown in Figure 13.7, where we have also displayed the histograms in order to emphasise the very rough nature of the approximation.

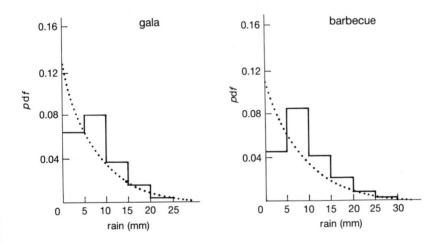

Figure 13.7

Knowing the profit curve $p(r)$ and the pdf $f(r)$ it is now simple to write down an expression for the expected profit

$$E(p) = \int_0^\infty p(r)\, f(r)\, dr.$$

In principle it is then straightforward to integrate numerically to obtain a graph similar to the previous ones. This is a very laborious task, however, and we are better - once again - to simulate.

Our problem, when simulating with the continuous pdf, is to generate a random rainfall with the correct distribution. This is a standard problem, and is solved by a simple trick.

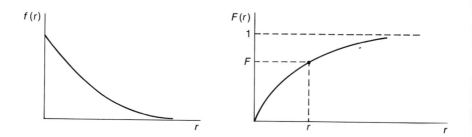

Figure 13.8

The plots in Figure 13.8 show the pdf f(r) and the cdf F(r)
- which, of course, is very easy to evaluate in our
demonstration example. We now generate a random number F
(uniform on the range $[0,1]$) and evaluate r so that F = F(r).
This value of r is the required random rainfall, having a
distribution f(r).

In our example we have probability density function

$$f(r) = \lambda\, e^{-\lambda r}$$

so that the cumulative distribution function is

$$F(r) = 1 - e^{-\lambda r}$$

and

$$r = -\ln(1 - F) / \lambda.$$

The simulation is now straightforward. For both the gala
and the barbecue we generate a random number as above, and
feed this into the appropriate profit formula p(r) to
obtain the profit. We add the two profits together to give
the total profit and plot the graph. The program
to do this together with sample output are shown in Figures
13.9 (a) and (b) respectively. The results are seen to be
similar to the previous ones, but the accuracy is now dependent
on how well we can fit the data with a continuous pdf (or cdf)
rather than on anything else.

We also emphasise that there is nothing special about the
negative exponential distribution used above - except its
simplicity. Any curve at all could be used to fit the data
(not just classical probability distributions) but care must

be taken to normalise it so that it has the correct probability
properties.

```
5     DIM L(27)
10    FOR J = O TO 27
12    L(J) = O
14    NEXT J
20    SEED = RND ( - 1)
22    DEF FN GP(R) = 25.91 * EXP (- O.188 * R)
24    DEF FN BP(R) = 7.789 - O.5957 * R + O.O13 * R * R
30    INPUT "NUMBER OF REPLICATIONS ? ";NMAX
40    FOR N = 1 TO NMAX
50    LAMDA = O.127
60    DEF FN G(T) = - LOG (1 - T) / LAMDA
70    MU = O.106
80    DEF FN B(T) = - LOG (1 - T) / MU
90    T = RND (1)
100   R = FN G(T)
110   GP = FN GP(R)
120   R = FN B(T)
130   BP = FN BP(R)
180   PROFIT = GP + BP
200   FOR J = O TO 23
210   IF J < PROFIT THEN L(J) = L(J) + 1
220   NEXT J
230   NEXT N
240   HGR
242   PRINT "% TIMES AMOUNT EXCEEDED"
244   PRINT "XMIN=O,XMAX=27OOO,YMIN=O,YMAX=1OO"
250   HCOLOR= 2
260   HPLOT O,O TO 270,O TO 270,159 TO O,159 TO O,O
270   FOR J = O TO 27
280   L(J) = L(J) / NMAX
290   X = 10 * J
300   Y = 159 * (1 - L(J))
310   HPLOT TO X,Y
320   NEXT J .
330   END
```

Figure 13.9(a)

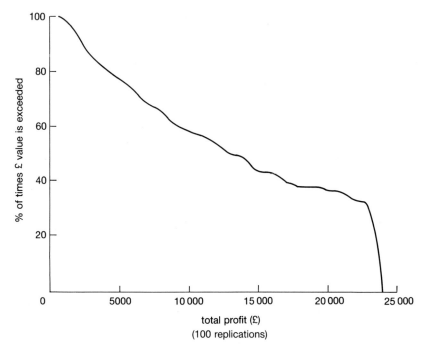

Figure 13.9(b)   100 replications

13.7   FINAL COMMENT TO LECTURER

In using this example with undergraduates, it has not been
found necessary that the students have previously studied
probability theory. The tabular method of solution is
available to any numerate student prepared to think about
the problem for a while, and our experience is that even
students with no knowledge of simulation will discover it
for themselves given the right sort of environment.

To aid this process of discovery, which is a highly
motivating experience for the student, we encourage group
work (3 seems ideal) and try to interfere as little as
possible. Our main contact with each group comes when a
question is asked: if this question is for further information
we supply it, otherwise we usually counter with a question
of our own.

The example above would usually be covered in two such 1
hour workshop sessions, and the groups asked to write the
Treasurer's report to the Sports and Social Club committee
over the next week. This would form a typical coursework
in a 100% continuously assessed modelling course.

14

Indian population projectories

IAN HUNTLEY and GRAHAM RAGGETT
Sheffield City Polytechnic

14.1 STATEMENT OF THE PROBLEM

In 1981 the Indian National Institute for Health and Family
Welfare, an Indian Government Department, declared the
following aims for limiting its population to the end of the
century.

(i)   Reduce the yearly birth rate from about 36 per
        thousand in 1981 to 21 per thousand in 2000. This
        is to be achieved by expenditure on birth control
        techniques comprising advertising of all forms and
        the extensive manufacture of contraceptives.

(ii)   Reduce the yearly death rate from about 14 per
        thousand in 1981 to 9 per thousand in 2000, achievable
        by more effective medical care.

(iii)   Limit the population in 2000 to one thousand
        million from its 1981 level of 684 million.

To what extent do you consider that the above aims are
compatible?

The problem statement is formulated so as to be given out to
small working groups with no initial help. One would
ultimately expect most students to use a differential or
difference equation approach. Students with less knowledge
than this may go a long way using graphs.

Our experience indicates that most students will opt for a
differential equation model (if only because difference
equations are omitted from many courses!), and so we here
concentrate on this approach.

Initially, various differential equation models are discussed, starting with a very simple model and introducing extra complications in order to cope with the various shortfalls of each model. At each stage an analytic solution is given. Then various computer-generated solutions to the models met so far are discussed. To illustrate the different approaches available, some of these use standard computer packages (as available in most universities and polytechnics) and others use programs in BASIC written for the BBC micro.

Finally, difference equation models are discussed, and the minor changes to the previous computer programs are noted.

14.2 A POSSIBLE BASIC DIFFERENTIAL EQUATION MODEL

We define the following necessary variables and conditions.

Time t, measured in years, over the period 1981 - 2000. Taking 1981 as our time origin t = 0, then t is defined on [0, 19]

Time dependent yearly birth rate $b(t)$ with $b(0) = 0.036$ and $b(19) = 0.021$ to satisfy (i).

Time dependent yearly death rate $d(t)$ with $d(0) = 0.014$ and $d(19) = 0.009$ to satisfy (ii).

Time dependent population $p(t)$ with $p(0) = 6.84 \times 10^8$ and $p(19) \leqslant 10^9$ to satisfy (iii).

In a small interval of time δt let the population increase from $p(t)$ to $p(t+\delta t)$, i.e. increase in population over $[t, t+\delta t]$ is $p(t+\delta t)-p(t)$.

This is brought on by an increase due to births over this time of approximately $b(t)p(t)\delta t$ and a corresponding decrease due to deaths of approximately $d(t)p(t)\delta t$, i.e.

$$p(t+\delta t)-p(t) = [b(t)-d(t)]p(t)\delta t,$$

i.e.   (1)

$$\frac{p(t+\delta t)-p(t)}{\delta t} = [b(t)-d(t)]p(t).$$

Although populations do indeed change by discrete integer amounts in practice, the vastness of the population makes it sensibly legitimate to take the limit as $\delta t \to 0$ in (1), giving the differential equation

$$\frac{dp}{dt} = [b(t) - d(t)]p(t). \tag{2}$$

14.3 CONSTANT BIRTH AND DEATH RATES

The problem, as stated, clearly does not assume either a
constant birth rate or a constant death rate. However, this
over-simplification is easy to consider and, furthermore, does
lead to extreme situations which give valuable insight into the
likely compatibility of the stated aims.

With constant yearly birth and death rates of B and D,
respectively, (2) becomes

$$\frac{dp}{dt} = [B-D]p(t) \tag{3}$$

and separation of variables gives

$$\int \frac{dp}{p} = \int [B-D]dt. \tag{4}$$

Integration of (4) and imposition of the initial condition

$$p(o) = 6.84 \times 10^{8}$$

yields the Malthusian type growth law

$$p(t) = 6.84 \times 10^{8} \exp[(B-D)t]. \tag{5}$$

Four extreme special choices of B and D are appropriate for the
problem, as follows.

Case 1

$$B = 0.036; \quad D = 0.014$$

This implies that the government merely 'stand-still' allowing
the current birth and death rates to go unchecked. Stand-still
in this context does not necessarily mean doing nothing, or
even continuing with present policies, as to do so could well
exacerbate the situation still further.

Substitution of these values of B and D into (5) gives

$$p(19) = 1.039 \times 10^{9}$$

as the projected population figure in 2000. This clearly violates condition (iii), even if only relatively marginally.

Case 2

$$B = 0.036; \ D = 0.009$$

In this situation the government have a stand-still policy in respect of birth rates, but persuade the developed countries immediately to input extensive medical care facilities so that the death rate is reduced and maintained at its ideal projected final figure over the whole period. This could nearly be achieved in principle, one would suspect.

These B and D values give , using (5),

$$p(19) = 1.142 \times 10^{9}$$

which clearly produces a larger projected figure than Case 1 due to the net increase in birth rate brought on by the reduced death rate. Such a solution would no doubt be quite popular for the people in the short term but hardly viable in the long term. One is left to wonder from a political standpoint if underdeveloped countries always willingly accept medical aid!

Case 3

$$B = 0.021; \ D = 0.014$$

This is totally the other extreme from Case 2, in which the government put massive funds into reducing the birth rate immediately to its ideal projected final figure while having a stand-still policy in respect of the death rate.

These B and D values give, using the same formula,

$$p(19) = 7.813 \times 10^{8}$$

which give, hardly surprisingly, a population figure well below that projected due to the effective minimisation of the net birth rate using the available figures.

This solution is clearly infeasible as the population would take a considerable time to be educated in the use of birth control techniques, (much longer than for effective medical care one would think), so that some delay would ensue before birth rate levels were substantially reduced. Even if implementable, one would imagine such a policy, with little or no regard for health care, being most unpopular.

Case 4

$$B = 0.021; \quad D = 0.009$$

This is the ideal situation in which both the birth and death
rates are immediately assumed to take on their ideal projected
values and then stay there for the whole period.

In this case (5) gives

$$p(19) = 8.592 \times 10^{8}$$

clearly within the required final population bound.

For the reasons already expounded, such a solution, though
acceptable, would not be practically possible.

General Comments

While the four cases above represent extremes in idealised
policies, they do at least indicate the possible projected
range in final population estimates. In particular, effectively
doing nothing as in Case 1 marginally violates condition (iii),
whereas achieving final birth and death rates immediately, as
in Case 4, predicts a significant success.

As the proposed situation lies somewhere between these two extremes,
the order of the final projected population figure seems
realistic. Furthermore, the above figures lead one to believe
that condition (iii) will be satisfied, but more work is
required to verify this related to variable birth and death
rates.

14.4 VARIABLE BIRTH AND DEATH RATES

Time dependent representatives for $b(t)$ and $d(t)$ are now
required to simulate the changing birth and death rates over
the period concerned. Since both rates are required to
decrease as time increases, we shall look for monotonic
decreasing functions to approximate these.

Linear Representations

The simplest possible approximations for $b(t)$ and $d(t)$ may be
taken as linear functions of time satisfying the desired
initial and final conditions. These give the relations

$$b(t) = 0.036 - \frac{0.015}{19} t, \quad d(t) = 0.014 - \frac{0.005}{19} t, \qquad (6)$$

as exhibited in Figure 14.1(a): substitution of (6) into (2) then yields

$$\frac{dp}{dt} = [\, 0.022 - \frac{0.01}{19}\, t]\, p \tag{7}$$

which separates to

$$\int \frac{dp}{p} = \int [\, 0.022 - \frac{0.01}{19}\, t]\, dt$$

and integrates to yield the solution.

$$p(t) = 6.84 \times 10^{8} \exp[\, 0.022t - \frac{0.01}{38}\, t^{2}] \tag{8}$$

which is shown in Figure 14.1(b).

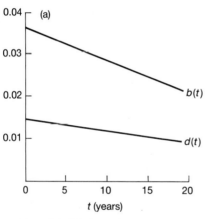

Fig. 14.1(a)

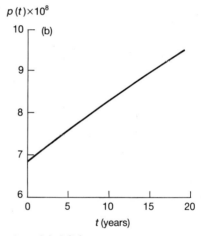

Fig. 14.1(b)

Evaluation of (8) at t = 19 gives

$$p(19) = 9.45 \times 10^{8}, \tag{9}$$

so that the three aims are indeed compatible under linear model assumptions over the applicable time span.
It should be realised that linear representations of the birth and death rates are hardly appropriate, as their very nature undermines the far more likely relatively slow reduction in these rates initially, when the population needs time to adjust to new ideas.

Quadratic Representations

To fit quadratic expressions for $b(t)$ and $d(t)$ over the range
considered requires the imposition of three conditions to
evaluate the appropriate constants. As for the linear case,
two conditions for each variable are immediately apparent
from the given information. The third condition may be
imposed in a variety of ways. However, to overcome the
main objection to the linear representations, the extra
condition is here imposed initially to retard any possible
rapid change in birth and death rates. Thus one imposes
that the initial rates of change of $b(t)$ and $d(t)$ are both
zero.

For example, $b(t)$ may be represented as

$$b(t) = a_0 + a_1 t + a_2 t^2 \tag{10}$$

and $b(0) = 0.036$ gives $a_0 = 0.036$.

Differentiation of (10) yields

$$\frac{db}{dt} = a_1 + 2 a_2 t$$

and imposition of the adjusting condition $\left.\dfrac{db}{dt}\right|_{t=0} = 0$ $\tag{11}$

gives $a_1 = 0$.

Finally, the condition $b(19) = 0.021$ gives $a_2 = \dfrac{-0.015}{19^2}$,

yielding for $b(t)$:

$$b(t) = 0.036 - \frac{0.015}{19^2} t^2. \tag{12}$$

Similar arguments for $d(t)$ give the quadratic expression

$$d(t) = 0.014 - \frac{0.005}{19^2} t^2, \tag{13}$$

and expressions for both $b(t)$ and $d(t)$ are illustrated in
Figure 14.2(a). Substitution of (12) and (13) into (2) and
separating the variables gives

$$\int \frac{dp}{p} = \int \left[0.022 - \frac{0.01}{19^2} t^2\right] dt,$$

which integrates to give the solution

$$p(t) = 6.84 \times 10^8 \exp\left[0.022\,t - \frac{0.01}{3(19)^2}\,t^3\right]$$ (14)

exhibited in Figure 14.2(b)

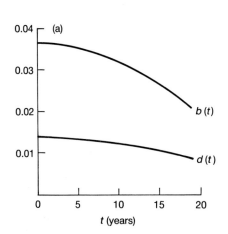
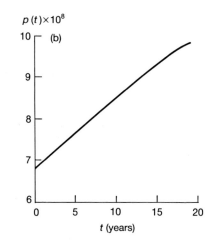

Fig. 14.2(a)   Fig. 14.2(b)

Substitution of t = 19 into (14) gives

$$p(19) = 9.75 \times 10^8,$$ (15)

which still predicts the three aims as compatible.   The
significant increase in the final population projections,
as given by (15) as compared with (9), is attributable to
the fact that the net birth rate function b(t) - d(t)
at any point $t \in (0,19)$ is always larger for the quadratic
representations than it is for the linear representations.

Exponential Representations

More meaningful representations for b(t) and d(t) over the
period concerned may be taken in the form

$$b(t) = \alpha_1 - \beta_1\,e^{\gamma_1 t}, \quad d(t) = \alpha_2 - \beta_2\,e^{\gamma_2 t}$$ (16)

with α_1, β_1, γ_1, α_2, β_2, γ_2 > 0. Such representations allow

for relatively slow initial changes in b(t) and d(t) (when the population is being educated) followed by later more major reductions once government policies take off.

Imposition of the birth rate conditions b(0) = 0.036, b(19) = 0.021 enables α_1 and β_1 to be eliminated yielding the birth rate function

$$b(t) = 0.036 - 0.015 \left[\frac{e^{-\gamma_1 t} - 1}{e^{19\gamma_1} - 1} \right], \tag{17}$$

where γ_1 > 0 is a free parameter.

Similarly, the condition $\alpha(0)$ = 0.014, $\alpha(19)$ = 0.009 yields the death rate function

$$d(t) = 0.014 - 0.005 \left[\frac{e^{-\gamma_2 t} - 1}{e^{19\gamma_2} - 1} \right] \tag{18}$$

where γ_2 > 0 is also a free parameter.

Clearly the choice of the parameters γ_1 and γ_2 reflects the impetus by the government for affecting birth and death rates. If, for example, $\gamma_1 > \gamma_2$ then for t ε (0,19) we have that

$$0 < \frac{e^{\gamma_1 t} - 1}{e^{19\gamma_1} - 1} < \frac{e^{\gamma_2 t} - 1}{e^{19\gamma_2} - 1} \tag{19}$$

due to the fact that the function $f(\gamma) = \frac{e^{\gamma t} - 1}{e^{19\gamma} - 1}$ clearly

decreases as γ increases for t ε (0,19). Thus, in real terms, $\gamma_1 > \gamma_2$ implies a relatively slower change in birth rate compared with death rate. The analogous condition $\gamma_2 > \gamma_1$ implies a relatively slower change in death rate compared with birth rate.

In order to maintain a relative equilibrium between changes in
birth rate and death rate effected by, respectively, birth
control techniques and medical care, it seems reasonable to
take $\gamma_1 = \gamma_2 = \gamma$ so that this desired equilibrium is applied
throughout the total period.

The above simplification still leads to a one degree of
freedom choice in the net birth rate function

$$b(t) - d(t) = 0.022 - 0.01 \left[\frac{e^{\gamma t} - 1}{e^{19\gamma} - 1} \right] . \tag{20}$$

Substitution of (20) into (2) and separating the variables
gives

$$\int \frac{dp}{p} = \int \left[0.022 - 0.01 \left| \frac{e^{\gamma t} - 1}{e^{19\gamma} - 1} \right| \right] dt, \tag{21}$$

which integrates to give the solution

$$p(t) = 6.84 \times 90^8 \exp \left[0.022\, t - 0.01\, \frac{(e^{\gamma t} - \gamma t - 1)}{\gamma (e^{19\gamma} - 1)} \right] . \tag{22}$$

Thus different choices of γ yield a family of possible
population functions leading to a final population projection
of

$$p(19) = 6.84 \times 10^8 \exp \left[0.418 - 0.01\, \frac{(e^{19\gamma} - 19\gamma - 1)}{\gamma (e^{19\gamma} - 1)} \right], \tag{23}$$

and, as γ increases, $p(19)$ increases.

Hence it may be seen that a critical choice γ_{MAX} of γ exists
such that

$$0 < \gamma \leqslant \gamma_{MAX} \tag{24}$$

give rise to the final required projected population condition
$p(19) \leqslant 10^9$. Substitution of a range of values into (23)
gives a value for γ_{MAX} of 0.251 to three decimal place accuracy.

Figure 14.3(a) shows the critical birth and death rate functions (17) and (18) with $\gamma_1 = \gamma_2 = 0.251$ produced with the given estimate for γ_{MAX}. The corresponding population function (22) with this same value of γ is given in Figure 14.3(b). Under the assumption of this model, families of p(t) satisfying (24) would lie under this graph, predicting success for the government aims.

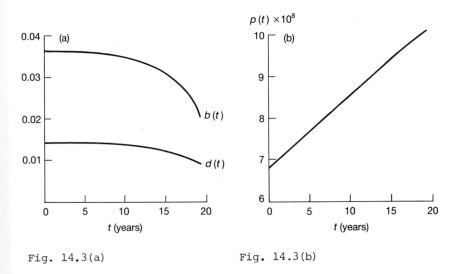

Fig. 14.3(a)   Fig. 14.3(b)

14.5   WHY BOTHER WITH COMPUTER-GENERATED SOLUTIONS?

We have seen above many equations of the form

$$\frac{dp}{dt} = br - dr$$

where the birth rate (br) and death rate (dr) have taken various forms. In each case we were able to solve the differential equation analytically to obtain the population (p) as a function of time (t).

The ability to solve the differential equation, however, was rather more luck than judgement - it is very easy indeed to write down equations which cannot be solved analytically. These are often nonlinear equations - ones involving terms like p^2 or a time delay $(t - \tau)$ - and, to obtain solutions, we have to resort to graphical methods, approximate methods, or computer methods. Here we examine the various ways of using a computer to generate solutions to the equations met earlier. As well as providing an interesting comparison of

the available techniques, this also allows the case study
to be used by a wider cross section of people - for instance,
those with little training in mathematics but with access to
certain computer packages.

In Section 14.6 we apply the package DYNAMO to the equations
above. This package is available on most mainframe computers
and on some micros, and was originally developed at MIT as
part of the Limits to Growth Study of the world ecosystem.

In Section 14.7 we utilise the package ISIS, written at
Salford University and especially designed to take full
advantage of the interactive graphics facilities available
on most mainframe computers.

In Section 14.8, by way of contrast, we develop a very
simple program written in BASIC for the BBC micro. This
illustrates that, with very little skill in programming,
large computer packages are not always essential - they
merely speed up the process.

14.6   USING DYNAMO TO SOLVE $\dfrac{dp}{dt} = br - dr$

Associated with DYNAMO is the notation of system dynamics
diagrams. Using the notation

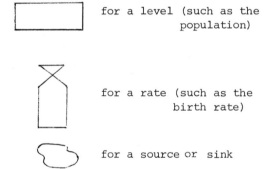

for a level (such as the
population)

for a rate (such as the
birth rate)

for a source or sink

gives the following system dynamics diagram for our simple
population models:

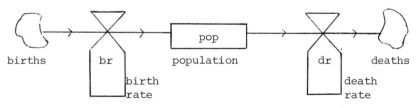

This is now very easily translated into a DYNAMO program.
For instance, in the case of constant birth and death rates,
where

br = b * pop

dr = d * pop ,

we have the following program.

```
*
NOTE INDIAN POPULATION PROJECTIONS
NOTE
NOTE CONSTANT BIRTH AND DEATH RATES
NOTE
L   POP=POP+DT*(BR-DR)
N   POP=684E6
R   BR=B*POP
C   B=0.036
R   DR=D*POP
C   D=0.014
N   TIME=1981
PRINT POP
PLOT POP=P(6E8,1OE8)
SPEC DT=0.1/LENGTH=2000/PRTPER=1/PLTPER=1
```

This gives the output shown in Figure 14.4(a), in agreement
with the results quoted above.

It is clear that the DYNAMO program is really a difference
equation formulation of the problem, rather than a differential
equation one:

$$p(t + dt) = p(t) + dt * \left[br(t) - dr(t) \right].$$

However, DYNAMO has a tremendous advantage over some other
packages, in that a minor change in the program converts
from differential equation to difference equation. As
written, the programme will run as a differential equation –
that is, with the step size DT chosen to be very small and
input to a Runge-Kutta integration routine. However, with
the addition of the statement

SPEC ITYPE = 2 /DT = 1

the programme runs as a difference equation with step size 1
year. This gives DYNAMO great versatility.

TIME E 00	POP E 06
1981.0	684.0
1982.0	699.2
1983.0	714.7
1984.0	730.6
1985.0	746.8
1986.0	763.4
1987.0	780.4
1988.0	797.7
1989.0	815.5
1990.0	833.6
1991.0	852.1
1992.0	871.0
1993.0	890.4
1994.0	910.2
1995.0	930.4
1996.0	951.1
1997.0	972.2
1998.0	993.8
1999.0	1015.9
2000.0	1038.5

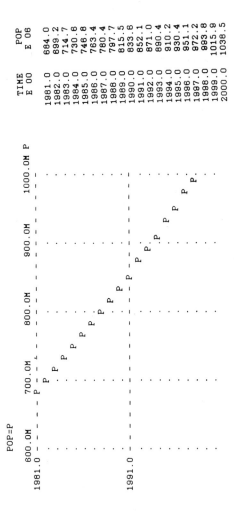

Shown in Figures 14.4(b) - 14.4(d) are the results for the
other equations considered earlier. Obviously the computer
results are the same as the (exact) analytic ones, but notice
how easy it would be to get DYNAMO to solve <u>any</u> equation -
even nonlinear ones.

```
NOTE    Indian population projections
NOTE
NOTE    Linear birth and death rates
NOTE
L   POP=POP+DT*(BR-DR)
N   POP=684E6
R   BR=B*POP
A   B=0.036-0.015*T/19
R   DR=D*POP
A   D=0.014-0.005*T/19
N   TIME=1981
A   T=TIME-1981
PRINT POP
PLOT POP=P(6E8,10E8)
SPEC DT=0.1/LENGTH=2000/PRTPER=1/PLTPER=1
```

| TIME | POP |
E 00	E 06
1981.0	684.00
1982.0	699.03
1983.0	714.02
1984.0	728.95
1985.0	743.80
1986.0	758.55
1987.0	773.19
1988.0	787.69
1989.0	802.05
1990.0	816.24
1991.0	830.25
1992.0	844.05
1993.0	857.63
1994.0	870.97
1995.0	884.06
1996.0	896.87
1997.0	909.39
1998.0	921.59
1999.0	933.47
2000.0	945.01

Fig. 14.4(b)

```
NOTE    Indian population projections
NOTE
NOTE    Quadratic birth and death rates
NOTE
L    POP=POP+DT*(BR-DR)
N    POP=684E6
R    BR=B*POP
A    B=0.036-0.015*(T/19)*(T/19)
R    DR=D*POP
A    D=0.014-0.005*(T/19)*(T/19)
N    TIME=1981
A    T=TIME-1981
PRINT POP
PLOT POP=P(6E8,10E8)
SPEC DT=0.1/LENGTH=2000/PRTPER=1/PLTPER=1
```

TIME E 00	POP E 06
1981.0	684.00
1982.0	699.19
1983.0	714.68
1984.0	730.44
1985.0	746.42
1986.0	762.59
1987.0	778.89
1988.0	795.28
1989.0	811.71
1990.0	828.10
1991.0	844.42
1992.0	860.57
1993.0	876.51
1994.0	892.16
1995.0	907.43
1996.0	922.25
1997.0	936.54
1998.0	950.22
1999.0	963.19
2000.0	975.37

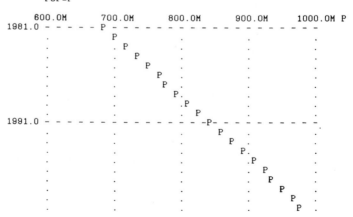

Fig. 14.4(c)

```
NOTE   Indian population projections
NOTE
NOTE   Exponential birth and death rates
NOTE
L   POP=POP+DT*(BR-DR)
N   POP=684E6
R   BR=B*POP
A   B=0.036-0.015*(EXP(GAMMA*T)-1)/(EXP(19*GAMMA)-1)
R   DR=D*POP
A   D=0.014-0.005*(EXP(GAMMA*T)-1)/(EXP(19*GAMMA)-1)
N   TIME=1981
A   T=TIME-1981
C   GAMMA=0.251
PRINT POP
PLOT POP=P(6E8,10E8)
SPEC DT=0.1/LENGTH=2000/PRTPER=1/PLTPER=1
```

TIME	POP
E 00	E 06
1981.0	684.0
1982.0	699.2
1983.0	714.7
1984.0	730.5
1985.0	746.7
1986.0	763.1
1987.0	779.9
1988.0	796.9
1989.0	814.3
1990.0	831.8
1991.0	849.6
1992.0	867.5
1993.0	885.5
1994.0	903.5
1995.0	921.4
1996.0	938.9
1997.0	955.9
1998.0	972.0
1999.0	986.9
2000.0	1000.1

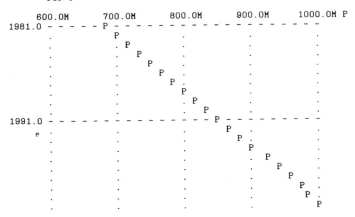

Fig. 14.4(d)

14.7   USING ISIS TO SOLVE $\frac{dp}{dt}$ = br - dr

In a similar way to DYNAMO, the package ISIS can solve both
differential and difference equations. However, in this
case, the equation written into the program looks more like
a differential equation.

For instance, in the case of linear birth and death rates
where,

    br = (b - c * tt) * pop

    dr = (d - e * tt) * pop

with

    tt = t - 1981,

we have the following program

```
:INDIAN POPULATION PROJECTIONS
:
:LINEAR BIRTH AND DEATH RATES
:
CONSTANT CINT=1,TFIN=2000
SIM
INITIAL
POP=684E6
T=1981
DYNAMIC
POP'=BR-DR
BR=(0.036-0.015*TT/19)*POP
DR=(0.014-0.005*TT/19)*POP
TT=T-1981
OUTPUT
PREPARE T,POP
```

This gives the output shown in Figure 14.5(b), where the
improved graphics are immediately evident.

Shown in Figures 14.5(a), 14.5(c), 14.5(d) are the results
for the other equations considered earlier.   Again, the ease
with which such a package can give tabular and graphical
output is clear.

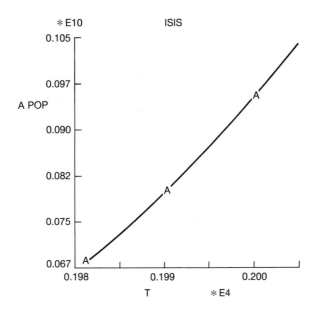

Figure 14.5(a)

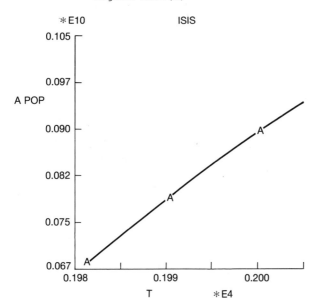

Figure 14.5(b)

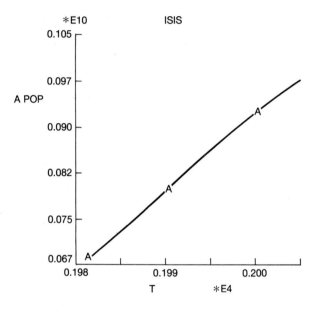

Figure 14.5(c)

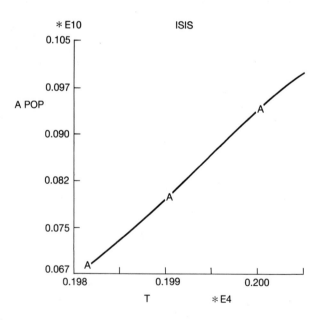

Figure 14.5(d)

14.8   USING BASIC TO SOLVE $\frac{dp}{dt} = br - dr$

The presentation above may have given the impression that
only those with access to expensive computer packages on micros or
mainframes can obtain generated solutions. This is certainly
not the case, and the programme in Figure 14.6 - written
for a BBC micro - illustrates one very simple form of
solution.

This program uses the Euler method

$$\text{pop}(t + \text{timestep}) = \text{pop}(t) + \text{timestep} * \left[br(t) - dr(t) \right]$$

with the timestep equal to a small constant value, as seen
in the procedure PROCEULER at line 960. The rest of the
program merely inputs the correct equations for the four
options (constant, linear, quadratic or exponential rates)
and controls the output.

A sample output from this program is shown in Figure 14.7,
where the results are seen to be very similar to those earlier.
With a smaller value of the parameter 'timestep', the answers
would be even closer to the ones above - but the program
would take rather longer to run.

Although not necessary with the very simple differential
equations considered here, more complicated equations would
require a more sophisticated procedure than the Euler method
used above. Then something like a 4th order Runge-Kutta
integration routine (with automatic stepsize) would be
used - as in both the DYNAMO and ISIS packages.

```
10 :REM INDIAN POPULATION PROJECTIONS
20 MODE4:VDU19 128,4,0,0
30 PRINTTAB(5,4)"INDIAN POPULATION PROJECTIONS"
40 PRINTTAB(2,10)"This program solves the"'" differential equation"
50 PRINTTAB(2,13)"d/dt(pop) = (b - d) * pop"
60 PRINTTAB(2,15)"in various situations"
70 REM EQNS AND DESCRIPTIONS ARE IN PROCFNn AND IN PROCNAMEn
80 PROCMORE
90 PRINTTAB(2,4)"You may choose between the following"
100 PRINTTAB(4,8)"1 Constant birth and death rates"
110 PRINTTAB(4,10)"2 Linear birth and death rates"
120 PRINTTAB(4,12)"3 Quadratic birth and death rates"
130 PRINTTAB(4,14)"4 Exponential birth and death rates"
140 PRINTTAB(2,20)"What NUMBER do you want?";
150 KEY=GET
160 PROCINT
170 IF KEY=ASC("1") THEN PROCNAME1
180 IF KEY=ASC("2") THEN PROCNAME2
190 IF KEY=ASC("3") THEN PROCNAME3
200 IF KEY=ASC("4") THEN PROCNAME4
210 ON ERROR CLS:GOTO 90
220 CLS
230 PROCINFO
240 PROCMORE
250 CLS
260 PRINTTAB(5,2)"YEAR(t)"TAB(12)"POPULATION(pop)":PRINT
270 PRINT T;TAB(20)POP
280 REPEAT PROCEULER
290 PRINT T;TAB(20)POP
300 IF T-INT(T)=0 THEN PRINT T;TAB(20)POP
310 PRINT:PRINT
320 UNTIL T>=2000
330 FINALPOP=INT(POP/1E8+0.5)
340 PRINT FINALPOP" million people"
350 END
360 DEF PROCINFO
370 PRINTTAB(2)"So our estimate of the Indian"'" population in the year 2000,
    using "NAME$" rates, is"
380 PRINTTAB(4,7)"b = "B$
390 PRINTTAB(4,9)"d = "D$
400 PRINTTAB(2,16)"We simulate from 1981 to 2000"
410 ENDPROC
420 DEF PROCMORE
430 PRINTTAB(2,28)"Press SPACE to continue"
440 A$=GET$:IF NOT(A$=" ")THEN 430
450 CLS
460 ENDPROC
470 DEF PROCINIT
480 POP=684E6
490 T=1981
500 TIMESTEP=0.25
510 ENDPROC

540 B$="0.036"
550 D$="0.014"
560 PROCFN1
570 ENDPROC
580 DEF PROCFN1
590 B=0.036
600 D=0.014
610 DERIV=(B-D)*POP
620 ENDPROC
630 DEF PROCNAME2
640 NAME$="linear"
650 B$="0.036-0.015*(t-1981)/19"
660 D$="0.014-0.005*(t-1981)/19"
670 PROCFN2
680 ENDPROC
690 DEF PROCFN2
700 B=0.036-0.015*(T-1981)/19
710 D=0.014-0.005*(T-1981)/19
720 DERIV=(B-D)*POP
730 ENDPROC
740 DEF PROCNAME3
750 NAME$="quadratic"
760 B$="0.036-0.015*((t-1981)/19)^2"
770 D$="0.014-0.005*((t-1981)/19)^2"
780 PROCFN3
790 ENDPROC
800 DEF PROCFN3
810 B=0.036-0.015*((T-1981)/19)^2
820 D=0.014-0.005*((T-1981)/19)^2
830 DERIV=(B-D)*POP
840 ENDPROC
850 DEF PROCNAME4
860 NAME$="exponential"
870 B$="UGH"
880 D$="UGH"
890 PROCFN4
900 ENDPROC
910 DEF PROCFN4
920 B=0.036-0.015*EXP(0.251*(T-1981)-1)/EXP(0.251*19-1)
930 D=0.014-0.005*EXP(0.251*(T-1981)-1)/EXP(0.251*19-1)
940 DERIV=(B-D)*POP
950 ENDPROC
960 DEF PROCEULER
970 T=T+TIMESTEP
980 IF KEY=ASC("1") THEN PROCFN1
990 IF KEY=ASC("2") THEN PROCFN2
1000 IF KEY=ASC("3") THEN PROCFN3
1010 IF KEY=ASC("4") THEN PROCFN4
1020 POP=POP+TIMESTEP*DERIV
1030 ENDPROC
```

Figure 14.6

```
RUN
INDIAN POPULATION PROJECTIONS
This program solves the
   differential equation
d/dt(pop) = (b - d) * pop
in various situations
Press SPACE to continue


You may choose between the following
1 Constant birth and death rates
2 Linear birth and death rates
3 Quadratic birth and death rates
4 Exponential birth and death rates
What NUMBER do you want?


In this case we have
   linear birth and death rates
b = 0.036-0.015*(t-1981)/19
d = 0.014-0.005*(t-1981)/19
We simulate from 1981 to 2000
Press SPACE to continue
```

YEAR(t)	POPULATION(pop)
1981	684000000
1982	698943895
1983	713840478
1984	728672931
1985	743424183
1986	758076934
1987	772613697
1988	787016822
1989	801268537
1990	815350978
1991	829246230
1992	842936360
1993	856403458
1994	869629672
1995	882597251
1996	895288579
1997	907686219
1998	919772949
1999	931531805
2000	942946115

```
So our estimate of the Indian
population in the year 2000,
using linear rates, is
      943 million people
```

Fig. 14.7

14.9   CONCLUSIONS

So far we have discussed only the differential equation model

$$\frac{dp}{dt} = br - dr.$$

However, as was obvious when we illustrated the use of DYNAMO, computer programs cannot deal with differential equations – they convert them from a continous form to a discrete form before applying the integration routine. Thus the above differential equation is actually converted to

$$p(t + dt) = p(t) + dt * \left[br(t) - dr(t) \right]$$

before the computer can proceed. This last equation is really a difference equation – as can be seen by writing it in the equivalent form

$$x_{n+1} = x_n + \left[b_n - d_n \right].$$

It is now not very surprising that DYNAMO and ISIS can convert so easily from differential equation solution to difference equation solution – the only difference is that in the continuous case dt is small, whereas in the discrete case dt is large.

The question remains, however, as to which method is "correct": should we use (continuous) differential equations or (discrete) difference equations? As in so many similar cases, the answer is: it depends. When dealing with a population of Red Deer, with one well-defined mating season each year, clearly we should use difference equations with dt = 1. When dealing with a population of Blue Whales, who breed only once every two years, we should use difference equations with dt = 2. However, when dealing with the Indian population, it is far more sensible to use a differential equation model. This is why we have concentrated on differential equations above

15

Biological cell populations

JOHN USHER and IAN MACKENZIE
Robert Gordon's Institute

15.1 INTRODUCTION

Usher and Abercrombie (1981) presented two case studies
involving tumour growth and the response of cells to
irradiation. The intention of the present work is to extend
the study of tumour growth models to general biological cell
populations in order to increase the student's awareness of
some of the different possible types of model available. For
convenience we shall employ the classification of Table 15.1
for the different types of model.

The case studies presented here will concentrate on the
formulation stage of the modelling process. They are intended
to aid the teaching of what is often a very difficult phase of
the general modelling process. At the same time it is hoped
that the students will become aware of the differences and links
between such models. This should then enable them to exercise
an extended range of weapons when attempting to model more
complex situations.

Type of Model	Illustrative examples of where such a model might be employed
Discrete – employed where changes occur in "jumps"	Effect of radiation treatment on a tumour when applied for short periods of time but at regular intervals
Continuous – employed where changes are "smooth"	Effect of chemotherapy drugs on a tumour when introduced into a patient for a given duration of time
Stochastic – "probabilistic"	The different possible effects on tumour cells that might occur when subjected to irradiation
	e.g. i) some tumour cells might escape damage and continue to grow as if no irradiation had taken place
	ii) some tumour cells might continue to grow in size but without division
Deterministic – "non probabilistic"	e.g. i) Determination of the time taken for a tumour, whose mass is increasing at a known rate, to double in size
	ii) Determination of the time taken for the number of tumour cells to reach a certain figure when the cells are dividing into two over a known time interval

TABLE 15.1 Classification of models

15.1.1. Statement of the General Problem

Develop a model for a biological cell population where birth
and death processes coexist.

15.1.2 Notes to the Lecturer

(i)   One of the most important exercises in modelling a complex
      situation is to try to break down the problem into a
      series of simpler problems in order to understand some of
      the underlying mechanisms and principles involved. It is
      with this idea in mind that Case Studies 1 to 4 are
      presented as a series of tasks. Synthesis of the ideas
      involved in these case studies then permits the student to
      attempt Case Study 5.

(ii) If the complete set of case studies 1 - 5 were presented
      as a task to a student then it would probably have to be
      at final year degree level. However it is possible to
      view these case studies as an extended exercise within a
      three year undergraduate mathematical modelling course.
      Elements of the complete set could be used as building
      blocks in different years of such a course, as outlined in
      the study guide presented below.

15.1.3 Study Guide

YEAR 1   Case Study 1M (Modified form of Case Study 1)
            Case Study 3

YEAR 2   Case Study 1

YEAR 3   Complete set of Case Studies 1 - 5

The natural extension of the above study guide is that, on
completion of the Case Studies 1 - 5, the student could
proceed to a final years honours project applying the ideas
developed to build appropriate models for investigating, for
example, the problem of tumour growth and treatment by
radiotherapy.

15.2   CASE STUDY 1

Consider a cell population which has the following properties.

      P1: each cell has the same fixed life-time c seconds

      P2: at an initial time of observation the number of cells
          in the population is n_o and c seconds later one of
          the following sets of events occurs

E1: all cells die with no daughter cells being
produced

E2: all cells produce one daughter cell

E3: all cells produce two daughter cells

E4: each cell produces 0, 1 or 2 daughter cells.

A cell population possessing such properties is said to be
SYNCHRONOUS.

Develop models, either deterministic or stochastic, to predict
the cell number at a particular time in each of the set of
events E1 - E4 designated above. In particular, combine the
models so developed in the first three cases into one
corporate model.

Discuss connections between these deterministic and stochastic
models.

Explain under what circumstances the models could be used to
describe tumour growth.

15.3 A SOLUTION

The discrete nature of the processes involved suggests that we
develop discrete models for all four sets of events. The
certainty of the events E1 - E3 further suggests that
deterministic models would be realistic, whereas in the last
case probabilistic aspects warrant investigation of a
stochastic model.

Set of Events E1

Assume each cell of the given population produces no daughter
cells, i.e. the cell population dies after time c seconds.

Then $\quad n(t) = n_0 \qquad 0 < t < c$

$\qquad\qquad = 0 \qquad t > c$

where $n(t)$ denotes the number of cells at time
t seconds.

An alternative model, which probably gives a better indication
of how to model more complex situations arising in the
synchronous growth of cell populations, is now given.

It is simply

$$n_1 = 0$$

where n_1 denotes the number of cells in the first generation (i.e. all daughter cells of the original, zeroth generation, cell population).

Set of Events E2

If each cell of each generation produces one daughter cell at the end of its life-time of c seconds then the population size remains static i.e.

$$n_k = n_o$$

where n_k denotes the total number of cells in the kth generation ($k = 0, 1, 2, \ldots$).

Set of Events E3

If all cells produce two daughter cells at the end of their life-time of c seconds then

$$n_k = 2n_{k-1} \qquad k = 1, 2, \ldots$$

$$\therefore \; n_k = n_o \, 2^{t/c} \qquad \text{where} \qquad t = ck \, .$$

Clearly, t represents the total time from the first generation of cells. The above result can be written in the form

$$n(t) = n_o \, e^{\left(\frac{\ln 2}{c}\right) t} \qquad \text{where } t = ck \, .$$

Clearly both this model and the continuous model for exponential growth discussed in Case Study 1 of Usher and Abercrombie (1981) agree exactly at times $0, c, 2c, \ldots$.

The models hereto developed may now be incorporated into a single corporate model.

$$n_k = \lambda^k n_o \qquad k = 1, 2, \ldots \qquad (1)$$

where the parameter λ denotes the number of daughter cells synchronously produced by each cell in the population when it dies.

Set of Events E4

For the reasons mentioned previously we shall develop a
stochastic model for this case. In fact, the set of events
that may occur for this case is referred to as a Galton-Watson
branching process (see Eisen (1979), pp. 46-51).

Assume that each cell, independently of every other cell,
gives birth randomly to 0, 1 or 2 offspring (and then dies)
with probability p_0, p_1, p_2 respectively. (Remember

$p_0 + p_1 + p_2 = 1$).

Let z_k denote the number of descendents of a single cell in
the kth generation.

It is suggested, at this stage, that a tree diagram is
developed only up to the second generation. Such a tree
diagram is shown in Figure 15.1.

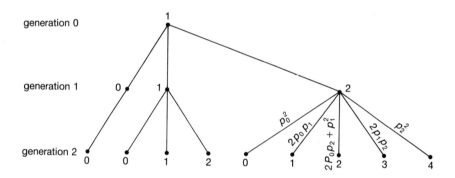

Figure 15.1 Tree diagram illustrating the number of
             daughter cells up to the second generation

The determination of the number of daughter cells in later
generations becomes more complex and the interested reader is
referred to Eisen (1979), Eisen and Eisen (1975) and Harris
(1963).

In order to compare the corporate deterministic model governed
by equation (1), which describes the sets of events E1 - E3,
with the stochastic model developed above, a measure must be
found for the size of the kth generation in the stochastic
model.

One such measure is the average or expected size of the kth generation.

By definition, $E[z_k] = \sum_{i=0}^{\infty} ip \ (z_k = i)$ and

the student should easily be able to verify

$$E[z_k] = \mu^k \qquad \text{for} \qquad k = 1, 2 \qquad\qquad (2)$$

where $\mu = p_1 + 2p_2$ (the expected size of the first generation).

The proof that result (2) is valid for larger values of k is more difficult (see Eisen and Eisen (1975)).

The student should now be able to deduce the result

$$N_k = n_o z_k \qquad k = 1, 2, \ldots$$

where N_k is the total number of cells in the kth generation,

and hence

$$E[N_k] = n_o \mu^k \qquad\qquad (3)$$

This result can now be compared with equation (1).

Thus the EXPECTED VALUE of the size of the kth generation predicted by the STOCHASTIC model agrees exactly with the prediction of the DETERMINISTIC model. However the stochastic model also provides a measure of the variation from this expected value, a measure which is unavailable if a deterministic model is employed.

The student should be able to use the result

$$VAR[N_k] = VAR[n_o z_k] = n_o^2 \ VAR[z_k]$$

in order to obtain the results

$$\text{VAR} [N_1] = n_o^2 \{ E [z_1^2] - \mu^2 \}$$

$$\text{VAR} [N_2] = n_o^2 \{ \mu (E [z_1^2] + 2p_2\mu) - \mu^4 \}$$

$$\text{where} \qquad E [z_1^2] = p_1 + 4p_2$$

$$E [z_1] = \mu = p_1 + 2p_2$$

Now let us address the problem as to the circumstances under which these models could be used to describe tumour growth (see Usher and Abercrombie (1981a) and (1981b) for background reading).

The stochastic model predicts that there is a positive probability of extinction of the population at the nth generation, (which would correspond to complete regression of tumour growth i.e. tumour death). The proof of ultimate extinction is a lengthy process, but it could be developed as a further case study (see discussion at the end of Case Study 5).

The stochastic model suggests the possibility of proportionally large random fluctuations in early generations whose effects may persist in later generations. Such behaviour is very rare (if non-existent!) in tumours. However if à large number of a particular type were observed the model could be employed to predict the average size of such tumours. This averaging not only reduces the effects of experimental errors but allows the possible use of deterministic models even when randomness is present.

15.4 CASE STUDY 1M

(This is a modified form of Case Study 1 and could be used as intimated in the suggested study guide earlier).

Consider a cell population which has the following properties.

> P1: each cell has the same fixed life-time c seconds

> P2: at an initial time of observation the number of cells in the population is n_o and c seconds later one of the following sets of events occurs

E1: all cells die with no daughter cells being
produced

E2: all cells produce one daughter cell

E3: all cells produce two daughter cells

Develop models to predict the cell number at a particular time
in each of the set of events E1 - E3 designated above.

Combine these models into a corporate model.

15.5 CASE STUDY 2

Develop a stochastic model for a biological cell population
where only deaths occur.

15.6 A SOLUTION

The death process may be either continuous or discrete, we do
not have enough information to decide which is appropriate.
However, let us proceed with building a model assuming a
continuous linear death process.

We shall make the following assumptions.

A1: During any time interval $(t, t + \Delta t)$ the probability
that a death occurs depends only on

a) the population at time t (the Markov property)

b) the length of the interval Δt.

We can further assume that this probability is proportional
to Δt (ie. linear property).

A2: At any moment in time each cell in the population has
a chance of dying (i.e. continuous death process) and
this chance is assumed constant and does not vary from
cell to cell

A3: Deaths occur independently (this is a consequence of
A1)

Assumption A1 $\Rightarrow$ that there exists a constant d>o such that in
any small time interval of duration Δt the
probability that any one cell dies is $d\Delta t$.

Firstly consider a population of just 1 cell.

In any time interval $(t, t + \Delta t)$ if there is one cell alive at time t then either

    a) the cell dies with probability $d\Delta t$

or

    b) at time $t + \Delta t$ the cell is still alive with probability $1 - d\Delta t$

Let $P_1(t) = $ Prob (cell alive at t), then

$$P_1(t + \Delta t) = [1 - d\Delta t] \, P_1(t) \qquad \text{by A1(a)}$$

so that

$$\frac{P_1(t + \Delta t) - P_1(t)}{\Delta t} = - d \, P_1(t)$$

which, on letting $\Delta t \to 0$, gives

$$\frac{dP_1(t)}{dt} = - d \, P_1(t) \qquad\qquad (4)$$

Since the cell was alive at t=0, $P_1(0) = 1$ so that the solution of (4) is

$$P_1(t) = e^{-dt}$$

Now consider a population of N cells at time t=0, and let $P_n(t) = $ Prob (n cells alive at time t).

It follows from assumption A2 that the probability of a death in time interval Δt among n cells must be $nd\Delta t$ so that

$$P_n(t + \Delta t) = (n+1) \, d\Delta t \, P_{n+1}(t) + (1 - nd\Delta t) \, P_n(t).$$

Hence we can obtain a differential-difference equation

$$\frac{dP_n(t)}{dt} = (n+1) \, d \, P_{n+1}(t) - nd \, P_n(t) \qquad\qquad (5)$$

To obtain a solution to this equation we must consider it as one of a system of differential-difference equations, starting at n=N since $P_{N+1}(t) = 0$ for all t. Then starting at n = N since $P_{N+1}(t) = 0$ for all t. Then

$$\frac{dP_N(t)}{dt} = -NdP_N(t), \qquad P_N(0) = 1$$

(6)

$$\frac{dP_n(t)}{dt} = (n+1) \; d \; P_{n+1}(t) \; - \; ndP_n(t), \; P_n(0) = 0$$

$$\text{for } n = N-1, \; N-2, \; \dots, \; 1.$$

This system of linear differential-difference equations is left to the student to solve   (e.g. using Laplace transforms.)

However, if we define the moment generating function by

$$P(\theta, t) = \sum_{n=1}^{N} e^{n\theta} \; P_n(t)$$

then the above system can be replaced by the single equation

$$\frac{\partial p}{\partial t} = \mu(e^{-\theta} - 1) \frac{\partial p}{\partial \theta}$$

with

$$P(\theta, 0) = e^{\theta N}$$

The students should show, as an exercise, that

$$P_n(t) = \binom{N}{n} e^{-ndt} (1 - e^{-dt})^{N-n}$$

(7)

for $n = N, \; N-1, \; N-2, \dots, \; 1.$

15.7   CASE STUDY 3

Develop a model for a cell population where, for each cell, the birth rate is constant and the death rate is constant.

15.8   A SOLUTION

Due to the constant birth and death rates it would seem sufficient to develop a deterministic continuous model.

For a pure birth process, with constant birth rate b, we have

$$\frac{dN}{dt} = bN$$

where $N(t)$ denotes the number of cells at time t, and b is a positive constant for each cell   (see Usher and Abercrombie (1981) Case Study 1)

For a pure death process, with constant death rate d,

$$\frac{dN}{dt} = -dN$$

where d is a positive constant for each cell.

Thus, the growth or decay of the population is governed by the differential equation

$$\frac{dN}{dt} = aN$$

where $a = b-d$ denotes the constant specific growth or decay rate of the population. This is readily solved to give

$$N(t) = N(0) \ e^{at}$$

and solutions corresponding to zero growth $(a = 0)$, exponential growth $(a>0)$ and exponential decay $(a<0)$ are illustrated in Figure 15.2.

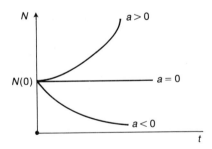

Fig. 15.2   Curves illustrating no growth, exponential growth and exponential decay.

15.9   CASE STUDY 4

Consider a biological cell population where the death process is stochastic, but the birth process is such that every c seconds all cells divide into two daughter cells.

15.10 A SOLUTION

The birth process here is deterministic and discrete, but the death process, although stochastic, may be either continuous or discrete. Again, as in Case Study 2, we do not have enough information with regard to the death process to make a decision as to whether continuous or discrete is appropriate.

The model developed here will involve a deterministic, discrete birth process but a continuous death process (as in Case Study 2). It will be based on assumptions A1, A2 and A3 of Case Study 2 in order to model the death process.

Thus, as in Case Study 2 equation (7), if we have no births then

$$P_n(t) = \binom{N}{n} e^{-ndt} (1-e^{-dt})^{N-n}$$

$$\text{for } n = N, N-1, N-2, \ldots 1$$

$$= \text{Prob (n cells alive at time t).}$$

This was found by solving the set of differential-difference equations (6) subject to initial conditions

$$P_N(0) = 1, \qquad P_n(0) = 0 \qquad \text{for} \qquad n = N-1, N-2, \ldots, 1.$$

However at c seconds all cells divide into two daughter cells. Hence at t = c we have a new set of linear differential-difference equations with the initial conditions

$$P_n(c) = \binom{N}{\frac{n}{2}} e^{-\frac{n}{2}P} (1-e^{-P})^{N-\frac{n}{2}}, \qquad n = 0, 2, \ldots, \quad 2N$$

$$P_n(c) = = 0, \qquad n = 1, 3, 5, \ldots, \quad 2N-1 \text{ where } p=dc$$

Evidently a new set of differential-difference equations with initial conditions at time 2c will have to be solved for 2c ⩽ t < 3c. The students should discuss the best way of solving such systems which restart at fixed intervals c, 2c, 3c ...

Possible methods of solution are

a) simulation,

b) an extension of moment - generating function techniques referred to in Case Study 2,

c) matrix methods of solution of linear differential - difference equations.

15.11   CASE STUDY 5

Develop a model for a biological cell population where birth and death processes coexist.

15.12   A SOLUTION

We shall develop one of the simplest possible stochastic models for the growth of a biological cell population, i.e. that which involves continuous linear birth and death processes.   The model will be based on the following assumptions.

A1: During any time interval (t, t + Δt) the probability that a birth or a death occurs depends only on the population at time t (Markov property)

A2: Each cell develops or dies independently of all other cells

A3: During any time interval (t, t + Δt) the probability that any one cell creates one, and only one, additional daughter cell is b Δt,   where b is a positive constant

A4: During any time interval (t, t + Δt) the probability that any one cell dies is d Δt , where d is a positive constant

Thus during a time interval of duration Δt an individual cell either

a) produces one additional daughter cell with probability bΔt,

or   b) dies with probability dΔt,

or   c) neither dies nor produces a daughter cell with probability 1 - bΔt - dΔt.

Hence, in a given population of N cells, we can select $\Delta t (>0)$ small enough so that

a) the probability of birth during a time interval of duration Δt is Nb Δt,

b) the probability of a death during a time interval of
   duration Δt is $Nd \, \Delta t$,

c) the probability of more than one birth or death is
   negligible.

Let $P_N(t)$ denote the probability of the event that the
population is of size N at time t. The event that the
population is of size N at time $t + \Delta t$ where we assume that
at most one birth or one death could occur in the time interval
$(t, \, t + \Delta \, t)$, can arise in one of the following ways.

1) At time t there were N-1 cells in the population and one
   birth occurred in the next Δt seonds but no deaths.

2) At time t there were N cells in the population and no
   births or deaths occurred in the next Δt seconds.

3) At time t there were N+1 cells in the population and
   then one death occurred in the next Δt seconds but no
   births.

The student is left to obtain the results.

$$P_N(t + \Delta t) = P_{N-1}(t) \; b(N-1) \; \Delta t + P_N(t) \; (1 - (b + d) \; N\Delta t)$$

$$+ \, P_{N+1}(t) \; d(N+1) \; \Delta t \qquad \text{for} \qquad N \geqslant 1 \tag{8}$$

$$P_o(t + \Delta t) = P_o(t) + P_1(t) \; d\Delta t \tag{9}$$

and hence deduce the following system of differential-difference
equations

$$\frac{dP_N(t)}{dt} = b(N-1) \; P_{N-1}(t) - (b+d) \; N \; P_N(t) + d(N+1) \; P_{N+1}(t)$$

$$\text{for} \qquad N \geqslant 1 \tag{10}$$

$$\frac{dP_o(t)}{dt} = d \; P_1(t)$$

The student should discuss appropriate boundary conditions for
this system of equations. The solution of a similar, but
simpler, system of equations was discussed in Case Study 2 (see
equations (6)) for a particular set of boundary conditions. A more
complete discussion of the methods of solution for systems of

equations such as (10) is given in Morgan (1979) and
Hoel et al. (1972). Since here we are trying to focus the
student's attention on the formulation and development of a
mathematical model, rather than mathematical techniques, we
shall make no attempt to solve these equations in general.
However the student can draw comparisons between the above
stochastic model and the deterministic model developed in Case
Study 3 by considering the three cases

    a) $b > d$

    b) $b = d$

    c) $b < d$

and discussing the behaviour of the population size in each
case.

In order to determine the ultimate behaviour of the
population, i.e. to see whether the population becomes extinct
or not, we consider the instants of time where a birth or a
death occurs.

Let $\quad P_{N,N+1}$ = Prob (population size increases
instantaneously from N to N+1)

$$= \text{Prob (birth)}$$

$P_{N,N-1}$ = Prob (population size decreases
instantaneously from N to N-1)

$$= \text{Prob (death)}.$$

Since each event is either a birth or a death

$$P_{N,\ N+1} + P_{N,\ N-1} = 1.$$

Now assume that

$$P_{N,\ N+1} = kNb$$

$$P_{N,\ N-1} = kNd$$

where k is a constant of proportionality. (Discuss these
assumptions.)

Then $\quad P_{N, N+1} = \dfrac{b}{b+d}$,

$$N \geqslant 1$$

$$P_{N, N-1} = \dfrac{d}{b+d}.$$

Let a_N = Prob (population ultimately becomes extinct/N cells initially)

Then a_N = Prob $P_{N, N+1} \, a_{N+1} + P_{N, N-1} \, a_{N-1}$, $\quad N \geqslant 1$.

The student should then show that

$$a_N - a_0 = (a_1 - a_0) \sum_{i=0}^{N-1} \left(\dfrac{d}{b}\right)^i \qquad N \geqslant 1 \qquad (11)$$

Hence if $b \geqslant d$ then the series $\displaystyle\sum_{i=0}^{N-1} \left(\dfrac{d}{b}\right)^i$ diverges as $N \to +\infty$.

In this case, since $a_0 = 1$ and $0 \leqslant a_N \leqslant 1 \, (N \geqslant 1)$, the only solution of (11) which does not cause a_N $(N \geqslant 1)$ to become either negative or larger than one as N increases is

$$a_N = a_0 = 1, \qquad N \geqslant 1,$$

i.e. the cell population ultimately becomes extinct.

If $b > d$ then (11) does not immediately provide a solution for a_N. However the student could apply simulation techniques to discover the behaviour of the model when $b > d$ for different values of N, the initial population size. It should be noted that this procedure is likely to become very involved.

15.13 FURTHER DISCUSSION

1. By considering the possibility of the coexistence of birth, death and enviromental-limiting processes, develop a model suitable for investigating tumour growth.

2. Investigate ways in which it might be possible to develop the various models considered in the above case studies and those considered in Usher and Abercrombie (1981a) and (1981b) in order to discuss the treatment of tumour cells by irradiation.

15.14   CONCLUSION

The distillation of the ideas discussed in the above case
studies should provide students with some knowledge of
distinctions and relationships between stochastic,
deterministic, continuous and discrete mathematical models.
This work should illuminate just a few facets of the
fascinating art of mathematical modelling. If, indeed,
students proceed to further investigations along the lines
mentioned in the preceding paragraph they will be walking along
the path leading to some of the current research work in the
field of cancer treatment.

REFERENCES

Eisen, M., 1979 Mathematical Models in Cell Biology and
    Cancer Chemotherapy, Lecture Notes in Biomathematics, Vol.
    30, ed. Levin, S., Springer-Verlag, Berlin, pp. 44-72.

Eisen, M. and Eisen, C., 1975 Probability and Its
    Applications, Quantum Publishers Inc., New York.

Harris, T., 1963 The Theory of Branching Processes, Springer-
    Verlag, Berlin.

Hoel, P.G., Port, S.C. and Stone, C.J., 1972 Introduction to
    Stochastic Processes, Houghton Mifflin Co., Boston.

Morgan, B.J.T., 1979 Four approaches to solveing the linear
    birth and death (and similar) processes, Int. J. Math.
    Educ. Sci. Technol. 10, No. 1, pp. 51 - 64.

Usher, J.R. and Abercrombie, D.A., 1981a Tumour Growth and
    the Response of Cells to Irradiation, In: Case Studies in
    Mathematical Modelling,(Eds. James, D.J.G. and
    McDonald, J.J.), S. Thornes (Pub) Ltd., Cheltenham, England,
    pp. 85 - 100.

Usher, J.R. and Abercrombie, D.A., 1981b Case Studies in
    Cancer and its Treatment by Radiotherapy, Int. J. Math.
    Educ. Sci. Technol., Vol. 12, No. 6, pp. 661 - 682.

16

Marketing a new variety of seed

JOHN BERRY   *Plymouth Polytechnic*

16.1   PROBLEM STATEMENT

Open Seeds Ltd have developed a new variety of plant and they
plan to sell the seed for the first time in 1985. Although
initially there is a shortage of seed, it is hoped that
eventually the variety will become established as a big seller.
Each year a small proportion of the seed produced will be
retained for producing more seed. In the early stages of
development, however, there is a choice between either
retaining a large proportion of seed and getting a small return
on sales or retaining a smaller proportion and inhibiting
future production.

The problem is to investigate the relative economics of
different methods of building up stocks of seed with a view
to maximising the profit.

16.2   TEACHING NOTES

In the problem statement one particular strategy for marketing
has been identified, that of maximising profits. There are
other possible approaches, for example, Open Seeds Ltd could
identify a target demand for the seed and aim to reach this
target in as short a time as possible.

This problem is suitable for students with a level of
mathematics equivalent to a G.C.E. Advanced level and requires
no specialist knowledge of biology or economics.

16.3   FORMULATING A MODEL

A useful technique for getting started on a problem like this
is to write down a list of the features that we may need to

take into account in formulating a model. The following list
of thirteen features is only one of the many lists that could
be suggested but it is sufficient for the possible solution to
the problem to be presented.

16.3.1 A possible feature list

When using this problem the group of students should be
encouraged to produce their own list and work with that. The
list given here is not meant to be a 'perfect answer.

(a)   time from sowing until the plant fruits and produces seeds

(b)   yield of seeds from one plant

(c)   is the plant a hybrid variety

(d)   effect on the yield of a poor growing season

(e)   initial cost of seed

(f)   land costs e.g. rates and rent

(g)   demand for the seeds

(h)   proportion of seed sold against that retained for sowing

(i)   amount of land available

(j)   overhead costs e.g. fertilizer, heating, etc.

(k)   selling price

(l)   effects of inflation

(m)   how long will the variety of plant remain popular?

To proceed to a model that can provide some predictions we
would need to make some assumptions about these features, so
as to simplify matters.

16.3.2 Assumptions

When using this problem the group of students should be
encouraged to make assumptions that apply to their feature
list. The following assumptions about the list in Section
16.3.1 will provide a simple model. We will assume that:-

1.   the plant is an annual, sown in the spring and harvested
     in the autumn, that it is a non-hybrid variety and
     each plant (obtained from one seed) produces r seeds on
     harvest (features a,b,c);

2. over the period of years under investigation there are no
    bad growing seasons so that r is taken as a constant
    (feature d);

3. a small amount of seed has been developed and tested in
    order to start production; development costs (i.e. the
    initial cost of seed) will be neglected (feature e);

4. the amount of land available is not restricted and the costs
    of producing and selling a quantity of seed are constants;
    (although this assumption appears to ignore the effects of
    inflation we could have assumed that the profit factor is
    constant over the period being investigated, so that the
    effects of inflation on costs are being taken care of by
    increasing the selling price); the cost of growing per unit
    weight of seed is £c and the selling price per unit weight
    is £s (features f, i, j, k, l);

5. there is a constant demand for the seed, for a period of
    m years after which the demand falls away due to an
    improved seed becoming available; constant demand is
    greater than the amount of seed produced;

6. all the seed produced within a growing season will be sold
    or planted for new stock for the following season and the
    proportion of seed sown in year n + 1 is α times the
    harvest in year n (feature h).

In this list of assumptions the feature(s) to which it applies
is included in brackets - this ensures that something is said
about all our features. The above assumptions are not defended
at this stage. The restrictions placed on the model by making
these assumptions will be apparent in the solution of the
problem that the model provides. The variables for use in the
model are underlined.

16.3.3 A simple model

The aim is to maximise the profit by investigating different
marketing strategies. We are interested in maximising the
profit over a period of m years, since then the demand begins
to fall away.

Consider the marketing strategy of sowing each year a fixed
proportion of the previous year's harvest i.e. choosing
α = constant. Let the amount of seed sown in year n be P_n so
that the initial seed available is P_1 (the units of P will be
an appropriate unit of weight).

At the end of year n, the seed harvested is rP_n (assumptions 1 and 2).

If the amount of seed sold is α times the year's harvest then at the beginning of year n + 1 the amount of seed to be sown is given by

$$P_{n+1} = \alpha r P_n$$

and the amount of seed sold is $(1 - \alpha) r P_n$ (assumption 6).

The profit in year n is £Y_n, where $Y_n = s(1 - \alpha) r P_n - c P_n$ (assumption 4)

$$\doteqdot P_n (rs(1 - \alpha) - c)$$

Total profit at the end of m years is £T, where

$$T = [rs(1 - \alpha) - c] [P_1 + P_2 + P_3 + \ldots + P_m]$$

(this assumes that all the seed put on the market at the end of year m is sold, although in practice the demand is beginning to fall).

Now $P_2 = \alpha r P_1$

$$P_3 = \alpha r P_2 = \alpha^2 r^2 P_1$$

$$P_4 = \alpha r P_3 = \alpha^3 r^3 P_1$$

$$\vdots$$

$$P_m = \alpha^{m-1} r^{m-1} P_1$$

Hence $\displaystyle\sum_{i=1}^{m} P_i = P_1 \sum_{i=1}^{m} \alpha^{i-1} r^{i-1} = P_1 \left\{ \dfrac{1 - \alpha^m r^m}{1 - \alpha r} \right\}$

The total profit at the end of m years is £T given by

$$T = \frac{[rs(1 - \alpha) - c]P_1[1 - \alpha^m r^m]}{1-\alpha r}$$

and the problem is to choose α, i.e. the proportion of the previous year's harvest that is to be sown, in order to maximise T.

16.3.4 Two consequences of the model

A: In order to increase the stock so that we have more seed
    to sell as the years go by (remember that this is a new
    stock of seed so that initial supplies will be well below
    demand)

$$P_{n+1} > P_n$$

i.e. $$\alpha r P_n > P_n$$

which gives $$\alpha > \frac{1}{r} \qquad\qquad (1)$$

(note that $r > 1$ and $\alpha < 1$ so that we harvest more seed
than is sown).

There may be a solution in which we could choose $\alpha = \frac{1}{r}$.
In this case the quantity of seed sown will just be
sufficient to meet a demand i.e. Open Seeds Ltd is selling
exactly the same amount of seed every year. This is a
steady state situation. If the initial quantity of seed
is not sufficient to meet the demand then for a few years
it will be important to increase stocks of seeds. This

requires $\alpha > \frac{1}{r}$. However when demand is satisfied in a
particular year then for future years we choose $\alpha = \frac{1}{r}$
(assuming constant demand), so that there is no seed left
unsold.

The solution presented here assumes that we do not satisfy
the demand until an improved variety becomes available.
With this approach $\alpha > \frac{1}{r}$ will always apply.

B: The profit in each year should be positive so that the
    profit £Y_n in year n is

$$Y_n = P_n[rs(1 - \alpha) - c] > 0$$

which gives $\alpha < 1 - \frac{c}{sr}$ (2)

Equations (1) and (2) provide bounds on α, and we have

$$1 - \frac{c}{sr} > \alpha > \frac{1}{r}$$

16.4   SOME SOLUTIONS FOR α

To proceed with the mathematical problem of finding a value
for α that maximises T, α_c, say, we choose some suitable values
for r, s and c and then investigate different values for m,
the number of years before the demand begins to drop.

In this problem, the important part of the modelling process,
namely data collection, can be left to the students.   The
values of r, s and c will depend on the plant under
investigation - the same model can be used for many
applications. For example, for potatoes r is about 10,
for winter wheat r is around 20 for cabbages r may be several
hundred.

It is possible to proceed to solve the mathematical problem
more generally than is done in the solution below by finding
α_c for various pairs of values of r and $\frac{c}{s}$.

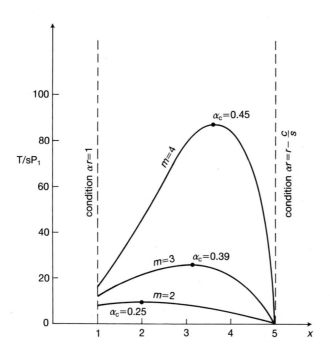

Figure 16.1 A graph of T/sP_1 against x for different values
of m

Suppose that for a variety of seed potato we have $r = 8$, and
$\frac{c}{s} = 3$. (These are dimensionless quantities.) This represents
a whole family of subcases. Let us consider one member of
this family. If we sow 1 ton of potatoes, and take the cost
of growing this amount to be £3 (i.e. $c = 3$) then the cost to
produce 8 tons is £3 and the revenue if we sold all 8 tons is
£8, since $s = 1$.

Now writing $\alpha r = x$ we have $T = \dfrac{sP_1[r - x - \frac{c}{s}](1 - x^m)}{1 - x}$ (in pounds)

and since $r - \frac{c}{s} = 8 - 3 = 5$ we have

$$T = sP_1\left[\frac{(5 - x)(1 - x^m)}{(1 - x)}\right]$$

The graph in Figure 16.1 shows plots of T/sP_1 against x for
different values of m. The values of α_c on each curve are
obtained by the usual calculus method of finding the value of
x for $\frac{dT}{dx} = 0$, x_c say, and then putting $\alpha_c = \frac{x_c}{r}$.

Table 16.1 shows values of α_c for different values of m.

TABLE 16.1

m	2	3	4	5	6	7
α_c	0.25	0.39	0.45	0.50	0.52	0.53

To interpret these results suppose that the marketing strategy
is to maximise the profit over a period of six years (i.e.
$m = 6$). To achieve the maximum profit, Open Seeds Ltd would
have to retain 52% of the seeds harvested each year for growing
the following year. The total profit is then £1377sP_1. Now
consider the land required for this six-year example. For
$\alpha = 0.52$ the amount of seed being sown each year is given in
Table 16.2. The values are calculated from the equation

$$P_{n+1} = \alpha r P_n$$

TABLE 16.2

Year	1	2	3	4	5	6
Amount of seed sown	P_1	$4.16P_1$	$17.3P_1$	$72P_1$	$300P_1$	$1246P_1$

Suppose that we begin with 1 ton of seed potatoes in year 1,
then at the beginning of year 6 we are planting 1246 tons of
seed potatoes. Roughly speaking potatoes are planted at about
1 ton per acre so that according to the marketing strategy
described above, Open Seeds Ltd would require an area of over
1200 acres. Now the average size of a farm in the United
Kingdom is about 260 acres. So our model is going to
require an area equivalent to about 5 farms in order to grow
the potatoes. This identifies one possible failing in the
marketing strategy adopted in this solution, in that the amount
of land required is being increased approximately four-fold
each year. We could amend the strategy in the following way.
If the total land available is limited, and a quantity of seed
A is sufficient to fill this land area, then when $P_{n+1} = A$,
we retain only the quantity of seed A each year for resowing.

This is then a steady state situation in which α is reduced
from the optimum value α_c to the value $\alpha = \frac{1}{r}$. For example,
the solution in Table 16.2, suppose that $A = 300P_1$ tons then in
year 5 the yield of seed potatoes is $2400P_1$ tons as before but
for year 6 we retain only $300P_1$ instead of $1246P_1$, and sell
2100 tons instead of 1154 tons. The quantity of seed potatoes
harvested in year 6 is then $2400P_1$ tons (as for year 5) which
is considerably less than the $9968P_1$ tons (i.e. $8 \times 1246P_1$)
for the original model. This amended strategy is unlikely to
satisfy the demand.

16.5 TWO ALTERNATIVE STRATEGIES TO EXPLORE

1. If the land available is sufficient to sow A tons of seed
   then do not sell any seed until the harvest is greater than
   A tons and retain A tons of seed per year, selling the
   rest.

2.   Consider the assumptions of section 16.3.2 but instead of
     a constant value for α, choose α as a function of n.
     (Clearly several possibilities are possible here both for
     α an increasing function and a decreasing function.)

REFERENCE

This problem formed one of the project specifications in 1982
for the mathematical modelling component of the Open University
second level course in Applied Mathematics, MST204.

17

Modelling plant growth

ALFREDO MOSCARDINI   *Sunderland Polytechnic*

17.1   DESCRIPTION OF THE PROBLEM

In all physical processes food is essential for growth, and the
two main sources for a plant are carbon and nitrogen. Carbon
is supplied by the atmosphere and is absorbed through the leaves
by a process called photosynthesis. Nitrogen is supplied from
the soil and is absorbed through the roots. The mechanisms by
which plants absorb, transport and combine these elements to
produce growth are not yet fully understood. Many complicated
biological models exist which attempt to explain them. Certain
hormones are thought to play a major role and this aspect is
the subject of considerable research at the present time.
However, certain basic observations can be made.

(a)   Carbon is absorbed by the leaves, known as the shoot, and
      nitrogen is absorbed by the root.

(b)   Both elements are needed in roughly fixed proportions for
      normal plant growth.

(c)   Carbon can be transported from shoot to root and likewise
      nitrogen from root to shoot.

(d)   At any time during plant growth, the carbon supply is
      related to the size of the shoot system and the nitrogen
      supply is related to the size of the root system.

(e)   Throughout growth, a balance is maintained between the size
      of the root and shoot systems.

Using these five observations, and without involving any more
complexities, could one construct a realistic mathematical
model of plant growth?

17.2 BACKGROUND INFORMATION

The energy required to produce new growth tissue in plants is
provided by photosynthesis, stimulating the chemical combination
of the carbon and nitrogen obtained from the atmosphere and
soil. For the purposes of this model, the effect of other
chemicals will be disregarded, as the two named above are dominant
in the following process.

The leaves of the plant intercept light and absorb carbon
dioxide to form sucrose during photosynthesis. The roots
absorb nitrates from the soil and convert them into amino acids,
which are the units from which proteins are formed. New cells
and tissues then result from the combination of the proteins
and the carbohydrates (sucrose). As sugar energy is used,
carbon dioxide is released back into the atmosphere.

The energy from the sugars can be used in several ways.

(1) Working Energy. This is required by the roots to absorb
     the nitrates and also to move the nitrogen and the carbon
     around the plant.

(2) Maintenance Energy. This is required to maintain the
     protein structure which is very unstable.

(3) Conversion Energy. Nitrates are converted into proteins
     and the sugar into other carbohydrates and fats.

(4) Building Energy. This is required to combine the large
     molecules into new tissue.

To give an estimate of the relative amounts of these energy
requirements, a typical unit block of energy would be divided
proportionally by area thus:

Conversion Energy	Maintenance Energy	Building Energy	Working Energy

Each plant cell is formed with a nearly fixed proportion of
carbon and nitrogen and any new cell produced will contain
similar proportions. One could imagine a plant making use of
carbon and nitrogen which are held in reservoirs, with movement
of carbon and nitrogen permitted between the reservoirs at
different positions in the plant. Although these reservoirs
do not actually exist as such, they could be helpful in
visualising the growth process.

Normally a plant is described in terms of its leaves, store and
roots but for the purpose of this problem, it is perhaps best
simplified to parts above ground (shoots) and parts below ground
(roots). This is now a two compartmental model of a plant
utilizing two essential elements which are shown diagrammatically
in Figure 17.5.

As this is a difficult model to build, a gradual approach is
suggested through three case studies. Each one is a model in
its own right, with exercises. It is strongly recommended that
a student follows this progression, although advanced students
could proceed directly to case study three. Many other models
could be constructed from this information, but it is felt that
this is a logical approach that yields sensible results.

17.3 MODEL 1

The simplest model is obtained if one does not distinguish
between the roots and the shoots or between the carbon and
nitrogen as food. One has then a single variable which depends
directly on how much food it can absorb. Whether the food is
carbon, which is absorbed by the shoots, or nitrogen, absorbed
by the roots, it seems a reasonable assumption that the amount
absorbed is directly proportional to the volume of the plant.

Thus one could write as a first equation

$\frac{dW}{dt} \propto V$, where W is the weight of the plant and V is its
volume.

Thus $\frac{dW}{dt} = kV = \frac{kW}{\rho}$ where ρ is the density of the plant, leading
to the solution $W = W_0 e^{kt/\rho}$.

The constant k will determine not only the amount of food
available but also how much of the energy from the food is
building energy as opposed to maintenance or working energy.
The solution obtained is simple exponential growth, which is
unrealistic as the plant does not grow indefinitely. What
happens is that, as the plant becomes larger, then the amount of
maintenance energy increases and thus building energy decreases.
This can be modelled by assuming that k is no longer constant
but a variable that changes with respect to time. The simplest
form of k would be linear, i.e. $k=a-2bt$. This leads to the
differential equation

$$\frac{dW}{dt} = (a-2bt) \frac{W}{\rho}$$

Thus growth would stop when $t = \frac{a}{2b}$, and $W = W_o e^{(at-bt^2)/\rho}$ for $t < \frac{a}{2b}$.

This gives a much more realistic approximation to growth. The plant will attain a maximum size of $W_o e^{a^2/4b\rho}$ when $t = \frac{a}{2b}$. After this time the model will actually start to decrease which is unrealistic, so the equation is taken to be valid for $t < \frac{a}{2b}$ only. The two major assumptions in this model are that

(a)   the plant is not differentiated into any specific parts,

(b)   the food is not divided into the two principal sources, i.e. carbon and nitrogen.

Two further models are considered in which these assumptions are relaxed.

17.3.1   Exercise 1

(a)   Consider other expressions for $k(t)$. How do these effect the results?

(b)   Assume that the amount of food absorbed is proportional to the surface area instead of volume. Analyse the result.

(c)   Have the parameters a and b any physical significance?

17.4   MODEL 2

The following assumptions are made.

(1)   The plant is not divided into specific parts but treated as one entity.

(2)   Both carbon and nitrogen are needed by the plant.

(3)   Growth depends on each of these being present. Thus the rate at which carbon is used by the plant depends not only on the amount of carbon present but also on the amount of nitrogen present.

(4)   A fixed proportion of the energy is used for building new tissue.

17.4.1 A possible formulation

If $C(t)$ and $N(t)$ represent the concentration levels per unit
volume of carbon and nitrogen then the food intake will involve
a function of these two variables, say $f(C,N)$. The form of this
function will be discussed later, but we define the rate of
carbon usage by the plant to be $Vf(C,N)$.

If it is assumed that any new material or tissue will contain
the same proportion of carbon and nitrogen as the old then, if
the ratio of nitrogen to carbon is λ, the rate of nitrogen usage
by the plant is $\lambda Vf(C,N)$. Let R_1 be the proportion of the
energy used for building and let γ be a conversion factor that
converts structural dry weight in terms of kg mole of carbon
to kg of structural material. Then our new growth equation
becomes

$$\frac{dw}{dt} = \gamma R_1 V(t) f(C(t),N(t))$$

which can be rewritten as

$$\frac{dw}{dt} = \gamma \frac{R_1 W(t)}{\rho} f(C(t),N(t))$$

17.4.2 The form of $f(C,N)$

Two conditions must be satisfied.

(a) As either the carbon or nitrogen levels decrease, the
utilization rate also decreases.

(b) When carbon and nitrogen are in abundance, the plant will
utilize the carbon at a genetically predetermined rate.

Several possibilities can be tried.

(1) Let $f(C,N)$ equal a constant, ie $f(C,N) = \alpha$.
This is, in essence, the model 1. It means that the plant
grows, independently of the carbon-nitrogen levels, and has
been fully discussed.

(2) Let $f(C,N)$ be linear in one variable, ie. $f(C,N) = \beta C$.
Utilisation would then be independent of N and would be
contrary to our initial assumption about the food.

(3) Let $f(c,N)$ be linear in both variables, ie.
$f(C,N) = \alpha + \beta C + \partial N$. As C and N increase, the value of
$f(C,N)$ increases and this would not satisfy condition (b).
Condition (a) would not be satisfied either, as a small
value of N or a large value of C would give a large value
for $f(C,N)$.

(4)   Let $f(C,N) = \alpha CN$.
      Condition (a) would now be satisfied but again condition
      (b) would not.

(5)   Let $f(C,N) = \dfrac{\alpha CN}{1+\beta CN}$.

      As C, N increase then $1+\beta CN \approx \beta CN$ and thus $f(C,N) \approx \dfrac{\alpha}{\beta}$.

      This satisfies condition (b). As either C or N decrease
      then CN decreases so condition (a) is also satisfied.
      Therefore, a possible form for the carbon utilization
      function is

$$f(C,N) = \frac{\alpha CN}{1+\beta CN}$$

Many more forms for this function could exist. It is hoped that
students will experiment with various forms until one that meets
the requirements is found.

To use this function in the growth equation, the concentration
levels must be known at any time. Two further equations are
needed which will determine those levels. A typical derivation
for these two equations is as follows.

Carbon present after (t+Δt) seconds	=	Carbon present after t seconds	+	Carbon obtained from photosynthesis in Δt seconds	−	Carbon used as various forms of energy in Δt seconds
Nitrogen present after (t+Δt) seconds.	=	Nitrogen present after t seconds.	+	Nitrogen obtained from soil in Δt seconds.	−	Nitrogen used as various for: of energy i Δt seconds

Most of these terms have already been identified. The amount of
carbon and nitrogen present at time t is $VC(t)$ and $VN(t)$
respectively. The rates of utilisation have been set as $Vf(C,N)$
and $\lambda Vf(C,N)$.

Carbon formed by photosynthesis can be assumed to be
proportional to the surface area of the plant. Knowing the
weight of a plant of certain surface area, this carbon can be
represented by $R_3 W(t) \Delta t$ where R_3 takes this conversion into
account.

The nitrogen obtained from the soil can be treated in a similar
manner and be represented by $R_5 W(t) \Delta t$.

The two equations can then be written in symbolic form as

$$V(t+\Delta t)C(t+\Delta t) = V(t)C(t) + R_3 W(t)\Delta t - Vf(C(t),N(t))\Delta t$$

$$V(t+\Delta t)N(t+\Delta t) = V(t)N(t) + R_5 W(t)\Delta t - \lambda Vf(C(t),N(t))\Delta t$$

i.e. $\dfrac{V(t+\Delta t)C(t+\Delta t)-V(t)C(t)}{\Delta t} = R_3 W(t) - V(t)f(C(t),N(t))$

$$\dfrac{V(t+\Delta t)N(t+\Delta t)-V(t)N(t)}{\Delta t} = R_5 W(t) - \lambda V(t)f(C(t),N(t))$$

Taking limits as $\Delta t \to 0$ and replacing $V(t)$ by $W(t)/\rho$ gives

$$\frac{d(WC)}{dt} = \rho R_3 W - Wf(C,N) \text{ and } \frac{d(WN)}{dt} = \rho R_5 W - \lambda Wf(C,N)$$

The model now consists of three linked simultaneous differential equations

$$\frac{dW}{dt} = \gamma\frac{R_1 W}{\rho} f(C,N)$$

$$\frac{d(WC)}{dt} = \rho R_3 W - Wf(C,N)$$

and $\dfrac{d(WN)}{dt} = \rho R_5 W - \lambda Wf(C,N)$

where $f(C,N) = \dfrac{\alpha CN}{1+\beta CN}$ and γ, ρ, λ, R_1, R_3 and R_5 are known constants.

17.4.3 Exercise 2

(a) How do these equations reduce to those of model 1 ?
(b) Consider the case $R_3 = 0$ (i.e. photosynthesis fails).
     Deduce that a maximum possible weight would be $W_0(1+\gamma\frac{R_1}{\rho}C_0)$
     where W_0, C_0 are initial values.
(c) What would a similar analysis yield if $R_5 = 0$ (i.e root failure).
(d) Consider special cases e.g. $R_5 = \lambda R_3$.

17.4.4 Units and Parameters

A common difficulty in problems such as this is the choice of
parameters in order to give realistic results. A system of units
can be agreed as follows. Time is measured in hours and plant
tissue is measured in kg of dry weight. This is defined as the
weight of the plant after it has been dried at a temperature of
$30^\circ C$. The carbon and nitrogen concentrations are measured in
kg mole m^{-3}, where 30kg of tissue result from 1kg mole of carbon.

R_1 Thornley (1976) gives a value of 0.05.

R_3, R_5 These parameters govern the intakes of carbon and
               nitrogen by the plant. Thornley   quotes a typical
               gross photosynthetic rate as $0.11 \times 10^{-3} gC\, m^{-2} s^{-1}$. This
               depends on surface area rather than volume.
               Assuming that 15 cm^2 of leaf weighs approximately 40mg,
               this rate can be converted to 0.5×10^{-6}kgC per kg per
               second. Thus R_3 = 0.0002 would represent a typical
               intake. R_5 will be about 10 times less.

ρ A typical density is ρ = 100 kg/m^3.

γ γ = 30 as stated above.

α, β These parameters are crucial to the model and govern
               the utilisation rates of carbon and nitrogen. When
               these elements are in abundance,

               $f(C,N) \to \dfrac{\alpha}{\beta}$ and thus $\dfrac{dW}{dt} = \gamma\dfrac{R_1\alpha}{\beta\rho} W.$ Solving this as in

               Section 17.3 we obtain

$$W = W_0 e^{\gamma R_1 \alpha t/\rho\beta} = W_0 e^{0.15\,\alpha\,t/\beta}$$

If the study is started after growth has commenced and
we assume that the plant doubles its size in a week
(say 90 sunlight hours) then $\dfrac{\alpha}{\beta}$ > 0.005. Assuming that
the utilisation rates are less than the photosynthetic
rates mentioned earlier then α and β can be estimated.
In this study the values of 0.08 and 1.6 are taken.

```
LI
20 DIM DW(100),DWC(100),DWN(100)
30 DIM W(100),C(100),N(100)
40 DIM GC(100),GN(100),GW(100)
50 FOR I=1 TO 3:READ R(I):NEXT I
60 FOR I=1 TO 5:READ A(I):NEXT I
70 READ W(0),C(0),N(0)
75 W=W(0)
80 DT=0.01
90 DEF FNP(X,Y)=(A(2)*X*Y)/(1+A(3)*X*Y)
96 FOR J=0 TO 99
100 FOR I=0 TO 99
106 KX=FNP(C(I),N(I))
110 DW(I)=A(5)*R(1)*W(I)*KX/A(4)
125  !PRINT "2";DW(I);KX
130 DWC(I)=(A(4)*R(2)*W(I))-(W(I)*KX)
135  !PRINT "3";A(4)*R(2)*W(I);W(I)*KX;DWC(I)
150 DWN(I)=(A(4)*R(3)*W(I))-(A(1)*W(I)*KX)
155  !PRINT "5";A(4)*R(3)*W(I);A(1)*W(I)*KX;DWN(I)
170 W(I+1)=W(I)+DW(I)*DT
190 WC=W(I)*C(I)+DWC(I)*DT
220 WN=W(I)*N(I)+DWN(I)*DT
230 C(I+1)=WC/W(I+1):   N(I+1)=WN/W(I+1)
242  !PRINT W(I);C(I);N(I);DW(I);DWC(I);DWN(I)
244  !PRINT:PRINT:PRINT
245 NEXT I
255 C(0)=C(I):N(0)=N(I):W(0)=W(I)
266 GC(J)=C(0):GN(J)=N(0):GW(J)=W(0)
270 NEXT J
282 FOR J=1 TO 99
285 PRINT GW(J);
290 NEXT J
300 INPUT"DO YOU WANT A GRAPH";A$
310 IF A$<>"Y" THEN 600
320 INPUT"LOWEST END OF SCALE IS ";L1
330 INPUT"HIGHEST END OF SCALE IS";L2
340 R=L2-L1
350 PRINT TAB(10);L1;TAB(68);L2
360 PRINT TAB(10);"----------------------------------------
370 FOR J=0 TO 99 STEP 3
380 Z1=INT((GW(J)-L1)*62/R)
400 PRINT 100*DT*J;TAB(Z1+10);"W"
430 NEXT J
440 STOP
450 DATA 0.5,0.0,0.0
460 DATA 0.222,0.08,1.6,100.0,30.0
470 DATA 0.6,0.35,0.49
600 END
```

Figure 17.1 Program listing for model 2

17.4.5 Method of Solution

Many methods exist to solve these equations. In this case a
computer program was written in which the equations were first
discretised. The time period, T, was divided into small
intervals $\Delta t (=0.01$ hour $)$.   Over this interval the growth rate,
$\bar{W}$, is assumed to be constant and so $W^{i+1} = W^i + \bar{W}\Delta t$, where i

denotes the ith time interval and $\bar{W} = \dfrac{YR_1 W^i}{\rho} f(C^i, N^i)$.

Using this approach for each equation, the program shown in
Figure 17.1 was devised. Initial values of 0.6, 0.35 and 0.49
were taken for W(0), C(0) and N(0).

17.4.6 Testing the Model

The first test was to provide abundant sunlight and nitrogen in
the soil. The appropriate values of R_3 and R_5 were set. Under
these conditions f(C,N) should tend to 0.05 and the growth will
be exponential. This is shown in Figure 17.2.

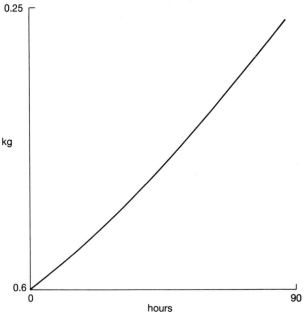

Figure 17.2 Abundant Carbon and Nitrogen

Low values of either nitrogen or carbon should result in minimal growth. Figure 17.3 shows R_3 = 0.0002 and R_5 = 0.00002.

This corresponds to reasonable sunlight but very little nitrogen. The plant grows at first but then levels off sharply. The growth period occurs as there is a considerable amount of nitrogen already available in the plant (see initial conditions) and this is being used at first. But when this runs out and very little comes in, the growth stops. Similar behaviour is noticeable in Figure 17.4, although at a much earlier stage, as there was less carbon originally present.

Many more runs can be performed with different data.

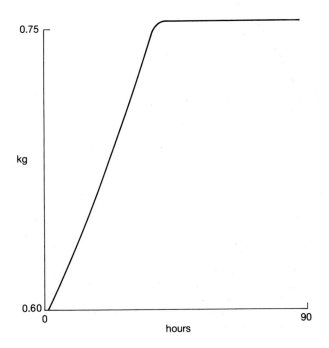

Figure 17.3   Low Nitrogen Intake

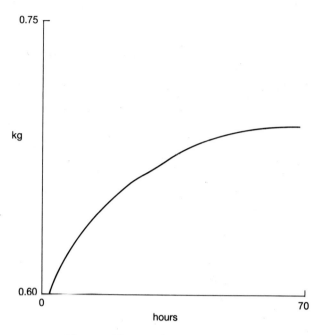

Figure 17.4   Low Carbon Intake

17.5 MODEL 3

In the last case study, carbon formed by photosynthesis was
assumed proportional to the surface area of the plant. It is
much more realistic to assume that it is proportional to the
surface area of the shoots only, and that the nitrogen is
proportional to the size of the roots. Thus it seems natural
to extend our model to include a two-compartment model of the
plant, i.e. shoots and roots. We must now allow for transfer
of carbon and nitrogen between the two areas, and a diagrammatic
representation of the model would be as in Figure 17.5.

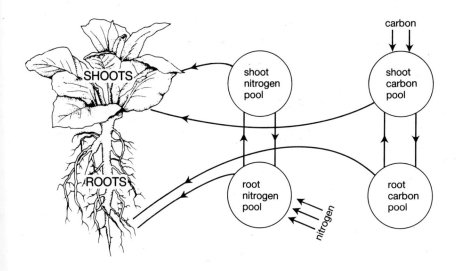

Figure 17.5

The diagram of Figure 17.5 derives from the penultimate
paragraph in the background material and contains all the
mechanisms for the model. Six variables are now needed, these
being the weights of the shoots (W_s) and roots (W_r) and the
concentrations of the carbon and nitrogen in the shoots and
roots which are C_s, N_s, C_r, N_r respectively. In all other
aspects the model is similar to model 2 and the same form
of the function $f(C,N)$ can be used.

17.5.1 A possible formulation

The equations will be derived in a similar manner as in model
2, but there will be three equations for the shoots and three
for the roots. The two growth equations are

$$\frac{dW_s}{dt} = \frac{\gamma R_1 W_s}{\rho_s} \; f(C_s, N_s)$$

and

$$\frac{dW_r}{dt} = \frac{\gamma R_1 W_r f(C_r N_r)}{\rho_r} \; ,$$

The shoot carbon equation will contain an extra term which will represent the flow of carbon from the shoot to the root. It is assumed that this flow will depend on the difference in the concentration levels i.e. $R_2(C_s-C_r)$. Thus the equation will be

$$\frac{d(W_s C_s)}{dt} = \rho_s R_3 W_s - \rho_s R_2 (C_s-C_r) - W_s f(C_s, N_s)$$

and similarly

$$\frac{d(W_r C_r)}{dt} = \rho_r R_3 W_r - \rho_r R_4 (C_r-C_s) - \lambda W_r f(C_r, N_r).$$

The change of nitrogen in the shoot will be the difference between the nitrogen transported from the root and the nitrogen used in building new material and maintenance. It is easy to derive

$$\frac{d(W_s N_s)}{dt} = \rho_s R_4 (N_r-N_s) - W_s f(C_s, N_s)$$

and

$$\frac{d(W_r C_r)}{dt} = \rho_r R_2 (C_s-C_r) - W_r f(C_r, N_r)$$

Our model now consists of six linked simultaneous non linear first order differential equations. The same values can be used for the constants, but we need values for the new parameters R_2 and R_4 which govern the transportation of the carbon and nitrogen around the plant. As concentrations are measured per volume, R_2, R_4 must relate to both volume and time. In this model, time is discretised into units of 0.01 hours and R_2 is chosen to have a value of 0.0003, i.e. this percentage of carbon is transported every 0.01 hour. R_4 is taken equal to R_2.

17.5.2   Method of Solution

Many computer packages exist for solving such equations (see Moscardini, Thorp and Cross 1980) but the program shown in Figure 17.6 was written especially for this example. The equations were treated exactly as before and initial values were $W_s(0) = 0.5$, $W_r(0) = 0.1$, $C_s(0) = 0.2$, $C_r(0) = 0.15$, $N_s(0) = 0.22$, $N_r(0) = 0.24$.

```
20 DIM DWS(100),DWR(100),DWCS(100),DWCR(100),DWNS(100),DWNR(100)
30 DIM WS(100),WR(100),CS(100),CR(100),NS(100),NR(100)
40 DIM GCS(100),GCR(100),GNS(100),GNR(100),GWS(100),GWR(100)
50 FOR I=1 TO 5:READ R(I):NEXT I
60 FOR I=1 TO 8:READ A(I):NEXT I
70 READ WS(0),WR(0),CS(0),CR(0),NS(0),NR(0)
75 WS=WS(0):WR=WR(0):DT=0.01
90 DEF FNP(X,Y)=(A(2)*X*Y)/(1+A(5)*X*Y)
96 FOR J=0 TO 99
100 FOR I=0 TO 99
106 KX=FNP(CS(I),NS(I)):KY=FNP(CR(I),NR(I))
110 DWS(I)=A(8)*R(1)*WS(I)*KX/A(7)
120 DWR(I)=A(8)*R(1)*WR(I)*KY/A(6)
130 DWCS(I)=A(7)*R(3)*WS(I)-A(7)*R(2)*(CS(I)-CR(I))-WS(I)*KX
140 DWCR(I)=A(6)*R(2)*(CS(I)-CR(I))-WR(I)*KY
150 DWNS(I)=A(7)*R(4)*(NR(I)-NS(I))-A(1)*WS(I)*KX
160 DWNR(I)=A(6)*R(5)*WR(I)-A(6)*R(4)*(NR(I)-NS(I))-A(1)*WR(I)*KY
170 WS(I+1)=WS(I)+DWS(I)*DT
180 WR(I+1)=WR(I)+DWR(I)*DT
190 WCS=WS(I)*CS(I)+DWCS(I)*DT
200 WCR=WR(I)*CR(I)+DWCR(I)*DT
210 WNS=WS(I)*NS(I)+DWNS(I)*DT
220 WNR=WR(I)*NR(I)+DWNR(I)*DT
230 CS(I+1)=WCS/WS(I+1):   CR(I+1)=WCR/WR(I+1)
240 NS(I+1)=WNS/WS(I+1):   NR(I+1)=WNR/WR(I+1)
244  !PRINT:PRINT:PRINT
245 NEXT I
255 CS(0)=CS(I):CR(0)=CR(I)
260 NS(0)=NS(I) :NR(0)=NR(I)
265 WS(0)=WS(I) :WR(0)=WR(I)
266 GCS(J)=CS(0):GCR(J)=CR(0):GNS(J)=NS(0)
267 GNR(J)=NR(0):GWS(J)=WS(0):GWR(J)=WR(0)
270 NEXT J
282 FOR J=1 TO 99
285 PRINT GWS(J);GWR(J);
290 NEXT J
291 PRINT
320 INPUT"LOWEST END OF SCALE IS ";L1
330 INPUT"HIGHEST END OF SCALE IS";L2
340 R=L2-L1
350 PRINT TAB(10);L1;TAB(68);L2
360 PRINT TAB(10);"-----------------------------------------------"
370 FOR J=0 TO 99 STEP 3
375 Z1=INT((GWS(J)/WS-1)*62/R):Z2=INT((GWR(J)/WR-1)*62/R)
390 IF Z1<>Z2 THEN 395
391 PRINT 100*DT*J;TAB(Z1+10);"RS"
392 GOTO 430
395 IF Z1<Z2 THEN 420
400 PRINT 100*DT*J;TAB(Z2+10);"R";TAB(Z1+10);"S"
410 GOTO 430
420 PRINT 100*DT*J;TAB(Z1+10);"S";TAB(Z2+10);"R"
430 NEXT J
440 STOP
500 DATA 0.5,3.0E-4,2.0E-4,3.0E-4,2.0E-5
510 DATA 0.222,0.08,0.0,0.0,1.6,100.0,100.0,30.0
520  DATA 0.5,0.1,0.2,0.05,0.2,0.05
600 END
```

Figure 17.6 Program listing for model 3

17.5.3 Testing the Model

The improvement of this model on the last is that it should show balanced growth between the roots and the shoots. The graphs thus show a variable called relative growth against time. The relative growth is $\frac{W(t)}{W(0)}$ i.e. the ratio of the weight at time t to the original weight. Similar graphs were plotted as in the last model. Figure 17.7 shows balanced growth under optimum conditions. Again these were represented by R_3 = 2.0E-4 and R_5 = 2.0E-5.

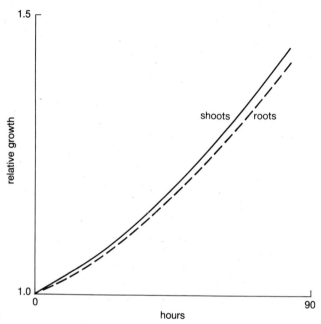

Figure 17.7 Abundant Carbon and Nitrogen

Figures 17.8 and 17.9 represent low intakes of carbon and nitrogen respectively. When carbon intake is low, the roots will suffer slightly more than the shoots and vice-versa in the other case. In both cases balanced growth is achieved. Figure 17.10 shows no growth when no food intake at all is available.

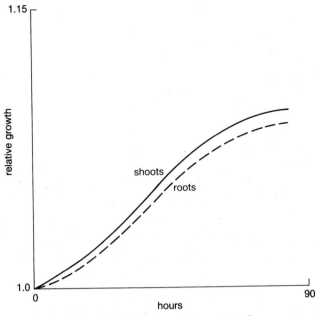

Figure 17.8   Low Carbon Intake

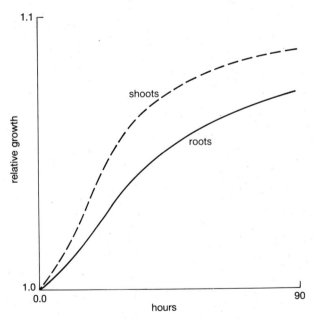

Figure 17.9   Low Nitrogen Intake

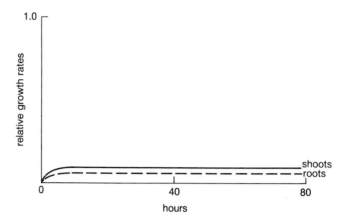

Figure 17.10   No carbon or nitrogen intake. $R_3 = R_5 = IE-10$.

17.6   CONCLUSION

The point of the exercise was to investigate whether a simple
mathematical model could be constructed that described balanced
growth between the roots and shoots of a plant.   Each section
of the plant obtained its own food, and transportation within
the plant was allowed.   Growth depended on both foods, and a
shortage of one could not be compensated by excess of another.

A crucial aspect in this exercise was the choice of parameters.
Some of these were estimated from published parameters,
Thornley (1976) was most useful, but some had to be decided on
an ad hoc basis, e.g. R_2 and R_4 which govern the transportation
rates.   The two parameters α and β which control the function
$f(C,N)$ also play an important role.

17.7   Further Work

(1)   The method of estimating the amount of carbon and nitrogen
      intake by the shoots and roots is rather crude.   Could
      this be improved?

(2)   The interrelationship of the parameters R_1, R_2, R_3, R_4 and
      R_5 is interesting.   Could the equations be
      non-dimensionalised to show the relative importance of
      these variables?

(3)   If $f(C,N)$ is set equal to a constant then the interdependence
      terms vanish from the equations.   Investigate the consequence

(4) Could one derive an equation describing the total weight
     $(W_s + W_N)$ and use more analytical methods for solution?

(5) Does the day and night cycle for photosynthesis have any
     effect?

(6) Would it be helpful to introduce a third compartment,
     i.e. the stem? What functions would it have?

REFERENCES

(1) Cross, M., Moscardini, A.O. and Thorp, M., 1982
     Interactive Computer Simulation Tools for use in Teaching
     Mathematical Modelling. Int. Jour. Math. Educ. Sci. Technol.
     Vol. 13, No. 6, 763-778.

(2) Moscardini, A.O., Thorp, M. and Cross, M., 1980
     Interactive Computer Simulation without Programming.
     Adv. Eng. Software, Vol. 2, No. 3, 117-130.

(3) Thornley, J.H.M., 1976   Mathematical Models in Plant
     Physiology, Academic Press.

Part III: Extended problems

18

Valve design in the treatment of hydrocephalus

DAVID BURLEY *Sheffield University*

18.1 INTRODUCTION TO LECTURER

This case study involves a complicated physiological process.
An attempt has been made to simplify the mechanism to a
level where a mathematical model can be usefully constructed.
The exercise is not a research project, so it is not worth
getting too involved in the detailed physiology or in trying
to compare too closely with experiment. There are features
of the valve which are omitted from the model but are important
for the useful operation of such a system.

The model has been used with final year undergraduates only,
but the development has been divided into three parts which
would probably correspond to first, second and third year
undergraduate level respectively. The model is essentially
a mechanical model, so students must have some understanding
of elementary mechanics and the idea of pressure to tackle
the first part. For the final part an understanding of flow
rates is needed, and some familiarity with spring and dashpot
systems is desirable.

18.2 BACKGROUND

A fluid, called the cerebospinal fluid, is continually
produced in the head, filling the spinal column and a cavity
around the brain. The fluid drains into the bloodstream
through a natural valve. A schematic view of the system is
illustrated in Figure 18.1. The natural valve is a very
delicate and complex mechanism which can cope easily with
changes in pressure depending on whether the person is
standing or lying down, normal variations in the production
rate, and so on. The analysis of these aspects involves
complicated hydraulic problems which require extensive knowledge of

the physiology of the fluid system, see Hakim and Burton (1974) or Davson (1967).

When the valve fails or works inefficiently there is a rapid increase in the amount of fluid in the head, which at best can cause severe discomfort and at worst swelling of the head, typical of hydrocephalus children. Such a condition clearly needs a relief system that will replace, either partially or totally, the natural valve. Such a relief valve would need to be inserted by an operation and would presumably be inaccessible until a replacement is necessary. Since such children are very susceptible to infection, the design life of such equipment must be as long as possible.

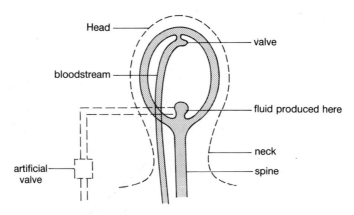

Figure 18.1 Schematic view of head with natural and artificial valve system

18.3 GENERAL PROBLEM

The basic problem is how you would design such a valve, discover which parameters are important and then study its operation under a wide range of conditions.

18.4 TEACHING NOTES

At this stage students should be given an opportunity to think about how valves work. The most familiar will be a bicycle tyre valve using rubber valve tubing, a car tyre valve and a toilet flush valve. A discussion of how they work and why they are designed that way should set the scene.

Some notes are given in the appendix which may help to structure a sensible discussion.

A general discussion should then be led to the requirements
of a valve for hydrocephalus children. It will become clear
that some features such as being of non-return type and
being very durable will be well understood while others such
as the exact nature of the fluid, the size of the system,
what are acceptable materials,will not be at all obvious.
It is not worth getting into too much detail of the medical
aspects since these are complicated and it is difficult to
obtain the necessary literature, Davson (1967). Here we
are more interested in studying the mechanics of the system
and identifying the key parameters. The further step of
using the model as a design tool is a major undertaking
and not suitable for work at this level. However it is
important to get an idea of typical sizes and Table 18.1
gives some indication. Students at this stage may be
encouraged to estimate how long it takes to replace the
whole fluid, how long it takes to fill an empty head, a
typical speed of flow through the valve.

TABLE 18.1

Total fluid (adult)	about 140 ml
Production of fluid flow rate	15 - 35 ml/hr
Pressures	up to 120 mm water
Valve deflection	up to 0.1 mm

To relieve the pressure build up, an artificial valve is
inserted into the part that produces the fluid and
drains the fluid down into the neck or chest, as indicated
in Figure 18.1. The comparison with non-return valves of
the tyre variety is not entirely relevant since the normal
position is closed by the excess pressure inside the tyre.
In the hydrocephalus valve it is necessary to drive fluid
into the bloodstream since the fluid pressure is higher than
ambient. Since there is not a natural return mechanism,
one must be designed into the system. A most natural method
is to use a spring. Students may well suggest an alternative,
but in the end it is likely to be equivalent to a spring.

18.5 A POSSIBLE VALVE

The valve in Figure 18.2 is that used by Hakim and Burton
(1974) and should serve as a basis for discussion.

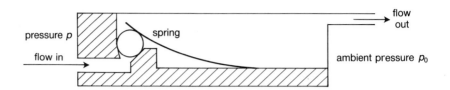

Figure 18.2 A possible valve design

18.6 STUDY 1

Having had a chance to think about valves in general and
suitable valves for hydrocephalus children, it is now
appropriate to consider the specific design in some detail.
Perhaps the first and simplest result that is needed is to
find when the valve will open.

The basic question is what is the pressure, called the
'popping pressure', required to open the closed valve. This
gives the simplest mathematics and needs the least physical
background. It leads to a series of subsidiary questions.
What parameters determine this pressure? How would you
measure these parameters? Which can be most easily
adjusted?

18.6.1 A Solution for the Valve Illustrated

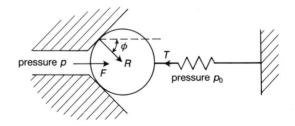

Figure 18.3 Schematic diagram of valve

For mathematical purposes it is convenient to replace
the spring in Figure 18.2 by an idealised version shown
in Figure 18.3. The three basic forces acting on the
bearing are F due to the pressure difference, R due to the
reaction on the seat and a tension force T due to the
compression of the spring. The system is symmetric so the

only interest is in forces and motion in the F-direction, so
the reaction R needs to be resolved.

Since force = pressure x area, F can be written

$$F = (p - p_0)A,$$

where A is the effective area of the bearing. Suppose
that the spring has natural length a and stiffness k and it
is compressed a distance x_0. Then making the usual assumption
that tension is proportional to extension gives

$$T = k(x_0 + a).$$

Thus, in equilibrium the balance of forces gives

$$k(x_0 + a) = (p - p_0)A + R \cos \phi$$

and the 'popping pressure', p_1, occurs when the reaction
R = O so

$$p_1 - p_0 = k(x_0 + a)/A \qquad (1)$$

The size of the device will limit the size of the bearing
and hence A, and the choice of spring will determine k and
a, so that the only parameter that can be changed easily is
x_0. In the valve illustrated in Figure 18.2 this will mean
presetting the spring appropriately. This can clearly be
done in the laboratory to match the required popping pressure.
Thus, provided the values of A, k and a give roughly the
correct values of pressure, the fine adjustment can be made by
presetting the x_0 value.

Over a period of time the contact between the bearing
and the cone becomes 'sticky', so that more pressure is
needed to open the valve. Thus, instead of just opening
slightly and then settling back on to its seat, the valve
opens fully, fluid pushes out and a comparatively long time
elapses before the valve closes. It becomes necessary
therefore to study the detailed dynamics of the system
to ensure, for instance, that the system is stable (see
Study 3). If the valve is open for any significant time
the system will settle down to a steady inflow/outflow
situation which gives an intermediate model which is
analysed in Study 2.

18.7 STUDY 2

From the background notes it is clear that to return a
child to normality the valve system must be able to operate
at a steady inflow/outflow situation. The problem is now
more complicated, but an analysis of the steady open valve
state is required.

The most difficult concept for this case is to work out the
amount of fluid leaking through the open valve as a
function of pressure drop and gap size, and then to calculate
the force on the bearing. The detailed fluid flow problem
is difficult and will produce a tricky lubrication problem.
To side-step this problem, a more simple minded approach
can be taken. Students should be encouraged to think about
the effect on the mass flow of a zero pressure drop, zero gap,
an increase of pressure, an increase of gap. The discussion
should be led along the lines of the next section to obtain a
mathematical formulation of these ideas. This can then
be fed into an equation for the balance of pressure and
spring forces. A study of the various parameters of the
system can then be undertaken and their relevance evaluated.

18.7.1 A Possible Solution for the Valve Illustrated

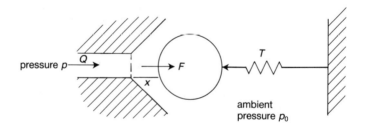

Figure 18.4 Schematic diagram of steady open valve situation

It may be assumed that deflection from the seat is small
so that p_0 remains unaltered and

$$F = (p - p_0)A$$

still gives the correct form for the pressure force. For
a given extra deflection, x, from the seat the tension is
given by

$$T = k(x + x_0 + a)$$

using the same notation as before for the spring. Finally
it is necessary to relate p and x for a given throughput, Q.

The following facts give some indication of this relationship.

$x = 0$ => on the seat   => no throughflow => $Q = 0$

$p = p_1$ => just about to open   => no throughflow => $Q = 0$

x bigger   => larger gap   => Q bigger

$(p - p_1)$ bigger => more pressure force => Q bigger

A mathematically convenient way of satisfying these observations is by an equation of the form

$$Q = \alpha \, x^n \, (p - p_1)^m, \tag{2}$$

where n and m are positive constants and α is a proportionality constant. It should be noted that $x < 0$ is not allowed in the design and $p < p_1$ will shut the valve so these facts should be used when necessary. The values of n, m and p must be determined either theoretically or experimentally and would be expected to depend on the fluid and velocity range. Once these are known the size of inlet tube, the size of bearing and cone angle are crucial and will determine the exact values of the parameters.

The equations for the steady situation are equation (2) and mechanical equation from the balance of F and T forces,

$$(p - p_0)A = k(x + x_0 + a) \tag{3}$$

Using equation (1) this can be rewritten

$$(p - p_1)A = kx \tag{4}$$

and for a steady throughput $Q = Q_2$, gap $x = x_2$ and pressure $p = p_2$ the two equations give

$$\left. \begin{array}{c} (p_2 - p_1)A = kx_2 \\ Q_2 = \alpha x_2 (p_2 - p_1) \end{array} \right\} \tag{5}$$

which can be solved to give

$$Q_2 = (\alpha k^m / A^m) \, x_2^{m+n}$$

or

$$Q_2 = (\alpha A^n / k^n) \, (p_2 - p_1)^{m+n}$$

For given parameters α, k, A, m, n, the gap x_2 and pressure $(p_2 - p_1)$ are determined by the throughput Q_2. While the gap x_2 can be adjusted easily, the values of Q_2 and $(p_2 - p_1)$ are prescribed within fairly well defined limits by the physiology of the system. Little can be done other than to ensure that the parameter $(\alpha A^n / k^n)$ has exactly the right value for steady operation at physiologically acceptable levels. For the previous study an easy adjustment could be made to ensure the popping pressure was correct, while in the present case there is no easy adjustment and the correct value of $(\alpha A^n / k^n)$ must be chosen first time at the design stage of the valve.

As indicated at the end of Study 1, the next goal is to look at the dynamic behaviour of the system.

18.8 STUDY 3

The previous two studies have looked at the static situations of zero gap and of a steady non-zero gap. Due to normal postural changes there will be variations from the static case. Sometimes the valve will be closed or steady but usually it will be changing from one situation to another.

Thus the next problem is to study the dynamic behaviour of the valve.

This case study is only useful for students who have a knowledge of spring and damper systems and experience of solving the resulting equations. Such people have little difficulty in extending equation (3) to the dynamic situation. The problem can be tried without a damper in the system but this leads to an unstable configuration and any realistic situation should certainly include some damping. Figure 18.4 should therefore be amended to include a damper at the start of this model.

The major problem is how to relate changes in pressure and gap to the build-up of pressure inside the head. The new idea is that the head itself now needs to be considered. A useful idea is to give the students a balloon and ask them to look at the effect of changes in pressure and volume and their effect on the airflow. If the balloon is blown up then the pressure inside the balloon increases, which in turn increases the volume. When the opening is released, air rushes out of the balloon, decreasing both the volume and pressure until the pressure inside and outside are the same.

The situation is similar in the head. If pressure builds
up due to an inefficient valve, the column of fluid will
increase and the head will act much like a rather stiff
balloon. Once the valve opens the fluid rushes out and thus
a relation is needed between the flow rate and the decrease
in volume. The pressure and volume at the same time
reduce to their steady values and a relation between volume
and pressure in the head is needed.

Both these equations prove to be the trickiest to establish
and considerable help and encouragement to the student are
needed to end up with equations such as (7) and (8) below.

18.8.1 A Possible Solution for the Illustrated Valve

The mechanical equation (3) is extended naturally to

$$M\ddot{x} = - k(x + x_0 + a) - c\dot{x} + (p - p_0)A \tag{6}$$

where M is the mass of the bearing and linear damping has
been inserted through the $c\dot{x}$ term. The throughflow equation
does not change and is given by equation (2).

Since we are now allowing variations in the pressure,
the pressure can build up in the head, which in turn will
increase the volume. If the head is regarded as a rather
stiff balloon the normal pressure in the steady state
will take the value p_2 and any increase will increase
the volume. Thus we may take as an approximation

$$p - p_2 = \beta(V - V_2)^{\ell} \tag{7}$$

where V_2 is normal volume at steady pressure p_2, ℓ (> 0) is
a constant and β a proportionality constant.

To connect the equations (2) and (7) we need an equation
relating Q and V. Now since Q_2 given by (5) is the
throughflow that maintains the steady pressure p_2, there will
be no change in V if $Q = Q_2$ but it will increase/decrease as
Q is smaller/larger than Q_2. The simplest possible assumption
that satisfies these facts is the linear relationship

$$Q - Q_2 = - dV/dt.$$

For simplicity of calculation, the values $m = n = \ell = 1$ in
equations (2) and (7) are chosen.

The calculation has proceeded on the assumption that the system is near to a steady inflow/outflow situation. Thus it seems sensible to perform the calculations as variations about the steady values x_2, p_2, Q_2, V_2. Writing

$$z = x - x_2, \quad P = p - p_2, \quad \overline{Q} = Q - Q_2, \quad \overline{V} = V - V_2$$

the equations (2), (6), (7), (8) then become

$$\overline{Q} = \alpha\left[x_2 P + z(p_2 - p_1) + zP\right] \tag{9}$$

$$M\ddot{z} = AP - kz - c\dot{z} \tag{10}$$

$$P = \beta\overline{V} \tag{11}$$

$$\overline{Q} = - d\overline{V}/dt \tag{12}$$

Eliminating $\overline{Q}$ and $\overline{V}$ gives the two equations

$$M\ddot{z} + c\dot{z} + kz = AP \tag{13}$$

$$\dot{P} = -\beta\alpha\left[x_2 P + z(p_2 - p_1) + zP\right] \tag{14}$$

In order to simplify equations (13), (14) a useful technique is to non-dimensionalise the variables, in this case z, P and t. There is a natural distance x_2 in the problem and a natural pressure difference $(p_2 - p_1)$, thus it seems reasonable to non-dimensionalise with respect to these parameters by putting

$$X = z/x_2, \quad \theta = P/(p_2 - p_1).$$

For the time, however, there is no obvious time parameter in the problem and a little more thought is needed. Taking equation (13) first, if P = O and c = O then the equation reduces to the simple harmonic equation

$$M\ddot{z} + kz = O$$

and hence the periodic time proportional to $t_1 = (M/k)^{\frac{1}{2}}$ is a natural candidate for normalisation. Equally if (14) is chosen with z = O then the equation reduces to the exponential equation

$$\dot{P} = - \beta\alpha\ x_2 P$$

and again a natural time parameter appears $t_2 = 1/(\beta\alpha x_2)$, this giving a measure of how fast the pressure will decay to steady. Thus there are two time parameters hidden in (13) and (14) and one of these must be chosen. The arbitrary decision is made to non-dimensionalise with respect to t_1 so put

$$\tau = t/t_1$$

The equations (13) and (14) become

$$X'' + CX' + X = D\theta \tag{15}$$

$$\theta' = - E(\theta + X + \theta X) \tag{16}$$

where there are three non-dimensional parameters C, D and E, and 'dash' denotes differentiation with respect to τ. The parameter $D = (p_2 - p_1)A/kx_2$ is exactly equation (5) and hence D = 1. It should be noted that equations (13) and (14) involve eight parameters M, c, k, A, α, β, x_2, $(p_2 - p_1)$ but the non-dimensionalisation has reduced these to two, C and E, and both of these can be interpreted usefully. Now $C = c/(Mk)^{\frac{1}{2}}$ involves only the spring parameters and does not involve the activating mechanism, in this case pressure changes. Thus C gives a measure of the damping in the system and is determined entirely by the spring/damper system. The other parameter $E = (Mk)^{\frac{1}{2}}/(1/\beta\alpha x_2) = t_1/t_2$, which is just the ratio of the two times introduced in the previous paragraph.

To evaluate C and E experimentally the spring/damper system can be studied independently to get C and t_1. Then, fixing the gap, the second time parameter t_2 can be measured independently of the spring.

A disadvantage of the non-dimensionalisation is that the case M = O needs special care since the non-dimensional time τ becomes infinite. It is best for this case to return to the original equations and start again (see Example 8 in Section 18.10).

18.8.2 *Small Oscillations about Steady State*

It is essential that any small oscillations about the
steady state do not grow, since this can lead to resonance
phenomena or uncontrolled behaviour which are very
undesirable in such a system. To establish the stability
of the system   see any book on vibrations, for instance
Den Hartog (1956). θ can be eliminated between (15) and (16)
and a third order equation can then be analysed. Alternatively
(15) and (16) can be attacked directly. Since the problem
is to look at small oscillations about the steady state, the
X term in (16) can be omitted. The stability of the system
can be determined by putting

$$X = re^{\lambda\tau}, \ \theta = se^{\lambda\tau}$$

and studying the values of λ. Substituting into (15)
and the linearised form of (16) gives

$$s = r(\lambda^2 + C\lambda + 1)$$

$$\lambda s = - E(r + s)$$

and to be consistent we must have

$$-E = (\lambda + E)(\lambda^2 + C\lambda + 1)$$

or

$$\lambda^3 + (E + C)\lambda^2 + (1 + CE)\lambda + 2E = 0.$$

The stability is determined if the three roots of this
cubic all have negative real parts. The condition, see Den
Hartog (1956) page 288, is that all the coefficients are
positive, which is certainly satisfied, and

$$(E + C)(1 + CE) > 2E$$

or

$$C + C^2E + CE^2 > E.$$

One immediate consequence of this inequality is that $C \neq 0$,
implying $c \neq 0$, so that there must be some damping in the
system or the system will be unstable. Fortunately in
practice there is always some damping. A graph of C against
E gives an idea of the stable region. It shows that the
damping c, must be large enough compared with $(Mk)^{1/2}$ to
ensure stability.

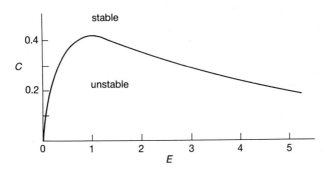

Figure 18.5   Stability of system about steady flow

18.9   FURTHER POSSIBLE STUDY

The above calculations are clearly only the start of a
study of valves. In the case studied the full equations
(13) and (14), including the non-linear term, have not
been tackled and it would be expected to be a difficult
job analytically. Only if simplifying assumptions are made
as in examples 7, 8 and 9 can such analytical solutions
be obtained easily.

Again it is clear that assumptions have been made on the
exact form of the flow Q in equation (2) and the
pressure/volume relationship in equation (7). These need
to be checked carefully by experiment and the precise values
of ℓ, m, n obtained. Special values of these parameters
have been chosen to make the mathematics simple, but this
is not the most helpful criterion. A sensitivity analysis
on the parameters might be a useful exercise.

The present work might lead to a study of valve systems
generally. Almost all machinery that handles fluids or
gases will involve a valve of some sort. Typically motor
cars contain a variety of valves and also any system that
requires a steady supply of fluid or gas without surges,
for example supply of domestic gas. An old fashioned but
first class book that contains such examples is Den
Hartog (1956).

18.10   FURTHER EXAMPLES

1. In Study 1 an additional practical problem is that the
    valve becomes "sticky". How would you feed this into
    the model, and how would it modify equation (1)?

2. In Study 2 it is assumed that the effective area A
    is a constant. In practice $A = A(x)$, so it is
    required to look for reasonable assumptions for $A(x)$.
    It is unlikely that this will vary greatly over small
    displacements, so $A(x) = A_0(1 - \gamma x)$ might be a suitable
    assumption. Look at the consequences on the steady
    pressure p_2.

3. In equation (2), putting $m = 0$ makes the throughflow
    pressure independent. Are there any advantages in
    making this change and does it affect the conclusions
    of Study 2?

4. Equation (7) needs further discussion, since if $\ell = 2$,
    then $p > p_2$ always. A better description would be

    $$p - p_2 = \beta(v - v_2)|v - v_2|^{\ell-1},$$

    but this makes the analysis more difficult unless
    $\ell = 1$. Even then this equation suggests that if
    $p < p_2$ then $V < V_2$, so that the head shrinks. Is this
    reasonable or is there some cut off value below which
    V will not decrease?

5. In the analysis of Study 3 consider the case $m = 0$,
    $n = \ell = 1$, ie. Q independent of the pressure and linear
    in x. Show that the system is linear with governing
    equation for z of

    $$M\ddot{z} + c\ddot{z} + k\dot{z} + \alpha\beta\ Az = 0.$$

    Investigate the behaviour of the system.

6. Take equation (14) with the situation $z = 0$, that is
    held fixed at the steady opening value $x = x_2$.
    Show that

    $$\dot{p} = -\ d\beta x_2 p$$

    and that the pressure decays to its steady value,
    with a natural decay time parameter $1/(\alpha\beta x_2)$.

7. Examine the case where $M = c = 0$ so that both the
    mass of the bearing and the damping is neglected.
    Show that

    $$P = 2(p_2 - p_1)/(Ke^{2t/t_2} - 1)$$

where K is an arbitrary constant.

8. If M = O, that is the mass is neglected, show that
    equations (13) and (14) are stable for small
    oscillations about the steady situation.

9. If M = O, look at the phase plane (or state space)
    for z and P. Show that

    $$\frac{dP}{dz} = - \alpha\beta c \, \frac{\left[zP + z(p_2 - p_1) + x_2 P\right]}{AP - kz}$$

    In the phase plane, plot dP/dz on the lines P = O,
    z = O, AP = kz and on the curve
    $(z + x_2)(P + p_2 - p_1) = x_2(p_2 - p_1)$. From this
    information plot out possible trajectories in the z, P
    plane.

10. Interpret physically the situation when E is very small
    in equation (16). Here $t_2 \gg t_1$, so that the pressure
    settling time is very much longer than the spring
    oscillation time. How is this reflected in the solution?

11. As in question 10 except for E very large.

12. An alternative assumption to equation (7) might be

    $$\frac{dP}{dt} = \beta \, (V - V_2)$$

    Argue the case for this assumption and work out the
    consequences for the case n = O, m = 1 in equation (2).

REFERENCES

(1)   Davson, H., 1967 , Physiology of the cerebrospinal
      fluid, Churchill.

(2)   Den Hartog, J.P., 1956 , Mechanical Vibrations,
      McGraw-Hill.

(3)   Hakim, S. and Burton, J.D., 1974 , Engineering
      in Medicine, Vol 3, pages 3-7.

APPENDIX

A schematic view of a variety of valves are illustrated
below. These could be shown to students and they could then
be asked to decide

(a) the overall purpose of the valve,

(b) the steady or resting position,

(c) the method of activation of the valve,

(d) whether the valve is of non-return type,

(e) what causes the valve to return to its steady or
    resting position.

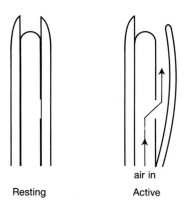

Resting   Active

air in

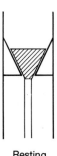   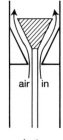

Resting   Active

air   in

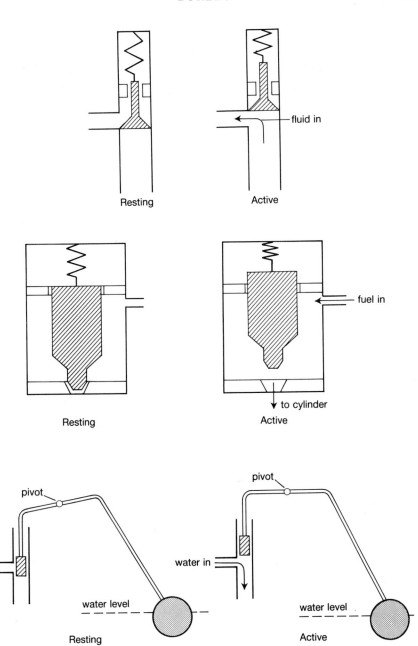

Resting   Active

fluid in

Resting   Active

fuel in

to cylinder

pivot

pivot

water in

water level   water level

Resting   Active

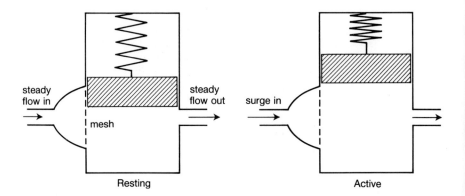

Resting   Active

19

Why airlines sometimes overbook flights

DICK CLEMENTS *Bristol University*

In presenting case studies in mathematical modelling in a
volume such as this, it is inevitable that a number of
different styles will emerge from different authors. I feel
that this is helpful to lecturers using this volume as
source material, in that these different styles will suggest
different ways in which they might present material to their
students. In using material from books similar to this in my
own teaching I have usually found it necessary to recast the
material in my own style. Hence the following presentation is
not intended to be pedagogically prescriptive. What I have
actually written reflects my own mental processes in creating
the model described; how lecturers present the problem to
their students depends on their perception of students'
capabilities and their own teaching style.

Again, some lecturers prefer to present concrete and specific
problems, others to propose an area of study and see what
emerges. In the case of this material I have adopted the
latter stance, since that is how I asked the question of myself.
That I should do it in this way probably reflects my own
mathematical style, and other people will have a different
style. The material could be recast in a more specific style
if the user wished to do so. Further, the style is also
probably best chosen in the light of the intended student
audience.

Having presented, in advance, these apologia let us proceed to
the problem area itself.

19.1 INTRODUCTION TO THE PROBLEM

We sometimes read, in the press, indignant letters from
travellers who have thought themselves booked onto a particular

flight with a particular airline and who, arriving at the airport and checking in at the airline reception, are horrified to be told "I'm sorry sir, the flight is now full and we will have to rebook you onto a later flight". Perhaps some of us have friends to whom this has happened, and the author can speak of it from personal experience - a well known British airline once compelled him to spend the first night of his holiday in Greece in an hotel at the end of the Gatwick airport runway! Such events cause considerable inconvenience and aggravation to the passengers concerned and it is often alleged that it ought to be possible, in these days of computerised bookings, to design a system that would not give rise to these errors.

The purpose of this chapter is to develop a model of the decisions facing an airline and, from this, to acquire an understanding of why it may indeed be beneficial to an airline to book more passengers onto a particular flight than the capacity of the airliner that is to make the flight. The model developed will allow us to explore the effects of the constraints facing an airline on their decision-making behaviour. In the absence of data relevant to any particular service or aircraft it is not possible for us to arrive at a solution specific to some service, but an exploration of the effects of variation of the various parameters involved in the model will yield valuable qualitative insights into the decision-making of the airlines.

19.2 NOTATION

Obviously it is necessary, in developing mathematical models, to define variables and keep a note of the notation being used. It is not possible, if one undertakes any moderately complex modelling exercise, to anticipate all the variables one will need before one starts. I find it essential to compile a notation for my own benefit and for that of others reading or using my model. To this end I always keep a separate sheet of paper on which I record my notation as I go along. I suggest that students be encouraged to develop such a habit. You, as tutor, will find it an enormous help in understanding what they have done. The notation below, then, was compiled not as it is presented, altogether, but bit by bit as I developed the model.

f - the cost of providing some flight
n - the number of passengers carried on a flight
g - the fare paid by each passenger
N - the capacity of the airliner making the flight
k - the number of 'no shows' for a flight
P_k - the probability of k 'no shows'
m - the number of passengers booked on a flight
S - the surplus generated by a flight
b - the cost of letting down (ie bumping) a passenger
     who had booked
p - the probability that a booked passenger arrives for
     the flight
q - the probability that a passenger 'no shows',
     [i.e. q = (1-p)]
j - the number of reduced fare tickets sold for a flight
r - the reduced fare rate as a fraction of the full fare.

19.3 DEVELOPMENT OF THE MODEL

When developing models I always find it natural, and helpful
to my understanding of the problem, to develop the model in
stages and check, at each stage, that the properties of the
model accord with my intuition about the real system being
modelled. In this vein I started off by modelling the profit
an airline might expect from an underbooked flight.

19.3.1 A First Attempt

The costs associated with running a particular flight are
largely independent of the number of passengers carried on the
flight. The airline must pay its pilots, navigators,
engineers and cabin staff regardless of whether the airplane
is full or not. The extra fuel consumed by a full airliner
compared to that consumed by a half empty one is very little
as a percentage of the gross fuel load. A very high
percentage of the take-off weight of an airliner is the fuel
it needs to carry to reach its destination, and much of that
fuel is required to enable the airliner to carry the remainder
of the fuel to the point in the flight where it will be used.
The take-off, landing and handling fees charged by airports
are independent of the number of passengers carried by an
aircraft. Thus, to a sufficient degree of accuracy, we may
ignore the variable costs of a flight and assume that the cost
to an airline of running a flight is a fixed sum £f. Each
passenger carried pays a fare and the difference between the
fares paid and the cost of the flight is the surplus or, in
some sense, the profit. Of course there are other costs (e.g.
maintenance of aircraft, cost of ground-based staff, cost of
publicity) which may already have been allocated in
determining f, or which may still have to be deducted from

this surplus before arriving at the final profit figure. For our purposes, however, determining the effect of certain decisions on the surplus, whether gross or net of such costs, will be adequate. Also different passengers pay different fares. There are First Class, Club Class, Tourist Class, Economy, Apex, Super Apex and a host of other options open to passengers. For the moment, though, let us suppose that all passengers are carried at one fare.

Here again, I would normally try to keep a model as simple as possible at first and go back to include more features once I had the basic model formulated. Such an approach is a good discipline for students as it compels them to develop basic models without being confused by a welter of detail. Once they have achieved a basic understanding of their model they can go back and include more detailed effects. I find that, left to their own devices, the most common stumbling block for students in their modelling activities is their determination to include all effects, great and small, right from the word go.

If a flight carries n passengers the surplus generated is £(ng - f) where £g is the fare paid by each passenger. Fairly obviously this simple model has the properties we would expect of it. As the number of passengers carried increases the profit increases. The maximum profit that can be made is £(Ng - f) where N is the passenger capacity of the airliner. There is a break-even point at which the fares paid by the passengers carried just covers the cost of the flight, $n = f/g$, and for fewer passengers than this the flight makes a loss. All these points are as we would expect.

At first sight this simple model suggests that, in order to make as much profit as possible, the airliner should aim to fill each flight. Once N bookings have been received the flight is full and no more bookings are accepted. The problem that arises is that some passengers may fail to turn up at the airport for their flight. The standard conditions of carriage for airline passengers allow full fare passengers to do this without penalty. They can turn up at the airport later and their tickets will be valid for another flight. This is not the case for certain other categories of passengers and we shall return to this point later. Each passenger who fails to turn up represents a loss of potential revenue. Such passengers are known in the business as 'no shows'.

19.3.2 A Better Model

Let us develop the simple model proposed above in the following way. Suppose that the probability of k 'no shows' is P_k. Let us denote the number of passengers booked onto a flight by m, and allow that m may exceed N. The surplus that the airline will make from the flight when there are k no shows is

$$S = (m - k)g - f \quad \text{if} \quad m - k \leqslant N$$
$$= Ng - f \quad \text{if} \quad m - k > N \tag{1}$$

The number of passengers who will fail to appear for their flight is a chance event so the appropriate indicator for the profit from a flight is the probabilistic expected profit. Let us denote it by S. Then

$$\bar{S} = \sum_{k=0}^{m} P_k \times [\text{surplus from a flight with (m-k) passengers}] \tag{2}$$

$$= \sum_{k=0}^{m-N-1} P_k (Ng - f) + \sum_{k=m-N}^{m} P_k [(m - k)g - f]$$

If $m \leqslant N$ then the first summation disappears and $\bar{S}$ is given by the second summation alone with the lower limit replaced by zero. Obviously the number of passengers booked onto a flight may be small because of a lack of demand. In such cases the airline has no problem in determining how many passengers to book or overbook onto a flight. Since the problem we want to elucidate is the airline's behaviour when there is excess demand we will assume now that such is the case and that, whatever maximum booking level m is set by the airline, it will always be achieved. Such would probably be the case on daytime flights on busy routes.

Now we can rewrite (2) as

$$\bar{S} = \sum_{k=0}^{m} P_k (Ng - f) + \sum_{k=m-N}^{m} P_k [(m - k)g - f - (Ng - f)]$$

$$= (Ng - f) \sum_{k=0}^{m} P_k + \sum_{k=m-N}^{m} P_k (m - N - k)g$$

By the definition of the P_k, $\sum_{k=0}^{m} P_k = 1$, so we have

$$\bar{S} = Ng - f + g \sum_{k=m-N}^{m} P_k (m - N - k)$$

$$= Ng - f - g \sum_{j=0}^{N} jP_{m - N + j}$$

Hence we find $\bar{S} \leqslant Ng - f$ since the terms of the summation are all positive. The only way to get the expected profit near to its maximum is to reduce all the $P_{m - N + j}$, for $0 < j < N$, to as near zero as possible.

This is achieved if the booking level m exceeds N substantially, for, as the pool of booked passengers increases, the probability of any large number of 'no shows' decreases.

The second model, then, predicts that an airline, in the presence of uncertainty as to the number of booked passengers who will actually turn up for their flights, will substantially overbook flights in order to achieve an expected profit somewhere near the theoretical maximum achievable with a full aircraft. There is no deterrent in this model to overbooking even at the level of many times the capacity of the flight. This strategy results, however, in a number of passengers being turned away from almost all flights and this number increases as the level of overbooking increases. Thus we begin to understand why an airline, in an attempt to operate as profitably as possible, may deliberately overbook flights. The prediction of a very substantial level of overbooking seems somewhat unrealistic, however, and further refinement of the model is necessary.

19.3.3 A Further Refinement

In cases where an airline has overbooked flights and has more passengers at the airport than the capacity of the aircraft, the excess passengers must be turned away and offered seats on later flights perhaps. The airline may be liable to pay certain expenses to the passenger resulting from his delay, or the passenger may decide to travel on another airline and the ticket will have to be transferred to that airline incurring some administrative costs and a loss of potential revenue. Also there is the accompanying bad publicity and loss of public image of the airline. Let us assume that, for each passenger who cannot be carried on the booked flight (the passenger is said, in the business, to have been 'bumped'), a cost of £b is incurred, in one way or another, by the airline. A more sophisticated model that takes the penalty for overbooking into account in arriving at the average revenue the airline expects from the flight may now be constructed. The number of passengers arriving at the airline desk at the airport hoping to travel on the flight is m-k. The profit from the flight is

$$S = (m - k)\, g - f \qquad\qquad \text{if} \qquad m - k \leqslant N$$
$$= Ng - f - (m - k - N)\, b \qquad \text{if} \qquad m - k > N \qquad\qquad (3)$$

The average or expected profit made by the airline from a flight is then the sum over all possible numbers of 'no shows' of the profit with that number of no shows multiplied by the probability of that number of no shows. Hence we have

$$\bar{S} = \sum_{k=0}^{m} P_k \,[\text{profit from } (m-k) \text{ passengers}] \qquad (3a)$$

$$= \sum_{k=0}^{m-N-1} P_k[\,(Ng-f) - (m-k-N)b\,] + \sum_{k=m-N}^{m} P_k[\,(m-k)g - f\,]$$

$$= \sum_{k=0}^{m-N-1} P_k[(N-m+k)g - (m-k-N)b] + (mg-f) \sum_{k=0}^{m} P_k - g \sum_{k=0}^{m} kP_k$$

Now $\sum_{k=0}^{m} P_k = 1$ and $\sum_{k=0}^{m} kP_k$ is the expected number of 'no shows', which we will denote $\bar{k}$.

$$\bar{S} = mg - f - \bar{k}g - (b + g) \sum_{k=0}^{m-N-1} P_k (m - N - k)$$

$$= (m - \bar{k})g - f - (b + g) \sum_{k=0}^{m-N-1} P_k (m - N - k) \qquad (4)$$

We now have a relatively complicated intermediate result which we would like to verify in some way. To check the validity of such results, and detect arithmetic errors, I often try out one or two special cases to see if the results are as I expect. When I was writing this I detected one such error at this stage. It is important to teach students to be constructively and continuously critical of their work.

To check this result let us put $P_0 = 1$ and $P_k = 0$ for $k \geqslant 1$ in (4).

This corresponds to a zero chance of any passenger failing to show up so all the passengers booked on the flight appear. In this case (4) reduces to

$$\bar{S} = (m - \bar{k})g - f - (b + g)(m - N)$$

$$= Ng - f - b(m - N) \quad \text{since } \bar{k} = 0$$

This shows, as we would expect, that if m passengers are booked onto a flight with a capacity of N and they all show up, the profit will be Ng-f, from flying a full aircraft, less the cost, $(m - N)b$, of bumping the $(m - N)$ surplus passengers. In this case the maximum average profit is achieved when $m = N$ which agrees with the first simple model.

So far we have made no assumptions about the form of the P_k.

In order to obtain more insight from the models developed it will be helpful to make some plausible assumptions about these probabilities. Perhaps the simplest assumption is to take the probability of any given passenger turning up as p. The probability of a 'no show' is then q.

Making the further assumption that the arrivals of passengers are independent of each other would lead to the binomial distribution for the P_k,

$$P_k = {}^{m}C_k \, q^k p^{m-k} \tag{5}$$

In fact, of course, the assumption of independence of 'no shows' is not entirely valid - a percentage of passengers tends to arrive (or to fail to arrive) in pairs or small groups. However, for the time being, let us put this added difficulty aside. With this distribution $\bar{k} = qm$ and (4) becomes

$$\bar{S} = pmg - f - (b + g) \sum_{k=0}^{m-N-1} P_k (m - N - k) \tag{6}$$

What an airline will try to do now is to maximise the average profit from the flight. The expression for the average profit in (6) is dependent on g,b,f,q,m and N. The costs and prices f,g and b are beyond the airline's short term control (fares are set by IATA not by the individual airlines), q and N are

external constraints which leaves the airline with the booking
level, m, as the controllable parameter. As a result of the
presence of the partial sum in (6) the problem can best be
solved by enumeration. However it is evident that the optimum
booking level must be at least N, the capacity of the aircraft,
since from (3a) the expected profit for m < n reduces to

$$\bar{S} = \sum_{k=0}^{m} P_k[(mg-f) - kg]$$

$$= (mg-f) \sum P_k - g \sum kP_k$$

$$= mg-f - q\, mg$$

$$= pmg - f$$

which is an increasing function of m.

The evaluation of the P_k from (5) involves different values for
each P_k for each booking level m. The evaluation of these will
be laborious by hand. If a computer is available students
could be encouraged to write a program which computes the
expected profit from any combination of g,b,f,q,N and m and
then use it to determine optimum booking level for some set of
g,b,f,q and N. If the computation is to be done by hand (or
using a non-programmable calculator) I would explore with them
first of all the possibilities of further simplification. For
instance if N is sufficiently large (and N ≈ 300 for an Airbus,
≈350 for a DC-10 or Lockheed Tristar, ≈450 for a Boeing 747)
the substitution of the terms of the Poisson distribution for
the binomial distribution will not make a great deal of
difference. On the other hand the number of terms in the
partial sum in (6) is (m - N) and the partial sum must be
evaluated for a range of m in order to find the optimum booking
level. The labour involved will be reduced by choosing a small
aircraft (say an 80 seater feederliner) which will yield only 8
terms for a 10% overbooking as opposed to a 450 seater jumbo
jet yielding 45 terms in the partial sum for a 10% booking.

The partial sum in (6) will be a function of q, N and m. A
computer program was written to evaluate the partial sums for
given values of q, N and m. The expected profit can then be
seen to be a function of q,m,g,f,b and N. Airlines operate
with a break-even load factor of around 60% so we could assume,
to a good approximation, that 0.6 Ng = f. Then we would have

$$\frac{\bar{S}}{f} = \frac{1}{.6N} \left[pm - (1 + \frac{b}{g}) \sum_{k=0}^{m-N-1} P_k (m - N - k) \right] - 1 \qquad (7)$$

The computer program has been used to compute expected profit against booking level for an aircraft with a capacity of 300 passengers assuming q = 0.05, 0.1 and b/g = 0.2 with the results shown in Table 19.1. It is apparent that the level of overbooking required to maximise the expected profit is substantial. We can also compute the probability that j or more passengers are bumped as

$$P[\text{j or more passengers bumped}] = \sum_{k=0}^{m-N-j} P_k$$

Included in Table 19.1 are the probabilities of bumping at least one passenger and of bumping 5 or more.

| $q = 0.05$ | | | | | $q = 0.1$ | | | |
m	$\bar{S}/f$	P{≥1bump}	P{≥5bumps}		m	$\bar{S}/f$	P{≥1bump}	P{≥5bumps}
300	0.58333	0.000	0.000		300	0.50000	0.000	0.000
301	0.58861	0.000	0.000		301	0.50500	0.000	0.000
302	0.59389	0.000	0.000		302	0.51000	0.000	0.000
303	0.59916	0.000	0.000		303	0.51500	0.000	0.000
304	0.60444	0.000	0.000		304	0.52000	0.000	0.000
305	0.60972	0.001	0.000		305	0.52500	0.000	0.000
306	0.61498	0.002	0.000		306	0.53000	0.000	0.000
307	0.62022	0.005	0.000		307	0.53500	0.000	0.000
308	0.62542	0.015	0.000		308	0.54000	0.000	0.000
309	0.63052	0.027	0.000		309	0.54500	0.000	0.000
310	0.63547	0.051	0.002		310	0.55000	0.000	0.000
311	0.64018	0.088	0.005		311	0.55500	0.000	0.000
312	0.64454	0.142	0.011		312	0.56000	0.000	0.000
313	0.64846	0.211	0.024		313	0.56500	0.000	0.000
314	0.65185	0.294	0.046		314	0.57000	0.000	0.000
315	0.65465	0.387	0.081		315	0.57500	0.000	0.000
316	0.65683	0.485	0.131		316	0.57999	0.001	0.000
317	0.65839	0.581	0.196		317	0.58499	0.001	0.000
318	0.65939	0.671	0.277		318	0.58997	0.002	0.000
319	0.65988	0.751	0.367		319	0.59495	0.004	0.000
320	0.65996	0.818	0.464		320	0.59991	0.007	0.000
321	0.65970	0.871	0.561		321	0.60483	0.012	0.001
322	0.65919	0.912	0.652		322	0.60971	0.019	0.002
323	0.65849	0.942	0.734		323	0.61453	0.030	0.003
324	0.65766	0.963	0.803		324	0.61925	0.045	0.006
325	0.65675	0.977	0.860		325	0.62385	0.065	0.010
326	0.65578	0.988	0.903		326	0.62828	0.091	0.016
					327	0.63251	0.125	0.025
					328	0.63650	0.165	0.039
					329	0.64019	0.212	0.057
					330	0.64357	0.265	0.080
					331	0.64659	0.324	0.111
					332	0.64922	0.386	0.148
					333	0.65147	0.451	0.192
					334	0.65333	0.517	0.242
					335	0.65480	0.581	0.298
					336	0.65590	0.643	0.359
					337	0.65665	0.701	0.423
					338	0.65710	0.753	0.488
					339	0.65727	0.800	0.553
					340	0.65720	0.840	0.615
					341	0.65693	0.875	0.675
					342	0.65649	0.903	0.729
					343	0.65592	0.927	0.778
					344	0.65523	0.945	0.821
					345	0.65447	0.960	0.859

Table 19.1 Expected profit and bump probabilities for 300 seat airliner with b = .2g and g = $\frac{f}{.6N}$

In these cases it is seen that the maximum expected profit arises when the flights are overbooked by 20 and 39 passengers respectively. The probability of bumping 5 or more passengers in 46% and 55%, substantial figures. An exploration of the effect of the cost of each bump yields the results in Table 19.2. The results agree with intuitive expectations. As the penalty associated with each bump increases the level of overbooking which maximises the expected profit from the flight decreases. The associated probability of bumping any given number of passengers (the probability of bumping five or more is given as an example here) is reduced.

b/g	booking level for maximum $\bar{S}/f$	$\bar{S}/f$	$p\{\geqslant 5 \text{bumps}\}$
.1	321	.663	.56
.2	320	.660	.46
.3	319	.658	.37
.4	318	.656	.28
.5	317	.655	.20

(a) $q = 0.05$

b/g	booking level for maximum $\bar{S}/f$	$\bar{S}/f$	$p\{\geqslant 5 \text{bumps}\}$
.1	342	.661	.73
.2	339	.657	.55
.3	338	.654	.49
.4	337	.652	.42
.5	336	.650	.36

(b) $q = 0.1$

b/g	booking level for maximum $\bar{S}/f$	$\bar{S}/f$	$p\{\geqslant 5 \text{bumps}\}$
.1	364	.660	.77
.2	361	.655	.64
.3	359	.652	.55
.4	357	.649	.44
.5	356	.646	.40

(c) $q = 0.15$

Table 19.2. Booking levels for maximum expected profit, as a fraction of fixed costs of flight, for a 300 seat airliner with $g = \dfrac{f}{.6N}$

A good exercise here would be to discuss with students how the
estimate of b would be arrived at by an airline. The cost is
probably composed of very tangible direct costs and some
relatively intangible indirect costs like loss of goodwill and
future custom. This discussion should lead on to a
consideration of sensitivity. One way to obtain a good
understanding and estimate of the likely errors in a model's
predictions is to vary the imput parameters and observe the
sensitivity of the output to these variations.

Another interesting avenue to explore here is possible
alternative criteria for choosing the level of overbooking.
An airline may decide that its criterion would be a certain,
presumably low, probability of having to bump any passengers.
It may wish, perhaps, to run an advertising campaign
emphasising that it, above all rivals, has the lowest bump
rate. Students could then be asked to formulate measures of
economic performance to evaluate this strategy. I would
suggest a comparison of the expected profit resulting from
this strategy for setting the overbooking level with the
maximum expected profit achievable from the overbooking
strategy already outlined. This leads one naturally into the
whole area of multi-criterion decision making and the problems
of trade-offs between incommensurable criteria.

The figures in Table 19.2 suggest that the probability of
bumping 5 or more passengers is extremely sensitive to
variation in the value of b as a proportion of g. On the other
hand the expected profit is relatively insensitive to such
variation. In practice this would suggest that the airline's
decision makers would err generously on the side of
overestimating b – it is rather hard to estimate b accurately
and the penalty, in terms of lower average profit, for
overestimating it is small whilst the benefit, in terms of
reduced probability of bumping a significant number of passengers,
is large.

19.3.4 Yet Another Refinement

If only one or two passengers are bumped from a flight it is
probable that the incident can be kept relatively quiet, but a
substantial group of dissatisfied passengers could cause an
ugly scene at the airline desk in the airport, and airlines
wish to minimise the risk of this. It may be that, in
formulating booking policy, the airline adopts a policy that
is less than optimal in terms of maximising expected profit
but which has the merit of reducing the probability of a large
number of bumps from one flight to an acceptably low level.
An alternative is to try to find ways of increasing the
likelihood of passengers booked onto a flight actually turning

up. This can be achieved by the use of APEX, ABC and other special fare schemes. With these schemes the passenger is offered a ticket valid only for a specified flight but at a reduced fare. If passengers fail to arrive for that flight the ticket is void and the passengers lose their money. Obviously some passengers (chiefly business travellers requiring some flexibil in their planning) will still be prepared to pay full fare to retain that flexibility, whilst other (chiefly holiday makers) will accept the restriction in return for the reduced fare. The second category of passengers will not miss their flight lightly so we can assume that their 'no show' probability is virtually zero. These passengers then form a solid base of passengers who can be relied on to turn up for the flight.

Suppose j such passengers are booked onto a flight at a fraction r of the full fare. Then the profit from j reduced rate and m-k-j full fare passengers is

$$S = rjg + (m-j-k)g-f \qquad \text{if} \qquad m-k \leqslant N$$
$$ = rjg + (N - j)g-f-(m-k-N)b \qquad \text{if} \qquad m-k > N \tag{8}$$

The probability of k no shows, however, is now the probability of k out of (m-j) full fare passengers failing to appear, i.e.

$$P_k = {}^{m-j}C_k \, q^k \, p^{m-j-k} \tag{9}$$

The expected profit from the flight is

$$\bar{S} = \sum_{k=0}^{m-N-1} P_k [\,(N-j(1-r))g-f-(m-k-N)b]$$

$$+ \sum_{k=m-N}^{m} P_k [\,(m-k-j(1-r))g-f]$$

$$= \sum_{k=0}^{m-N-1} P_k [\,(N-m-k)g-(m-k-N)b]$$

$$+ [\,(m-j(1-r))g-f]\sum_{k=0}^{m} P_k - g \sum_{0}^{m} k \, P_k$$

$$= m-j(1+r)g-f-qmg-(b+g) \sum_{k=0}^{m-N-1} P_k (m-N-k)$$

$$= pmg-(1+r)jg-f-(b+g) \sum_{k=0}^{m-N-1} P_k (m-N-k) \tag{10}$$

This equation could be programmed as it stands and an
exploration of the effects of changes in p,m,g,j,r,b,g and N
undertaken. The complication of this can be reduced if, as
before, we make a plausible assumption about the relationship
of g, the full rate fare, to f, the cost of the flight.

In this case we might assume that the break-even load consisted
of a flight with 60% of the seats filled with proportionate
numbers of full fare and reduced fare passengers. The result of
this is that, as the proportion of reduced fare passengers is
increased, the basic full fare also increases since the
proportion of passengers paying it is decreased. The break even
condition is then

$$.6 \ (jrg+(N-j)g) = f$$

$$\text{i.e.} \qquad \frac{g}{f} = \frac{1}{.6(N-(1-r)j)}$$

So, deriving the equation equivalent to (7) from (10), leads to

$$\frac{\bar{s}}{f} = \frac{1}{.6(N-(1-r)j)} \left[pm-(1-r)j-(1+b) \frac{1}{g} \sum_{0}^{m-N-1} P_k(m-N-k) \right] -1. \quad (11)$$

The previous program was modified to compute $\bar{s}/f$ under these
circumstances. The model has been developed now to the point
where there are sufficient variables and parameters to make the
presentation of the results in a useful and clear way an
increasing problem. This, in itself, is a useful teaching
point. One of the skills needed by mathematicians in industrial
and commercial environments is the ability to present and
communicate their findings to non-mathematicians in a clear and
lucid fashion. This model illustrates well one of the problems
that arises in so doing.

Table 19.3 presents some typical results from the use of the
model embodied in (11). The choice of the parameters q,N,b/g,
and r is made just for illustrative purposes. It would be
possible to evaluate the effects on $\bar{s}$ for various booking levels
of varying any of these as well as varying j. From Table 19.3
we see, as we would expect, that as j increases the booking
level that maximises $\bar{s}/f$ decreases and the probability of
bumping passengers decreases also.

m	$\bar{S}/f$	p{$\geqslant$1bump}	p{$\geqslant$5bumps}
300	0.58333	0.000	0.000
301	0.58861	0.000	0.000
302	0.59389	0.000	0.000
303	0.59916	0.000	0.000
304	0.60444	0.000	·0.000
305	0.60972	0.001	0.000
306	0.61498	0.002	0.000
307	0.62022	0.005	0.000
308	0.62541	0.013	0.000
309	0.63050	0.027	0.000
310	0.63542	0.051	0.002
311	0.64008	0.088	0.005
312	0.64436	0.142	0.011
313	0.64817	0.211	0.024
314	0.65140	0.294	0.046
315	0.65400	0.387	0.081
316	0.65591	0.485	0.131
317	0.65717	0.581	0.196
318	0.65781	0.671	0.277
319	0.65790	0.751	0.367
320	0.65755	0.818	0.464

(a) $j = 0$

m	$\bar{S}/f$	p{$\geqslant$1bump}	p{$\geqslant$5bumps}
300	0.57971	0.000	0.000
301	0.58522	0.000	0.000
302	0.59072	0.000	0.000
303	0.59623	0.000	0.000
304	0.60173	0.001	0.000
305	0.60721	0.004	0.000
306	0.61263	0.011	0.000
307	0.61795	0.025	0.000
308	0.62307	0.053	0.001
309	0.62788	0.096	0.003
310	0.63222	0.159	0.009
311	0.63597	0.241	0.023
312	0.63903	0.338	0.047
313	0.64132	0.443	0.087
314	0.64284	0.551	0.146
315	0.64365	0.651	0.224
316	0.64382	0.741	0.318
317	0.64347	0.815	0.421

(b) $j = 50$

m	$\bar{S}/f$	p{≥1bump}	p{≥5bumps}
300	0.57576	0.000	0.000
301	0.58151	0.000	0.000
302	0.58727	0.000	0.000
303	0.59301	0.002	0.000
304	0.59871	0.008	0.000
305	0.60429	0.022	0.000
306	0.60965	0.052	0.000
307	0.61461	0.104	0.002
308	0.61899	0.179	0.007
309	0.62263	0.278	0.020
310	0.62541	0.393	0.046
311	0.62728	0.513	0.093
312	0.62829	0.628	0.164
313	0.62854	0.730	0.258
314	0.62817	0.813	0.369

(c) j = 100

m	$\bar{S}/f$	p{≥1bump}	p{≥5bumps}
300	0.57143	0.000	0.000
301	0.57746	0.000	0.000
302	0.58346	0.004	0.000
303	0.58936	0.016	0.000
304	0.59500	0.048	0.000
305	0.60016	0.109	0.000
306	0.60456	0.203	0.003
307	0.60798	0.328	0.014
308	0.61032	0.464	0.047
309	0.61159	0.600	0.097
310	0.61193	0.720	0.184
311	0.61152	0.816	0.301

(d) j = 150

Table 19.3 Variation of expected profits and bump probabilities with booking level for different levels of reduced fare ticket sales. 300 seat airliner, b =.3g, r = .75, q = 0.05. $\frac{g}{f} = \frac{1}{.6(N-(1-r)j)}$.

The models developed in this chapter do not lead to any definite conclusions because there are many external parameters to which we cannot assign definite values without further research. The chapter does however illustrate the process of model building by successive refinement, the use of models to obtain qualitative results (e.g. trends and sensitivities) and the problems of organising conclusions concerning parameters which are functions of many variables.

19.4 SUGGESTIONS FOR FURTHER MODELLING WORK

The problem considered in this chapter is just one of a number of similar situations in which an owner of a resource which is lent, hired or sold to the public has to make decisions concerning future promises of goods to customers who may or may not materialise. Listed below are a selection of similar problems which should provide fruitful ground for modelling exercises.

1. THE HOTEL

Hotels accept future bookings largely on trust. They have very little come-back on clients who fail to materialise. Some hotels demand a deposit on booking to secure a higher probability that the customer will materialise. (These tend to be the lower price hotels whose operating margins may be tighter.) Other hotels may offer reduced rates for longer term bookings or for prepaid bookings. Some so-called 'bargain breaks' where lower rates are offered involve an element of prepayment. The operation of such multiple rate systems could be considered.

2. THE CAR HIRE FIRM

Car hire firms have a fixed number of cars (at least in the short term) to allocate to customers. Hire firms may have arrangements with customers (chiefly companies) who hire vehicles frequently whereby they offer reduced rates in return for a guaranteed minimum amount of business. Reduced rates are offered for longer term rentals (weekly or monthly rental) since such business gives a measure of certainty at least a few days into the future. A firm may well allocate rather more cars than they actually have available in the expectation that some bookings will not materialise.

3. THE LIBRARY

Libraries may purchase multiple copies of popular books. This applies particularly to course texts in college and university libraries. Some copies may be confined to the library in order to maximise their availablity to students. A model of book availablility could be attempted.

20

Estimating fertilizer requirements of vegetable crops

TONY BARNES *University of Queensland*

20.1 STATEMENT OF THE PROBLEM

A series of field experiments has been carried out at a crop Research Institute to investigate how the yields of crops of the different vegetables are related to the amounts of various types of fertilizer added to the soil in which the crops were grown. These experiments were all carried out on the same type of soil, the characteristics of which were fairly well recorded. Unlike important agricultural crops such as wheat, barley and sugar beet, it is not considered economically justifiable to repeat similar experiments covering all the different types of soil on which vegetables are grown throughout the country. From the results of this limited set of vegetable experiments and other relevant information, how can the relationship between yields and fertilizer levels be estimated for all possible combinations of vegetable species and soil types?

20.2 BACKGROUND INFORMATION

Synthetic fertilizer is a vital part of modern agriculture. Fertilizers are applied to the soil before most agricultural and horticultural crops are grown. Without them, crop yields would be drastically reduced; indeed, there would be more starvation throughout much of the world. It is, therefore, extremely important that sufficient quantities of the correct types of fertilizer are applied to fields when they are being prepared for a crop. However, fertilizers are expensive and their costs are rising all the time, so, it is important that fertilizers should not be squandered. Other problems also arise if too much fertilizer is used - pollution of underground aquifers and lakes can occur when excess fertilizer is washed away in drainage water and, for certain types of fertilizer, too high concentrations in the soil can directly reduce yields due to toxic effects on plants. So, besides supplying enough fertilizer, it is important that excessive applications are avoided.

The purpose of adding fertilizer to soil is to augment the amounts of certain inorganic chemical nutrients in the soil. Amongst the many chemical elements necessary for proper plant growth there are three that are required in larger quantities than the others (nitrogen, N, potassium, K, phosphorus , P) and these are often in short supply in farm soils in this country. Corresponding to these three nutrients there are fertilizers, each consisting of chemicals containing one or more of these nutrients.

Although there are many differences between soil types that affect plant growth, it is often suggested by soil scientists that soils can be graded on the basis of the amounts of each of the three major nutrients they contain at the beginning of a growing season, when no fertilizer has been added. These base levels of nutrients tend to remain fairly constant from one year to the next and may be thought of as arising because equilibrium is established between fixation and release of chemicals by clay particles and soil micro-organisms. This is an over simplification, for N in particular, but will suffice for t present purposes. One approach often adopted by farmers to the application of fertilizers is that sufficient fertilizer of each type is added to the soil each season to bring the soil up to a minimum nutrient status. This will be wasteful if some crops require more or less than these fairly arbitrarily chosen minimum nutrient levels.

Growing plants in a crop take up nutrients and water from the soil through their root systems. For this to occur it is obviously necessary for the nutrients to come into contact with the roots. This comes about partly because roots proliferate throughout the soil and partly because nutrients, in water solution, move towards roots by a combination of the process of diffusion down concentration gradients and as a consequence of water moving towards roots. Plants require the nutrients N, P and K to construct new tissues and if these are insufficiently supplied the rate of growth of the plants will be reduced, sometimes severely. When very high concentrations of N are present in soils, particularly at low water contents, the movement of water into roots can be hindered, resulting in restrictions of growth.

In order that farmers may be advised accurately about what quantities of fertilizer should be applied, a great deal of effort has been put into extensive field experimental programmes, carried out throughout the country and over many

years. Not unnaturally, this work has concentrated on the
major agricultural crops such as wheat, sugar beet and grass.
The aims of each of these experiments have been to observe,
for the particular combination of crop species, soil type and
climatic conditions under which the experiment is carried out,
the crop yields resulting when different amounts of the three
nutrients, as fertilizer, are added. From the results of these
experiments it has been possible to arrive at estimates of the
expected relationship between crop yields and quantities of
applied fertilizer, for any crop species and soil type.
Agricultural Advisory Officers use these relations when advising
farmers on fertilizer application rates for the more important
agricultural crops.

One observation made repeatedly during the course of the
experimental programme with agricultural crops was that if a
crop species was more responsive than another crop to a
particular type of fertilizer on one soil in one year (ie. it
gave a larger percentage increase in yield following a given
fertilizer application), it was generally more
responsive to that fertilizer type on other soils in the same
or other years. So, although there was considerable variation
in the absolute magnitudes of the yields across soil types and
seasons, the relative responsiveness of different crop species
remained reasonably consistent.

Ideally, a similar experimental programme would have been
carried out for each of the vegetable species,but this cannot
be justified economically. As a compromise, a series of
experiments covering all vegetable types was conducted at one
site. A commonly used format for these vegetable experiments
was to apply various quantities of one fertilizer type to
different field plots and to apply fixed quantities of the other
two types of fertilizer to all the plots. A small selection of
some of the yield data collected from these studies is shown
in Table 20.1. Only the levels of one fertilizer type were
varied in each experiment, the quantities of the other two
fertilizers being equal to the seventh level when they
themselves were varied. For example, in the N study on broad
beans, 196 kg/ha P and 372 kg/ha K were applied to the soil
irrespective of the level of N fertilizer.

The information gained about the behaviour of vegetable yields
at different fertilizer levels in these experiments is of rather
limited value to a vegetable grower with the problem of deciding
how much fertilizer to apply to his vegetable crops growing on
his particular soil, which may not have the same characteristics
as the experimental soil. From the more extensive experimental
programme on agricultural crops, some knowledge of the general
differences between soil types with respect to fertilizer
requirements was gained. The purpose of this modelling exercise

FERTILIZERS FOR VEGETABLE CROPS

	N		P		K	
	Fertilizer (kg/ha)	Yield (t/ha)	Fertilizer (kg/ha)	Yield (t/ha)	Fertilizer (kg/ha)	Yield (t/ha)
Broad beans	0	12.20	0	12.68	0	9.69
	28	13.01	24	12.45	47	10.67
	56	12.73	49	12.63	93	12.43
	84	12.73	73	13.38	140	13.01
	112	12.25	98	13.61	186	13.48
	168	12.43	147	13.78	179	13.68
	224	12.30	196	13.36	372	12.83
	280	12.28	245	13.06	465	12.93
	336	12.45	294	13.83	558	12.85
	396	12.93	342	13.86	651	13.21
Brussel sprouts	0	2.59	0	8.21	0	8.21
	45	4.10	12	8.75	23	8.28
	90	4.87	24	8.72	47	9.25
	135	6.25	37	8.43	70	8.74
	179	7.21	49	8.09	93	8.86
	269	8.82	73	9.36	140	8.36
	359	9.52	98	9.29	186	9.27
	448	9.56	122	9.21	233	8.72
	538	8.24	147	9.07	279	7.96
	629	7.77	171	9.74	326	7.65
Potatoes	0	15.18	0	33.46	0	18.98
	34	21.36	24	32.47	47	27.35
	67	25.72	49	36.06	93	34.86
	101	32.29	73	37.96	140	38.52
	135	34.03	98	41.04	186	38.44
	202	39.45	147	40.09	279	37.73
	259	43.15	196	41.26	372	38.43
	336	43.46	245	42.17	465	43.87
	404	40.83	294	40.36	558	42.77
	471	30.75	342	42.73	651	46.22
Lettuce	0	11.02	0	6.39	0	15.75
	28	12.70	49	9.48	47	16.76
	56	14.56	98	12.46	93	16.89
	84	16.27	147	14.33	140	16.24
	112	17.75	196	17.10	186	17.56
	168	22.59	294	21.94	179	19.20
	224	21.63	391	22.64	372	17.97
	280	19.34	489	21.34	465	15.84
	336	16.12	587	22.07	558	20.11
	392	14.11	685	24.53	651	19.40
Spinach	0	9.21	0	3.33	0	5.06
	56	19.41	24	6.35	56	8.59
	182	25.18	49	10.49	112	13.46
	168	27.04	73	13.78	167	17.27
	224	28.27	98	15.21	223	19.88
	336	28.25	147	20.66	335	23.20
	448	24.71	196	23.88	447	24.53
	560	23.34	245	24.33	558	28.17
	673	19.88	294	25.46	670	27.92
	785	18.35	342	26.11	782	28.35

Table 20.1 A small selection of results from fertilizer experimen
on vegetable crops. The initial amounts of nutrients
the soil on which these experiments were carried out w
56 kg/ha N, 49 kg/ha P and 65 kg/ha K.

is to find some way of combining what can be deduced from the
agricultural experiments about soil difference with what can
be deduced about vegetable species differences from the results
of the vegetable fertilizer experiments, and thus extend the
usefulness of these results beyond the single soil type on which
they were carried out.

20.3   NOTES TO LECTURERS

1.   Some students may wish to consider the problem in an
     economic context. It may be helpful to suggest that in the
     first instance only the relationship between crop yield
     and fertilizer application rates should be considered.
     Some interesting economic considerations are discussed as
     further extensions in Section 20.6.

2.   There are probably two types of approach to tackling the
     problem that may occur to students. Firstly, it may be
     suggested that the growth of plants, with special reference
     to the influence of nutrients, should be simulated. This
     could be done by identifying relevant biological processes
     occurring in the soil and plants, and attempting to formulate
     algebraic descriptions of them. Linking the resulting
     equations to provide a full model would probably require a
     computer program. This is a perfectly valid approach and
     some references are supplied which indicate some research
     workers' attempts along these lines. Models of this type
     very quickly become quite large, because of the many
     biological processes involved, and they contain large
     number of parameters, requiring realistic values which are
     difficult to obtain. Information given here is not
     sufficient for this approach to be successful and it is
     doubtful whether mathematics students would successfully
     search the biological/agricultural literature without being
     able to devote a great deal of time to this problem. In
     fact, even professional agricultural research workers have
     not been able to produce usable models based on this
     approach because of the complexity and number of processes
     involved.

     The second approach is much more empirically based and
     would be centred around examining the data provided. An
     attack along these lines would probably start with a
     graphical examination of the data provided. One version of
     this approach is provided in the solution presented here.
     An important feature about this approach is that it is
     necessary to appreciate that no information about the
     behaviour of vegetable yields at different levels of
     fertilizer application over a range of soil types is
     available in the results of the vegetable experiments. A

means of dealing with soil effects must be derived from the
brief account of major soil differences given in Section
20.2. The comment about the behaviour of agricultural crop
yields from different soils provides an indication of
roughly what might be expected of vegetable species in
different soils. It will also be necessary to find a means
of incorporating soil effects into the chosen procedure
for summarising vegetables species' yields at different
fertilizer levels.

3. It may be necessary to point out to students that constructing
an initial model, with only one type of fertilizer
varying, greatly simplifies the problem. In the modelling
exercise that follows only one fertilizer type is considered;
extensions, to include more than one fertilizer, are
suggested as a further exercise. It should be apparent
from the data and background information that the
relationship between yields and P and K fertilizer levels
is simpler than that for N. Nothing has been said to
suggest that the general nature of the behaviour of yields
with respect to P and K fertilizer is different.

4. Note that the data provided are real experimental results
and contain random experimental errors. However, although
statistical techniques could be used they are not an
essential part of the modelling exercise.

5. This problem definitely does not have a 'correct' answer.
All answers will be approximations; in fact most approaches
of reasonable simplicity may be expected to arrive at
estimated relationships which are quite incorrect for some
combinations of soil type and species. What is required
here is something that will be roughly correct most of the
time.

20.4 A MODEL OF THE RELATIONSHIPS BETWEEN YIELDS AND P
      FERTILIZER

20.4.1 *Fertilizer Requirements on Different Types of Soil*

It was indicated above that the major part of the influence of
soil type on yield-fertilizer relationships came about as a
consequence of the different quantities of nutrients in the
soils prior to the addition of any fertilizer. This suggests
that we may reasonably consider the different base nutrient
levels of the soils as being equivalent to a corresponding
amount of fertilizer. So that a soil with a base level of
phosphorus nutrient of P_o would be equivalent to a soil with a

zero base level but with a quantity, P_o, of phosphorus

fertilizer added. Thus, where a quantity, P, of phosphorus
fertilizer is applied to a soil with base level P_o, the amount
of phosphorus nutrient available to the crop will be
$p = P + P_o$. This assumption is used from hereon and is crucial
to the model.

20.4.2 Deriving an Equation for the Relationship Between Yields for Applied Amount of P Fertilizers

Absolute levels of yield can vary quite considerably from
one crop to another and from one year to another for the same crop
types. Typical shapes of the observed relationships are shown
in Figure 20.1, derived from the raw data provided. It will be
noted that experiments were not carried out over identical
ranges of P fertilizer levels.

The method by which a model will be constructed here is
based on inspection of the data in Figure 20.1. Following
graphical examination it is intended to construct algebraic
equations that describe the observed yield-fertilizer level
relationships. These equations will have two variables,
yield (y) and fertilizer level (P), and will depend on a number
of parameters.

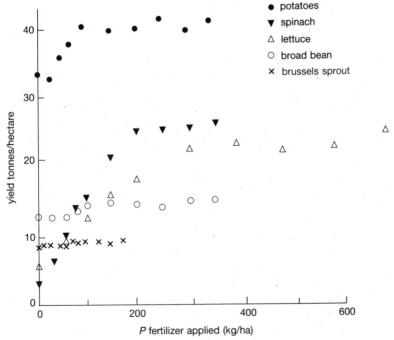

Figure 20.1 Yield v applied P fertilizer for 5 vegetable crops

Bearing in mind that the data in Figure 20.1 include
experimental errors it will be appreciated that the form of
the relationship between the variables y and P vary from (i)
a constant value of y irrespective of P (this would require only
one parameter), (ii) relationships which could be described
reasonably adequately by a straight line, with y increasing
as P increases (two parameters required) and (iii) relationships
which show some evidence of curvature, y increases at a
diminishing rate as P increases (at least three parameters
required).

Some thought about the way plants grow will suggest that
even for those crops which show yield increases at the highest
fertilizer level, this cannot go on indefinitely - yields
cannot be infinite. A second important point is that all
plants require P to grow; so if the experiments had been
carried out on a soil containing very little natural P, all
crops would have had near-zero yields when no P fertilizer was
applied.

To progress further it is necessary to give some sort of
mathematical expression to the shape of these curves. Many
alternatives are obviously possible but, irrespective of the
apparent simplicity of the observed relations in Figures 20.1,
it will clearly help our purposes if a single family of curves
could be used to describe the various types of relationship,
with different parameter values of these curves providing the
means of generating the different shapes.

Further inspection of the curves in Figure 20.1 and
consideration of the likely behaviour of crop yields with
respect to applied fertilizer rates reveals two important
characteristics of these curves.

(i) When no fertilizer is added, yields are at a minimum.
This suggests one important characteristic of the curves is
this minimum yields or, alternatively, this feature of the
curves could be expressed as the effective amount of fertilizer
(nutrients) already in the soil before any is supplied. It
would be convenient if this feature could be identified as a
parameter of our chosen equation.

(ii) At relatively high levels of fertilizer the increase in
yield which is attained, following a given increment in added
fertilizer, tends to be much smaller than the corresponding
yield increase at lower fertilizer rates. Further, there is
no suggestion in the curves that yields show any signs of
diminishing at extremely high fertilizer rates. So, a second
important characteristic of the curves is this maximum, or
asymptotic, yield achieved at very high fertilizer application

rates.   Again, this would make a useful parameter.

At least one further parameter will be required to allow for
the different relative rates at which the asymptotic yield
is approached.   As there is not a great deal of underlying
difference in behaviour of these curves, it will probably be
unnecessary to use more than one shape parameter.   At least,
it seems sensible to investigate the possibility of using only
three parameters first, if only because of the advantages
associated with simplicity.

Many algebraic functions based on three parameters could be
used to describe the main features of the relationships between
y and P as illustrated in Figure 20.1.   Three possible
approached are discussed below, all of which have been used
with varying degrees of success by agricultural scientists.

(i)   The most obvious three parameter equation for
relationships such as those of Figure 20.1 is y as a quadratic
expression in terms of P.   Readers familiar with statistical
curve fitting procedures will see the advantages of a quadratic
expression over most other three parameter equations.   However,
the quadratic has serious limitations for our present purposes.
A quadratic expression either becomes indefinitely large as P
increases, which is not sensible for plant growth, or must have
a maximum in y for some value of P - something not observed in
Figure 20.1.   More seriously, y must decrease after the
maximum, eventually to zero at some high value of P and nothing
like this is observed in the data.   Further, it is not obvious
how the three characteristics mentioned above could be
identified with parameters in a quadratic expression of P for
y.

(ii)   Relationships based on two straight lines, intersecting
at the optimum fertilizer application rate.   One line would
follow the approximate linear increase in yield at low application
rates and the other would be the constant asymptotic yield,
parallel to the P axis.   This approach has the apparent
advantage of generating estimates of the best possible
fertilizer application rate, the point of intersection of the
two lines.   However, as the maximum yield is not usually
approached sharply, as would be implied with two intersecting
straight lines, the point of intersection of the two lines
often gives a biased underestimate of the optimum fertilizer
application rate.

(iii)   A continuous algebraic function with three parameters
might be preferable, monotonically increasing but asymptotic.
Many functions could be considered, but two simple functions
commonly used to describe curves of this shape are ⌐

based on the negative exponential expression

$$y = a(1 - c.\exp(-bP))$$

or based on the hyperbola

$$y = \frac{aP + c}{d + P} \qquad (1)$$

Each of these functions has advantages over the other but these
and many other similar functions have been used by agricultural
research workers in this type of modelling problem. The main
advantage of the exponentially based expression is that the
curves generated by this function tend to have more pronounced
curvature than the hyperbolas and extensive inspection of
experimental data suggests that this type of behaviour may be
more generally appropriate to yield-fertilizer relationships.
The advantages of the hyperbola are mainly associated with the
useful interpretation of its parameters and ease of estimating
values for them (see below). The hyperbolic function will be
used here but it must be stressed that other three-parameter
equations would do almost, if not equally, well.

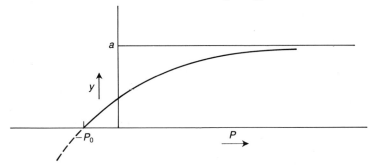

Figure 20.2   The hyperbola chosen to describe yield-fertilizer
relationships

20.4.3   Parameter Identification and Estimation for a Model
Based on the Hyperbola

An implication of the way in which soil differences are to be
represented is that when the curve in Figure 20.2 is traced
back to $y = 0$ the value of P must be $-P_0$. Thus from equation (1)

$$0 = \frac{-aP_0 + c}{d - P_0} \quad \text{giving}$$

$$c = aP_0 .$$

So

$$y = \frac{a(P + P_0)}{d + P} \qquad (2)$$

It is convenient to rewrite (2) as

$$y = \frac{a(P + P_o)}{b + P + P_o}$$

where $d = b + P_o$, so that y is a hyperbola in both P and $P + P_o$.

Different years or seasons tend to influence the relationship
between yields and fertilizer levels mainly by increasing by
reducing yields, irrespective of the amount of added fertilizer.
It is, therefore, reasonable to suppose that the majority of
year differences will be incorporated into the asymptote, a, of
increasing (3). As the intention is to derive relationships
applicable to future years, with as yet unknown weather conditions,
the parameter a is of no direct interest and it is helpful to
estimate it by working in terms of Z = (y/a), which is the
fraction of the maximum yield attained by applying an amount
of fertilizer to P.

$$Z = \frac{P + P_o}{b + P + P_o} \quad . \tag{4}$$

The only remaining parameter in (4) is b. By setting $Z = \frac{1}{2}$
in (4), it will be seen that b can be interpreted as the amount
of P fertilizer that must be added to a zero base soil for the
yield to be equal to half the maximum possible. This is a
very reasonable way of assessing differences between crop
species with respect to fertilizer requirements.

As all vegetable experiments were carried out on a common soil
type, with a known value of P_o, values for b, for all vegetable
crops, can be estimated by plotting the reciprocal of the yield
against added fertilizer plus P_o. From (3) we have

$$\frac{1}{y} = \frac{1}{a} + \frac{b}{a} \cdot \frac{1}{P + P_{oI}} \tag{5}$$

where the subscript I refers to the particular soil used.

Estimates of b are then given by the slope of (5) divided by
the intercept at $\frac{1}{y} = 0$ (Figure 20.3). More exact parameter
estimates can be obtained by statistical curve fitting techniques
which take into account the nature of the experimental
variation in the data.

Inspection of the fitted curves, derived from the data of
Figure 20.1 using equation (5), and the observed crop data
generally shows good agreement. However, occasions do arise

where a strict adherence to the previously suggested
interpretation of the parameters could be misleading. For
instance, the fitted curves for lettuce shown in Figure 20.4
suggest that only 70% of the maximum possible yield is being
achieved at fertilizer rates of 400 kg/ha P; this might be
incorrectly interpreted to mean that much higher rates of
added fertilizer would produce further substantial yield
increases. This situation arises because a , the maximum
yield, has been overestimated for lettuce due to inflexibility
of the hyperbolic functions used here. In this instance, the
maximum yield would have been estimated more precisely had an
exponential family of curves been used. However, failures of
this type in the model can be allowed for provided it is
recognised that they may occur, even though their occurrence
may be infrequent.

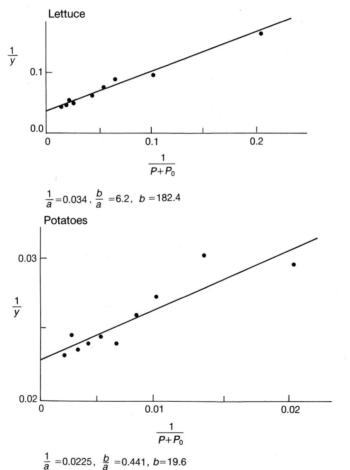

Figure 20.3   Graphs of reciprocals of yield and total nutrients
available to crops derived from the potatoes and
lettuce data supplied.

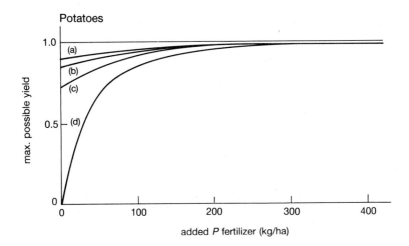

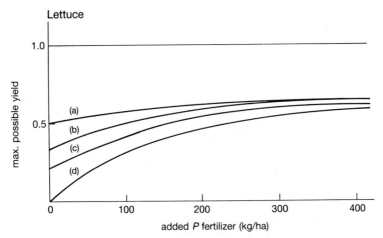

Figure 20.4   Estimated relationships between the proportion of
the maximum possible yield attained and applied
P fertilizer, for potatoes and lettuce.   The
letters indicate relationships appropriate to
different soil types (a) P_o = 200, (b) P_o = 100,
(c) P_o = 50 and (d) P_o = 0 kg/ha.

20.4.4 *Using the Yield-Fertilizer Relationships*

It is now a straightforward exercise to arrive at estimates of
the relationship between fertilizer application rates and
relative crop yields for any vegetable species and soil type,
provided a measurement is available of the amount of
phosphorus in the soil before fertilizer application, P_o .

This is done by substituting this value of P_o and the value of
 b appropriate to the crop concerned (derived from the
experiments on soil type I using equation (5)) into equation
4 (Figure 20.4).

The equations resulting from an extensive experimental and
modelling exercise, along the lines outlined here, have proved
sufficiently useful to be used as a basis for arriving at
officially sanctioned recommendations for P fertilizer application
rates for vegetable growers throughout England and Wales.

20.5 FINAL NOTE

This approach to modelling the yield-fertilizer relationship
proves useful because it was recognised at the outset that soil
type effects must be described by a single parameter which did
not depend on specific vegetable species. If this separation
had not been made it would not have been possible to quantify
soil effects from the known information; and without a method
for dealing with soil effects, the results of the vegetable
experiments could not have been generalised beyond the soil on
which they were done.

20.6 FURTHER PROBLEMS AND EXTENSIONS

1. The model devised for P fertilizer is also appropriate to
    K fertilizer but is not adequate for applications of N.
    Suggest an appropriate extension to take account of the
    depression in yields often observed at high N fertilizer
    rates.

2. In practice situations will rarely occur where only one
    type of fertilizer is in short supply. It is therefore
    necessary to be able to establish the relationship between
    crop yields and fertilizer levels when the rates of
    application of more than one type of fertilizer are varied.
    Suggest a way to combine or extend the single fertilizer
    models to cover this situation. The data provided in
    Table 20.2 are the yields obtained from an experiment with
    French beans in which all possible combinations of five
    rates of application of each of the three main fertilizer
    types were applied to field plots. These data might be

Yield of pods (lb/acre)
K fertilizer applied (kg/ha)

N fertilizer applied	P fertilizer applied		0	168	336	504	672
0	P fertilizer applied	0	7038	10064	10224	10350	11452
		168	7778	10540	10116	10044	10762
		336	7857	10883	10858	10842	11342
		504	8270	11331	10903	11754	10441
		672	6831	10078	10542	10439	10831
168	"	0	9827	15917	14839	15111	16810
		168	9814	17388	16637	16008	16996
		336	8790	18651	16894	17783	17119
		504	8109	19354	19636	17247	16720
		672	8119	18841	17631	18824	30584
336	"	0	9659	14464	14777	15960	14817
		168	8645	18428	19281	18191	20744
		336	9881	18185	20317	19629	20261
		504	8107	18844	20621	19305	20781
		672	8285	22415	18920	20174	22461
504	"	0	8690	14180	12813	14984	14417
		168	7820	18917	18326	19908	18679
		336	10433	18271	19863	19940	19972
		504	7491	18299	19439	17922	22367
		672	8137	19383	18501	20164	19118
672	"	0	9262	10360	13220	13657	14170
		168	9846	16753	16056	18772	19341
		336	10947	17546	19412	23242	20354
		504	8129	17770	19828	21034	19492
		672	9844	19469	20038	20413	21774

Table 20.2   Yield from a French bean experiment carried out on
the same site as the other vegetable experiments.

used either to construct an appropriate multi-fertilizer
model or to check the validity of a model constructed by
combining individual fertilizer models.

3. Students may well have given some thought to what might be
   the most appropriate methods of providing farmers and
   growers with advice on fertilizer application rates.
   There are two basically different approaches. Firstly,
   farmers might be provided with information derived
   exclusively from the estimated yield-fertilizer application
   rate relationship, omitting any economic considerations and
   without suggesting particular optimum fertilizer
   applications. Farmers would then have to make their own
   decisions on precise application rates on the basis of
   their own economic and environmental assessments. A second
   approach would carry out economic analysis relating
   fertilizer costs to profits from expected yield increases.
   Related points that would need to be considered here are
   that cost and profit functions change with time. Also,
   fertilizers are usually sold as compound mixes, i.e. a
   mixture of N, P and K fertilizers in fixed proportions, and
   the number of combinations of mixtures commercially
   available is limited. Discounts might well be given for
   bulk buying of a given mixture and, in addition, dealing
   with a small number of fertilizer combinations simplifies
   application, which may be important for a vegetable grower
   with a large number of different crops requiring differing
   amounts of fertilizers. Suggest an appropriate model for
   estimating optimum fertilizer applications. What information
   would be necessary to enable recommendations based on
   economic considerations to be derived?

SUGGESTED READING

Boyd, D.A., Lowing, T.K., Yuen, and Needham, P., 1976,
    Nitrogen requirements of cereals. *J. Agric. Sci.*, Camb. 87,
    149-162.

Cleaver, T.J., 1971, The use of a modified Mitscherlich model
    to interpret fertilizer experiments. *J. hort. Sci.*, 46,
    403-411.

Greenwood, D.J., Cleaver, T.J. and Turner, M.K., 1974,
    Fertilizer requirements of vegetable crops. Proceeding
    No. 145 of the Fertilizer Society, 5-31.

Greenwood, D.J., Wood, T.J. and Cleaver, T.J., 1974 A dynamic
    model for the effects of soil and weather conditions on
    nitrogen response. *J. Agric. Sci.*, Cambs. 82, 455-467.

Thornley, J.H.M., 1978 Crop response to fertilizers. *Ann. Bot.*
    42, 817-826.

21

Leylandia vehicles required
General Insurance

MARTIN WILSON *Coventry Polytechnic*

21.1 PROBLEM STATEMENT

LEYLANDIA is a country of mixed economy. There is a state run
car industry whose only product for the private owner is the
TORMENT. The industry is protected by legislation that forbids
other cars on the public highway. Car repairs and servicing
operate in the private sector as does, surprisingly, medicine.
Insurance is nationalised, and the main object of our study is
the motor vehicle division of this enterprise termed the LVRGI.

The LVRGI only offers one-year comprehensive insurance policies
which have a no-claims bonus scheme associated with them.
Customers fall into four categories for this no-claims system;
groups 0, 1, 2 and 3. The higher the group number, the more
discount they obtain on their premium.

For premium calculations, new customers are generally placed
in group 0. Customers renewing their policies who have made
no claim in the previous year are promoted one group if
possible before having their premium determined. Customers
who have made claims in the previous year drop back two groups,
or to group 0 when this is impossible, when renewing their
policies. Some customers withdraw from the scheme either
naturally or by accident deaths, where this occurs an appropriate portion of their premium is refunded.

A major item of public interest in LEYLANDIA at present is the
Government proposal to institute seat belt legislation.
Should such legislation be brought in then it is believed that
though the number of accidents per year will not go down, the
physical damage to the drivers and passengers involved in
them will be reduced with a consequent reduction in the cost
of medical services. Such an outcome is foreseen by the

Government and has led to the question of the expected
reduction in insurance premiums being asked. An answer to this
question is just one of the problems occupying the LVRGI
executives at present.

Studies of statistics from countries where such legislation
has been introduced indicate that driver deaths will be
reduced by about 40% from current levels. Unfortunately the
decrease in medical costs is not so readily determined. The
opinion has been expressed that this reduction will be about
20 to 40 percent of the previous costs.

The LVRGI are currently implementing their new computer
system and have no-one available for data searches at the
moment, especially since once the system is on-line then many
summary reports will become available which will give this
information rapidly. Specimens of these reports are given in
Tables 21.1 and 21.2, though the values shown on them are of
dubious worth.

In your position as a very junior, and therefore expendable,
executive at LVRGI, you are expected to produce a technique
for dealing with the Government's enquiry and demonstrate its
working with the figures provided in Tables 21.1 and 21.2, so
that an answer may be provided as quickly as possible after
the actual summaries become available.

TABLE 21.1

Summary: Policies terminating in 1984/85

```
BASE PREMIUM $775

GROUP    NO CLAIM    RENEWALS    NEW      CANC'LD    TOTAL
         BONUS (%)

  0         0        1280708    384620    18264     1665328
  1        25        1764897         1    28240     1764898
  2        40        1154461         0    13857     1154461
  3        50        8760058         0   324114     8760058

                     TOTAL INCOME  (M$)           6182
            LESS     REFUNDS       (M$)             70
                                                  ----
                     NET INCOME    (M$)           6112
            LESS     COSTS  (M$)        149
                     CLAIMS (M$)       6093        6242
                                                  ----
                     LOSS          (M$)            130   ****
                                                  ----
```

TABLE 21.2

Summary: Claims from policies terminating in 1984/85

GROUP	NUMBER OF CLAIMS	DRIVER DEATH	AV. COST REPAIR($)	AV. COST MEDICI($)	AV. COST ($)
0	582756	11652	1020	1526	3195
1	582463	23315	1223	1231	3886
2	115857	2292	947	823	2941
3	700872	7013	805	814	2321

TOTAL REPAIR COSTS	(M$)	1981
TOTAL MEDICAL COSTS	(M$)	2218
TOTAL DEATH PAYMENTS	(M$)	1894

TOTAL CLAIMS MADE	(M$)	6093

21.2   INITIAL REACTION

On being faced with the problem a typical student reaction is
to check the tables; figures seem to hold this fascination!
This is not a bad activity in that it helps the student to
understand the problem better and may also lead to the
discovery of oversights in a practical situation. This type
of investigation should result in the eventual discovery of
the following discrepancy in Table 21.1.

Total Income - Given in Table 21.1   6182(M$)

Total Income - Calculated from Table 21.1

    1.665328 x 775   1290.(6)
    1.764898 x 775 x .75   1025.(8)
    1.154461 x 775 x .6   536.(8)
    8.760058 x 775 x .5   3394.(5)
                            _____
                            6248(M$)

This is intentional to emphasise the point that oversights
often occur in real situations. Special six-month policies
exist within the scheme, whose existence the author
deliberately forgot to mention.

360 GENERAL INSURANCE FOR VEHICLES

The difficulty may be dealt with in a variety of common-sense ways. The method adopted here is to assume that only a proportion of the premium is obtained; another alternative is to increase total income to 6248 (M$) and refunds to 136 (M$) in Table 21.1.

It next appears that the problem can be dealt with by elementary algebra and careful arithmetic along the following lines .

(a) Use the data in Table 21.2 to find the average payment on death in each group. For group O we have

Total paid out   .582756 x 3195   = 1861.9

Medical costs   (.582756 - .011652) x 1526

Repair⁺ costs   + .582756 x 1020   = 1465.9

Total death payments   396.0

Average death payment 396/.011652 = $33,985
(The values occur as the Djs in Appendix 21.2)

(b) Make appropriate changes to the figures in Table 21.2 to meet the seat belt situation. With, for instance, deaths down by 40% and medical costs by 20% the new claims total can be determined.

Group O deaths are reduced by 4661 to 6991 and average medical costs become $1221. Medical costs become (.582756 - .006991) x 1221 and death payments .006991 x 33985 to give total cost for the group of 1535 (M$). Similarly obtained values for the other groups will lead to the new total claims value.

(c) In Table 21.1 alter the cancelled totals by the reduction in deaths as a result of seat belts.

For group O this will become 18264 - 4661 giving 13603. Again, alter other figures by the appropriate reduction in deaths.

(d) Assume a premium P and determine the new net income as a multiple of P. Some change to the refunds figure will need to be made as well; this too will be a multiple of P.

Income is now in form KP

(e) From net income and total outgoings find the new value
     for P.

        Total costs C are now known and premium determined
        as C/K.

Unfortunately, this simple approach is inadequate in that it
ignores an important process that is at work here. This is
the changing distribution of the numbers in the various
no-claims groups. Introducing the legislation will alter the
manner in which this distribution will change. We need to
know how to deal with these changes since they may be large
in effect. One line of approach is to investigate the
performance of the scheme over a few years operation. Having
done this, introduce the effect of the legislation and see
the operation of the new scheme over the same period and then
make a judgement.

A word of caution is necessary here; to manage more than just
"what will happen next year?" types of enquiry will need the
assistance of a computer program to avoid the horrible
arithmetic.

21.3 MODELLING ASPECTS

The basis of a lot of mathematical modelling is comprehending
the underlying processes and expressing them in mathematical
form. To do this we start by introducing certain parameters
together with some explanation. These are

    α , an accident rate

    w ; a natural withdrawal rate

    δ , the proportion of accidents involving driver death

Hence, if we have x policy holders then we can say αx of them
will have accidents and of these $\alpha \delta x$ will die with the result
that $(w + \alpha\delta)x$ of them will leave the scheme. These comments
are introduced to give clear definition to the term   rates
in what follows. In actual fact we need a more precise form
of notation and a simplifying assumption to progress.

We firstly are going to assume that all renewals take place in
a short period of time at the start of the year. (As there
are only 13 million of them it can easily be coped with by the
efficient LEYLANDIA Post Office system!) Next we introduce
the following notation.

α_k , the accident rate in group k

w_k , the withdrawal rate in group k

δ_k , proportion of accidents in group k involving driver death

$x_{k,j}$, the number of premium payers in group k for year j

$N_{k,j}$, the number of new entrants to group k in year j

where k can take values 0, 1, 2 and 3 and j = 0 denotes 1984/5.

By considering the rules of the scheme we can now describe the numbers in each of the groups in year (j + 1) in terms of the numbers in each of the groups in the previous year as follows:-

$$x_{0,j+1} = N_{0,j+1} + \alpha_0(1-\delta_0)x_{0,j} + \alpha_1(1-\delta_1)x_{1,j} + \alpha_2(1-\delta_2)x_{2,j}$$

$$x_{1,j+1} = N_{1,j+1} + (1-\alpha_0-w_0)x_{0,j} + \alpha_3(1-\delta_3)x_{3,j}$$

$$x_{2,j+1} = N_{2,j+1} + (1-\alpha_1-w_1)x_{1,j}$$

$$x_{3,j+1} = N_{3,j+1} + (1-\alpha_2-w_2)x_{2,j} + (1-\alpha_3-w_3)x_{3,j}$$

Or, using matrix form

$$
\begin{bmatrix} x_{0,j+1} \\ x_{1,j+1} \\ x_{2,j+1} \\ x_{3,j+1} \end{bmatrix}
=
\begin{bmatrix} N_{0,j+1} \\ N_{1,j+1} \\ N_{2,j+1} \\ N_{3,j+1} \end{bmatrix}
$$

$$
+
\begin{bmatrix}
\alpha_0(1-\delta_0) & \alpha_1(1-\delta_1) & \alpha_2(1-\delta_2) & 0 \\
(1-\alpha_0-w_0) & 0 & 0 & \alpha_3(1-\delta_3) \\
0 & (1-\alpha_1-w_1) & 0 & 0 \\
0 & 0 & (1-\alpha_2-w_2) & (1-\alpha_3-w_3)
\end{bmatrix}
\begin{bmatrix} x_{0,j} \\ x_{1,j} \\ x_{2,j} \\ x_{3,j} \end{bmatrix}
$$

or, in more succinct style as

$$\underline{x}_{j+1} = \underline{N}_{j+1} + T \underline{x}_j \tag{1}$$

So, provided we know T and the various $\underline{N}_j$ s we can start from the given pattern of numbers in each group, $\underline{x}_0$, and then calculate first $\underline{x}_1$, then $\underline{x}_2$, and so on.

In terms of our situation we would probably obtain the $\underline{N}_j$ s from some forecasting system within the LVRGI. For the purposes of this exercise I shall assume that the number of new entrants each year is constant, and that all new entrants go into group O. This leaves us with the matrix T, or dealing with its elements separately then the α_k s, w_k s and δ_k s.

For convenience I shall comment on one parameter in particular, α_0 say, then proceed to generalise.

It must be realised that α_0 is not a constant. It is something we must hold a view on, and then express that view mathematically. In practice α_0 depends on a whole variety of factors and is certainly stochastic. Even if we knew all the factors we would still only be in the area of reducing its uncertainty. All we can do is take a simple view and see what happens. One such view could be that it is slowly varying with time and subject to slight perturbations from year to year.

How much of this view one uses is to some extent dictated by convenience; as an initial approach we might decide that the variations were negligible and treat α_0 as a constant, analyse the model and then see how sensitive it is to small changes in α_0. Taking such a view and similar ones for the w_k s and δ_k s then T becomes a matrix with constant elements and the numbers in each group in each year can now be calculated.

Having determined the numbers in each group for each of the next few years there are various values to be determined. These are costs and income.

We look first at the cost of the claims.

Defining

R_k , average repair costs per vehicle for group k

M_k , average medical costs per (living) driver for group k

D_k , average payment on death of a group k driver

$C_{k,j}$, cost of claims for group k in year j

then we can find $C_{k,j}$ since it will be the average cost of an accident multiplied by the number of accidents, i.e.

$$C_{k,j} = \alpha_k (R_k + (1-\delta_k) M_k + \delta_k D_k) x_{k,j}$$

or if we let

$$v_{kk} = \alpha_k (R_k + (1-\delta_k) M_k + \delta_k D_k)$$

then $C_{k,j} = v_{kk} x_{kj}$

or, employing the same notation as in equation (1),
$\underline{C}_j = V \underline{x}_j$ where V is the diagonal matrix with elements v_{kk}.
Pre-multiplying by [1,1,1,1] will give the total cost of the claims for year j.

Income can be dealt with in a similar manner. Introducing

P , basic premium

b_k , no-claims allowance (fraction) for group k

q , average proportion of premium refunded (on withdrawal)

η , average proportion of premium collected

$I_{k,j}$; income from group k in year j

then $I_{k,j} = (1-b_k) (1-(1-q)(w_k + \alpha_k \delta_k))\eta x_{k,j} P$

Employing the same technique as with cost of claims we have

$\underline{I}_j = P U \underline{x}_j$ where U is the appropriate (diagonal) matrix.

Pre-multiplying by [1,1,1,1] will give the total income for
each year as a multiple of P.

With regard to operating expenses I have taken the view that
these will be roughly the same over the duration of any
investigation (they can equally well be made some multiple of
the total number of premium payers, or even some more complex
form). Using

$$F \quad ; \quad \text{operating cost per year}$$

$$\underline{g}' \quad ; \quad [1,1,1,1]$$

then the income, $\underline{g}' \underline{I}_j P$, and the costs, $\underline{g}' \underline{C}_j + F$, can be
evaluated over the next few periods.

21.4 MODEL ANALYSIS

Having established a model some analysis is now required. One
look at the matrix work involved suggests the rejection of
hand methods. Our task thus becomes the production of a
computer program of our model and the estimation of the
parameters to use within it.

A program of the model is supplied (Appendix 21.1). It was
written to go on an 8K Commodore PET computer, though it
should fit on any small machine supplied with BASIC (after
altering the output statements appropriately). The awkward
output statements are merely to make the results match
Tables 21.1 and 21.2.

Parameter estimation is outlined in Appendix 21.2. For the
purposes of this explanation, the program was run several
times with different items of data changed to make a few basic
checks. Which runs should be chosen will be determined by
how the modeller is expecting to report in such a situation.
I should add here that when using this type of case study with
students, I suggest that they produce their efforts in the
form of a report suitable for use in the supplied situation.
I have not found that this makes the problem of assessment any
easier, but it does give them a chance to tidy up what they
have done as opposed to an inconclusive bundle of loose ends.

The first run used was the precisely calculated values
obtained in Appendix 21.2 to check the results against
Tables 21.1 and 21.2 for validity. The program was then used
to display the corresponding tables for years 1 to 5. The
premium was next increased by $5 to $780 and the tables for
years 1 to 5 again displayed.

These two runs were repeated after altering the parameters to
their rounded values. The resulting yearly profits from these
runs are displayed in Table 21.3.

TABLE 21.3

PARAMETERS	YEAR	0	1	2	3	4	5
	PREMIUM						
PRECISE	775	-130	-114	-89	-80	-73	-69
	780	-90	-75	-50	-41	-34	-30
	DIFFERENCE	40	39	39	39	39	39
ROUNDED	775	-125	-110	-83	-74	-66	-62
	780	-85	-70	-43	-34	-27	-22
	DIFFERENCE	40	40	40	40	39	40

entries show overall profit for
year (M$)

As can be seen the rounding leads to modest discrepancies; the
main point to perceive being that for this situation a $5 base
premium increase leads to a $40 million increase in annual
profits.   Considering a premium of $780 then a total loss over
the five years of 196(M$) will result. With a $5 premium
increase then 200(M$) increase will occur to reach the break
even point over this period.   (If desired, ideas on the time
value of money can be introduced here, outlined under the
heading discounted cash flow in many accountancy textbooks).
Hence we can see that without the seat belt legislation a
premium of about $785 is needed over the next five years.

The second investigation was to see the results of the
legislation. Using precise values for the parameters, the
death rate was reduced by 40% and the medical costs by 20% then
40% with the results shown in Table 21.4.

TABLE 21.4

REDUCTION (MED.EXP.)	YEAR	0	1	2	3	4	5
	PREMIUM						
-20%	775	1059	1066	1080	1085	1090	1094
	770	1019	1027	1041	1046	1050	1054
	DIFFERENCE	40	39	39	39	40	40
-40%	775	1507	1513	1525	1531	1536	1540
	770	1467	1474	1486	1492	1496	1500
	DIFFERENCE	40	39	39	39	40	40

entries show overall profit for year (M$)

Again we note that a $5 premium increase leads to a $40 million increase in annual profits. Accumulated profits in the two cases when premium is $775 are $5415 and $7645 (million) respectively. This needs a premium reduction of $135 and $190 respectively to get to break even, i.e. premium in range $585 to $640.

Hence as a rough and ready summary we can say that for years 1985-1989, if the legislation is not introduced an insurance premium of $785 per annum will be needed. Introducing the legislation will result in this falling by about 150 to 200 dollars.

21.5 FURTHER INVESTIGATION

Two ideas for further work on the problem stem from the views expressed in the discussion on α_0 in Section 21.3. While not restricting anyone's imagination on what should occur, these changes can be easily incorporated by suitably altering the subroutine (lines 300-480) of the given program. The two ideas I offer are to make the accident rates proportional to some power (squared springs to mind if we consider the number of 'meetings' that can take place) of the number of policy holders and secondly to operate the withdrawal rates on the residual living drivers instead of the original number of policy holders. Other questions that might be investigated

are the no-claims bonuses offered: Should they be altered?,
Are they fair?, What values should be used?

APPENDIX 21.1

```
5 HM$="J"
10 LF$=CHR$(13)
15 SC=0
20 DEF FNFI(X)=INT(X+.5)
30 DEF FNSC(X)=FNFI(X/1000000)
40 DIM NC,AL,W,DE,R,M,D,S1,S2(3)
50 DIM V,T,U(3,3)
60 DIM X,N,I(3,5)
80 FOR J=0 TO 3 :READ NC(J) :NEXT J
100 FOR J=0 TO 3 :READ AL(J) :NEXT J
120 FOR J=0 TO 3 :READ W(J)  :NEXT J
140 FOR J=0 TO 3 :READ S2(J) :NEXT J
160 FOR J=0 TO 3 :READ R(J)  :NEXT J
180 FOR J=0 TO 3 :READ S1(J) :NEXT J
200 FOR J=0 TO 3 :READ D(J)  :NEXT J
230 READ Q,NE
240 READ RC
241 RC=FNSC(RC)
249 X$="ILLEGAL, PLEASE REPEAT."
250 INPUT "ENTER % SAVING MED. COSTS      ";SV
251 IF ABS(50-SV)>50 THEN PRINT X$:GOTO 250
252 SV=1-SV/100
260 INPUT "ENTER % REDUCTION IN DEATH RATE";DR
261 IF ABS(50-DR)>50 THEN PRINT X$: GOTTO 260
262 DR=1-DR/100
270 FOR J=0 TO 3
280 DE(J)=S2(J)*DR :M(J)=S1(J)*SV
290 NEXT J
295 GOTO 495
300 FOR L=0 TO 3:FOR K=0 TO 3
310 T(L,K)=0:U(L,K)=0:V(L,K)=0
320 NEXT K:NEXT L
340 FOR L=0 TO 3
350 U(L,L)+(1-NC(L))*(1-(1-Q)*(W(L)+AL(L)*DE(L)))
360 V(L,L)=AL(L)*(R(L)+(1-DE(L))*M(L)+DE(L)*D(L))
370 NEXT L
400 T(0,0)=AL(0)*(1-DE(0)):T(0,1)=AL(1)*(1-DE(1))
420 T(0,2)=AL(2)*(1-DE(2)):T(1,3)=AL(3)*(1-DE(3))
440 T(1,0)=1-AL(0)-W(0):T(2,1)=1-AL(1)-W(1)
460 T(3,2)=1-AL(2)-W(2):T(3,3)=1-AL(3)-W(3)
480 RETURN
495 IF SC>0 THEN 560
500 FOR J=0 TO 3:READ X(J,0) :NEXT J
510 FOR J=0 TO 3:FOR K=0 TO 5
```

```
515 N(J,K)=O
540 IF J=O THEN READ N(J,K)
550 NEXT K:NEXT J
555 N(1,O)=1:N(O,O)=N(O,O)-1
560 SC=1
590 FOR J=1 TO 5
600 GOSUB 300
610 FOR K=O TO 3
620 X(K,J)=N(K,J)
630 FOR L=O TO 3
640 X(K,J)=X(K,J)+T(K,L)*X(L,J-1)
650 NEXT L:X(K,J)=FNFI(X(K,J)):NEXT K:NEXT J
700 FOR J=O TO 5:FOR K=O TO 3
720 I(K,J)=O
730 FOR L=O TO 3
740 I(K,J)=I(K,J)+U(K,L)*X(L,J)
755 NEXT L:NEXT K:NEXT J
800 BP=O:PRINTHM$
805 INPUT "ENTER BASE PREMIUM   ";BP
806 INPUT "ENTER YEAR OF INTEREST";J
810 PRINT HM$;LF$;LF$;"REDUCTION MED. COSTS",FNFI((1-SV)*100);"%"
815 PRINT "REDUCTION DEATH RATE", FNFI((1-DR)*100);"%"
820 PRINT LF$;LF$;"TABLE 2"
821 PRINTLF$;"YEAR";1984+J;"/";85+J
822 PRINT"GP CLAIMS DEATHS REPC MEDC AV.C"
840 EM=O:ED=O:EX=O:
850 FOR K=O TO 3
860 A=AL(K)*X(K,J):B=A*DE(K):F=FNFI(V(K,K)/AL(K))
865 EX=EX+A*R(K):ED=ED+B*D(K):EM=EM+(A-B)*M(K)
870 A=FNFI(A):B=FNFI(B)
875 PRINTSTR$(K);SPC(8-LEN(STR$(A)));A;SPC(7-LEN(STR$(B)));B;
879 A=FNFI(M(K))
880 PRINTSPC(6-LEN(STR$(R(k))));R(K);SPC(6-LEN(STR$(A)));A;
885 PRINTSPC(6-LEN(STR$(F)));STR$(F)
890 NEXT K
900 PRINT LF$;LF$;"REPAIRS";FNSC(EX):PRINT "MEDICAL";FNSC(EM)
920 PRINT "DEATH   ";FNSC(ED)
930 CL=FNSC(EX+ED+EM)
940 PRINT LF$;"TOTAL CL";CL;LF$;LF$
950 INPUT "ENTER X TO CONTINUE   ";X$
960 B=BP
990 PRINT HM$;LF$;LF$; LF$; "TABLE 1"
991 PRINT"YEAR";1984+J;"/";85+J
1010 IF BP=O THEN B=(RC+CL)*1000000/NE/(I(O,J)+I(1,J)+I(2,J)+
     I(3,J))
1015 B=-5*INT(-B/5)
1016 PRINT LF$;LF$;"BASE PREMIUM "B;"$"
1018 PRINTLF$;"GP NC RENEWALS NEW LEAVE TOTAL"
1019 CI=O:CO=O
```

```
1020 FOR K=0 TO 3
1030 A=(W(K)+AL(K)*DE(K))*X(K,J):CO=CO+A*(1-NC(K))*NE*Q*B
1040 CI=CI+X(K,J)*(1-NC(K))*NE*B
1045 F=FNFI(100*NC(k))
1050 PRINTSTR$(K);SPC(4-LEN(STR$(F)));STR$(F);
1055 F=X(K,J)-N(K,J)
1060 PRINTSPC(9-LEN(STR$(F)));STR$(F);SPC(8-LEN(STR$(N(K,J))));
     STR$(N(K,J));
1065 A=FNFI(A)
1070 PRINTSPC(8-LEN(STR$(A)));STR$(A);SPC(9-LEN(STR$(X(K,J))));
     STR$(X(K,J))
1080 NEXT K
1090 CO=FNSC(CO):CI=FNSC(CI)
1100 PRINT LF$;LF$;TAB(20);"INCOME   ";SPC(6-LEN(STR$(CI)));CI
1110 PRINT TAB(20);"RETURNS ";SPC(6-LEN(STR$(CO)));CO
1115 PRINT TAB(20);"NET     ";SPC(6-LEN(STR$(CI-CO)));CI-CO
1120 PRINT "LESS COSTS";SPC(5-LEN(STR$(RC)));RC
1130 PRINT "    CLAIMS";CL;TAB(28);SPC(6-LEN(STR$(CL+RC)));CL+RC
1135 A=CI-CO-RC-CL
1140 PRINTTAB(20);"PROFIT  ";SPC(6-LEN(STR$(A)));A;LF$;LF$
1200 INPUT "ENTER Y TO CHANGE YEAR";Y$
1205 IF LEFT$(Y$,1)="Y" THEN 806
1220 INPUT "ENTER Y TO ALTER PRE'M";Y$
1225 IF LEFT$(Y$,1)="Y" THEN 805
1250 INPUT "ENTER F TO TERMINATE  ";Y$
1260 IF LEFT$(Y$,1)="F" THEN 9999
1270 GOTO 250
8000 REM ALPHA
8010 DATA . 3499347,.3300264,.1003559,.0800077
8100 REM WITHDRAW
8110 DATA .0039704,.0027905,.0100177,.0361985
8150 REM DELTA
8160 DATA .0199946,.040028,.019783,.010006
8400 REM REPAIR
8410 DATA 1020,1223,947,805
8450 REM MEDICAL
8460 DATA 1526,1231,0823,0814
8500 REM DEATH
8510 DATA 33985,37006,60015,70971
8550 REM RETURN/COLLECT/EXPENSES
8560 DATA .435087,.989465,149000000
8600 REM START X
8610 DATA 1665328,1764898,1154461,8760058
8650 REM ENTER
8660 DATA 384621,384621,384621,384621,384621,384621
9999 END
```

APPENDIX 21.2

PARAMETER ESTIMATION

α_0 582756/1665328 = 0.3499347 say 0.35

α_1 = 0.3300264 say 0.33

α_2 = 0.1003559 say 0.10

α_3 = 0.0800077 say 0.08

δ_0 11652/582756   = 0.019946 say 0.02

δ_1 = 0.040028 say 0.04

δ_2 = 0.019783 say 0.02

δ_3 = 0.010006 say 0.01

w_0 (18264-11652)/1665328= 0.0039704 say 0.004

w_1 = 0.0027905 say 0.0028

w_2 = 0.0100177 say 0.010

w_3 = 0.0361985 say 0.036

$x_{0,0}$ = 1665328 $x_{1,0}$ = 1764898 $x_{2,0}$ = 1154461

$x_{3,0}$ = 8760058

$N_{0,j}$ = 384621, all other $N_{k,j}$ = 0 (except $N_{1,0}$ = 1)

R_0 = 1020 say 1025 M_0 = 1526 say 1525

R_1 = 1223 say 1225 M_1 = 1231 say 1225

R_2 = 947 say 950 M_2 = 823 say 825

R_3 = 805 say 800 M_3 = 814 say 825

D_0 = (3195 x 582756-582756x1020-(582756-11652)x1526)/11652

                                      = 33985 say 34000

D_1 =   = 37006 say 37000

D_2 =   = 60015 say 60000

D_3 =   = 70971 say 70000

q = 0.435087(0.44) η = 0.989465(0.99) F = 149000000

22

Windmill power

KEITH OKE   *South Bank Polytechnic*

22.1   STATEMENT OF THE PROBLEM

Wind power, harnessed centuries ago by man, is fast gaining
new popularity due to soaring costs of the use of
coventional fuels. Windmills are, of course, only one
way of obtaining power; apart from the use of oil, coal
and wood, other newer sources of power include nuclear,
solar, wave and geothermal power. No doubt, in the years to
come, we shall see a combination of methods of producing
energy and power suited to the varying needs of the world's
regions.

Windmills come in all shapes and sizes these days. Designs
range from relatively large many-bladed machines used for
pumping water to small-scale two/three bladed aerogenerators
for producing modest amounts of electricity as back-up for
individual domestic use. There are also some very ambitious
schemes afoot to build and operate windmills capable of
producing several megawatts of electrical power which, in
turn, can be fed into the national grid. Typical of such
schemes is the Taylor-Woodrow/British Aerospace/GEC-Marconi
endeavour to produce some three to five megawatts of
electricity for the Scottish Electricity Authority. The
windmill involved is a horizontal-axis machine with two blades
(fixed pitch) that is to be mounted in the Orkneys where
winds speeds can be up to 100 miles per hour.

Strangely enough, little is understood of the basic physics
of the air flow around a moving blade. Most windmill designs
depend on an accumulated body of empirical knowledge - the
knowledge gained from operating smaller-sized windmills,
consisting of measured data and many graphs and tables of
this data. It would therefore save much computer time and

effort if a simple mathematical model could be devised in
the initial studies of air-flow around moving blades.

Figure 22.1 is a photograph of a simple flat-bladed
horizontal-axis windmill that might be used for the
generation of small amounts of electricity (say 200 - 300 W for
a small workshop). Moderate wind speeds can be assumed
(5 - 10 ms^{-1}, ie. approximately 12 - 24 mph).

Figure 22.1 Simple two bladed windmill

Studying a flat rectangular bladed windmill is just one step
in many in trying to understand how windmills work. The
mathematics and physics for flat blades (stationary or
moving) is expected to be simpler than for the conventional
twisted blades with aerofoil cross-section.

Find a mathematical model to represent the motion of the
simple two bladed windmill described above. Use this model
to suggest ways of improving the design of horizontal axis

windmills.   What quantities are likely to be involved in
determining the power developed by the windmill?

The blades could be made from a light material, aluminium
say, and for cheapness will be rectangular, flat and set
at a fixed pitch.   See Figure 22.2 for the definition of pitch
angle.

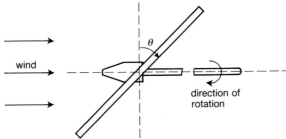

Figure 22.2   Definition of pitch angle (Plan view, looking
along one blade from tip to axle)

Owing to the rotation about the axis, each point on the
blade surface will start to move downwards in the plane of
the paper (see Figure 22.3).

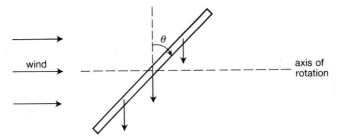

Figure 22.3   Linear velocity of blade when windmill is
allowed to rotate

Note that: (i)   the linear velocity of each portion of the
blade is (angular velocity of blade) x (distance
from axis).

(ii)   no rotation can take place if we set θ at
$0°$ or $90°$.

22.2   NOTES FOR THE LECTURER

The problem as posed is a difficult one.   However, students
enjoy meeting the challenge; contributions range from simple
descriptions to quite extensive aerodynamic analyses.   The

problem has the merit of being topical, and students are
easily motivated in the fields of alternative technology.
As with all modelling exercises, student response depends
very largely on two factors.

(i)   The enthusiasm and skill of the lecturer; giving too
      many hints reduces the problem to a conventionally
      structured one. No guidance at all, except for
      students with extensive modelling experience, can
      be most daunting.

(ii) Student background and ability. Those students with
      a strong mathematics and physics background tend
      to try to use the Kutta-Joukowski aerofoil theory.
      Students weaker in physics consider pressure on a
      blade to be some simple function of wind velocity.

Clearly there are numerous approaches to tackling the
problem. One that, for all its drawbacks, has produced
interesting student reaction is to consider the analogous
situation of a water jet being directed onto a flat sheet
of metal. This is the approach used in subsequent sections
of this chapter. Students usually need to be encouraged to
consider a single fixed blade initially (ie. no rotation).
So, one of the first things to calculate is the force acting
on a blade due to the momentum change of the air impinging
upon it.

For those students who already have some experience of
mathematical modelling, it is suggested that the statement
of the problem in Section 22.1 is handed out. The class could
then be split up into groups and each group be required to
model the problem as far as it is able and to hand in a
report of its work in perhaps a month's time. Little or no
mathematical or physical hints should be provided - each
group should be allowed to formulate, solve and interpret
in its own way.

For those students with little or no experience in modelling,
it is suggested that the lecturer works interactively with
a class. It is important whilst doing this not to stultify
ideas - write down important features of the problem as
identified by the students on the blackboard. Later on in
the session (of perhaps one hour), the lecturer may guide
the students in attempting to select the most relevant
variables and formulating relationships between them. Once
some mathematical relationships, preferably of the most simple
kind initially (eg. force on fixed blade with pitch angle θ),
have been derived, leave students to continue as far as they
can manage to produce some results for homework . Students

at this stage, may only get as far as a mathematical
expression for the starting torque (blades fixed) - this is
considered good progress for the inexperienced. Others may
start considering rotating blades in their attempts to find
the power harnessed by the windmill. Many different (usually
erroneous) results creep in at this stage and hence the
necessity of emphasising checking and interpretation at each
stage of the model development.

Finally, any model should be validated; mathematical
predictions should be compared with measured values from a
full-scale or model of an actual windmill. Unfortunately,
it is often difficult within the time and resource constraints
of a teaching programme to provide realistic data for some
problems, including this one. The author has just had
constructed a model flat-bladed windmill for the purpose of
preliminary wind tunnel tests (see Figure 22.1); however,
there are difficulties with designing a suitable dynamometer
which can be used for measuring torque produced by the
windmill shaft. As a result, numerical values for torque
and power are unfortunately not available as yet. Common sense
interpretation of the mathematical model is vital in spite of
the above difficulties; for example, if a starting torque

(with $\theta = 15°$, say) is calculated to be in the region of 10^6 N m
then the blades will break!

Sections 22.3.2 and 22.3.3 may be considered as a complete
case study; these sections consider the force and torque on
stationary blades only. Sections 22.3.4 to 22.3.6 may be
considered as an extended case study; these sections extend
the results for force and torque to those for rotating blades,
and consequently lead to expressions for the power developed.

22.3 MODEL DEVELOPMENT

Using the elementary momentum approach, as mentioned in the
previous section, the problem may be split up into the
following parts.

> (i)   Identification of quantities likely to be
>   involved; major assumptions.
>
> (ii)   Force on a fixed blade.
>
> (iii) Torque produced by a fixed blade about horizontal
>   shaft.
>
> (iv)   Force on a moving blade.
>
> (v)   Torque produced by a moving blade about horizontal
>   shaft.

    (vi)   Power produced = Torque $\times$ angular velocity of
            shaft.

It should be realised, as pointed out earlier, that students
do not suggest the above list initially. Only after
considerable effort has been expended on the problem does
the above tidy list become apparent.

22.3.1 *Identification of Quantities; Major Assumptions*

It is soon realised that the following quantities are likely
to be involved:

    surface area of blades

    blade angle (pitch)

    speed of wind

    density of air

    rotational speed

    mass of blades

    friction in bearings

    mechanical load on windmill (eg. due to electric
    generator).

The important assumptions made in the following are:

    (a) the windmill blades are smooth,

    (b) the air hitting the blades has no viscosity.

It follows from the assumptions that the air, having struck
the blade, moves off along the surface without causing a
tangential frictional force.

Further important assumptions are also made:

    (c) the mass (and moment of inertia) of the blade and
    shaft assembly are neglected,

    (d) the speed of the wind is assumed constant,

    (e) air is incompressible and has a constant density ρ.

22.3.2 *Force on a Fixed Blade*

By Newton's second law, the force acting on the front (or
windward) surface of the blade is due to the rate of change

of momentum of the air which strikes it.   Thus,

$$\frac{d}{dt} \text{(momentum)} = \frac{d}{dt}(m\ v) = \frac{dm}{dt} v = \dot{m}v \qquad (1)$$

since $\dot{v} = 0$, assumption (d).

To determine the mass flow rate $\dot{m}$, let us look first of all at the case when the pitch angle θ is zero - ie. when the air strikes the blade normally.

Weaker students might prefer a dimensional argument at this stage: as area of blade (A) increases then force increases (other parameters fixed),   as v increases again force increases (other parameters fixed).   So, force $\alpha\ A^n v^m$, m,n > 0.
Comparing dimensions, force $\alpha\ Av^2$.

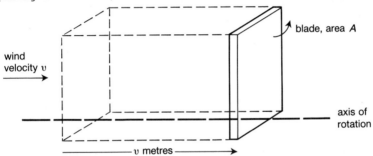

Figure 22.4   Air impinging normally on a fixed blade ($\theta = 0°$)

The air striking the blade in one second is contained within the prism shown in Figure 22.4.   Its volume is thus Av and its mass is ρ Av, where ρ is constant (see assumption (e)).

Equation (1)   therefore becomes

$$\frac{d}{dt} \text{(momentum)} = \dot{m}v = \rho Av.v = \rho Av^2 \qquad (2)$$

where A is the area of one blade.

This result is now generalised for a non-zero value of θ.

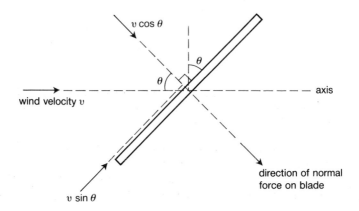

Figure 22.5   Plan view of one blade (fixed), showing velocity components of incident air stream

Referring to Figure 22.5, we note that:

(i)   the resolved components of air velocity are as shown,

(ii) the blade "sees" an approaching air stream having a normal velocity of only v cos θ.

Equation (2) therefore becomes

$$\frac{d}{dt} \text{ (air momentum)} = \rho A \, (v \cos \theta)^2 = \rho A v^2 \cos^2 \theta \qquad (3)$$

Expression (3) gives the force acting normal to the blade, but it is the component F perpendicular to the windmill shaft (axis) that produces motion.

The force component F is given by

$$F = \rho A v^2 \cos^2 \theta \, \sin\theta \qquad (4)$$

and illustrated in Figure 22.6

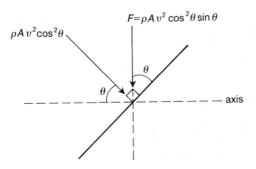

Figure 22.6   Force component F acting on a stationary blade

The result in (4) fits in well, on a qualitative basis,
with the known behaviour of windmills in spite of the
somewhat unrealistic air-flow pattern adopted for this early
stage of the modelling.   A sketch graph of F against θ is
shown in Figure 22.7 (the sketch was in fact suggested by
some students before result (4) was derived).   Note that for
a given ρ, A and·v, F varies as $\cos^2\theta \sin\theta$; the maximum

value of F occurs when θ = 35.3°.

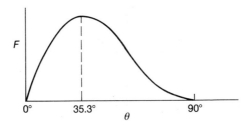

Figure 22.7   Variation of F with θ

It seems worth mentioning that the result (4) is unlike that
which would be suggested by treating the blade as an
aerofoil at the outset.   In the aerofoil approach, the
Kutta-Joukowski law predicts that F, referred to as a "lift"
force, is given by

$$F = \pi\rho A v^2 \cos\theta \quad (\text{for } \theta \to \pi/2) \tag{5}$$

Comparing this result with (4) it is seen that the
trigonometrical factor (apart from the π) is quite
different and does not fit in with the graph in Figure 22.7.
There is in fact no reason why we should expect the aerofoil
approach to give a realistic model in the case of a windmill.
This is because:

(i)   windmill blades are set for small θ
      (certainly not θ = $\frac{\pi}{2}$),
(ii) the air circulation patterns assumed for the
      aerofoil approach cannot be expected to hold
      for windmill blades.

23.3.3   Torque Produced by Fixed Blade about Horizontal Shaft

Since the blade is held fixed or stationary, then if the
torque about the horizontal shaft is multiplied by the
number of blades present (2 in this case), we obtain an
expression for what is termed the starting torque. Clearly,
the minimum value for the starting torque must be equal to
the torque required to start turning a machine (electric
generator) plus any frictional torques (eg due to shaft
bearings).

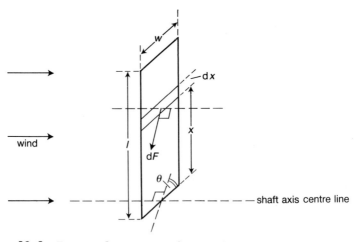

Figure 22.8   Torque due to stationary blade

Consider a blade of width w and length ℓ and an element of
the blade of area wdx; see Figure 22.8.   Then the force dF
on the element tending to cause rotation is, from (4),

$$dF = \rho w \, dx \, v^2 \cos^2 \theta \sin \theta. \qquad (6)$$

The torque, dT, produced by dF about the shaft is therefore given by

$$dT = x\ dF,$$

and hence the total torque T about the shaft is

$$T = \rho v^2 \cos^2 \theta \sin \theta w \int_{0}^{\ell} x\ dx,$$

for given ρ, w, v and θ. That is

$$T = \frac{1}{2} \rho\ w\ \ell^2\ v^2 \cos^2 \theta \sin \theta. \tag{7}$$

So, for two blades, the starting torque is given by

$$\text{Starting torque} = 2T = \rho w\ \ell^2\ v^2 \cos^2 \theta \sin \theta \tag{8}$$

Note that the maximum value for starting torque for a given blade size, pitch angle and wind speed and density, is where $\theta = 35.3°$; furthermore, the sketch graph shown in Figure 22.7 for the driving force F is essentially the same for starting torque.

Consider a numerical example with the following values:

$$\rho = 1.2\ \text{kg m}^{-3}\ (\text{at } 760\ \text{mm Hg},\ 20°\text{C})$$

$$w = 0.1\ \text{m}$$

$$\ell = 0.5\ \text{m}$$

$$v = 5\ \text{ms}^{-1}$$

$$\theta = 35.3°$$

Then, maximum value for the starting torque is given by (8):

$$\text{Starting torque} \bigg|_{\text{max}} = 1.2 \times 0.1 \times 0.5^2 \times 5^2 \cos^2 35.3° \sin 35.3°$$

$$= 0.29\ \text{Nm}.$$

Note that a doubling of wind speed implies a quadrupling of torque; so with $v = 10\ \text{ms}^{-1}$, starting torque becomes $4 \times 0.29 = 1.16\ \text{Nm}$.

Since the starting torque is just sufficient to overcome the
resistance of the windmill/generator combination, we can
already see the advantage of working in higher wind speeds.
Such torques are easily measured in practice (for a model, a
string wrapped around the shaft with a weight attached to
one end would suffice), and so provide an opportunity for
checking our simple model.

As pointed out in Section 22.2, it is considered that students
who have little or no experience of mathematical modelling who
can reach this stage without further hints are making good
progress.

Exercises

1. Drawn sketch graphs showing how the driving force F
    varies with

    (a) wind speed

    (b) length of blade

other quantities remaining constant. Repeat the exercise
for the starting torque.

2. Show that the component of stress in the direction of
    rotation at points distance x from the shaft is given by

    $$\frac{1}{w} \frac{dF}{dx}$$

    and is independent of x (why?). (Use expression (6)).
    Sketch a graph showing how stress varies with pitch
    angle θ, other quantities remaining constant.

22.3.4 *Force on a Moving Blade*

This entails a consideration of the oncoming air relative
to the front surface, and the effect of the air on the
rear surface of the blade.

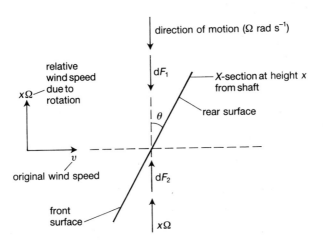

Figure 22.9   Forces on a moving blade element

It is assumed that, for a stationary blade, the wind
speed at the rear surface is zero. However, for a moving blade,
the wind speed will be made up of two velocities v and
$x\Omega$ at the front surface on an element of area wdx at a
distance x from the shaft (see Figure 22.9); for the rear
surface, it is assumed that a relative wind speed of $x\Omega$ is
the only speed to be considered (due to rotation of the
blade). dF_1 and dF_2 are the forces producing motion:

dF_1 due to v and $x\Omega$ velocity components on the front
surface.

dF_2 due to the $x\Omega$ velocity on the rear surface.

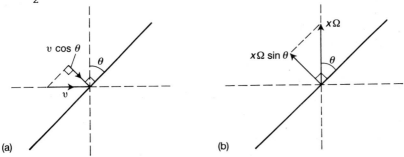

(a)   (b)

Figure 22.10 Front surface of blad element; normal components
of velocity.
(a) normal component of v   (b) normal component of $x\Omega$

Referring to Figure 22.10, net normal component of velocity of air on front surface of blade is

$$v \cos\theta - x\Omega \sin\theta \tag{9}$$

Hence, normal force is

$$\dot{m}(v \cos\theta - x\Omega \sin\theta) \tag{10}$$

where $\dot{m}$ is given by

$$\dot{m} = \rho w\, d\, x\ (v \cos\theta - x\Omega \sin\theta) \tag{11}$$

Hence from (10), (11), normal force on an element of area wdx is given by

$$\rho wdx\ (v \cos\theta - x\Omega \sin\theta)^2 \tag{12}$$

Hence, force dF_1 on element in direction of rotation is given by

$$dF_1 = \rho wdx\ (v \cos\theta - x\Omega \sin\theta)^2 \sin\theta \tag{13}$$

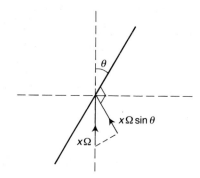

Figure 22.11   Rear surface of blade element; normal component of velocity.

Referring to Figure 22.11, normal component of velocity of air on rear surface of blade is

$$x\Omega \sin\theta \tag{14}$$

Therefore, normal force is

$$\dot{m}x\Omega \sin\theta \tag{15}$$

where $\dot{m}$ is given by

$$\dot{m} = \rho w \, dx \, x\Omega \, \sin\theta \qquad (16)$$

Thus, normal force on an element of area wdx is

$$\rho w \, dx \, x^2\Omega^2 \, \sin^2\theta \qquad (17)$$

Consequently, force dF_2 on element opposing motion is given by

$$dF_2 = \rho w dx \, x^2 \, \Omega^2 \, \sin^3\theta \qquad (18)$$

Hence, from (13) and (18), net driving force $dF_1 - dF_2$ (=dF, say) is given by

$$dF = \rho w dx \left[(v\cos\theta - x\Omega\sin\theta)^2 \sin\theta - x^2 \Omega^2 \sin^3\theta \right]$$

ie. $dF = \rho w dx \, v \sin 2\theta \, (\tfrac{1}{2} v \cos\theta - x\Omega \sin\theta)$ $\qquad (19)$

The total force F on a whole blade is of little interest (except for stress analysis purposes) and so we move on to find the torque produced. Note as a check, however, that with $\Omega = 0$, expression (19) reduces to expression (4) for a stationary blade.

23.3.5 Torque Produced by a Moving Blade about Horizontal Shaft

The torque, dT, produced by the force dF on the element at a distance x from the shaft is given by

$$dT = xdF \qquad (20)$$

and so the total torque T about the shaft is

$$T = \rho w \, v \sin 2\theta \int_0^\ell (\tfrac{1}{2} v \cos\theta - x\Omega \sin\theta) x dx,$$

for given ρ, w, v and θ. That is,

$$T = \rho w \, v \sin2\theta \, (\tfrac{1}{4} v \ell^2 \cos\theta - \tfrac{1}{3} \Omega \ell^3 \sin\theta) \qquad (21)$$

So, total torque (2 blades) is

$$\rho w \, \ell^2 \, v \sin 2\theta \, (\tfrac{1}{2} v \cos\theta - \tfrac{2}{3} \Omega \ell \sin\theta) \qquad (22)$$

Check: with $\Omega = 0$ in (22), we obtain agreement with expression (8) for a stationary blade.

In the usual type of design problem, the required electrical
power is specified. The design engineer can then pin down to
a small range of generators those which will provide the
specified power. Manufacturers of such generators usually
state the amount of electrical power that can be produced for
a given input of mechanical power; such generators need to
be run at a constant r.p.m., for peak performance, and hence
the input torque can be calculated. So for a given (average?)
wind speed v, density of air ρ, and pitch angle θ, several
values of w and ℓ (w < ℓ) may be calculated from (22) for a
given power requirement. The whole process should of course
be repeated for several v and θ values.

Note that students often have difficulty in distinguishing
between variables (w and ℓ in this case) and parameters
(v and θ).

From (21) and (22), we note that for the torque to be
positive, we must have

$$\tfrac{1}{2} v \cos\theta - \frac{2}{3} \Omega \ell \sin\theta > 0$$

$$\text{ie. } \tan\theta < \frac{3v}{4\Omega\ell} \tag{23}$$

So, for a given generator where Ω is given, the pitch angle
is limited in size according to (23) for a given wind speed
and length of blade.

Suppose v = 20 m s^{-1}, ℓ = 0.5 m, and a generator is designed
to be driven at 350 r.p.m. Then,

$$\Omega = \frac{350 \times 2\pi}{60} = 36.65 \text{ rad s}^{-1}$$

and

$$\tan\theta < \frac{3 \times 20}{4 \times 36.65 \times 0.5} = 0.8186$$

ie.

$$\theta < 39.3° \tag{24}$$

So, as to be expected for a fairly modest rotational speed,
the windmill must be run at a modest pitch. Anything near
39° for the pitch angle will produce very little torque and
hence negligible power.

In the next section, we consider for this example what sort of power output we might obtain.

22.3.6. *Power Produced by Windmill*

Since power, P, is given by $P = \text{torque} \times \Omega$, we have from (22):

$$P = \rho w \, \ell^2 \, v \, \sin2\theta \, (\tfrac{1}{2} \, v \, \cos\theta - \tfrac{2}{3} \, \Omega \, \ell \, \sin\theta) \, \Omega \qquad (25)$$

Note that this last expression is of the form

$$P = \sin2\theta \, (A \, \cos\theta - B \, \sin\theta) \, \Omega \qquad (26)$$

so that for a given Ω we can find the pitch angle θ that will provide maximum power, where

$$A = \tfrac{1}{2} \, \rho w \, \ell^2 \, v^2, \; B = \tfrac{2}{3} \, \rho w \, \ell^3 \, v \, \Omega \qquad (27)$$

For a given Ω, we need to maximise E, where

$$E = \sin2\theta \, (A \, \cos\theta - B \, \sin\theta) \qquad (28)$$

For a maximum, $\dfrac{dE}{d\theta} = 0$ and therefore

$$\sin2\theta \, (-A \, \sin\theta - B \, \cos\theta) + 2 \, \cos2\theta \, (A \, \cos\theta - B \, \sin\theta) = 0$$

ie.

$$\tan 2\theta = \frac{2(A \, \cos\theta - B \, \sin\theta)}{A \, \sin\theta + B \, \cos\theta} = \frac{2(A - B \, \tan\theta)}{A \, \tan\theta + B},$$

and writing t for $\tan\theta$, this reduces to

$$Bt^3 - 2At^2 - 2Bt + A = 0, \qquad (29)$$

which may be solved for $t = \tan\theta$ using the Newton-Raphson rule. For example, using the values from the last section, viz $v = 20 \text{ m s}^{-1}$, $\ell = 0.5\text{m}$, $\Omega = 36.65 \text{ rad s}^{-1}$, together with $w = 0.15\text{m}$, we obtain from (27) and (29):

$$11t^3 - 18t^2 - 22t + 9 = 0,$$

and the Newton-Raphson rule provides

$$t_{r+1} = t_r - \frac{(11t_r^3 - 18t_r^2 - 22t_r + 9)}{(33t_r^2 - 36t_r - 22)} \; ; \; r = 0, 1, 2, \ldots$$

Starting with $\theta_o = 20°$, which satisfies the inequality in (24), we obtain t_3 (= $\tan\theta_3$) = 0.3358, correct to 4SF. So θ is taken to be the value of θ_3, which is 18.6°. Substituting this value for θ into (26), we obtain

$$P_{max} = \sin 37.2° (9\cos 18.6° - 11 \sin 18.6°) \times 36.65$$

ie. P_{max} = 111.3   watts   (30)

Of course, the value given in (30) represents mechanical power of the shaft and only about 80% of this, or 89 watts, would be output by an electrical generator - not much given the wind speed involved!

As pointed out in Section 22.3.5 however, the usual design problem is posed in the form where the electrical power to be generated is specified together with the r.p.m. of the generator. This is left to one of the exercises.

22.4   CONCLUSIONS

The modelling exercise has been developed in six parts, and each part may be considered as a small model itself. Thus, the attempt has been to develop some understanding of how windmills work, using simple momentum theory, by a step-by-step or hierarchical process. As explained in Section 22.2, it has not been possible to validate or check any of the mathematical predictions against measured data from a physical model of a flat-bladed windmill. However, an attempt has been made of common sense interpretation by working with some reasonable numerical values. In fact, some interesting numerical and analytical methods do suggest themselves in such interpretation, and have some scope for development by computer programs.

22.5   EXERCISES

1. Given a value for the required electrical power (take $\frac{5}{4}$ times this value for mechanical input) and the r.p.m. of a generator, devise a method for finding the pitch angle of the windmill blades for given blade size and wind speed. Try out your procedure, given that if the required electrical power is 80 W to be produced by a generator running at 350 r.p.m., with blades (2) with w = 0.15m, ℓ = 0.5 m, and a wind speed of 20 ms^{-1}, the pitch angle is calculated to be 12.7°.

2.   By considering a velocity diagram for the air impinging
on the front surface of a moving blade, find a condition for
the minimum angle of attack ℓ (See Figure 22.12).

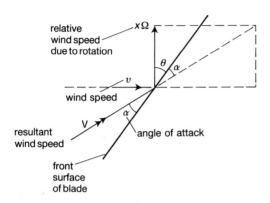

Figure 22.12

Hint: Also use expression (23)

Deduce from your condition, that twisted blades will
provide more power than flat blades (in which sense
(direction) should the blade be twisted?)

3.   Draw sketch graphs showing how power, for flat-blades,
varies with
      (a) pitch angle
      (b) angular rotation
      (c) wind speed

other quantities remaining constant. Can you determine how
sensitive power is to variations in each of the above
quantities (one at a time)?

4.   Show that the stress at points distance x from the shaft
is proportional to $\dfrac{dF}{dx}$.

By using expression (19), derive an expression for the stress at any point on the blade. Show by plotting $\frac{dF}{dx}$ against x, how stress varies along the length of a flat windmill blade.

5. Since pitch angles for starting torque and given power requirements are often different, try to devise a procedure for finding a compromise. How would your procedure be modified for twisted blades?

Suggested reading

Golding, E.W., 1976, The Generation of Electricity by Wind Power, E. and F.N. Spon Ltd.

Massey, B.S., 1979, Mechanics of Fluids, Van Nostrand Reinbold Co

Oke, K.H. and Jones, A.L., 1982, Mathematical Modelling in Physics and Engineering I, Physics Education (July)

Oke, K.H. and Jones, A.L., 1982, Mathematical Modelling in Physics and Engineering II, Physics Education (September)

23

Arcrite Pipework Limited

KEN JUKES *Bristol Polytechnic* and
DON THATCHER *Leicester Polytechnic*

23.1 BACKGROUND

Arcrite is a very small firm which amongst other things
manufactures, upon request, closed metal cylindrical tanks (the
tops being constructed from circles and the sides from
rectangles) for use within the chemical industry. Arcrite use
circular and rectangular metal plates for the construction of
these cylinders. The circles and rectangles are cut from large
steel plates of thickness 6mm. These plates are obtained as
offcuts from BSC and consequently the availability of given
sizes is variable. It is claimed that the size of plates which
can be supplied varies continuously from 6' x 3' to 20' x 8',
all sizes in between are equally likely to be offered by the
supplier at any one time, but the actual sizes that are
available at any one time is totally unpredictable.

The circular plates, or caps, which are cut by Arcrite from the
large rectangular offcuts are required in 4 possible diameters,
namely: 2'11"; 3'5.5"; 3'9.5"; 4'9 ". The cutting
process is carried out with a 1" separation of caps. It is
estimated that the demand for caps is in the ratio 2:1:1:1.
Stocking policy is to hold 8-10 caps in stock of any one size
to meet an order and to replenish stocks from new plate
ordered. Having cut the caps Arcrite then send them to Leeds
for finishing, to have them trimmed and shaped correctly.
This causes a time delay.

The rectangles used for the cylinder sides are not cut by
Arcrite but by the supplier of the offcuts. This supplier cuts
the rectangles to the required size from an offcut, but also
forwards the trim from the offcut which is charged at the same
rate. The 4 sizes of rectangles required are 72" x 95.375
151.75 x 84"; 114" x 84"; 123.5   x 84" and estimated demand

is in the ratio 2:1:1:1 with a minimum stock requirement of 6
of any one size.

Trim from the supplier when producing these rectangles (which
at present may be up to 1/3 in area) can of course be used by
Arcrite to cut further caps.

Unusable plate is eventually sold off as scrap.

Costs

6mm plate weighing 11.51 lb/sq ft costs £220 per tonne
(1000kg). Scrap yields approximately £22 per tonne (10% of
the cost price).

Current Situation

Mr. Taylor, the proprietor, receives orders for cylinders from
the chemical industry for certain tank sizes. In some cases he
will be able to satisfy the order from circles and rectangles
in stock, and may then, in his own time, buy back in the
necessary cut rectangles and offcuts to produce circles.
Occasionally the order requires sizes that he cannot supply
immediately from stock and he must then contact the supplier to
meet his needs; in this situation he will have no alternative
but to accept the offcut sizes that are available.

Problems

(1)   Currently Mr. Taylor faces difficulty, when ordering
       from the stockholders, in deciding which 'randoms'
       (offcuts) to purchase of those offered. Can some guide
       be given as to the best purchase, preferably taking into
       account the particular order and Arcrite stock
       situations? It must be remembered that Mr. Taylor often
       has to make very quick decisions over the phone and hence
       a complicated solution would not be useful.

(2)   The firm wishes to minimise waste by deciding how best to
       cut caps from given rectangular plate that was ordered
       for caps. Suggest possible minimisation techniques.

(3)   The firm also wishes to minimise waste from the trim that
       the supplier sends having cut rectangles from the
       offcuts. Again suggest suitable techniques.

Initial Comments

It is important to remember throughout that this is a real
current problem and that Mr. Taylor often has to 'solve' the

problem of placing orders and cutting caps at a minute's notice.
It is essential that any rules/guidelines that are given should
be relatively easy to follow and adopt. That does not mean, of
course, that the process by which these rules are obtained is
necessarily simple. Equally there is no reason why this
problem should not lead to others which are interesting and
challenging but of little use to Mr. Taylor.

As with most real problems it is not possible completely to
define the situation, there will always be questions that arise
while attempting a solution. In a truly realistic situation
Mr. Taylor would naturally be consulted, but in class it must be
left to the teacher to act upon behalf of Mr. Taylor and offer
answers as he thinks fit. The details that are given here
follow personal contact and some correspondence with Mr. Taylor.

23.2 GETTING STARTED

The problem statement has to be read several times before a full
grasp of the situation is achieved. As with most problems
progress is best made by individual reading followed by group
discussion and then discussion with the originator of the
problem (usually the teacher).

It is soon realised that the problem contains several different
aspects:-

> Purchasing of randoms to meet a particular order
> Cutting of caps from randoms already bought
> Maintaining a reasonable stock level - to meet small orders
>   - to minimise tied up
>   capital (an
>   economics problem)

Having identified the main features of the problem it is good
modelling practice to identify one small/simple aspect and to
solve that rather than the whole problem in one go. Another
useful technique at the beginning is to draw a picture and this
problem is no exception. In order to obtain a feel for the
relative sizes of the caps, scale drawings can be made. An
alternative, and an improvement over a scale drawing, is the
use of suitably scaled discs which may be placed upon scaled
rectangles. This readily shows the amount of freedom available
when attempting to arrange the required discs on a given
rectangle. It is worth remembering at this point that
Mr. Taylor or one of his workers currently performs this task
by drawing the discs full size onto the actual sheet to be cut.
The approach of using a physical model will be discussed in
more detail later.

Although, as already mentioned, one aspect of getting started
is that of searching for extra information, this is not possible
in a class situation. Following an attempt by one group of
students contact with Mr. Taylor was made, and given below are
some of the questions and answers.

QN.   Is it possible to leave a smaller gap than 1" between
       discs when they are being cut?

ANS.   Yes. A 1/2" gap rather than 1" would be possible (Does
       this make any significant difference?).

QN.   Are randoms ever ordered to build up stocks of either
       plates or caps?

ANS.   No. Randoms are only ordered from the stock holders on
       receipt of order for drums.

QN.   What is a typical order for drums?

ANS.   A typical order might be
             1 large vessel   (4'9" discs)
             1 size 3 vessel   (3'5.5" discs)
             2 small vessels   (2'11" discs).

QN.   As larger randoms are more likely to result in lower
       losses when cutting discs than from smaller randoms,
       what are the chances that large randoms are available?

ANS.   Very large plates are not usually available; the range
       being random up to those 16' long.

23.3   CUTTING OF RANDOM PLATES ALREADY DELIVERED

The cutting plan to be selected, whilst attempting to minimise
waste, has to take into account current orders and stock levels.
Following the idea mentioned previously it seems that it would
be useful and practical to have available on the shop floor a
kit consisting of a scaled down calibrated rectangle and a set
of scaled down discs. The rectangle could have two adjustable
strips to allow the workman to focus easily on any random
rectangle and then use this plan to guide him through the cuts
to be made.

For a given plate the number of cutting options is relatively
small since the caps are quite large relative to random sizes
available.

Since the caps are to be separated by 1" (note that a possible
1/2" gap is referred to above but 1" is used in all subsequent

results) then it may be best to take this into account in the
kit by considering caps of diameter 3', 3'6", 3'10.5", 4'10",
the corresponding scaled caps then being allowed to touch.
These caps are referred to as D1, D2, D3, D4 later. In a class
situation cardboard discs may be cut fairly accurately and
placed upon graph paper, but under proper work conditions a
calibrated metallic or plastic version would of course be
necessary for durability and ease of use. Using such a model
the maximum number of caps that could be cut from the largest
possible (i.e. 20'x8') random is found to be 18D1, or 11D2, or
10D3 or 4D4.

(Incidentally the largest number of D1 s for this plate is
obtained by cutting as in Figure 23.1.)

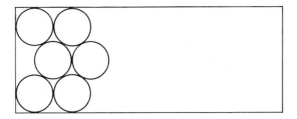

Fig. 23.1

A large initial waste occurs (offset of second row) which
might lead to the cutter not following this plan and so
yielding only 16 or 17 D1 s).

One group showed great interest in this particular aspect of
the problem; that being to find the most efficient method
for packing discs of the one size onto a given random plate.
Although not of direct interest to Mr. Taylor the group of
students who did study this found it sufficiently challenging
and rewarding for it to be included here. The details are
given at the end.

23.4 CONCERNING THE ORDERING OF RANDOMS

Once again ordering has to take into account current
Arcrite stocks, current orders and wastage, and is
complicated by the fact that selection of the 'best' plate
has to be made from randoms offered rather than being able
to order a specific sized plate. What would seem to be ideal
would be a set of tables listing: length and breadth of
random, full range of caps that can be cut from it, a
cutting plan, and wastage incurred. This could be
utilised to ensure that the random offered met the immediate
requirements, and then selecting the cutting plan which

satisfies the stock requirements taking into account wastage.
There would still be some play in that randoms falling between
sizes in the tables would allow some reassessment using the
kit. It will be seen in the later section on compact packing,
however, that the much simpler problem of producing a list
of the number of discs of one size from a given random is not
trivial and it is unlikely that the stated ideal will ever
be achieved. Some specific comments about randoms bought
for rectangles and caps have been detailed later. One
observation worth noting concerns the fact that demand for
drum sizes is in the ratio 2:1:1:1. Given a full width
(8') plate, then caps can be cut in this ratio with relatively
little waste (Figure 23.2).

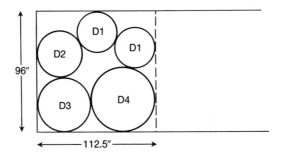

Fig. 23.2 (not to scale)

The number of caps can be doubled, maintaining the same
ratio by having a 96"/218.5" plate. Once again the inability
to order a specific size of plate makes this observation not
as useful as it might appear at first sight.

23.5 COMMENTS ON ORDERING RANDOMS

Rectangles

Plates of dimensions 72" x 95", 114" x 84", 123.5" x 84',
and 151" x 84" are referred to as R1-R4 respectively. In
all cases the suppliers should use the extreme left hand
edge (or as close to it as possible) for one side of the
rectangle.

Remember that Mr. Taylor buys the whole of the random - he
thus requires the minimum offcut possible or one which allows
him to cut a disc from it. If 8' wide plate is available
then R1 can be cut as in Figure 23.3.

Fig. 23.3

The length should be as close to 72" as possible, otherwise
a length of at least 108" is required which allows a D1 to
be cut in addition. If an 8' wide sheet is not available
then

Plate	Minimum Width (ins)	Minimum length (ins)		
R1	72	95	if not close	131
R2	84	114	close to min.	150
R3	84	123.5	length then	159.5
R4	84	151	need at least	187
	For R2-R4 anything in excess leads to automatic wastage			

Circles

Widths between 36" and 42" allow no real greater flexibility
for cutting caps than does 36", and so lead to greater waste
the further from 36".

For widths above 42.5" there is some flexibility in what can
be cut but there will always be a fair amount of waste due to
the relatively large sizes of the caps being cut.

This is highlighted in the next section.

23.6 COMPACT PACKING

The first aspect of this 'diversion' was to answer the
question - is packing based on an equilateral triangle or on

a square the more efficient?

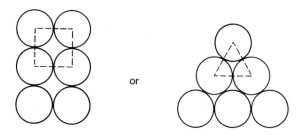

or

Fig. 23.4

When dealing with an infinite area the problem is trivial.
In both cases the following was calculated:

$$\text{Usage} = \frac{\text{Area covered by disc}}{\text{Area of sample}}$$

For square arrangement

$$\text{Usage} = \frac{\pi r^2}{(2r)^2} = \frac{\pi}{4} = 78.5\%$$

for triangle arrangement

$$\text{Usage} = \frac{\pi r^2}{2r.2r.\sin 60} = \frac{\pi}{2\sqrt{3}} = 90.7\%;$$

Once again this is a good modelling technique, that of
solving a relatively simple problem in order to give a feeling
for the problem being considered. In this case the 90.7%
also gives an upper bound for the solution. The next step
taken was that of introducing a bounded region. In
considering the two basic patterns the most suitable width
and length were chosen for each.

For square pattern:

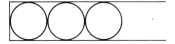
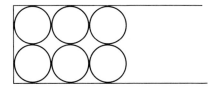

Fig. 23.5

For triangular pattern:

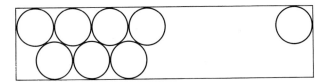

Fig. 23.6

Again the percentage of useful material is calculated.
In the case of the square pattern the only restriction on
the length is that it should be a multiple of 2r - say 2nr.

Thus

$$\text{Usage} = \frac{n\pi r^2}{2r2nr} = \frac{\pi}{4} = 78.5\% \text{ as before}$$

For the triangular pattern, assuming no more than 2 rows
wide (reasonable for most of the caps required and randoms
available). Assuming that the top row is exactly 2nr
long then

$$\text{Usage} = \frac{(2n-1)\pi r^2}{2nr(2+\sqrt{3})r} = \frac{(2n-1)}{2n} \frac{\pi}{(2+\sqrt{3})} \to \frac{\pi}{2+\sqrt{3}} = 84.2\%$$

In the worst case for this pattern with, n=2, the

$$\text{Usage} = 63.1\%$$

and in the case of the smallest cap from a long (18') random
(n=6)

$$\text{Uaage} = 77.2\%$$

Once again a good modelling technique has been adopted whereby
the model has been made slightly more realistic and the answers
could be compared to those obtained previously to see if they
were of the right order. It was, of course, apparent that
only on rare occasions would either of the above patterns ever
occur and that in most cases the pattern would be somewhere
in between   this is best explained by a few diagrams, as in
Figure 23.7

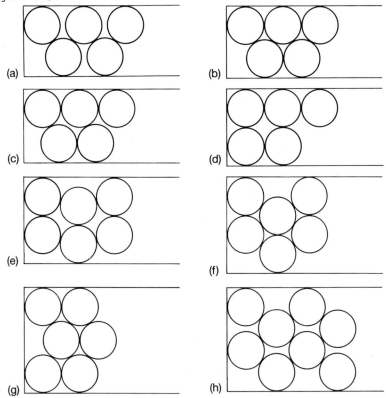

Fig. 23.7

As no plates are wider than 8' no other arrangements are
possible although the extension is fairly obvious to wider
plates. Note how (e) is exactly double (a), (f) is the
same as (b) with the addition of a 'full row' and (g) is
as (d) with a middle row.

The only remaining problem was that of the length.   In
general the technique was to establish how many discs could
be got on the 'top' row and then find if the second row had
the same number or one less (due to the offset). Only in
rare cases, as in (c), do any further complications arise as an

extra cap may be cut that does not follow the pattern.

In general it is possible to find an expression of the form
$N = f(r, w, \ell)$ where N is the number of discs of a given size
that can be cut from a plate of size w by ℓ.   The details for
each case are now presented.

The different categories are related to the width w, so that

(a) $2r < w < (2+\sqrt{3})r$

(b) $w = (2+\sqrt{3})r$

(c) $(2+\sqrt{3})r < w < 4r$

(d) $w = 4r$

(e) $4r < w < (4+\sqrt{3})r$

(f) $w = (4+\sqrt{3})r$

(g) $(4+\sqrt{3})r < w$

(h) $4r < w$

Consider case (a)

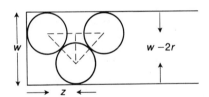

Fig. 23.8

Thus $z = \sqrt{4r^2 - (w - 2r)^2}$

$\qquad = \sqrt{4wr - w^2}$

and $N = INT\ [(\ell - 2\ r)/z] + 1$

Case (b) has already been covered

Case (c)

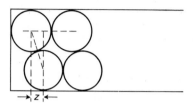

Fig 23.9

Again $z = \sqrt{4wr - w^2}$

Number of discs on top row = INT $(\ell/2r)$ = N_1 say

As the offset of the bottom row is z then if $\ell - N_1 2r \geqslant z$ the bottom row will have same as top row, otherwise it will have one less.

Case (d) is trivial.

Case (e) Number of discs N = 2 x (result for width $(w - 2r)$ as in (a)).

Case (f) is trivial.

Case (g)

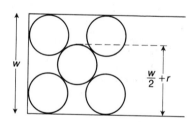

Fig. 23.10

Calculate number of discs that can fit width $\frac{w}{2} + r$ as in case (a) say N_1

Then number of discs N = N_1 + INT $\left(\dfrac{N_1 + 1}{2}\right)$

Case (h)

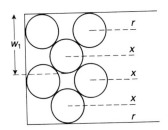

Fig. 23.11

$2r + 3x = w$

$$\therefore \quad x = \frac{1}{3}(w - 2r)$$

hence $w_1 = x + 2r$

$$= \frac{1}{3}(w + 4r)$$

Thus number of discs is found by using a width of w, as in case (a), and doubling the answer.

It is not clear whether case (g) or (h) will provide the greatest number of discs but it is a simple matter to calculate both and select the maximum.

As previously mentioned a slight problem can occasionally occur at the end when an additional disc may be cut but not following the pattern.

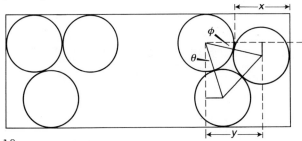

Fig. 23.12

x is the amount required for the extra disc. If $x \geqslant y$ then sufficient space is available.

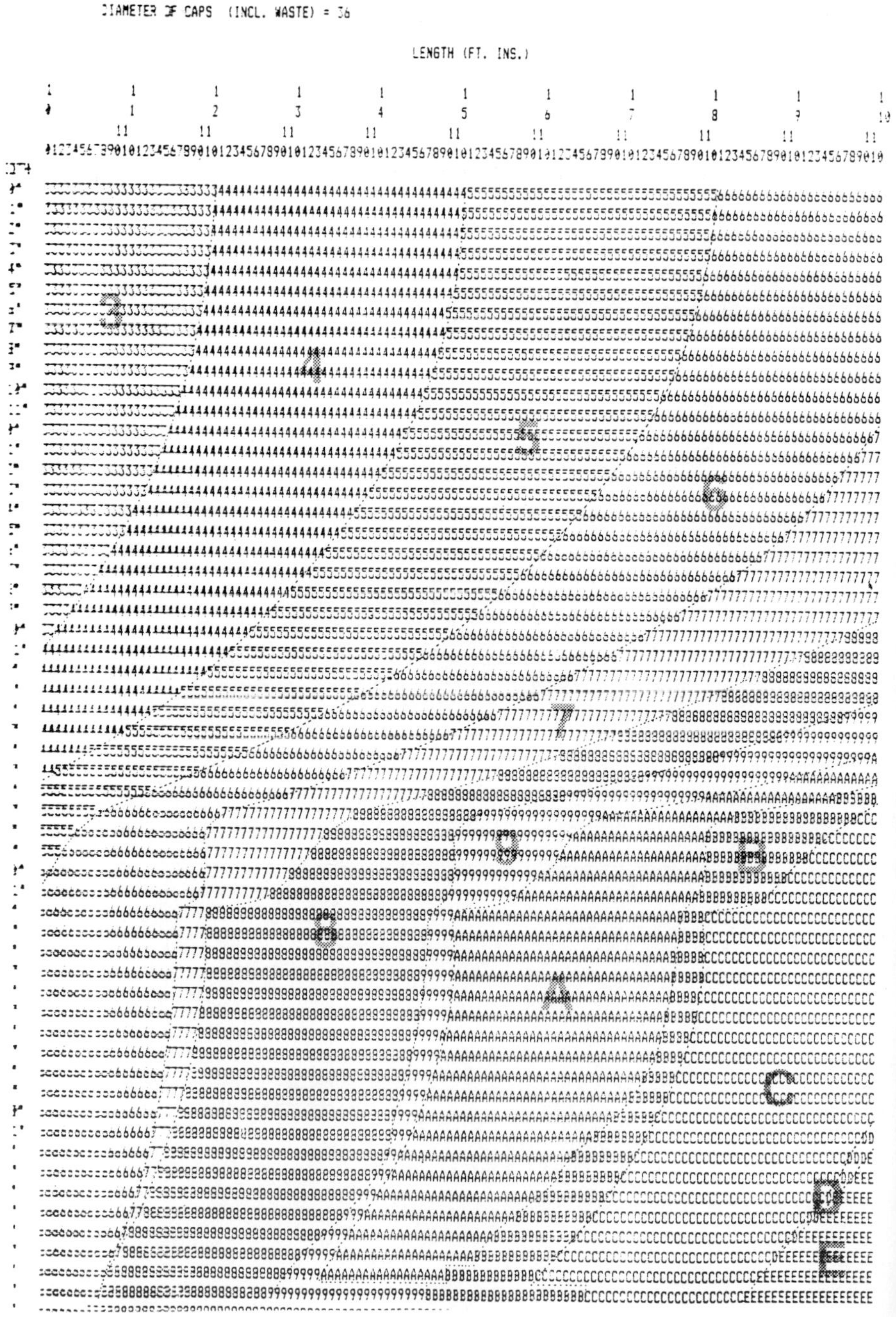

DIAMETER OF CAPS (INCL. WASTE) = 36

LENGTH (FT. INS.)

Fig. 23.13

NUMBER OF DISCS THAT MAY BE CUT FROM A GIVEN RECTANGLE

DIAMETER OF CAPS (INCL. WASTE) = 46.5

LENGTH (FT. INS.)

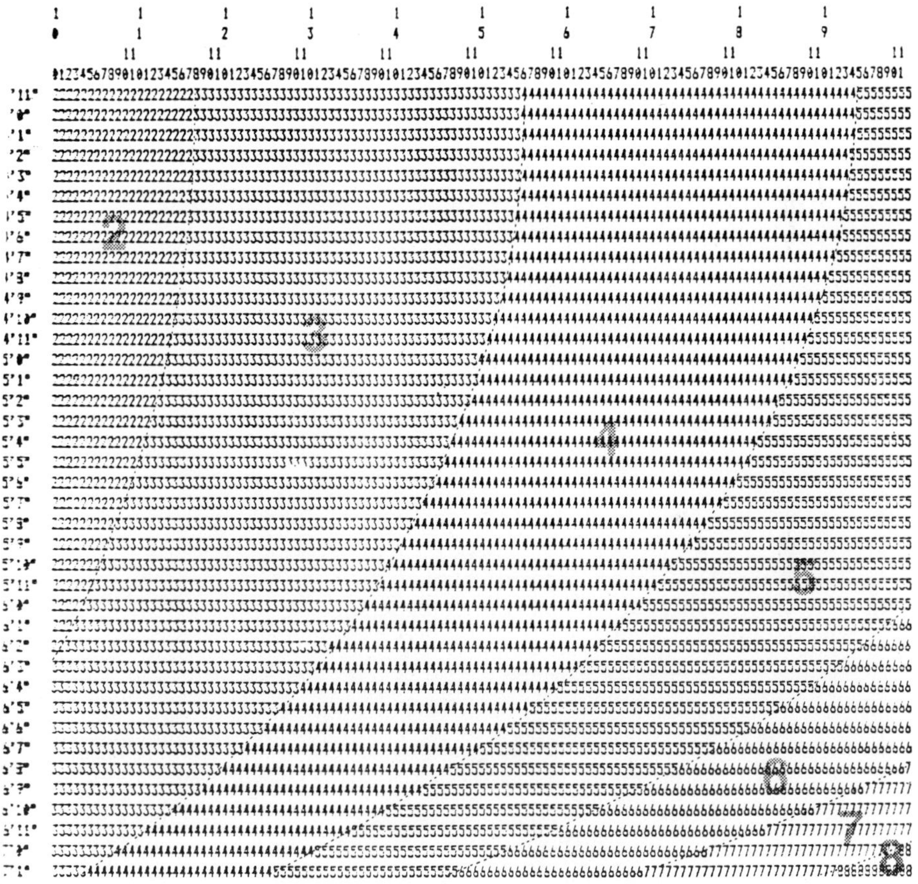

Figure 23.14

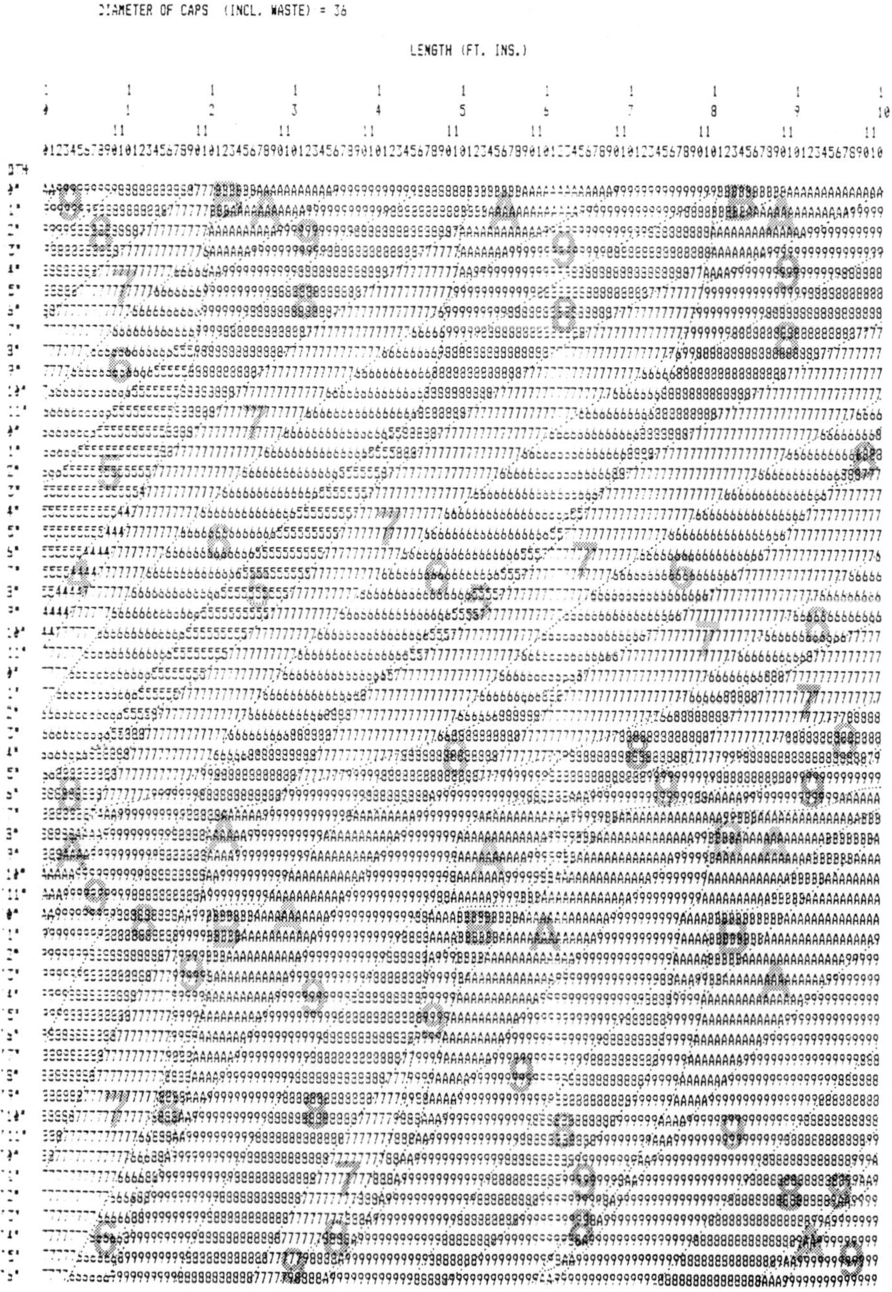

ARCRITE PIPEWORK

DIAMETER OF CAPS (INCL. WASTE) = 36

LENGTH (FT. INS.)

Figure 23.15

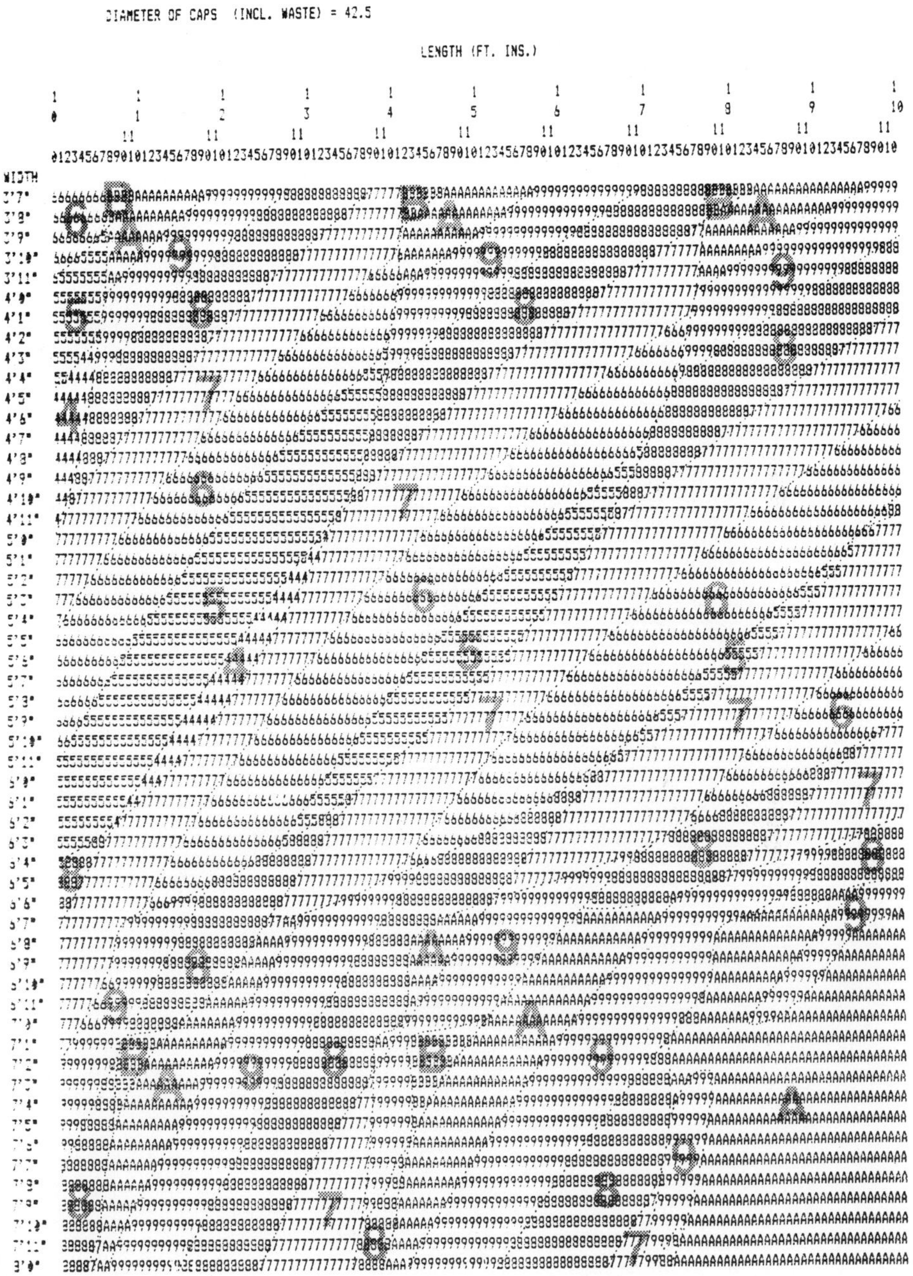

DIAMETER OF CAPS (INCL. WASTE) = 42.5

LENGTH (FT. INS.)

Figure 23.16

USEFUL METAL CUT AS DISCS FROM A GIVEN RECTANGLE

```
      0  =  20% - 25%
      1  =  25% - 30%  ETC.


         DIAMETER OF CAPS  (INCL. WASTE) = 46.5


                                    LENGTH (FT. INS.)

      !           !           !           !           !           !           !           !           !
      0           !           !           !           !           !           !           !           !
                  1           2           3           4           5           6           7           8           9
                  !!          !!          !!          !!          !!          !!          !!          !!          !!
      0123456789010123456789010123456789010123456789010123456789010123456789010123456789010123456789010123456789010123456789010
:DTH
  11"  877777777777766666666-8888AAAAAAAAA99999999999988888383888988777778888BBAAAAAAAAAAAAAA9999999999999998888888888888898888
   0"  777777777766666666658888AAAAAAAA99999999999988888888888888777777777BBBAAAAAAAAAAAAA99999999999999988888888888888BBAAA
   1"  777777776666666666666665AAAAAAAAA999999999988888888888888877777777777AAAAAAAAAA99999999999999998888888888888888887AAAAAA
   2"  77778668666666665555AAAAAA99999999999888888888888888877777777777777AAAAAAAAAA99999999999999998888888888888888877777AAAAAA
   3"  776666666666655555555AAA(99999999998888888888888877777777777777766666AAAAA9999999999999988888888888888888887777777AAAAAA
   4"  66666666666655555555A999999999998888888888888887777777777777766666666A99999999999999988888888888888877777777777777AA9999
   5"  666666666655555555555599999999998888888888888887777777777777766666666666999999999999988888888888888888887777777777777779999999
   6"  66666655555555555599999998888888888888887777777777777766666666666999999999999988888888888888888887777777777777779996666
   7"  66665555555555555599999998888888888888877777777777777666666666666999999998888888888888888777777777777777777666669999999
   8"  5655555555555444998888888888388887777777777777777666666666666665599988888888888888888777777777777777777666666669999998888
   9"  555555555555555443333333338888877777777777776666666666666666665555588888888888888888877777777777777777766666666666998888
  10"  555555555544444488833388888877777777777776666666666666666655555588888888888888889877777777777777777666666666666698888888888
  11"  555555554444444488833388977777777777777776666666666666665555558888888888888877777777777777776666666666666668889888888888888
   0"  5555554444444444488888877777777777777666666666666666655555555588888888877777777777777766666666666666665888888888877777777
   1"  55554444444444444888888877777777777777666666666666666655555555558888888877777777777777776666666666666666666888888888887777
   2"  5544444444444446877777777777776666666666666655555555555888887777777777777776666666666666666666665588888887777777777
   3"  44444444444449877777777776666666666666655555555555559887777777777777776666666666666666665555588887777777777777
   4"  44444444444498777777777776666666666666655555555555558877777777777777666666666666666665555588887777777777777777
   5"  44444444448777777777776666666666666855555555555555577777777777777766666666666666666665555588887777777777777777
   6"  44444444433777777777756666666666665555555555555547777777777776666666666666666665555555557777777777777777777666666
   7"  444444433377777777776665556666666665555555555555444777777777776666666666666666665555555557777777777777777777766666
   8"  444443333777777776666666666665555555555555544477777777777776666666666666666665555555555577777777777777777766666666
   9"  444433337777777766666666666655555555555555544447777777776666666666666665555555555557777777777777777777766666666666
  10"  443333327777766666666666666555555555555544447777777776666666666666665555555555557777777777777777777666666666666666
  11"  333333777766666666666665555555555555544447777777776666666666666666655555555555577777777777777776666666666666666
   0"  333337777666666666666655555555555555544447777777776666666666666666555555555555577777777777776666666666666666
   1"  3337777666666666666655555555555555544444777777776666666666666666555555555555557777777777777776666666666666666666
   2"  337777666666666666655555555555555444444777777776666666666666666555555555555557777777777777776666666666666666665557
   3"  37777666666666666655555555555555544444777777776666666666666665555555555555577777777777777776666666666666666665557777
   4"  777666666666666555555555555555444444777777776666666666666665555555555555577777777777777766666666666666666665557777777
   5"  766666666666655555555555555554444777777776666666666666655555555555577777777777766666666666666666666577777777777777
   6"  666666666665555555555555555444477777777766666666666666655555555555577777777777776666666666666666666577777777777777
   7"  6666666666555555555555555544477777777776666666666666666555555555557777777777777766666666666666666667777777777777777776
   8"  6666666666555555555555555544777777777766666666666666555555587777777777777776666666666666888887777777777777777777777776666
   9"  6666665555555555555555477777777777776666666666666665555888777777777777777766666666666888888877777777777777777766666666
  10"  66666555555555555555288777777777777766666666666666555888977777777777777776666666666688888888877777777777777776688888888
  11"  6665555555555588887777777777777766666666666688888888977777777776666888888888877777777777777776688888888888888
   0"  6655555555888888777777777777777766666666688888888888877777777777779998888888888888888777777777779998888888888888888
   1"  5555558899888877777777777777777766666669988888888888887777777777779998888888888888888777799999999999988888888888888887
   2"  5988888888877777777777769999998888888888888777777777799999999988888888888889877799999999999988888888888889999999
   3"  99888888888877777777777799999999999888888888AAAAA999999999998888888AAAAAAAA999999999999AAAAAAAAAAAAAA999999999999
   4"  9988888888877777777777799999999998888888888AAAA9999999999988888AAAAAAAAA999999999999AAAAAAAAAAAAA9999999999AAAAA
   5"  99888889877777777777779999999988888888888AAAAA999999999988888AAAAAAAA999999999999AAAAAAAAAAAAA999999999999AAAAAA
   6"  88988877777777776999999888888888AAAAA99999999999988888BBBBAAAA999999999999AAAAAAAAAAAAA9999999999AAAAAA
   7"  38888777777777766699999888888888AAAAA99999999888888888AA999999999999AAAAAAAAAAAAA99999999999998AAAAAAA
   8"  888877777777766699999888888888AAAAAAA99999999999888888888BAA9999999999AAAAAAAAAAAAA99999999999998AAAAAAA
   9"  8877777777776999988888888BBBAAAAAAAA99999999999988888888888A9999999999BAAAAAAAAAAAAA99999999999998888AAAAAAABBBBB
  10"  8777777AAA9999999998888BBBAAAAAAAAA999999999999988888888888A99999BBBBBAAAAAAAAAAAAA9999999999999988888AAAAAABBBBBB
  11"  777777AA99999999998888BBBAAAAAAAAAA99999999999968888888888877999998BBBBAAAAAAAAAAAAA99999999999999888888BBAAAA779BBBBBBB
 3'0"  777777A999999999998858BAAAAAAAAAA99999999999988888888888877799999988BBAAAAAAAAAAAAA99999999999999888888AA99888BBBAAA
```

Figure 23.17

```
USEFUL METAL CUT AS DISCS FROM A GIVEN RECTANGLE
------------------------------------------------

    0  =  20% - 25%
    1  =  25% - 30%  ETC.

         DIAMETER OF CAPS  (INCL. WASTE) = 5B

                              LENGTH (FT. INS.)

      1        1        1        1        1        1        1        1        1        1        1
      0        1        2        3        4        5        6        7        8        9        10
      11       11       11       11       11       11       11       11       11       11       11
      0123456789010123456789010123456789010123456789010123456789010123456789010123456789010123456789010123456789010123456789010
WIDTH
4'10"  BBAAAAAAAAA9999999999988888888888877777777777776666666668B83B8B3AAAAAAAAAAAAA99999999999999988888888888888888877777BBBBBBBB
4'11"  AAAAAAAA99999999999888888888888877777777777776666666666666BB83B8AAAAAAAAAAA99999999999999998888888888888888887777777BBBBBBAA
5'0"   AAAAAAA99999999999888888888888877777777777777666666666666BBBAAAAAAAAAA99999999999999998888888888888888877777777777BBBAAAAAA
5'1"   AAAA999999999999888888888888877777777777777666666666666566AAAAAAAAAA799999999999999988888888888888888877777777777777AAAAAAAA
5'2"   AA99999999999888888888888877777777777777666666666666666566EE5AAAAAAAA7999999999999988888888888888888877777777777777AAAAAAAA
5'3"   99999999999988888888882277777777777777666666666666666666555555AAAAAAA3999999999999998888888888888888877777777777777766AAAAAAAA9
5'4"   9999999998888B88888877777777777777666666666666666666555555AAA99999999999999999888888888888888887777777777777777766666AAAA99999
5'5"   999999988888888888777777777777766666666666666666555555555A999999999999999988888888888888888877777777777777777766666666AA99999999
5'6"   999998888888889977777777777777666666666666666666555555555999999999999988888888888888888877777777777777777766666666666669999999999
5'7"   998888888889977777777777776666666666666666555555555559999999999998888888888888888877777777777777777766666666666666669999999999
5'8"   88888888887777777777777766666666666666666655555555555559999999888888888888888877777777777777777766666666666666666669999999998
5'9"   88888888977777777777776666666666666666655555555555555549999998888888888888888877777777777777777766666666666666666669999999998888
5'10"  988888877777777777766666666666666666655555555555555544449999888888888888888877777777777777777766666666666666666655599999988888888
5'11"  98888877777777777766666666666666666555555555555555544444499999888888888888888777777777777777777666666666666666666655599999888888888
6'0"   998877777777776666666666666666655555555555555555444444443999888888888877777777777777777766666666666666666666555555589888888888888
6'1"   377777777776666666666666666555555555555555544444444443988888888877777777777777777776666666666666666666655555555558888888008B888
6'2"   77777777776666666666666666555555555555555444444444443398888888877777777777777777766666666666666666655555555555888888888888777777
6'3"   777777777766666666666666655555555555555544444444444393888888877777777777777777766666666666666666555555555555888888888887777777
6'4"   7777777566666666666666555555555555555444444444444439398887777777777777776666666666666666555555555555555888888888877777777
6'5"   77777666666666666655555555555555544444444444444333337777777777776666666666666666555555555555555555899977777777777777
6'6"   7777666666666665555555555555544444444444444333397777777776666666666666666555555555555555555889977777777777777777
6'7"   77766666666665555555555555555444444444444444439077777777775666666666666666655555555555555555555889977777777777777777
6'8"   766666666665555555555555555544444444444444444277777777777766666666666666666555555555555555555555598877777777777777777777
6'9"   66666666665555555555555554444444444444444444277777777777766666666666666666555555555555555555555557777777777777777777666
6'10"  66666666555555555555554444444444444444444337777777777766666666666666665555555555555555555555544777777777777777776666
6'11"  66666666555555555555544444444444444444444333377777777766666666666666666555555555555555555555544777777777777777777666666666
7'0"   666660655555555555555444444444444444444333337777777766666666666666666555555555555555555444477777777777777777766666666666
7'1"   666666555555555555554444444444444444443333377777777766666666666666665555555555555554444777777777777777766666666666666
7'2"   6666555555555555554444444444444444443333337777777666666666666666665555555555555544444777777777777776666666666666666
7'3"   665555555555555544444444444444444433333337777777666666666666666655555555555555444447777777777777776666666666666666
7'4"   65555555555554444444444444444444433333337777766666666666666665555555555555544444477777777777766666666666666666
7'5"   55555555554444444444444444444333333377776666666666660666555555555555555544444477777777777666666666666666666555
7'6"   555555555544444444444444444333333337777766666666666666666555555555555555444444477777777777666666666666666666555
7'7"   5555555554444444444444444433333333377766666666666666666555555555555544444447777777777766666666666666666555555555
7'8"   555555554444444444444444443333333337777666666666666655555555555555555444444477777777776666666666666666666555555555
7'9"   5555554444444444444444443333333377776666666666666655555555555555555444444477777777776666666666666666655555555555
7'10"  555554444444444444444443333333377776666666666665555555555555555444444477777777666666666666666666555555555555557
7'11"  55554444444444444444433333333777766666666666666555555555555554444447777777777666666666666666666655555555555557777
8'0"   5554444444444444444433333333377776666666666666665555555555555555444447777777777766666666666666666655555555555557777777
```

Figure 23.18

$$y = 2r \cos \phi$$

$$= 2r \cos (90 - (60 + \theta))$$

$$= 2r \sin (60 + \theta)$$

$$z = \sqrt{4wr - w^2} \qquad\qquad \text{as before}$$

$$\theta = \tan^{-1} \left(\frac{z}{w - 2r} \right)$$

The main purpose of this exercise was to be able to produce
a table of all possible lengths and widths which would
indicate the number of discs that could be cut. All the
different cases were entered into a computer program from
which tables for each disc size were obtained. It is
interesting to speculate why the patterns that are shown
in Figures 23.13 to 23.18 take their particular form.

The program was modified slightly in order to output the
amount of useful metal, ie. that in the form of discs, that
is obtained in each case. The variation in 'usage' is large,
but the table indicates the general principle that in general
larger plates offer a greater efficiency than do smaller ones.

24

Signal flags

GEORGE HALL *Nottingham University*

24.1 PROBLEM STATEMENT

Ships communicate with one another by radio, nowadays, but the
older system of using signal flags has not disappeared. For
colour illustrations of the flags and comments on their present
use see Dent (1981). A black and white version is given in
Figure 24.1. Flags have an obvious advantage when a message
has to be conveyed to all comers over an extended period.
Since contemporary sailors are less familiar with these flags
than their predecessors there is a serious problem of
identifying them, especially under difficult stormy conditions.
This is our problem. Coding a message into flags is made easy
by the alphabetical ordering of the flags. Decoding flags into
the message is very much slower unless an ordering based on how
the flags are recognised is also available. We look for an
ordering which will promote faster recognition.

This cannot be a wholly objective problem. The ease with which
individuals can distinguish a feature of a flag depends to a
considerable extent on the acuity of their eyesight, their
familiarity with the context of a particular signal and their
habits of mind. There can, therefore, be alternative solutions
based on the selection of different features as most
significant.

One way of identifying a particular flag is to ask questions
about it. One group of questions can be used to identify the
colours present and another the features of the flags. There
are 5 colours used, white, blue, red, yellow and black. The
description of the features is somewhat arbitrary but 7 are
readily identified - vertical bars, horizontal bars, diagonal
lines, a saltire, a cross, hatchwork and an enclosed area.

It seems to correspond to experience to allow for 3 responses
to the question of whether a colour or feature is present.
Absence of a colour or a feature is denoted by 0 and its
presence by 1 or 2. A colour which is 60% or more of a flag is
given 2 and a smaller amount gets 1. Similarly a feature which
occurs more that once is given 2. These weightings are
subjective but can be unambiguously applied and correspond to
real distinctions that can be made in practice. Thus each flag
is described by the answer (0, 1 or 2) to 12 questions and
these answers are conveniently taken as the components of a
column vector. The 26 signal flags then produce 26 column
vectors which may be collected together to form a 12 x 26
matrix M containing all the answers.

24.4 THE MODELS

24.4.1 *A map of the flags*
The 12 dimensional vectors mentioned above give a description
of the flags which is more than sufficient to distinguish them.
The problem of reducing the dimensionality of the space, while
retaining the maximum amount of distinction, is a standard one
in factor analysis and is discussed in a beautifully simple

manner in Fletcher (1972). From the matrix M, the matrix MM^T and
then its eigenvalues and eigenvectors are calculated. The largest
eigenvalues are the most significant for our purpose. The
corresponding eigenvectors are normalized, each to the square
root of the appropriate eigenvalue, and can then be regarded as
a set of weights. These weights can be multiplied into M to
give weighted answers for each flag. Two such weight vectors
enable us to produce a two-dimensional map of the flags. In
general, in factor analysis, the two largest eigenvalues are
selected but the next largest may become significant if it is
of comparable magnitude. The test must be the dispersion of
the points corresponding to flags. The two selected
eigenvectors are known as principal components. The larger the
distance between the points the more easily they are
distinguished.

In this example the greatest two-dimensional dispersion comes
from the second and third largest eigenvalues. The two sets of
weights are

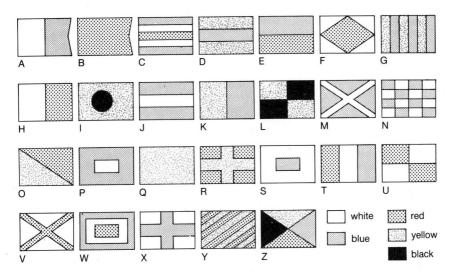

Figure 24.1

24.2 TEACHING COMMENTS

Students who have no experience of describing objects by the presence or absence of qualities, as in Section 24.3, will need help in starting this problem. A few experiments using cut out pictures of flags and recording every step in identifying the letters would help motivate the selection of different features.

The first solution in Section 24.4 below, arose during a course which included some factor analysis. It would not otherwise be appropriate. Note that this 'solution' is too complicated to be used practically. The second solution, in Section 24.5, has many variants. It is essential to press for a classification which is easy to understand and unambiguous to apply. An experiment to verify that the suggested classification is faster for decoding than the alphabetical list would be a suitable final stage.

24.3 DESCRIBING FLAGS

Signal flags differ from one another in three respects. They may differ in colour, in features and in shape. Of these shape is clearly the least useful, since all but two of the 26 flags are rectangular and these two are not easily distinguished from rectangular. Shape will be disregarded here, but it should be noted that it does distinguish readily the alphabetic flags from the numeric pennants which are ignored in this discussion.

x	y	colour/feature
1.72	-1.32	white
-1.47	-1.42	blue
1.64	2.46	red
-2.04	2.78	yellow
-0.50	0.74	black
-0.59	0.17	vertical bar
-1.67	-0.56	horizontal bar
0.68	1.89	diagonal bar
0.27	-0.22	saltire
0.22	0.18	cross
0.13	-0.05	hatch
0.56	0.17	hollow

The weights corresponding to the largest eigenvalues are of
comparable magnitude but, since they are all positive, their
range is less than these. The resulting map is shown in
Figure 24.2. It shows a good scattering of the points, though
there are a few pairs close to one another.

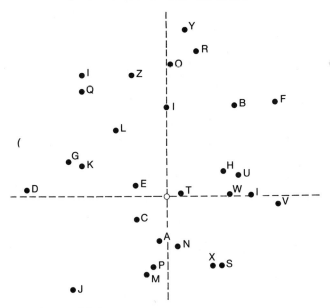

Figure 24.2 Principal component analysis

Although this method provides a theoretical solution to the
problem, it has very little practical value. It establishes
that, by using the eigenvectors to weight the colours and
features, a good map can be produced. This allows us to
conclude that certain letters will be easy to identify and

others difficult, but because of the awkward weights it does
not provide the means to do so in real working conditions.

24.4.2 A practical simplification

In stormy weather it will be more difficult to distinguish
features on a flag than its colours, so it seems appropriate
to consider how colour alone can be used. A quick examination
of the flags shows that the distinction between black and blue,
which is the most difficult pair to distinguish, is never
critical. Whether black is totally ignored or put with blue
into a common category makes little difference. The four
remaining colours will be the primary means of classifying the
flags. An inspection of the two eigenvectors mentioned above
shows how to proceed.

If the two principal components are reduced to their four
largest terms and the coefficients simplified to ± 1

$$x = \ \ (\text{white}) - (\text{blue}) + (\text{red}) - (\text{yellow})$$

$$y = -(\text{white}) - (\text{blue}) + (\text{red}) + (\text{yellow})$$

A rotation by $\pi/4$ then gives the easier form

$$x' = \tfrac{1}{2}(x-y) = (\text{white}) - (\text{yellow})$$

$$y' = \tfrac{1}{2}(x+y) = (\text{red}) - (\text{blue}).$$

Thus a pairing of white with yellow and of red with blue is
suggested.

As a first attempt at a practical identification procedure we
now take these variables x', y' and apply them to the 0, 1, 2
entries under the colours for each flag. The result is a two-
dimensional map of the flags according to colour alone, as in
Figure 24.3. Since these variables are a rough approximation
to the eigenvectors after the latter have been rotated by $\pi/4$, it
is not unexpected that Figure 24.2 and Figure 24.3 are
similarly related.

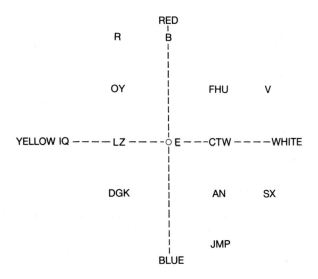

Figure 24.3   Flags classified by colour alone

Figure 24.3 enables 4 flags to be distinguished but the remainder are in groups of 2 or 3 and require some further means of identification. By examining the feature parts of the two eigenvectors above, and also of the next largest eigenvalue, it can be seen that certain features are given greater weight than others and so are good candidates for another variable. From this consideration, and with a certain amount of trial and error, the suggestion can be made that the variable

Z = 2 (Horizontal bar)+(Vertical bar)-(Diagonal bar)-(Hollow)

is an appropriate one. Clearly many other variables can be used,but this has sufficient power to divide all the previous groups while retaining simple arithmetic. This three-dimensional map of the flags can be projected down to a two-dimensional map very simply by replacing y' by y'-$\frac{1}{6}$z. This map is shown in Figure 24.4.

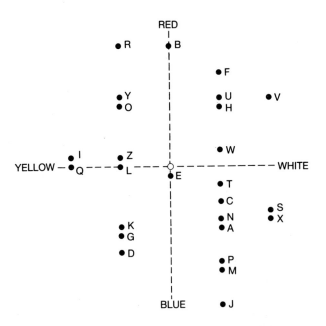

Figure 24.4   Flags classified by colour and features

24.5   A DIRECT SOLUTION

It is also possible to approach this directly as a
classification problem. The colours themselves can be used to
define classes. Clearly, single colours, since there are only
five of them, do not give a sufficiently large number of
classes for a good classification. A better method is to use
pairs of colours,which doubles the categories. A count of the
number of flags containing two specified colours shows that
yellow and white never occur together and that red and blue are
found together infrequently. Only three flags involve three
colours and only one has four. We can take advantage of this,
and of the 0, 1, 2 score for a colour, to plot all four colours
together in a two-dimensional map. This is exactly equivalent
to using the variables

$$x' = (white)-(yellow)$$

$$y' = (red)-(blue)$$

and so leads again to Figure 24.4.

To separate individual flags within the categories defined by
colour we require another variable. An inspection of one of

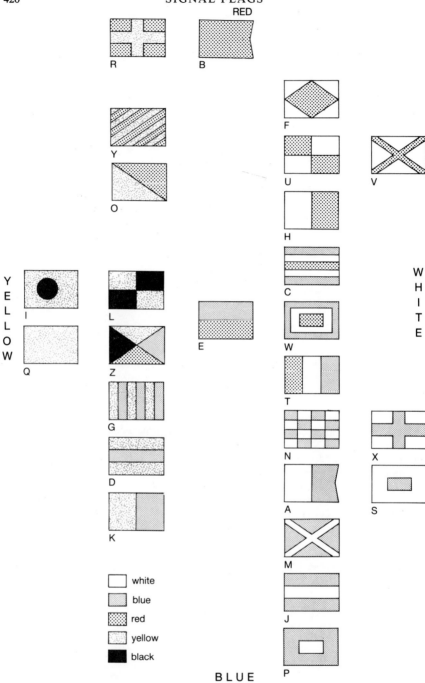

Figure 24.5   Final classification

these groups, e.g. FHU, suggests that the number of connected
coloured areas a flag contains might be a useful variable. For
this purpose five or more areas count as one class. With this
extra variable almost every flag can be given a distinct label.
The exceptions are the pairs T, W and L, Z. These pairs can be
split by adding 1 to L and W because of their higher symmetry.
The resulting classification is shown in Figure 24.5. An
incidental advantage of this classification is that it brings
together the three flags that contain black. Although the
classification of Figure 24.5 is very similar to that of
Figure 24.4 it does permute some groups. The version in Figure
24.5 would seem to be the easier to use in practice, since it
quantifies the 'complexity' of the flag so this is the
preferred solution.

A practical procedure for identifying signal flags under
difficult conditions has been devised. In the first instance
it relies on the correct recognition of the colours of the flag
and secondly it uses the complexity of its design to complete
the identification. The final result is a two-dimensional map
of the flags which specifies each one uniquely and brings
together those with which it could most easily be confused.

REFERENCES

Dent, N., 1981 , Yachtsman's Pocket Almanac , Mitchell Beazley.

Fletcher, T.J., 1972 , Linear Algebra through its Applications ,
    Van Nostrand Reinhold.

Part IV: Further problem statements

25

Emergency evacuation times
for educational buildings

MIKE O'CARROLL   *Sunderland Polytechnic*

25.1   INTRODUCTION

This case study is based on an exercise included in a new
educational development. Students are required to work in
teams within a formal procedural framework, so that the
exercise is equally one of communication as well as of
modelling. Teachers reading this may be interested in both
aspects of the exercise.

In the course of doing the project, students take part in such
things as acting as chairman and secretary of progress
meetings, organising work to meet a strict schedule and report
writing. Teams are left to their own devices on technical or
mathematical matters.

Much of the work in this example is in formulating concepts
and quantifiable variables, and later in determining significant variables and validating results. The mathematical
nature of the relationships involved is simple.

The first sheet of the Project Guide (Figure 25.1) issued to
students indicates the context of the exercise. The statement
of the project as issued to students is reproduced as Figure
25.2. The new building was due to be opened in July 1982 and
at the time of this exercise it was under construction. There
is a clear numerical objective: how long will it take to
evacuate the new building? In addition it is important to
know the level of confidence which can be placed in this
prediction, or the likely error involved. As Head of
Department in the new building I am interested in the result
both for safety in a real emergency and so I can judge how
successful we are with fire drills. It will be useful to
have a target time to aim at.

HND Mathematical Modelling Projects

PROJECT GUIDE

1. Objectives of this course

A study of the employer's view of the average mathematics
graduate in industry gave this summary

"Good at solving problems, not so good at formulating
them, the graduate has reasonable knowledge of
literature and technique, he has some ingenuity and is
capable of seeking out further knowledge. On the other
hand, the graduate is not good at planning his work or
making a critical evaluation of it when completed;
and in any event he has to keep his work to himself as
he has apparently little idea of how to communicate it
to others."

R.R. McLone, The Training of Mathematicians, SSRC
Report, London, 1973

This course sets out to provide experience both of the
processes of communication and the practices of mathematical modelling relevant to the mathematician in
industry and commerce. There are three main features.

FUN - This is an active course. You do not learn about
it . You do it. There is no pressure of preparing for
examination nor grasping new theory. The requirement is
simply to be there and to be involved in the experience.
You have a great deal of freedom in how you tackle problems.
There is usually no single correct answer. The work is
creative and social and it should complement the more usual
lecture-tutorial activities.

COMMUNICATION - You will gain experience in written and
oral communication. You will be involved in formal and
informal meetings, working in a team to strict deadlines,
and writing reports.

MODELLING - The skill of mathematical modelling is
acquired by experience more than by learning about it. It
is an art as well as a science. It concerns understanding
a practical problem (often poorly presented), formulating
it mathematically, solving the mathematical problem and
interpreting the result. There are more elaborate models
of modelling. None of them applies in every case.

Figure 25.1 First page of Project Guide

HND 1 Mathematics, Statistics and Computing, 1981–82

Building Evacuation Times   Project 11 January 1982 – 12 February 1982

Construct a model to determine evacuation times for educational building and apply it to the new Mathematical and Computer Sciences Building.

Deadline for presenting report: Friday 12 February 1982.

Information available for reference:

(a) Fire Drill Reports 1980/81, Teesside Polytechnic

(b) Fire Precautions Act 1971, Section 3:   Means of Escape

(c) Plans for Mathematical and Computer Sciences Building (due for completion and occupation August 1982)

Extract from Fire Drill Reports [item (a)]:

Evacuation Times in Min-Sec

Date/ Building	May 1980	Jan/Feb 1981	May 1981	Oct 1981
Clarendon	4-36	3-55	3-59	4-20
Multi-Storey	5-55	5-16	5-03	4-25
Social Amenities	2-15	1-55	2-45	2-25

Figure 25.2 Statement of Problem

Teachers wishing to use this project are encouraged to
relate it to a local building or a fictitious new one at their
institution. We found our Safety Officer to be more than willing
to supply details of fire drill times in various buildings
and other material. He was glad of the opportunity to speak
to the class about safety in general and his experiences of
evacuation.

25.2 GETTING STARTED - BACKGROUND INFORMATION

Our students had been encouraged, through a mini-project
exercise beforehand and in the Project Guide, to start out by
seeking clarification on the general objective of the problem.
They may decide their immediate objective is to predict the
evacuation time for the new building; but what evacuation
time? A real one, the first official fire practice, assuming
the building is full to capacity, the worst (longest) possible
time, ...? It is soon clear that the detailed identification
of the question is not trivial, never mind the answer. More
detailed determination of the question is left until later
when a better understanding is built up.

The next step they are advised to take is to note down any
ideas of things which may be relevant to the problem. Here
they are encouraged to be open minded and to venture even
unlikely ideas, with a view to reconsidering them later. Such
a set of ideas is called a features list . In this example
the information provided also acts as a source of ideas.

The extract from the Fire Precautions Act considers nearest
exits, positions of alarms, escape path length, etc.,
although it does not give escape times so it does not provide
the answers.

Figure 25.3 shows an example of a features list and its later
revised and grouped form as actually devised by one of our
student teams.

The Fire Drill Reports dealt with many buildings, but most
teams readily settled on the Clarendon Building as being.
broadly comparable with the new building. Both are 2-storey
buildings with a mixture of lecture rooms and staff rooms.
The Clarendon has a total capacity variously estimated or
calculated by the teams at from 1200 to 2000 persons whereas
the new building is roughly half that size with a capacity of
about 600. The multi-storey building has 10 floors and the
long escape path down the stairway may require any model for
escape times to be qualitatively different for it.

```
                        FEATURES LIST

Initial Features List

1.   Building's use
2.   Size of building and rooms
3.   Number of people using building at any one moment
4.   Number of exits and distances from rooms
5.   Number of sirens and loudness
6.   Facilities for disabled people
7.   Fire exits have to lead into safe area
8.   Type and size of fire doors and direction of opening
9.   Width of corridors
10.  Width of stairs
11.  Standard of stairs
12.  Type of windows
13.  Position of building, whether it has easy access e.g.
     for emergency services.

After some discussion certain aspects of the initial
features list were grouped together to be used when
calculating evacuation times and some features were omitted
as, after further consideration, they were found to be
irrelevant.

Revised Features List

1.   Building's use, age of people, physical capabilities
2.   Fire exits leading to a safe area, position of
     building
3.   Number of people using building at any one moment
4.   Number of sirens and loudness
5.   Size of building and rooms
6.   Number of exits
7.   Distance the exits are from rooms
8.   Standard of stairs.
```

Figure 25.3   Features Lists

As work proceeded, and teams were calculating room capacities
and measuring times, further information was provided in
response to requests, from the students, particularly a report
on the occupancy of class rooms throughout the Polytechnic
(typically below 50% of total capacity when averaged over all
buildings and times in the normal working day). At a later
stage the Polytechnic Safety Officer gave a general talk on
fire safety and answered questions about the fire drills.

25.3 A SIMPLE EMPIRICAL MODEL

One team's line of thought led it quickly to the following
preliminary model, which it later replaced by a more detailed
one. The team conceptualised the notion of time per person
for evacuation and felt that it should be almost constant for
buildings of similar type. This is tantamount to the assumption (ignoring the possibility of different occupancy levels)

$$\text{total evacuation time} \propto \text{total capacity} \qquad (1)$$

The team's figures gave an estimate by comparison with the
average time for the Clarendon Building of about 76 seconds,
although that would have been 2 minutes using some estimates
of capacity. This of course takes no account of the number
and distribution of exits or of the process of escape.

We can call this model empirical since it uses the measured
Fire Drill times, and relates them to the new building, without
considering the fundamentals of how the evacuation takes place
(or barely so). It would then be sensible to validate the
empirical model by examining whether the above assumptions
were borne out by observation. One way to proceed would be to
plot the Fire Drill times for all buildings on a graph of time
against capacity, to see if similar buildings gave points on a line
through the origin, although the team concerned did not do so
because figures of capacity were not readily available.

25.4 A SINGLE CONGESTION-POINT MODEL

Although it took some conceiving, most teams developed the
idea that there would be two main types of time involved in
evacuation. The first is travel time which depends on the
speed of travel and the distance, for example walking along
corridors and down stairs. The second is queueing time at
bottlenecks or congestion points such as the doors out of
classrooms and the final exits. This depends on the rate of
flow of people through the bottleneck, which in turn depends
on its width.

Some teams decided that there would be one main congestion
point on each exit route, that is at the final exit, where they
decided there would be a queue (backed up by now by their own
experience of fire drills). Thus the evacuation time for the
whole building would be the sum of a lead time, that is the
time before a queue starts to form at the exit, plus a
queueing time at the exit. Although teams approached this
entirely differently the conceptual implications of this idea
were manifested in more than one team's work.

One team included a third type of time, response time, which
allowed for delayed reaction to the alarm and preparing to
move. This could be included in the lead time so fits in with
this model.

The lead time then consisted of a response time T_O (if any)
plus an internal travel time equal to the average walking speed
S divided into the distance D between the exit and the nearest
classroom. It was supposed that the queue would only start
with the arrival of people from the nearest classroom, not
from staff rooms or corridors.

One team at least went on to suggest that all longer escape
paths would be insignificant since people taking them would
merely join the queue at the exit anyway. They justified this
assumption later (see below).

The queue time at the exit was taken as the rate R of flow of
people per unit time which the exit could admit (measured by
the students directly) divided into a total number N of people
using the exit. Thus the composite model is embodied in

$$\text{Evacuation time} = \max_{\text{(exits)}} [T_O + D/S + N/R]. \qquad (2)$$

There is still a little work involved in estimating N. Some
teams apportioned the total capacity (multiplied in some cases
by an occupancy factor) equally between all exits. Others
took each room to evacuate to the nearest exit; then the
building was notionally partitioned according to the exit used
and, since the exits are of equal size and roughly equal lead
times, the one with the largest number of evacuees was chosen
for the calculation.

Now this model depends on the assumption that a continuous
queue will form at the exit and will render the longer internal
travel times insignificant. This was justified by one team

which calculated the longest internal travel time at about 78 seconds, as compared with queueing time of between 100 and 150 seconds with a lead time of 22 seconds.

This is a theoretical rather than empirical model. It works out a description of the processes involved in the evacuation and it makes no use whatever of the drill times or any recorded evacuation times. Consequently it needs validating to see if the end result is consistent with observed times for a whole evacuation. This can be done by applying the model to the other buildings and comparing the result with the measured drill times (see later).

25.5 A MULTI-STAGE CRITICAL-PATH MODEL

Most teams contemplated the range of times and escape routes and some considered a convergent tree-structured set of routes leading to the nearest exit. It was then easy to conceive of a furthest point or longest escape path. In general it may not be obvious which is the furthest point and one way of proceeding would be to assign escape times to each intermediate point working in from the exits, finally determining accumulated times at the furthest points. For the new building under consideration this general problem did not materialise and it was easy enough to locate a furthest point.

Consideration of this model would be easy if it were limited to travel times and ignored queueing times at congestion points. It becomes more difficult when two routes merge at a bottleneck so that the longest path is interfered with by queues from other paths. The last person then suffers an additional delay due to the swollen queue. One team dealt with this by accumulating the travel and queue times at each of four stages on the longest route, estimating the queue size N_i at the four congestion points.

Thus

$$\text{Evacuation time} = \sum_{i=1}^{4} (D_i/S_i + N_i/R_i), \qquad (3)$$

where i=1 refers to the classroom length and congestion at its single door ($R_1 \sim 1 \text{ s}^{-1}$), i=2 to travel along corridors and through the double fire doors, i=3 to travel down stairs and through double doors at their foot, and i=4 to travel thence to the double exit doors ($R_2 = R_3 = R_4 \sim 2 \text{ s}^{-1}$).

The basis of the estimation of queue sizes N_i was not very clear, but you might take the total number of people expected to pass through the point, less the number of them who could have passed in the time elapsed so far. Then, of course, N_i depends on the elapsed time

$$T_{i-1} = \sum_{j=1}^{i-1} (D_j/S_j + N_j/R_j).$$

You can see that a general model for a complex building would need to work out these merging times at many route junctions in order to determine which is the longest path.

As with the previous model, this one is theoretical and needs to be validated by application to buildings for which there are some measured evacuation times. One of the teams did this and compared both the models (2) and (3) as follows in Table 25.1.

25.6   ERRORS

It is important in producing any prediction to have an idea of the confidence which can be placed in it, or of the likely extent of error. This can be approached in two ways.

Firstly in conjunction with the validation comparison with fire drills, an assessment is available of the difference between the model and drill times (in these cases typically an underestimate of up to 20%) and also of the variation between drills on different occasions (here typically up to ± 15%).

Secondly the errors implicit in the quantities in the fundamental formula can be considered. Here distances were known fairly accurately, but speeds and rates of flow through doors quite roughly (even up to 50% errors).

Consequently most teams concluded that their results gave only an outline indication of escape times and could be out by as much as 50%. The teams complemented their conclusions with a discussion of the factors most contributing to the uncertainties and variations.

TABLE 25.1

Comparison of models with fire drills

Building	Capacity	No. of Exits	No. of Storeys	Evacuation Time (seconds)		
				Model (2)	Model (3)	Fire Drill
Multi-storey	1600	6	10	285	277	307
Clarendon	1200	6	2	237	199	253
New Building	600	3	2	162	182	–

25.7 DISCRIMINATION BETWEEN EXIT-QUEUE DOMINANCE AND INTERNAL-TRAVEL DOMINANCE

The project captured the interest of one student, Mr. Peter Holmes, sufficiently for him to draft this note (unsolicited and reproduced here unaltered) after the project had finished.

Consider an educational building containing a number of floors above ground level. Let each floor have a similar arrangement of rooms, and equal student capacity.

The maximum time for one person to leave the building would be the time taken to travel the furthest distance to a final exit via the staircase (in this case, from a point P on the top floor).

This would not alter if one person were to set out from each room, since each person would be sufficiently separated to avoid any congestion along the exit route.

However, as the number of people increases on each floor, then delays will occur due to the following factors.

(a)   Suppose that the door of each lecture room allows p persons to pass through per second. Then if the room contains n number of people it will take n/p seconds for them to pass through the doorway.

(b)   If the access corridors on each floor are not narrower than the staircase, the flow of people will be restricted mainly by the aggregate width of the available staircases.

(c)   As people from different floor levels converge, this will further restrict progress, both on the staircases and along the corridors. This would occur approximately after the first groups of people have reached the staircase, and descended one floor of the building.

Proposition (c), above, implies that the evacuation time will be governed by the linear flow of people down the staircases. However, it assumes that the majority of people in the building are above ground level, otherwise the aggregate width of the final exits would be more significant.

This can be expressed as an inequality

$$\frac{S}{E-S} > \frac{N}{G}$$

for the point at which the final exits could become
significant.

S = aggregate width of staircases (or flow rate of people down
    the staircases)

E = aggregate width of final exits (or flow rate of people
    through the final exits)

N = the number of people above ground level

G = the number of people at ground level.

25.8 POST MORTEM AND CONCLUSIONS

The discussion of the various models above reports ideas from
the five student teams and includes some lecturers' comments.
Each team's report was less comprehensive taken on its own.
The approaches taken by the teams were different, some in their
emphasis of features and some more fundamentally.

Most of the teams arrived at some form of model 2 with a
travel time and queue time. One team developed a similar
formula combining queue time to evacuate a room plus travel
time in corridors and stairs, but then abandoned it when they
were unable to evaluate coefficients. They went on to rely on
travel times determined from the Fire Drill data, and
multiplied them by congestion factors.

Apart from one team's range of prediction from 56 seconds to
3 minutes, all the predicted ranges were between 2 minutes
2 seconds and 3 minutes 39 seconds. All teams completed their
reports on time. After that we held a very lively post
mortem meeting where teams took turns to present a summary of
their results and to be questioned by the rest of the class.
This event was well received in a good humoured and competitive
spirit. It was important that it was organised with a strict
schedule: 3 minutes presentation and 7 minutes questioning
for each group in this case.

As a supervisor the author felt that the models of type 2 were
the most appropriate ones for the exercise. Anything more
sophisticated would not be justified in view of the inherent
uncertainty of empirical data. It was something of a surprise
at the first fire drill in the new building in October 1982 to
find that evacuation was quite smooth with no apparent queuing.
There were probably between 100 and 200 people in the building
at the time. Almost all were out within three minutes but one
class (of mature students) was later than the rest and the

drill time was 3 minutes 25 seconds. I feel that we could
and should improve on that in future. Three minutes would seem
to be a very reasonable target.

Finally feed-back from students showed that they felt they
had gained confidence in tackling real problems and in working
in teams. They generally much preferred the project work to
the prospect of an alternative lecture course.

26

Road safety

DOUG HAYNES   *Liverpool Polytechnic*

26.1 SAFETY IN FAIRFIELD

A recent death resulting from a road accident in Fairfield,
a suburb of Pugworth, has caused the issue of safety in
Fairfield to be tabled to Pugworth Town Council. "Put some
speed bumps in; that'll stop 'em!" was Councillor
Higginbottom's response. "Not likely" shouted Councillor
Banks. (His car's suspension had recently broken when
negotiating a speed bump at some speed). "Those things
ought to be banned". A third spokesman tried to intervene
and point out that people's lives were at stake in this
issue. The matter was eventually placed in the hands of
the town's department of the Environment and the Engineering
department.

1) Consider how you would measure safety in Fairfield.
2) Assess what factors might relate to safety in Fairfield.
3) Draw up two lists.

    List A: Those factors for which data probably exists
    and its most likely source.

    List B: Those factors for which data probably does
    not exist but which could be determined.

4) Identify any potential "solutions" which may improve
    the level of safety in Fairfield.

5) Choose one of your potential solutions in question 4
    and discuss the criteria which you would use to justify
    its implementation.

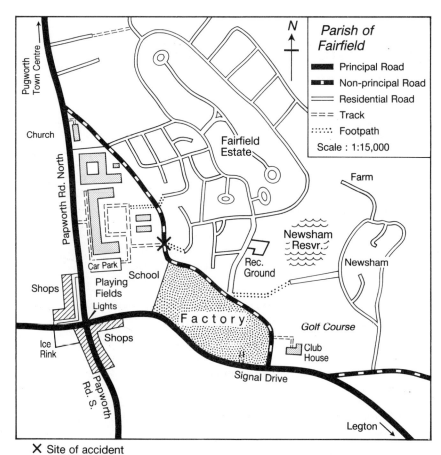

X Site of accident

Figure 26.1 Map of Fairfield

26.2 BACKGROUND INFORMATION

We here provide some extra information on the 5 questions
posed above.

a)   Students will normally choose factors which can be easily
     measured. This might be accident numbers and traffic
     flows, though others are possible. Traffic flows are
     generally known for principal roads, where a "link and
     node" network is used as a grid for recording this
     information. Approximately 85% of accidents occur on
     such grids . Flows are also recorded (for each hour of
     the day) for any non-principal road having a high level
     of accidents.

b)   A very large list of factors is possible here, some more
     plausible than others.

c)   The police collate information on reported accidents,
     though there is no legal requirement for people to report
     accidents unless a fatality is involved. Approximately
     70% of all injury accidents are reported to the police.
     However, accident information is very confidential and
     would not be released in any form where it could be used
     to ascribe any blame. Hence information provided by the
     police, or by the local authority, to whom the police
     forward collated accident information, would be of a
     summary "linear" form.

     List A might include information summarising the
     "accident cluster" (ie. how many accidents have occurred
     in the fatal, serious, slight and damage-only categories),
     and information on traffic flows. It may further include
     a list of "engineering measures" which have been
     implemented over the last 10 years ; for example, signs,
     road widening, traffic signals, pedestrian crossings.

     List B might include features specific to the accident
     site and area, such as visibility, roadside parking,
     lighting, location of signs etc. These could be
     determined by visiting the area and site.

d)   See extended problem which follows.

e)   See extended problem - the criteria would normally
     include some costs.

26.3 EXTENDED PROBLEM

i) An accident investigation team would first try to assess
    whether the recent accident presented a "real" or an
    "apparent" safety problem.

    What types of accident might present an "apparent" rather
    than a "real" problem?

ii) If the accidents were considered "real", the team would go
     on to investigate the priority status of the relevant
     stretch of road. Two possible measures are:
     ACCIDENT NUMBERS: the number of accidents on a given
     stretch of road over a period of time.
     ACCIDENT RATES: the number of accidents per million
     vehicle miles or per million vehicle kilometres.

 In Pugworth, a section of road gains a **PRIORITY STATUS** if

 a) there have been $\geqslant$ 20 injury accidents on a 200 metre
     stretch over the last 3 years.

 b) there have been $\geqslant$ 15 injury accidents in a 200 metre
     stretch over the last 3 years and there is an accident
     rate of at least one injury accident per million vehicle
     kilometres.

     What is the relevance of the second category as
     opposed to the first category?

iii) Whether or not the stretch of road were on the priority
     list, the team would further investigate the cluster of
     accidents at the site, since elected representatives
     (councillors) have power to override the priority list.
     This would involve listing the number of various accident
     types over the last 3 years:

          Fatal injury
          Serious injury
          Slight injury
          Damage only.

     Nationally 70% of all "injury" accidents are reported
     to the police, but most "damage only" accidents are never
     reported. Investigations suggest that there are 6 or 7
     "damage only" accidents for each "injury" accident. All
     accident information is passed on to the local authority
     by the police.

A "severity rate" could be measured for a site by using records to calculate

$$\text{SEVERITY RATE} = \frac{\text{no. of Fatal + Serious Accidents}}{\text{Total no. of accidents}} \times 100\%$$

Does this measure over-estimate or under-estimate the true severity rate of accidents?

What practical significance will errors in this measure have?

iv) Statistics compiled nationally give the average costs for accidents. These contain the following components:

Lost output
Medical and Ambulance
Police and Administration
Damage to property
Pain, Grief and Suffering

The average costs per accident on urban roads are given in Table 26.1

TABLE 26.1

Category	Cost	
Fatal accidents	£141,100	Average for all
Serious accidents	£7,180	injury accidents
Slight accidents	£930	is £4,460.

A summary of the "accident cluster" over the last 3 years at the Fairfield site of the recent accident is as follows:-

    FATAL   1
    SERIOUS 5
    SLIGHT 12

a) Estimate the average cost per annum of injury accidents at this site.

b) What would the estimate be if the reporting rate (70%) is taken into account?

c) What would the estimate be if "damage only" accidents were assumed to be 6 times the number of injury accidents, and that a "damage only" accident costs £640 on average?

v) The accident investigation team decides to consider several "engineering measures" as potential options for improving safety at the site. These measures and their estimated capital costs are summarised in Table 26.2.

    However, they are aware that they must justify a rate of return of at least 50% of the capital outlay in the first year of operation. Capital expenditure spent on safety measures is allocated from a "safety items" budget, but will only be released if the expected annual savings in accident costs anticipated at the relevant site form over 50% of the investment.

vi) For which of these measures could a 50% return on capital investment be advocated? The team would have to evaluate causal factors in the historical accidents and determine how many accidents the engineering measures would probably have eliminated if they had been in operation. Their estimates are summarised in Table 26.3

TABLE 26.2

Engineering measures and their estimated costs at this site

MEASURE	COST(£)	REMARKS
A) Pelican Crossing	6,200	Not considered appropriate for "peaky demand" near a school.
B) Speed Bumps/Ramps	2,800	Several would be required to contain maximum speeds.
C) Patrol (Revenue cost)	600	Appointed by police; these patrols (lollipop men/women) already exist at peak times - 4 times a day.
D) Improve Warning Signs	550	Improved siting for signs.
E) Access Restriction (Signs)	750	Requires police enforcement measures rather than self-enforcement measures.
F) Pedestrian Guard Rails (Approx. 200 metres)	11,200	Designed to stop haphazard crossing near school gates.
G) Bridge/Underpass	94,500	Children (and adults) often don't use them.
H) Improve Alternative Route	38,600	Improvements at the principal road junction, easing flows both ways between Signal Dr. and Papworth Rd. North.
I) Improving Visibility across bend	280	Clearing bushes and a few small trees.
J) Easing bend	96,000	Levelling and constructing a short section of road to cut across the severe bend.
K) One Way System	940	Several signs and road markings: increase in vehicle speeds likely.
L) Width Restrictions (narrow entry)	6,250	Prevents HGVs and heavy traffic.
M) Road closure		Cuts out "through" traffic. Non-principal road would be degraded to a residential road.
- End	8,750	Unpopular (car owning residents)
- Central	6,400	More acceptable for residents since route through estate. (Awkward for "through" traffic).

TABLE 26.3

	Estimated number of injuries saved over last 3 years			Expected Accident Savings (1st year)	Captial of Cost	% Rate of Return
	Fatal	Serious	Slight			
A) Pelican Crossing	–	1	1		6,200	
B) Speed Bumps/Ramps	–	–	3		2,800	
C) Patrol	–	–	–		600	
D) Improve Signs	–	–	1		550	
E) Access Restriction	–	–	1		750	
F) Guard Rails	–	2	6		11,200	
G) Bridge/Underpass	–	2	8		94,500	
H) Improve alt. route	–	1	3		38,600	
I) Improve Visibility	–	1	2		280	
J) Easing Bend	–	3	2		96,000	
K) One Way System	–	–	1		940	
L) Width Restrictions	–	–	3		6,250	
M) Road Closure – End	–	–	3		8,750	
– Middle	–	2	4		6,400	

a)   Use Table 26.3, in conjunction with the information in
     Table 26.1, to calculate the expected annual saving in
     accident costs and the corresponding rate of return on
     the capital expenditure involved.

b)   What further analysis would be necessary if you are
     considering recommending more than one engineering measure?

c)   Write a short report for the Council presenting your
     recommendations for improving safety. Give adequate
     justification for your chosen recommendations in the report.

CREDIT

We are grateful to Alan Stilwell (Accident investigation,
Merseyside County Engineers Department) for his assistance.

REFERENCES

Dept. of Transport - Road accident costs and statistics

Transport and Road Research Lab., Crowthorne - Lab Reports

27

Sheep farming

DILWYN EDWARDS   *Thames Polytechnic*

27.1   PROBLEM STATEMENT

A prospective sheep farmer has L m^2 of land for grazing and wishes to have answers to the following questions:

(1)   How many sheep should he keep?
(2)   How much of the summer grass should he store as feed for the winter months?
(3)   What proportion of female lambs should he retain each year for breeding?

27.2   DISCUSSION

This is obviously a difficult problem because of the large number of factors which need to be considered but by leaving out much of the detail we can set up a simple model which can give us useful answers.

Essentially, what we have to do is produce models for the two living populations (sheep and grass) and also to model the interaction between them (sheep eating the grass). We need data for the growth rate of grass, the reproduction rate of sheep and also the nutritional requirements of the sheep.

27.3   BACKGROUND INFORMATION

To simplify matters we can consider the year to be divided into four seasons. The daily growth rate of grass depends on the type of grass, the nature of the soil and the amounts of sunlight and water available. The last two factors will obviously vary with the seasons. For a particular type of grass (Perennial Ryegrass) on a lowland site the following are approximations to the average growth rate

	Winter	Spring	Summer	Autumn
Daily growth rate (gm^{-2})	0	3	7	4

In most common breeds of sheep the ewes produce one, two or
three lambs each year until they are about 5 to 8 years old
when they are sold. To replace them the farmer either has to
buy ewes from other farmers or keep some of his own female
lambs each year to maintain the breeding flock. If we assume
that ewes are kept until they are five years old then the
following are the average numbers of lambs born per ewe in
each age group

Age (years)	0-1	1-2	2-3	3-4	4-5
Lambs born	0	1.8	2.4	2.0	1.8

We also need information on the probability of survival of
female sheep from year to year and the following are fairly
typical values for a flock in Britain.

From age	to age	Probability of survival
1-2	2-3	0.98
2-3	3-4	0.95
3-4	4-5	0.80

Finally we shall assume that the following are average feeding
requirements per animal during the year.

Daily requirements (kg of grass)	lambs	ewes
Winter	0	2.10
Spring	1.00	2.40
Summer	1.65	1.15
Autumn	0	1.35

This case study provides an opportunity to introduce or
reinforce the distinction between discrete and continuous
growth in living populations. It also poses the problem of
modelling the interaction between the two. In modelling the
sheep population we are not concerned with the weight gain of
individual animals but in the total flock size which is subject
to additions in Spring in the form of new lambs and deletions
in the Autumn when we assume all male lambs and a certain
percentage of female lambs are killed. One part of the problem
is to determine what this percentage should be in order for the
flock size to remain at a constant size N. The second part is
to decide what N should be, given L m^2 of land.

27.4 POSSIBLE SOLUTIONS

A useful technique for modelling changes in the sheep flock
from year to year is by means of a transition matrix. We can
represent our current flock by means of a population vector
which shows the number of sheep in each of the age ranges
0-1, 1-2, 2-3, 3-4 and 4-5. For example suppose we have an
initial flock of forty ewes with ten in every age group and
forty lambs (0-1 year old) then our population vector is
$X = [40,10,10,10,10]^T$. If we sell 90% of the female lambs
i.e. 95% of the total lambs, the corresponding matrix will be

$$P = \begin{bmatrix} 0 & 1.8 & 2.4 & 2.0 & 1.8 \\ 0.05 & 0 & 0 & 0 & 0 \\ 0 & 0.98 & 0 & 0 & 0 \\ 0 & 0 & 0.95 & 0 & 0 \\ 0 & 0 & 0 & 0.80 & 0 \end{bmatrix}$$

To predict next year's flock we calculate
$PX = [80,2,9.8,9.5,8.0]^T$ and this gives a total flock size of
109.3 for next year.

The controllable factor in our model is the culling percentage
which determines the (2,1) element of the matrix P.   It is
easy to write a short program for a microcomputer to carry out
successive multiplications by the transition matrix and
investigate the consequences of various culling rates.   For
the data we have used above we find that the flock size
remains constant when about 86% of all the lambs are killed,
that is, all the male lambs and 72% of the females.   In the
steady state the stable population vector is a multiple of
$[1000, 136, 133, 127, 101]^T$.   This implies that in a stable
flock of N animals the number of lambs born every year is
0.668N and the number of ewes present during the Autumn and
Winter is 0.332N.

Using the information from section 27.3 we can now write down the
feed requirements for a flock of total Summer size N.

Winter:	2.10 x 0.332N	= 0.697N
Spring:	0.668N + 2.40 x 0.332N	= 1.465N
Summer:	1.65 x 0.668N + 1.15 x 0.332N	= 1.484N
Autumn:	1.35 x 0.332N	= 0.448N

If we apply the condition that the rate of grass growth in
Spring, Summer and Autumn must exceed the rate at which the
sheep are grazing we have

$$
\begin{array}{lll}
\text{Spring:} & 1.465N < 0.003L \\
\text{Summer:} & 1.484N < 0.007L \\
\text{Autumn:} & 0.448N < 0.004L
\end{array}
$$

These give us the following limits on N/L, the number of
animals per m^2 of land.

$$
\begin{array}{lll}
\text{Spring:} & N/L < 0.00205 \text{ per } m^2 & \text{or } 20.5 \text{ per ha} \\
\text{Summer:} & N/L < 0.00472 \text{ per } m^2 & \text{or } 47.2 \text{ per ha} \\
\text{Autumn:} & N/L < 0.00893 \text{ per } m^2 & \text{or } 89.3 \text{ per ha}
\end{array}
$$

The figure of 20.5 animals per ha in Spring is equivalent to
6.8 ewes per ha and provided we do not exceed this stocking
density there will be sufficient feed in Spring, Summer and
Autumn.

Suppose that we cut y kg/m^2 of the Summer grass to keep for
winter feeding then the summer criterion is

$$
1.484 \frac{N}{L} < 0.007 - y
$$

with $N/L = 0.00205$ per m^2 we must have $y < 0.0039$ kg/m^2.

The requirement for Winter feeding at this stocking rate is
0.0014 kg/m^2 so that the stored grass should be sufficient
even allowing for the fact that its nutritional value will be
below that of the fresh grass.

27.5 EXTENSIONS

We can develop a more detailed model of grass growth if we
assume that the rate of growth depends on the leaf area and on the
amount of light received. The amount of light received by a
particular leaf in a canopy will be reduced by the amount
which has already been trapped by the leaves above it. If
this rate of trapping is proportional to the leaf area then
the weight w of an average leaf in the middle of the canopy
grows at a rate given by

$$
\frac{dw}{dt} = kw(m-w)
$$

where k is constant, if we take the incoming light intensity
to be constant, and m is a constant representing the maximum
weight that the canopy can achieve.   If we assume that the
sheep are eating the grass at a constant rate R kg/m^2 then
we have the following first order differential equation for w,

$$\frac{dw}{dt} = kw(m-w) - R$$

with a solution of the form

$$w = \frac{\alpha_1 - A\alpha_2 e^{(\alpha_1-\alpha_2)kt}}{1 - Ae^{(\alpha_1-\alpha_2)kt}}$$

where A is a constant and α_1, α_2 are the roots of the quadratic
$\alpha^2 - m\alpha + R = 0$.

Taking different values for R and k in the four seasons we
could try to produce a graph of w against t which looks
something like Figure 27.1 with the grass weight per m^2
returning to its previous level at the end of the twelve
months.

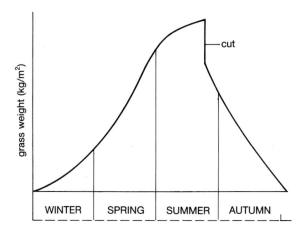

Figure 27.1

28

Loading tiles into boxes

GEORGE HALL *Nottingham University*

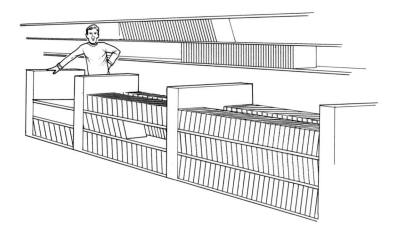

28.1 STATEMENT OF THE PROBLEM

Roofing tiles fresh from the kiln are stacked in columns five
tiles high. A week later they are packed into boxes for
transport to building sites. This packing is done manually
and, since the work is heavy (3 tons/hour), it is necessary
that it should be efficient. How should it be done?

Since many starting configuratons are possible and many
decisions have to be taken quickly, simple tactical rules which
are tolerably efficient are of more value than strictly optimal,
but complicated, solutions.

* This problem was first suggested by David Lee whilst a student
at the University of Nottingham, and arose from his experience
with Redland Roof Tiles, Westerham.

Each tile is 15" x 9". It remains on edge throughout the
packing. The initial stack has parallel layers and tiles can
be taken from the top of the three nearest columns. The box
stretches alongside the stack and is filled from adjacent
columns. Once a column has been exhausted boxes are placed
close to the next column. The vertical cross-sections of these
are shown in Figure 28.1.

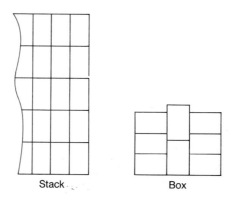

Figure 28.1 Vertical cross-section of tiles in stack and box

28.2 TEACHING COMMENTS

The problem of packing library books into a packing case is a
very similar one and may be easier to use to illustrate the
manual operations. It has only one column but books can be
taken from different shelves.

The solution suggested has three different phases representing
three stages in coming to grips with the problem. In the first,
a measure of difficulty of an individual move is set up. Using
potential energy and ignoring horizontal movements make this
solution easier. More elaborate measures may well be tried.
The second phase looks at the sequencing of moves so that by
foresight really awkward moves are avoided, and the third
relates this to the full day's work. It is possible to
abbreviate the second part at the expense of making the third
part longer.

A network model is by no means necessary, but a simulation model
seems almost inescapable. It can be carried out by computer,
by hand or even by using child's bricks!

The library problem could be taken as a follow-up problem.

28.3 FACTORS

The heaviness of the labour depends on many factors. Among
these the principal ones can be listed as

1. Differences in vertical height
2. Horizontal distance moved
3. Lifting over intervening columns of tiles
4. Rotating of some tiles
5. Ambidexterity of worker

Since we are concerned with tactical comparisons rather than
absolute measures of effort, factors 2, 4 and 5 can be taken as
constant and ignored.

To simplify the problem in a realistic way, and to eliminate the
effect of the third factor inside the box, a standard order of
loading will be assumed. In this, each column in the box is
finished before the next is started. Similarly, the most
awkward consequences of this factor for the stack can be
eliminated by imposing the restrictions that no more than 3
columns of the stack are to be involved at any one time and that
successive columns inwards will have non-decreasing heights.

The significant factor that remains is the first, the vertical
height moved.

The problem can now be reformulated as one of selecting from the
stack to fill the box so that lifting up the tiles is minimised.

28.4 THE POTENTIAL MODEL

Since vertical height is the significant variable the simplest
model of the situation is in terms of the potential energy
difference. If the potential energy of the tiles in the box is
higher than in the three nearest columns of the stack then some
lifting up is inevitable. If it is lower, then it is worthwhile
to look for a tactical procedure which achieves the transfer
without lifting up at any stage.

Thus we look for a minimum to the sum of the positive energy
differences.

It is useful to measure the potential energy in units of the
energy required to raise a tile 15" to rest on another tile. If
the zero of energy corresponds to tiles stacked on the ground
then the box has a potential energy of 4 units.

This figure is approximate since it depends on the lowest tiles
being given a zero energy irrespective of orientation. Note

that the dimensions of the tiles ensure that the remaining
energies are correct.   Potential energy levels are shown in
Figure 28.2.

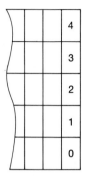

Figure 28.2   Potential energy levels in stack and box

The potential energy of the tiles removed from the stack is the
difference in potential energy of the initial and final
configuration of the stack.   For convenience the notation
(x,y,z) will describe a stack configuration with the column
nearest the box x tiles high, the next column y tiles high and
the third z tiles high.   The constraints above imply that
$x \le y \le z$.   Note that if, at any stage, $x = 0$ then the next
full column must be included.   The potential energy differences
are now relatively easy to evaluate, e.g.

Initial	Final	Δ(P.E.)
(5,5,5)	(0,2,5)	19
(3,5,5)	(0,0,5)	13
(2,5,5)	(0,0,4)	15
(2,3,3)	(0,0,0)	7

The last of these examples is the configuration with the lowest
initial potential energy consistent with the restriction to
three columns and the final configuration which minimizes the
potential difference, Δ.   Even this configuration has ample
potential energy to exceed 4, the value of the potential energy
of the tiles in the box.

Not only does this model suggest that lifting up can be avoided
but it also provides an ordering of initial stack configuration
which gives some measure of how easy it will be to avoid
lifting up.

28.5   THE NETWORK MODEL

The potential model suggests that an efficient loading sequence
may exist but it does not help to find it.   To do this the
alternatives need to be investigated systematically.   It is
convenient to use the (2,3,3) configuration to illustrate one
way in which this can be done.   The process is represented by a
network, Figure 28.4, with vertices corresponding to the
different configurations.   At each vertex outgoing edges (i.e.
downwards) are labelled by the alternative positions (3 at most)
from which tiles can be removed.   Since configurations can be
reached in various ways a vertex may have several incoming
edges.   Configurations with the same number of tiles are
represented by vertices at the same horizontal level.

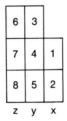

Figure 28.3   Labelling of tiles in (2,3,3) configurations.

The same network (see Figure 28.5) can also be labelled on each
edge with the potential energy difference between the tiles in
the stack and in the box.   In this, lifting down will be a
negative label and lifting up a positive one.

To avoid lifting up, a path must be traced from start to stop
without using positive edges.   Since the final edge is unique
and is positive, this is not entirely possible here.   There are,
however, several alternative paths that have no other positive
edge.   One of these is shown by the dashed line and corresponds
to removal in the order 1, 3, 4, 2, 6, 5, 7, 8.   Note that,
since potential energy is conservative, different routes
between vertices have the same totals.

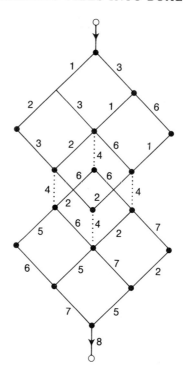

Figure 28.4   Alternative sequences for removing tiles

Each of the other initial configurations can be analysed in the
same way, though the networks become rather more complex.
Optimization by this procedure is not a practical working
method.   We require a procedure which can be applied to an
arbitrary configuration in the few moments that the task gives
and without computer assistance!   We are helped by several
observations.   The advantages of horizontal movement, with no
change of energy, is obviously great.   The path chosen in
Figure 28.5 has 3 such segments.   Because of conservation of
energy, a positive edge is often preceded, or followed, by a
large negative one.   Thus, avoiding a large lift down makes a
lift up less likely.   This is equivalent to minimising both
lift up and lift down, though with smaller weight given to a
lift down.

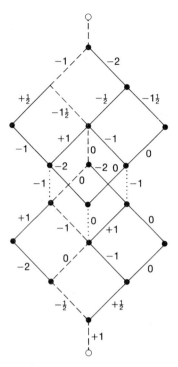

Figure 28.5   Potential energy differences.

The working algorithm that can be applied generally and rapidly,
follows from these considerations. It can be applied to each
row of tiles and is summarised in the rules:

1.   Select an edge with 0 if there is one, i.e. move tiles
     horizontally
2.   If not, select the edge with least negative value i.e.
     lift down the smallest amount
3.   If neither, select smallest positive edge i.e. lift up
     the least

The route shown in Figure 28.5 is reproduced by starting from
the top and following these rules at every vertex.

It is interesting to note that the advice given to novices
includes 'leave a few for later', e.g. avoid lifting tiles from
the top row of the stack to the bottom of the box.

28.6   THE SIMULATION MODEL

The process of loading boxes is continuous, with the final
configuration after loading one box becoming the initial

configuration for the next box. The optimum strategy cannot be decided by considering just one box. A realistic model will have to involve a run of several boxes, and be long enough to give typical results. The simplest practical way of investigating this is to simulate the loading on a computer.

The computer can be programmed to load according to various decision rules. One of these will be the rule given in the previous section. Another might be to select the nearest column every time. A comparison could also be made with a random choice at each point.

By a run of about 20 boxes (a day's work) the influence of the first initial configuration could be reduced and proper comparisons made.

A simulation of this kind in which the difficulty of lifting up was rated at twice the difficulty of lifting down, which was measured by the potential energy change, gave the following results when averaged over a number of different starting configurations.

Method	Average difficulty
Suggested role	11.2
Nearest column	12.3
Random column	13.1

This suggests that the choice of the nearest column is about 10% worse than the suggested rule, and a random choice about 20% worse. Although small, these precentages are significant to a hard-working individual.

An advantage of this model is that if experience suggests other decision rules they can be rapidly evaluated.